The Dilemmas of Statebuilding

Confronting the contradictions of postwar peace operations

**Edited by
Roland Paris and Timothy D. Sisk**

LONDON AND NEW YORK

First published 2009
by Routledge
2 Park Square Milton Park Abingdon Oxon OX14 4RN

Simultaneously published in the USA and Canada
by Routledge
270 Madison Avenue, New York, NY 10016

Routledge is an imprint of the Taylor & Francis Group, an informa business.

Typeset in Times New Roman by
Taylor & Francis Books
Printed and bound in Great Britain by
CPI Antony Rowe, Chippenham, Wiltshire

British Library Cataloguing in Publication Data
A catalogue record for this book is available from the British Library

Library of Congress Cataloging in Publication Data
The dilemmas of statebuilding : confronting the contradictions of postwar
  peace operations / [edited by] Roland Paris and Timothy D. Sisk.
    p. cm. – (Security and governance)
  Includes bibliographical references and index.
    1. Nation-building. 2. Postwar reconstruction. 3. Peace-building. I. Paris,
  Roland, 1967– II. Sisk, Timothy D., 1960–
  JZ6300.D55 2008
327.1′72–dc22   2008027276

ISBN 978-0-415-77628-8 (hbk)
ISBN 978-0-415-77629-5 (pbk)
ISBN 978-0-203-88483-6 (ebk)

Contents

Illustrations

Figures

Tables

Box

Contributors

Deborah Avant is Professor of Political Science and Director of International Studies at the University of California at Irvine. Her research (funded by the Institute for Global Conflict and Cooperation, the John D. and Catherine T. MacArthur Foundation, the Olin Foundation, and the Smith Richardson Foundation, among others) has focused on civil–military relations, military change, and the politics of controlling violence. Her recent work on the privatization of security has appeared in *The Market for Force: the Consequences of Privatizing Security* (Cambridge University Press, 2005) as well as articles in academic and popular journals such as *Perspective on Politics, Review of International Studies, Foreign Policy,* and *International Studies Perspectives.* She is also the author of *Political Institutions and Military Change: Lessons from Peripheral Wars* (Cornell University Press, 1994) along with other articles on military change in such journals as *International Organization, International Studies Quarterly,* and *Armed Forces and Society.*

Michael Barnett is the Harold Stassen Professor of International Affairs at the Humphrey Institute and Professor of Political Science at the University of Minnesota. He teaches and publishes in the areas of international relations, international organizations, humanitarianism, and Middle Eastern politics. Among his books are *Dialogues in Arab Politics: Negotiations in Regional Order* (Columbia University Press, 1998), *Security Communities* (co-edited with Emanuel Adler, Cambridge University Press, 1998), and *Eyewitness to a Genocide: The United Nations and Rwanda* (Cornell University Press, 2002), *Rules for the World: International Organizations and World Politics* (with Martha Finnemore, Cornell University Press, 2004), and *Humanitarianism in Question: Politics, Power, and Ethics* (co-edited with Tom Weiss, Cornell University Press, 2008).

Christopher Cramer is Senior Lecturer in Political Economy at the School of Oriental and African Studies (SOAS), in the University of London, where he teaches in the Department of Development Studies. He created and convenes the MSc in Violence, Conflict and Development and chairs the University of London's Centre for African Studies. The two main prongs of his research interest in recent years have been rural labor markets in sub-Saharan Africa (especially Mozambique) and the political economy of violence in developing countries. His book *Civil War is Not a Stupid Thing: Accounting for Violence in Developing Countries* was published in the UK by C. Hurst in 2006 and in the USA by Indiana University Press.

David M. Edelstein is an Assistant Professor in the Edmund A. Walsh School of Foreign Service and the Department of Government at Georgetown University. In addition, he is a core faculty member in Georgetown's Security Studies Program and Center for Peace and Security Studies. Prior to arriving at Georgetown, he was a pre-doctoral fellow at Stanford University's Center for International Security and Cooperation and a post-doctoral fellow at Harvard University's Belfer Center for Science and International Affairs. He is the author of *Occupational Hazards: Success and Failure in Military Occupation* (Cornell University Press, 2008), and his work has been published in *International Security, Security Studies*, and *Survival*.

Miles Kahler is Rohr Professor of Pacific International Relations at the Graduate School of International Relations and Pacific Studies and Professor of Political Science at the University of California, San Diego (UCSD). From 2001 to 2005, he served as Interim Director and Founding Director of the Institute for International, Comparative, and Area Studies at UCSD. His recent publications include *Territoriality and Conflict in an Era of Globalization* (co-edited with Barbara Walter, Cambridge University Press, 2006), *Governance in a Global Economy* (co-edited with David Lake, Princeton University Press, 2003), and *Leadership Selection in the Major Multilaterals* (Institute for International Economics, 2001). Current research interests include international institutions and global governance, the evolution of the nation-state, multilateral strategies toward failed states, and the political economy of international finance.

Jens Narten is a Ph.D. candidate at the University of Hamburg's Institute for Peace Research and Security Policy. From 2001 to 2004, he was a Senior Human Rights Officer and Human Rights Training Coordinator for the OSCE Mission in Kosovo, seconded by the German Foreign Office. He has lectured at the Universities of Prishtina, Hanover and Marburg on conflict resolution and human rights, and has written several articles and book chapters on human rights and democracy in the Balkans. The topic of his Ph.D. dissertation is Post-Conflict Peacebuilding and Local Ownership, focusing on Kosovo.

Roland Paris is University Research Chair in International Security and Governance, and Associate Professor of Public and International Affairs, at the University of Ottawa, Canada. He is also the founding Director of the university's Centre for International Policy Studies. Previously, he was Assistant Professor of Political Science and International Affairs at the

University of Colorado, Director of Research at the Conference Board of Canada, Policy Advisor in the Department of Foreign Affairs and the Privy Council Office of the Canadian government, and Visiting Researcher at the Johns Hopkins School of Advanced International Studies in Washington, D.C. His research focuses on international security, peacekeeping operations, and international governance. His book *At War's End: Building Peace After Civil Conflict* (Cambridge University Press, 2004) won three awards including the International Studies Association's 2005 Chadwick Alger Award for best book on international organization and the 2007 Grawemeyer Award for Ideas Improving World Order. Paris's other writings have appeared in *International Security, Review of International Studies, European Journal of International Relations, International Studies Quarterly, Political Science Quarterly, International Studies Review*, and elsewhere.

David Roberts is Lecturer in Peace and Conflict Studies and Course Director for the International Politics Degree at Magee College, University of Ulster, Northern Ireland. He has taught at the University of Nottingham, the School of Oriental and African Studies (SOAS), and King's College London. His current research areas are global governance, peacebuilding, and human insecurity. He has published a monograph *Human Insecurity: Global Structures of Violence* (Zed, 2008) and will publish a second work *Remapping Global Governance: Biopolitics and Human Security* (Zed, 2009). He is convenor and chair of the Human Security Working Group of the British International Studies Association, and is presently writing a new volume on peacebuilding, entitled *Recapturing Peace from Global Governance: the Limits of Liberal Peace*, to appear in 2010. He also wrote *Political Transition in Cambodia, 1991–1999: Power, Elitism and Democracy* (Curzon Routledge, 2001) and has published more than 30 articles in refereed journals and in the knowledge transfer sector.

Kirsti Samuels is a Constitution Building and Peacebuilding specialist. She is currently the Lead Constitution Building Specialist at International IDEA, an intergovernmental organization that supports sustainable democracy worldwide, and was the Senior Programme Manager of the Constitution Building Processes Programme from 2007. In 2006, she worked in Somalia and Kenya as the lead legal consultant to UNDP on a constitution-building process for Somalia, where she assisted the interim-government and later the Constitutional Commission in developing and implementing an inclusive and participatory process. Dr Samuels holds a Law degree and Science degree from the University of Sydney, and a Masters in Law and a Doctorate from Oxford University. Her recent publications include *Political Violence and the International Community: Developments in International Law and Policy* (Martinus Nijhoff Publishers, 2007), "Rule of Law Reform in Post-Conflict Countries: Operational Initiatives and Lessons Learnt" (World Bank Social Development Papers series, October 2006), "Post-Conflict Peace-Building and Constitution-Making" (*Chicago*

Journal of International Law, Vol. 6, No. 2, Winter 2006), "Constitution Building Processes and Democratization: A Discussion of Twelve Case Studies" (International IDEA, 2006), "Constitutional Engineering After Conflict: The Consequences of Governance Choices in Post-Conflict Constitutions" (IPA, 2006), "Sustainability and Peace-building: A Key Challenge" (*Journal of Development in Practice*, Vol. 15, No. 6 November, 2005) and "State-building and the Political Transition after Conflict" (*Proceedings of the American Society of International Law Annual Conference*, 2005).

Timothy D. Sisk is Associate Dean and Associate Professor at the Josef Korbel School of International Studies, University of Denver, and Director of the Center for Sustainable Development and International Peace, a research and policy development institute at GSIS. He also serves as an Associate Fellow of the Geneva Centre for Security Policy in Geneva, Switzerland. He has conducted extensive research on the role of international and regional organizations, particularly the United Nations, on peace operations, peacemaking, and peacebuilding. Sisk has just published a major scholarly book titled *International Mediation in Civil Wars: Bargaining with Bullets* (Routledge, 2008). Prior to joining the University of Denver in 1998, Sisk was a Program Officer in the Grant Program of the United States Institute of Peace in Washington and, prior to that, a staff member for a United States Senator. Sisk earned a Ph.D. "with distinction" in Political Science (comparative politics, research methods) from The George Washington University in 1992, and an M.A. in International Journalism (1984) and a B.A. in Foreign Service and German (1982) from Baylor University.

Astri Suhrke is Senior Researcher at the Christian Michelsen Institute in Bergen, Norway. She has written widely on the politics of humanitarian policies in international organizations and the UN system, the concepts of human security and humanitarian intervention, and refugee movements. She recently completed a multi-year project funded by the Research Council of Norway on aid strategies in postwar situations. Currently she is working on a Ford Foundation project dealing with strategies of postwar reconstruction with particular reference to Afghanistan. Her most recent books are *Eroding Local Capacity: International Humanitarian Action in Africa* (co-authored with Monica Kathina Juma, Nordic Africa Institute, 2003) and *The Path of a Genocide: The Rwanda Crisis from Uganda to Zaire* (co-authored with Howard Adelman, Transaction Publishers, 1999).

Christoph Zürcher is Professor of Political Science in the Graduate School of Public and International Affairs at the University of Ottawa. He received his Ph.D. from the University of Bern, Switzerland. His previous teaching and research appointments include the University of Konstanz, the Institut d'Études Politiques d'Aix-en-Provence, Stanford University, and Free University Berlin. His research and teaching interests include conflict research, methods of empirical conflict research, statebuilding and intervention, international governance and development. His regional focus is on the former Soviet Union especially on Russia, the Caucasus, and Central Asia including Afghanistan. He has worked as a consultant for various development organizations in Central Asia and the Caucasus. He is the editor of *Potentials of Disorder: Explaining Violence in the Caucasus and in the Former Yugoslavia* (Manchester University Press, 2003) and the author of *The Post-Soviet Wars: Rebellion, Ethnic Conflict and Nationhood in the Post-Soviet Era* (New York University Press, 2007).

Acknowledgments

The editors would like to thank the Carnegie Corporation of New York's Program in International Peace and Security for funding the Research Partnership on Postwar Statebuilding (RPPS) on which this book is based, and especially Steven J. Del Rosso, Jr. for his unwavering support for the project.

We would also wish to thank the Government of Norway for sponsoring a symposium in Oslo in September 2007 at which the initial findings of the project were deliberated.

Similarly, the Geneva Centre for Security Policy graciously hosted an event in Geneva in October 2007 where our work was presented and discussed among a group of specialists involved in the Geneva Peacebuilding Platform.

In November 2007, the International Peace Academy (now International Peace Institute) co-hosted a workshop in which the findings of the research were presented to UN policymakers and other specialists. Thanks are due to Jenna Slotin for her professional management of this event and to Adam Lupel for leading the team that produced a superb policy-briefing document.

We also had the opportunity to present our research at seminars organized by the UN Peacebuilding Support Office in New York, the Fragile States Group of the Organization for Economic Cooperation and Development in Paris, and the Graduate School of Public and International Affairs in Ottawa. We benefited enormously from the comments and reactions from participants in those meetings.

Routledge's Security and Governance Series editors, Fiona Adamson and Stefan Wolff, as well as two anonymous reviewers, read the initial manuscript and provided insightful and invaluable comments, for which we are grateful.

Finally, we wish to thank two hard-working University of Denver Master of Arts students. Marc Weiner served as a research assistant for the project and staffed the dissemination events and Sarah Hoffman ably assisted in the final preparation of the manuscript.

Roland Paris and Timothy D. Sisk

1 Introduction

Understanding the contradictions of postwar statebuilding

Roland Paris and Timothy D. Sisk

Since the end of the Cold War, an enormous international experiment has been underway. A shifting constellation of international and regional organizations, national governments, and non-governmental organizations has conducted a series of complex "peacebuilding" operations aimed at stabilizing countries just emerging from periods of internal war. From Namibia in 1989 to Darfur in 2007, more than 20 major multilateral peacebuilding missions were deployed to post-conflict societies with the goal of preventing the resumption of violence (see Table 1.1). Nor is the demand for these operations likely to abate in the near future, given the increased tendency of armed conflicts to end in negotiated settlements rather than military victory.[1]

Why characterize these missions as an experiment? For one thing, there is still no reliable formula for transforming a fragile ceasefire into a stable and lasting peace. Nor should this observation come as a surprise. It is difficult to imagine a more complex or demanding task than post-conflict peacebuilding, which combines three separate yet simultaneous transitions, each posing its own tremendous challenges: a social transition from internecine fighting to peace; a political transition from wartime government (or the absence of government) to postwar government; and an economic transition from war-warped accumulation and distribution to equitable, transparent postwar development that in turn reinforces peace. Peacebuilding also resembles an experiment in the sense that its methods have been evolving over the past two decades in response to the perceived lessons—and short-comings—of preceding missions. Much of this policy evolution has occurred within sectoral or "micro" areas of peacebuilding, such as specific techniques for organizing and administering elections, but there has also been policy evolution at the "macro" level of the missions as a whole, and in the broad approaches they pursue.

One of the most important macro-level shifts in peacebuilding strategy occurred in the late 1990s and early 2000s, when major peacebuilding agencies began emphasizing the construction or strengthening of legitimate governmental institutions in countries emerging from civil conflict, or what we call "statebuilding" in this book. Statebuilding is a particular approach to peacebuilding, premised on the recognition that achieving security and

Table 1.1 Major post-civil conflict peacebuilding operations, 1989–2007

Location	Duration (military component)
Namibia	1989–1990
Nicaragua	1989–1992
Angola	1991–1997
Cambodia	1991–1993
El Salvador	1991–1995
Mozambique	1992–1994
Liberia	1992–1997
Rwanda	1993–1997
Bosnia	1995–present
Croatia (E. Slavonia)	1995–1998
Guatemala	1997
Timor Leste	1999–2002
Sierra Leone	1999–2005
Kosovo	1999–present
DR Congo	1999–present
Afghanistan	2002–present
Liberia	2003–present
Burundi	2004–present
Côte d'Ivoire	2004–present
Sudan (Southern)	2005–present
Sudan (Darfur)	2007–present

Note: Excludes missions with fewer than 200 military personnel (e.g., Georgia) and those not following an armed conflict (e.g., Haiti).

development in societies emerging from civil war partly depends on the existence of capable, autonomous and legitimate governmental institutions. One of the lessons from the preceding years was that peacebuilding operations tended to rely on quick fixes, such as rapid elections and bursts of economic privatization, while paying too little attention to constructing the institutional foundations for functioning postwar governments and markets. Without mechanisms such as pre-election power-sharing pacts and institutions to uphold election results, for example, balloting initially served as a catalyst for renewed conflict in Angola in 1992. Without arrangements to ensure that newly elected officials would themselves respect the rule of law, autocratic elites reverted to despotic forms of rule in Cambodia during the 1990s and in Liberia after 1997. Without institutions to govern the market, economic reform initiatives were diverted by powerful black marketers in Bosnia in the years following the negotiation of the 1995 Dayton Accords. In response to these and other lessons, international agencies such as the United Nations (UN) began to reorient their peacebuilding strategies towards the construction of effective, legitimate governmental institutions in transitional states. Because such institutional reform required more time, moreover, missions began to be deployed for longer periods, including in Timor Leste, Kosovo, and Sierra Leone.

Increased attention on statebuilding as a foundation for peacebuilding made good sense. The assumption that political and economic liberalization could be achieved in the absence of functioning, legitimate institutions—an assumption that implicitly underpinned the design and conduct of peacebuilding in its early years—was deeply flawed (Paris 2004). In other development-related fields, too, weak governance was increasingly recognized as a contributing factor to a range of social ills: from poverty[2] and famine[3] to disease.[4] Institutional strengthening, alone, would not produce peace and prosperity, but without adequate attention to the statebuilding requirements of peacebuilding, war-torn states would be less likely to escape the multiple and mutually reinforcing "traps" of violence and under-development.

As the mandates and time-frames of postconflict missions expanded, however, the problematic aspects of externally-assisted statebuilding became more apparent. Longer-term international deployments, for instance, risked being perceived by local actors as foreign intrusions in domestic affairs. How could international actors promote the goals of statebuilding without creating real or perceived "neo-trusteeship" arrangements over the host state? How could "local ownership" be achieved in the presence of powerful external actors? What about the danger of creating dependency on foreign actors or resources? How could international agencies promote statebuilding in a manner that respected local traditions and expectations in political, social and economic life? What were the long-run effects of different statebuilding strategies, including different electoral systems? How could postwar constitutions be designed to keep the peace in the short term and to lay the foundation for an effective, legitimate state in the longer-term? Postwar statebuilding is rife with these—and many other—vexing dilemmas.

To be sure, practitioners of statebuilding in the United Nations and other international organizations have been aware of many of these challenges. Issues such as coordination and coherence, local ownership, legitimacy, capacity-building, dependency, accountability, and exit are now commonly discussed in meetings of the new UN Peacebuilding Commission and elsewhere. But one of the arguments of this book is that such official discussions still tend to superficial, relying more on catch phrases than substance.[5] Meanwhile, the underlying sources of statebuilding's problems are rarely explored—or even directly acknowledged.

We believe that the time has come for a closer examination of the dilemmas and contradictions that lurk beneath the more visible, day-to-day challenges of statebuilding. Fundamental and unresolved tensions in the idea of externally-assisted statebuilding have given rise to a recurring series of policy problems facing peacebuilding actors in the field. Directly acknowledging and confronting these problems is crucial to the future success of the international community's peacebuilding efforts. The principal objective of this book is to investigate these contradictions and the policy dilemmas they generate.

The evolution of peacebuilding practice and theory

During the Cold War, the UN's principal security function was traditional peacekeeping, which typically involved deploying lightly-armed military forces to monitor ceasefires or patrol neutral buffer zones between former combatants. With rare exceptions, UN peacekeepers restricted themselves to the role of ceasefire observers, and stayed out of the domestic politics of their host states. They did so for several reasons: First, the UN Charter expressly prohibited the organization from intervening in matters "essentially within the domestic jurisdiction of any state."[6] Second, the Soviet Union and United States—both veto-wielding members of the UN Security Council— were wary of outside meddling in their respective Cold War spheres of influence, which in turn limited the UN's opportunities to play a more active role in addressing domestic security problems, particularly in strategically important countries. Third, even when the Soviets and Americans saw little threat to their strategic interests, the intense ideological differences of the Cold War made it virtually impossible to reach agreement on supporting any particular model of domestic governance—democracy or otherwise—within the states hosting peacekeepers.

Faced with these constraints, successive UN Secretaries-General held that international peacekeepers "must not take on responsibilities which fall under the Government of the country" in which they were operating.[7] But changing conditions at the end of the Cold War offered the UN a new entrée into domestic affairs which quickly revolutionized the organization's peace operations. Neither the US nor the Soviet Union (later Russia) was willing to maintain previous levels of military and economic assistance to their respective clients, particularly in many parts of the world, including most of Africa, which were now deemed strategic backwaters. This created a demand and an opening for the UN and other international organizations to become more directly involved in efforts to end several long-standing conflicts.

In 1989, the UN sent a mission to Namibia to monitor the conduct of local police and disarm former fighters, while preparing the country for its first democratic election and assisting in the drafting of a new national constitution. These functions went well beyond the constraints that had traditionally been imposed on peacekeepers, including the prohibition on involvement in the domestic affairs of host states. In 1991, new missions were launched in Angola, El Salvador, and Cambodia, involving the organization of elections, human-rights training and monitoring, and even (in Cambodia) temporarily taking over the administration of an entire country. In 1992, the UN deployed personnel to Bosnia and Somalia in the midst of ongoing civil conflicts, with formal Security Council authorization to use force for purposes other than their own self-defense—another contrast from traditional peacekeeping. In the same year, the UN sent a mission in Mozambique with wide-ranging responsibilities paralleling those in Angola, El Salvador, and Cambodia, including the preparation and supervision of democratic elections.

In his 1992 policy statement *An Agenda for Peace,* UN Secretary-General Boutros Boutros-Ghali presented a conceptual map of these new mission types (Boutros-Ghali 1992). He defined "peacekeeping" in traditional terms, as lightly armed missions that would mainly perform observation functions. His second category of operations—peace enforcement—involved more heavily armed contingents authorized to use force to achieve purposes other than self-protection. A third category of missions—post-conflict peacebuilding— aimed "to strengthen and solidify peace" in the aftermath of "civil strife." According to Boutros-Ghali, peacebuilding might include such functions as "disarming the previously warring parties and the restoration of order, the custody and possible destruction of weapons, repatriating refugees, advisory and training support for security personnel, monitoring elections, advancing efforts to protect human rights, reforming or strengthening governmental institutions and promoting formal and informal processes of political participation" (1992, para. 55). In addition, Boutros-Ghali underlined the importance of preventive diplomacy, or efforts to ease tensions before they result in conflict, which might include the "preventive deployment" of UN forces in order to avert violence.

The distinction between these different mission types was never absolute— nor could it be. The UN was moving in the direction of more complex multifunctional operations which sometimes displayed elements of all these mission types combined. The contradictions manifested themselves in an especially important way in Bosnia, where the ill-fated UN Protection Force (UNPROFOR) ended with peacekeepers unable to establish zones of safety that could stop crimes against humanity. In the ensuing years, some actors broadened the definition of "peacebuilding" to include everything from preventive diplomacy and humanitarian aid to different types of civilian assistance, military operations, development activities, and post-conflict reconstruction.[8] This was, in some respects, understandable: post-conflict peacebuilding aimed not only to consolidate peace after war, but also to prevent renewed violence in countries that had recently experienced conflict, and it therefore had simultaneously preventive and remedial purposes. On the other hand, such definitional broadening risked deflecting attention away from the special challenges and circumstances of *postwar* reconstruction, which is the focus of this volume.

Definitional nuances aside, peacebuilding in its post-conflict form became the UN's principal peace and security activity after the Cold War. Between 1989 and 1993 alone, eight major peacebuilding missions were deployed into territories emerging from war: Namibia, Nicaragua, Angola, Cambodia, El Salvador, Mozambique, Liberia, and Rwanda (see Table 1.1). The apparent failure of subsequent peace-enforcement operations in Somalia and Bosnia in 1993–94 had a chilling effect on UN operations through the mid-1990s, creating a lull on the deployment of new missions that lasted until the latter part of the decade. Nevertheless, three new operations were created during this relatively slow period: in Bosnia (1995), Croatia (1995), and Guatemala (1997).

In hindsight, the missions launched between 1989 and 1997 may be viewed as a first generation of peacebuilding operations following the Cold War, and they revealed the international community's relative inexperience in dealing with the task of post-conflict stabilization. Initial mandates tended to be for very limited periods, focusing primarily on holding a successful post-conflict election, usually within the first one or two years of peace, after which it was hoped that the host societies would be on their way to a lasting peace based on democracy and functioning free-market economies. Relatively little attention was paid to the longer-term tasks of constructing or strengthening the institutional structures necessary for democratic governance and market reforms—and, arguably, a durable peace—to take root.

Scholarship on peacebuilding during this initial period was also nascent. Most of the literature provided detailed descriptions of particular operations and countries, offering relatively little systematic, cross-case analysis, or theorizing about the strategies or nature of the peacebuilding enterprise.[9] Even studies that treated multiple cases tended to present a series of largely disconnected descriptive accounts rather than developing more general hypotheses about peacebuilding and evaluating these hypotheses through structured cross-case analysis. Two major volumes edited by William Durch published in 1993 and 1996, respectively, exemplified this early scholarship. Durch and his colleagues provided the most comprehensive surveys of peace operations to date and an invaluable reference on these missions, but shed little light on the over-arching objectives and underlying assumptions of peacebuilding. To be sure, the novelty of peacebuilding in the early and mid-1990s required defining and itemizing the characteristics of these operations, particularly in relation to traditional forms of peacekeeping that were more familiar to scholars of international security and the UN. Nevertheless, the first generation of academic writing on peacebuilding (with some important exceptions) tended to be heavy on description and light on comparative or theoretical analysis.

By the end of the 1990s and early 2000s, however, the practice and study of peacebuilding underwent parallel transformations. The experience of implementing the Dayton Accords in Bosnia in the latter half of the 1990s prompted several peacebuilding agencies including the United Nations to reconsider the time-lines and benchmarks of "success" in such operations. Launched in December 1995, the post-Dayton Bosnia mission was scheduled to last just one year—a timeframe that grossly underestimated what would be required. Although national elections were completed by the end of 1996, it was obvious to all that only preliminary progress had been made in other areas including refugee resettlement, and that the newly constituted Bosnian government was deeply dysfunctional: several elected officials initially refused even to meet with their counterparts in other ethnic communities. As a consequence, the operation was extended first for 18 additional months, and later for an indefinite period.

Thus, even though the mid-to-late 1990s was a period of relative quiescence in the creation of new peacebuilding efforts, it was nevertheless a time of learning for peacebuilding agencies. This learning manifested itself in two ways. First, three new operations were deployed in 1999—in Kosovo, Timor Leste and Sierra Leone—marking the end of the mid-1990s lull in new peacebuilding deployments. The mandates of these missions—particularly Kosovo and Timor Leste—were more expansive than their predecessors, reflecting a recognition that such operations needed to focus less on exit deadlines, and more on achieving the conditions for basic stability in these societies, including the functioning systems of public administration.[10] Second, these lessons were openly articulated in official discussions and documents of major peacebuilding agencies, most notably the United Nations. After the publication of a major report critiquing the peacebuilding methods of the 1990s,[11] the UN Security Council, for example, held a series of discussions on "exit strategies."[12] The near-universal consensus shared by national delegates at the meeting was pithily summarized by the Argentine representative: "[Exits] must not be determined by pre-established timetables, but by attainable objectives."[13] This position also became the central theme of Secretary-General Kofi Annan's ensuing policy statement, the title of which captured its main message: "No Exit without Strategy."[14]

In parallel with the changing practices of peacebuilding, a second-generation scholarship was coming to fruition in the late 1990s and early 2000s, including more theoretical treatments and systematic cross-case comparisons. One branch of this new literature focused on the durability of peace after civil wars, comparing the effects of different types of international post-conflict interventions with countries that had not hosted peacebuilding or peacekeeping missions.[15] Another group of analysts examined the role of natural resources and "conflict economies" in explaining peacebuilding outcomes, expanding upon Paul Collier's and Anke Hoeffler's work on "greed and grievance" as drivers of civil war.[16] Others examined peacebuilding through the lens of "critical" theories including neo-Marxist approaches, securitization theory, cosmopolitanism, and post-structuralism.[17] A number of scholars focused on the role of "spoilers" or local actors who seek to undermine peace processes, building on Stephen John Stedman's earlier conceptual writing,[18] while others examined the regional dimensions of peacebuilding,[19] the impacts of transitional justice mechanisms on post-conflict recovery,[20] or the role of women and gender in peacebuilding[21]—to name just a few sub-areas of the second-generation peacebuilding literature which blossomed around the turn of the century and thereafter.[22] Specific findings emerging from this scholarly activity were diverse—reflecting the multiple sub-areas and approaches to the subject. However, the argument that peacebuilders needed to pay more attention to statebuilding goals soon gained prominence, as we shall see below.

Statebuilding as a neglected element in peacebuilding

There are moments in every scholarly field when different writers independently arrive at similar conclusions at approximately the same time. This happened in 2004 with the publication of three books and two articles offering parallel critiques of peacebuilding theory and practice. In different ways, Francis Fukuyama, Simon Chesterman, James Fearon and David Laitin, Stephen Krasner, and Roland Paris all argued that the operational concepts and implementation of peacebuilding had under-emphasized the creation or strengthening of governmental institutions as a foundation for successful transitions from war to peace.[23]

Francis Fukuyama's book was not focused on peacebuilding per se, but more generally on "the problem of weak governance and missing or inadequate institutions at the nation-state level" as a critical obstacle to the economic and social development of their own societies and a source of insecurity to other countries: "Weak or failing states commit human rights abuses, provoke humanitarian disasters, drive massive waves of immigration, and attack their neighbors."[24] Specifically, Fukuyama criticized the international community's peacebuilding record in Haiti, Cambodia, and Bosnia, along with the more ambitious missions of Kosovo and Timor Leste, for having failed to make "much headway in creating self-sustaining states in any of the countries it has set out to rebuild."[25] While acknowledging the limitations of outsiders' abilities to create governmental structures *de novo*, he maintained that strengthening the capacity of a postwar government to perform basic functions of public administration, such that the government can eventually "wean itself from outside assistance," should be treated as a crucial goal of peacebuilding.[26]

Simon Chesterman's volume analyzed the history and dynamics of internationally-run "transitional administrations" from the League of Nations mandates system to the post-Cold War era, or instances in which international actors have exercised varying degrees of governing authority over a territory and its people. One of the leitmotifs of his historical account was tension between the means and ends of international administration: "Is it possible to establish the conditions for legitimate and sustainable national governance through a period of benevolent foreign autocracy?"[27] Although he expressed deep reservations about transitional administration and especially the troubling character and implications of international authority over the domestic affairs of their host states, he did not condemn peacebuilding as a form of neo-colonialism, as some other commentators were doing.[28] Rather, Chesterman sought to understand the evolution of transitional administration and some of its inherent problems, and he was thus among the first commentators to offer a serious analysis of statebuilding's contradictions and dilemmas, which is the principal topic of this book. Further, in spite of his reservations about statebuilding, he argued peacebuilders had not focused sufficiently on the importance of establishing sustainable institutions and economic stability.[29] He criticized the Bosnia and Kosovo missions, in particular, for not moving quickly enough to create a "functioning law enforcement and judicial system," which were among the governmental structures he viewed as necessary to consolidate peace and to implement other peacebuilding goals.[30] In this sense, Chesterman's conclusions about the importance of statebuilding loosley paralleled those of Fukuyama.

James Fearon and David Laitin approached this subject from yet another perspective in their widely read article on "Neotrusteeship and the Problem of Weak States" (Fearon and Laitin 2004). Their purpose was twofold. First, they presented a "realist" case for statebuilding, pointing out that countries with very weak governmental institutions (or low "state capacity") are not only particularly prone to civil war, but that the political disorder and economic collapse creates international security risks, including the proliferation of weapons of mass destruction, transnational terrorism, drug smuggling, and health threats. Second, they argued that the international community lacked the capacities to conduct effective statebuilding missions. The existing statebuilding tools were too ad hoc, disorganized and poorly resourced to deal with the challenges of collapsed states. Previous peacebuilding operations, they claimed, had attempted to promote reconciliation and to mediate political differences without paying enough attention to institutional strengthening or construction: Providing public goods through functioning governmental institutions were a precondition for "political and economic progress of any kind," they maintained.[31]

In the same year, Stephen Krasner authored "Sharing Sovereignty: New Institutions for Collapsed and Failing States," an article that caused something of a stir, less for its diagnosis of peacebuilding's problems and more for its unorthodox prescriptions (Krasner 2004). Krasner recommended "shared sovereignty" arrangements for the most dangerously fragile states, with external actors taking responsibility for some of the "domestic authority structures of the target state for an indefinite period of time."[32] The controversial element of this proposal was not the idea of international governance arrangements in fragile states but the notion that such arrangements should be viewed as permanent in some cases, and that countries in question should cease to be recognized as fully sovereign in international law. These recommendations went considerably further than Fearon and Laitin's call for a stronger international statebuilding role;[33] nor were they likely to be endorsed by either Chesterman or Fukuyama, both of whom insisted that peacebuilders should transfer sovereign powers back to the local population without delay because of the need to avoid creating destructive conditions of dependency and the perception (or reality) of foreign occupation. In spite of these important prescriptive differences, however, Krasner's diagnosis of peacebuilding's problems shared much in common with these other writers' analyses. Building effective governmental institutions, Krasner argued, was a necessary (but not a sufficient) condition for peacebuilding efforts to produce lasting results. "Failed, inadequate, incompetent, or abusive national authority structures," he wrote, "have sabotaged the economic well-being, violated the basic human rights, and undermined the physical security of their countries' populations" (Krasner 2004: 90).

Roland Paris offered another version of this critique in *At War's End: Building Peace After Civil Conflict*, which also appeared in 2004. Peace-building actors, Paris argued, had under-estimated the destabilizing effects of the political and economic reforms that were touted as remedies for civil violence. Those reforms promoted political liberalization or democratization (i.e., the promotion of elections and respect for basic civil liberties) and economic liberalization or marketization (i.e., movement toward a market-oriented economic model). The international community's efforts to promote stability in war-torn states by encouraging democratization and marketization in the 1990s had created not a liberal peace but instead renewed competition and violence in part because peacebuilders had not made sufficient efforts to build the basic institutional structures (including, most importantly, rule of law institutions) that both democracy and market economics required to function well. By contrast, Paris argued the need for effective governance was well understood by the eighteenth-century liberal philosophers who first advocated for free markets and representative political institutions as a for-mula for peace and prosperity, including John Locke, Immanuel Kant, and Adam Smith. All of these philosophers had written that reaping the benefits of liberalization required the existence of functioning state institutions to manage the destructive potential inherent in the idea of political and eco-nomic liberalization. Now, Paris wrote, this lesson needed to be recalled and reinstated in contemporary peacebuilding strategy—specifically, by recogniz-ing the need to devote more attention to the institution-building requirements of war-to-peace transitions.

In the wake of these and other publications, statebuilding became a grow-ing topic of interest within the peacebuilding scholarship[34] and in documents produced by and for major intergovernmental and national development agencies, including the Organization for Economic Cooperation and Devel-opment (OECD),[35] the United Nations Development Program (UNDP), and the United States Agency for International Development (USAID).[36] The OECD's Principles for Good International Engagement in Fragile States and Situations, for example, included advice to the organization's member countries (the largest donor nations in the world) that international efforts in fragile states should "focus on statebuilding as the central objec-tive."[37] Echoing these principles, one of the UN's most highly-regarded former diplomats, Lakhdar Brahimi, offered the following assessment in 2007:

> The concept of statebuilding is becoming more and more accepted within the international community and is actually far more apt as a descrip-tion of exactly what it is that we should be trying to do in postconflict countries—building effective systems and institutions of government. Indeed, acceptance of statebuilding as a generic term to describe our activities will help to concentrate international support on those very activities.[38]

While by no means universally embraced, statebuilding had clearly become an important part of the peacebuilding discourse—both for analysts and practitioners.

Whither statebuilding? Retreat, reinvest, reorganize or rethink?

Today, the future of postwar peacebuilding and statebuilding is uncertain, for several reasons. First, the record of these missions since 1989 has been mixed.[39] Most of the countries that have hosted these missions have not reverted to war, but the durability of peace even in the most "successful" cases is less clear. How should we judge, for example, the outcome of peacebuilding in Central America where missions did little to address deep socio-economic inequalities, which have arguably been among the root causes of the region's violence past? What about the utter failure of peacebuilding in Rwanda prior to the 1994 genocide, or the on-again, off-again progress in Angola or Sierra Leone? And what should we make of the burst of renewed fighting in Timor Leste in 2006, in a country that was widely touted as one of the most notable peacebuilding successes? Such outcomes have raised doubts about prospects for peacebuilding and statebuilding even in relatively favorable settings. Although most experts hold that these operations have, on the whole, done considerably more good than harm, serious doubts persist about the ability of international agencies to create the conditions for sustainable peace.

Second, the movement toward statebuilding—with its emphasis on longer-lasting missions and institutional strengthening—has raised additional concerns for some observers, including the charge that such missions represent a new form of colonial control over the territory of the war-torn state. The strongest versions of this critique portray statebuilding as a form of neo-imperial or capitalist exploitation of vulnerable societies.[40] Less extreme versions highlight the dangers of fostering a "culture of dependency" in the host society due to the international community's extended and seemingly intrusive role, which is contrary to the goal of promoting sustainable self-rule built on domestic governing capacities.[41] Whatever one may think of these critiques, the difficulties faced, for example, by the continued presence of international peacebuilders in Bosnia, well over a decade after their initial deployment, raises doubts about whether statebuilding efforts open a Pandora's Box of perpetual deployments and unending dependency.

Third, in the post-9/11 period—and particularly since the 2003 invasion of Iraq—it has become increasingly difficult to separate discussions of statebuilding in war-torn states from the ill-fated attempt to stabilize post-invasion Iraq. In fact, the circumstances of peacebuilding in Iraq (and Afghanistan) are profoundly different from those of most statebuilding operations: almost all of these operations have been deployed after civil wars (not external invasions) and at the request of local parties who have sought international assistance to help implement peace settlements. However, this distinction between post-invasion and post-settlement statebuilding is often unrecognized or deliberately blurred. As a result, exasperation over the deterioration of conditions in Iraq can spill over into skepticism about the potential effectiveness or desirability of *any* kind of post-conflict statebuilding operation.

In the face of these diverse criticisms and doubts, the historic experiment in peacebuilding and statebuilding appears to have arrived at a crossroads, and it is unclear what direction this experiment will take, or indeed whether it will proceed at all. Few observers seem willing to endorse the status quo, but there is little agreement beyond that. Some analysts warn that the entire enterprise is too ambitious and too interventionist, and recommend scaling back or eliminating international statebuilding efforts. Jeffrey Herbst, for instance, argues that seeking to reconstitute functioning states within existing borders, particularly in Africa where national borders were often arbitrarily drawn during the colonial era, can freeze in place arrangements that do not reflect underlying social patterns and are therefore unsustainable (Herbst 2003). His advice is to "let states fail": allow new forms and centers of political authority to emerge through conflict and cooperation without outside direction or intrusion, and then redraw national boundaries to reflect these new arrangements, rather than seeking to perpetuate the untenable fictions of many existing states.[42]

Similarly, Jeremy Weinstein endorses a strategy of promoting "autonomous recovery" in which states can achieve "a lasting peace, a systematic reduction in violence, and postwar political and economic development in the absence of international intervention."[43] He maintains that international efforts to end wars through negotiated settlements, and to rebuild states on the basis of these settlements, can serve to "freeze unstable distributions of power and to provide a respite from hostilities for groups that are intent on continuing the conflict when the international community departs."[44] Instead, allowing conflicts to take their natural course, sorting out the winners from the losers, is a surer basis for peace in the longer-term. This argument builds upon the research of some scholars who have found that civil wars ending in military victories tend to produce longer-lasting peace than those ending in negotiated agreements.[45] These positions, combined with earlier-mentioned critiques from those who reject large-scale peacebuilding on normative grounds as a new form of Western colonialism, represent a "counsel of retreat" from postwar statebuilding.

Others argue that the existing model is sound but that statebuilding operations have suffered from an under-commitment of international resources, and that even deeper and longer-lasting international intervention is the avenue to greater success. This is a "counsel of reinvestment" in peacebuilding and statebuilding—and it is based on the contention, as one high-level UN panel concluded, that "failure to invest adequately in peacebuilding increases the odds that a country will relapse into conflict."[46] In fact, the "gap between mission needs and the resources supplied by international interveners in collapsed states" is commonly identified as an impediment to more effective missions.[47] Investing resources means not just commitment of funds, but also personnel, equipment, and time; and even the more robust, longer-term missions launched since 1999 have been criticized as inadequate on these grounds. The resurgence of violence in Timor Leste in 2006, for instance, led Secretary-General Kofi Annan to acknowledge that the preceding peacebuilding mission had been terminated prematurely, before efforts to restore basic state functions (especially, in this case, the rule of law elements of the police and judiciary) were far enough along. In recommending the deployment of a new UN mission to the territory later that year, Annan made a point of explaining that strengthening public institutions in post-conflict societies is "inevitably a long-term process," requiring the international community to make a correspondingly long-term commitment to the new mission in Timor Leste.[48]

According to other observers, however, the primary problem of statebuilding is not the mismatch of resources and objectives but, rather, the lack of strategic coherence among international peacebuilders themselves. This critique often leads to a "counsel of reorganization," focusing on the need for a greater coordination.[49] Such concerns have in fact given rise to institutional reforms within the United Nations and elsewhere. In 2006, the UN launched its new Peacebuilding Commission, tasked with helping to coordinate peacebuilding actors and strategies and to mobilize resources for countries on its agenda (which, at the time of this writing, were Burundi, Sierra Leone, and Guinea-Bissau). The UN has also been developing "integrated missions" frameworks, which seek to "[link] the different dimensions of peacebuilding (political, development, humanitarian, human rights, rule of law, social and security aspects) into a coherent support strategy."[50] Further, several national governments have launched initiatives aimed at improving "whole of government" or "linked-up" approaches to peacebuilding, reflecting a widespread perception that inadequate communication and coordination among different branches of the same government (in particular, the ministries responsible for foreign affairs, development, and defense) were undermining their effectiveness in the field.[51]

The contributors to this volume have varying opinions on the three broad approaches outlined above, but one thing they all share in common is a belief that each of these options is a largely superficial response to the challenges and shortcomings of postwar statebuilding. The deeper problem, we argue, is insufficient understanding of statebuilding's complexities—in particular, its intrinsic tensions and contradictions. What the statebuilding "project" needs now is not simply reinvestment or reorganization, but careful rethinking. Scholars and practitioners have only recently begun to explore the competing (and sometimes contradictory) imperatives facing those who attempt to reconstitute effective and legitimate governmental structures in war-torn states. Conceiving of postwar statebuilding in this way—as an inherently contradiction-filled enterprise rather than as a sequence of mutually reinforcing steps—allows us to focus on the nature of the tensions and contradictions themselves. Only by doing so can we gain a better understanding of the forces that might sustain—or derail—future operations.

Most of the contributors to this volume also share the conviction that postwar statebuilding efforts are too important to abandon, in spite of their many shortcomings and frustrations. Today, a plethora of states—certainly more than 70 of the 190-plus states in the international system—are vulnerable to so-called state failure in the context of economic crisis, demographic instabilities, factionalized leaders, availability of arms, and other indicators of fragility;[52] and virtually all the countries at the top of states-likely-to-fail lists are those where there has been, or which are highly vulnerable to, armed conflict. Retreating from the postwar statebuilding project would be tantamount to abandoning tens of millions of people to lawlessness, predation, disease, and fear. Beyond their humanitarian effects, state weakness and state failure are global concerns because of the spillovers, contagions, instabilities, and vitiation of international norms that occurs when authority and order disappear. The international community may not be able to address every case of state fragility or failure, but it should, at least, help countries that are emerging from civil wars, since these are the countries at greatest risk of falling into a pernicious cycle of chronic violence. Capable states are also needed as partners in the "global public policy networks" needed to address global interdendencies such as climate change, disease mitigation, or transnational criminal networks.

What is statebuilding? And what is it not?

In this volume, postwar statebuilding refers to the strengthening or construction of legitimate governmental institutions in countries that are emerging from conflicts.[53] Four features of this definition should be noted:

1 Statebuilding is not synonymous with peacebuilding. Post-conflict peacebuilding refers to efforts to create conditions in which violence will not recur. Statebuilding, by contrast, is a sub-component of peacebuilding. Support for postwar statebuilding should thus not be misconstrued as an attempt to supplant peacebuilding, but rather, as a call for paying greater attention to strengthening or constructing effective and legitimate governmental institutions as an important element of peacebuilding.

2 Statebuilding is not limited to "top-down" approaches of institution-strengthening (i.e., those focusing on national elites), nor does it preclude "bottom-up" approaches (i.e., working through civil-society groups, or promoting measures to facilitate the accountability of state structures to their societies). This is a common but misplaced criticism of statebuilding.[54] Because statebuilding refers to the construction of *legitimate* governmental institutions, it necessarily requires attentiveness to the relationship between these institutions and civil society. States gain legitimacy from

both international and domestic sources (Bukovansky 2002). In the domestic realm, legitimacy derives from a belief among a state's people that public institutions possess a rightful authority to govern. This is the essence of legitimacy. It is a "subjective quality, relational between actor and institution, and defined by the actor's perception of the institution."[55]

3   Statebuilding is not synonymous with nation-building. Although the two concepts are related, statebuilding focuses primarily on public institutions— the machinery of the state, from courts and legislatures to laws and bureaucrats—whereas nation-building refers to the strengthening of a national population's collective identity, including its sense of national distinctiveness and unity.

4   Although we do attempt to provide an a priori list of "core" state functions, in part because the contributors to this volume have different views on this matter, most definitions of core functions include some or all of the following: the provision of security, the rule of law (including a codified and promulgated body of laws with a reasonably effective police and justice system), basic services (including emergency relief, support for the poorest, and essential healthcare), and at least a rudimentary ability to formulate and implement budget plans and to collect revenues through taxation. None of these functions requires Western-style democracy or "neoliberal" market ideologies. Although democratization and marketization have been routine features of peacebuilding to date, they are analytically distinct from the concept of statebuilding used in this volume.

Towards a better understanding of statebuilding's contradictions

By investigating the underlying tensions of statebuilding, this book contributes to an emerging, third generation of peacebuilding scholarship. As noted above, the first generation focused largely on describing the characteristics of peacebuilding missions in the years immediately following the Cold War. The second generation took a step back, analyzing the record of peacebuilding more systematically, and scrutinizing its purposes, strategies, and assumptions, including the relative neglect of institutional strengthening or statebuilding in countries emerging from conflict. Yet, statebuilding is no panacea; although analysts and international organizations have increasingly recognized the importance of statebuilding as a core element of peacebuilding, ongoing efforts to build effective, legitimate government institutions in war-torn countries rely on a limited foundation of knowledge. Understanding what works in postwar statebuilding, and what does not work, will require more than lists of lessons learned from previous missions. Indeed, officials in international organizations and national governments would err if they were simply to embrace statebuilding as a "solution" without recognizing that it is still poorly understood. Our objective in this book, therefore, is neither to bury statebuilding, nor simply to praise it. Rather, we regard the operational challenges of statebuilding as visible manifestations of deeper tensions, and we seek to dissect these tensions so that they may be better understood—and, ultimately, better managed.

The volume is divided into six parts. The first part analyzes the context of statebuilding operations, both in the field and in the relations among the principal international actors. In Chapter 2, Michael Barnett and Christoph Zürcher contend that international actors strike informal "contracts" with local protagonists as a means of reconciling some of the contradictory imperatives of statebuilding. Paradoxically, however, these negotiations sometimes lead to the reinforcement of weak statehood because both the international peacebuilders and the local elites share an interest in creating the appearance of change while leaving existing state–society relations largely intact. In Chapter 3, Roland Paris examines the international context for statebuilding, focusing on the problem of coordination that arises among the plethora of institutions, agencies, and individuals that constitute the "international community" in any given case. He argues that many of these coordination problems are mislabeled because they are not simply management failures but a reflection of deeper philosophical differences among the main peacebuilding actors. Efforts to "fix" these differences through procedural reforms are important, but they also serve to deflect attention away from the more substantive (and, arguably, more important) task of confronting the contradictions of statebuilding and thinking through strategies for managing these contradictions.

The book's second part focuses on the quintessential Weberian task of balancing the effectiveness and legitimacy of security forces in postwar countries. In Chapter 4, David M. Edelstein delves into the difficult role of foreign militaries and the challenges of providing security while forces face an "obsolescing welcome" from local populations. At a broader level, the chapter addresses the apparent contradiction in postwar statebuilding between the need for comprehensive, long-term international assistance, and the distorting and grating effects that an international presence can have on the host society over time. In Chapter 5, Deborah Avant tackles one of the most perplexing challenges of security sector reform: Under what conditions does the reliance on private security companies by international organizations for military training yield successful outcomes in terms of developing responsible, civilian controlled, local military forces? In some cases, it seems, private security companies can contribute to the creation or strengthening of effective and legitimate government institutions in the host state, but in other cases it can have the reverse effect.

If wars are fueled by and fundamentally shape economic systems, a critical element in peacebuilding is the transformation of markets and their associated flow and accumulation of wealth and distribution of poverty and destitution. In Chapter 6, Christopher Cramer explores the tensions between change and continuity in the economic patterns of transitional countries as they emerge from war. Rather than seeking to remake the economies of such countries, Cramer argues, peacebuilders should recognize that important elements of wartime economies can contribute to longer-term institution-building and economic development. The challenge is to move beyond the simplistic notion that war is "development in reverse," and to identify those elements in the wartime "trajectories of accumulation" that can facilitate, rather than undermine, statebuilding objectives. In a similar vein, David Roberts' analysis of Cambodia in Chapter 7 reveals a deep persistence in patterns of patronage before, during and after the country hosted a major peace operation in the early 1990s. In some ways, he argues, international efforts aimed at creating "modern" economic institutions and reducing corruption in Cambodia have weakened traditional patterns of regulation and social-service delivery without replacing them with effective alternatives. For both Cramer and Roberts, therefore, the tensions between continuity versus change, and deeply-rooted local patterns versus externally-driven reform, require a great deal more attention from peacebuilding practitioners.

It has been argued that peacebuilding should be viewed "as politics" (Cousens et al. 2000). In Chapter 8, Kirsti Samuels identifies the principal choices that guide the making of new constitutional dispensations and the critical role that constitution-making plays in the creation of new rules of the political game in postwar environments. Of particular interest to Samuels is the tension between the short-term versus long-term imperatives of effective statebuilding as they inform the process of constitution making, and how these imperatives might be reconciled. In Chapter 9, Timothy Sisk hones in on one of the most contentious areas of disagreement among analysts and practitioners: whether, when, and how the initial postwar election is held in order to legitimate new governments after war. He argues that choices and interventions made at the initial electoral moment fundamentally shape the nature of the postwar state, once again highlighting the need for international actors to reconcile tensions between the short-term and longer-term requirements of effective statebuilding, since even the earliest decisions affect the nature of the state that emerges for years to follow.

Two chapters in this volume address head-on the impact of statebuilding missions on local autonomy and dependence. Astri Suhrke's analysis of the Afghanistan case in Chapter 10 contends that, in this instance, less international intrusion would be better: peacebuilding following the 2001 toppling of the Taliban regime has been a story of fostering the dependency of the Karzai regime and of Afghan society on international assistance. In Chapter 11, Jens Narten evaluates one of the most important cases where the international "footprint" has been quite large—Kosovo—and where the principal challenge has been to create local ownership for a process of statebuilding in which the ultimate outcome remains uncertain. Both chapters offer important insights into a core contradiction of statebuilding and how it plays out in practice: namely, the use of outside intervention as a means of promoting domestic self-government.

The closing part of the book offers reflections and conclusions on the volume as a whole. In Chapter 12, Miles Kahler characterizes the book as an exploration and plea for a "revisionist" approach to peacebuilding—one that rejects the idea of abandoning societies emerging from conflict but that seeks rethink and revise prevailing approaches in order to make "international intervention more effective and less self-defeating over time." Kahler also notes that "the debate over statebuilding has only begun" and offers his own thoughts on how the revisionist option for statebuilding might be pursued. Finally, in Chapter 13, Roland Paris and Timothy Sisk organize the findings of the authors and weave their arguments into a set of observations about the key contradictions of statebuilding and the policy dilemmas they generate, along with some advice on navigating the pitfalls of statebuilding. We do not purport to offer "solutions" because these are true dilemmas that cannot be resolved in any definitive sense. But we do believe that these dilemmas could be better managed, based on careful analysis and greater knowledge of their sources and dynamics.

While varied in their approaches, methodology, case analysis, and recommendations, the essays in this volume do reflect a consensus. They all recognize the enormity and complexity of the task of "building" states in the aftermath of war, the difficulties of action and coordination in difficult environments, and the dilemmas, contradictions, and conundrums that emerge for the international community as it engages in a statebuilding enterprise. They also contend that the answer to these challenges is not resignation or retreat, nor simply reinvestment or "doing more" of what is already being done. Instead, the answers to the myriad of problems facing statebuilders can be found, first and foremost, in a deeper understanding of the dilemmas of statebuilding. This is a critical task of the third generation of scholarship on peacebuilding—and of this book.

Notes

1 Human Security Centre 2008.
2 Keefer and Knack 1997.
3 Sen 1999.
4 Menon-Johansson 2005.
5 For example, see the Security Council's discussion of peacebuilding in S/PV.5895 and S/PV.5895 (Resumption 1), May 20, 2008.
6 Article 2 (7).
7 *Report of the Secretary-General on the Implementation of Security Council Resolution 425*, (Security Council document S/12611), March 19, 1978.
8 See Lund 2003, pp. 26–27; Call 2005, pp. 3–5; and Barnett, Kim, O'Donnell and Sitea 2007.
9 For example, Durch 1993; Diehl 1994; Heininger 1994; Ratner 1995; Durch 1996; Mayall 1996; and Hillen 2000.
10 Norberg 2003.
11 "Report of the Panel on United Nations Peace Operations," also known as the "Brahimi Report," in 2000. A/55/305—S/2000/809 August 21, 2000.
12 Security Council documents S/PV.4223 and S/PV.4223 (Resumption 1) (November 15, 2000).
13 Security Council document S/PV.4223 (November 15, 2000), p. 12.

14 "No Exit without Strategy: Security Council Decision-Making and the Closure or Transition of United Nations Peacekeeping Operations," Report of the Secretary-General, UN document S/2001/394 (April 20, 2001).

15 For example, Doyle and Sambanis 2000 and 2006; and Fortna 2003 and 2004. Much of this literature built upon earlier work by Licklider 1995.

16 For example, Collier and Hoeffler 2001; Milliken and Krause 2002; Ross 2004; Cooper 2005; and Wennmann 2005.

17 For example, Chandler 2000; Duffield 2001; Pugh 2004; Woodhouse and Ramsbotham 2005; Richmond 2006; and Zanotti 2006.

18 For example, Stedman 1997; Zahar 2004; Newman and Richmond 2006; and Greenhill and Major 2006/07.

19 For example, Maclean 1999; Tschirgi 2002; Pugh and Waheguru 2003; Bellamy and Williams 2005; and Bures 2006.

20 For a review of the literature on the empirical effects of transitional justice in states undergoing transitions from conflict or authoritarianism, see Thoms, Ron and Paris 2008.

21 For example, Nakaya 2004; and De la Rey and McKay 2006.

22 Readers interested in examining other examples and sub-areas of this literature should consult two specialized journals that regularly produce high-quality articles on this subject: *International Peacekeeping* and the *Journal of Intervention and Statebuilding*.

23 See Fukuyama 2004; Chesterman 2004; Fearon and Laitin 2004; Krasner 2004; and Paris 2004.

24 Fukuyama 2004, pp. 92–93.

25 Ibid., p. 103.

26 Ibid., pp. 100 and 102.

27 Chesterman 2004, p. 1.

28 For example, see Chandler 2000 on Bosnia.

29 Chesterman 2004, p. 234.

30 Ibid., Chap. 3 and pp. 181–82.

31 Ibid., p. 23.

32 Ibid., p. 108.

33 Fearon and Laitin (2004, p. 41) suggested that some form of long-term "international surveillance through [the host state's] membership in a plethora of organizations" might be necessary. By contrast, Krasner (2004, p. 106) recommended developing "an alternative to conventional [national] sovereignty, one that explicitly recognizes that international legal sovereignty will be withdrawn and that external actors will control many aspects of domestic sovereignty for an indefinite period of time."

34 For example, Martin and Mayer-Rieckh 2005; Boyce and O'Donnell 2006; Chandler 2006; Ghani et al. 2006; Rubin 2006; Thies 2006; Weller and Wolff 2006; Fritz and Rocha Menochal 2007; *International Peacekeeping* 2007; and Marten 2007. Arguments about the importance of institutional strengthening for the consolidation of peace also coincided with work on the importance of "good governance" as a facilitating condition for economic development.

35 OECD 2007, p. 2.

36 Blair and Ammitzboell 2007.

37 OECD 2007.

38 Brahimi 2007.

39 See Doyle and Sambanis 2006; and Paris 2004.

40 For example, Bendaña 2005.

41 For example, Chandler 2006, Chap. 6.

42 Ibid. See also Atzili 2007; and Englebert and Tull 2008.

43 Weinstein 2005, p. 5.

44 Ibid., p. 9.
45 For example, Luttwak 1999; and Toft 2003.
46 High Level Panel on Threats, Challenges and Change 2004, para. 224.
47 Fearon and Laitin 2004, p. 20. See also Chesterman 2005, pp. 161–64.
48 "Report of the Secretary-General on Timor-Leste Pursuant to Security Council resolution 1690 (2006)," UN Security Council document S/2006/628 (August 8, 2006), paras. 40 and 142.
49 See Chapter 3 for details.
50 Note from the Secretary General Kofi A. Annan, "Guidance on Integrated Missions," 9 February 2006.
51 See Chapter 3.
52 See the work of the Fund for Peace's Failed States Index, at www.fundforpeace.org.
53 For other definitions of "statebuilding," see Jones et al. 2008; Call and Cousens 2008; and Suhrke et al. 2007.
54 For example, Chandler 2006; Richmond 2006; and Hameiri 2007.
55 Hurd 2003, p. 381.

Part I
Domestic and international context

2 The peacebuilder's contract

How external statebuilding reinforces weak statehood

Michael Barnett and Christoph Zürcher

Complex peacebuilding operations are reasonably successful at ending violence.[1] Yet they generally aspire to do more than end violence—they also intend to remove the root causes of violence and create the conditions for a positive peace. It is not enough that former combatants go to their respective corners, disarm, or recognize that a resumption of violence will generate more costs than benefits. In order for there to be a stable peace, war-torn societies must develop the institutions, intellectual tools, and civic culture that generates the expectation that individuals and groups will settle their conflicts through non-violent means. Peacebuilders seek to remove the root causes of violence and create this pacific disposition by investing these post-conflict societies with various qualities, including democracy in order to reduce the tendency toward arbitrary power and give voice to all segments of society; the rule of law in order to reduce human rights violations; a market economy free from corruption in order to discourage individuals from believing that the surest path to fortune is by capturing the state; conflict management tools; and a culture of tolerance and respect.

There are various explanations for why peacebuilding operations have fallen far short of this ambitious goal of creating the good society. Perhaps the simplest explanation is that peacebuilders are expecting to achieve the impossible dream, attempting to engineer in years what took centuries for West European states and doing so under very unfavorable conditions. Peacebuilding operations confront highly difficult conditions, including a lack of local assets, high levels of destruction from the violence, continuing conflict, and minimal support from powerful donors and benefactors (Chesterman 2004; Doyle and Sambanis 2006; Orr 2004). Another explanation faults the peacebuilders, failing to realize that their goal of transplanting a liberal-democracy in war-torn soil has allowed former combatants to aggressively pursue their existing interests to the point that it rekindles the conflict. In their effort to radically transform major aspects of state, society, and economy in a matter of months, complex peacebuilding missions are subjecting these fragile societies to tremendous stress. States emerging from war do not have the necessary institutional framework or civic culture to absorb the potential pressures associated with political and market competition.

Consequently, as peacebuilders push for instant liberalization, they are sowing the seeds of conflict, encouraging rivals to wage their struggle for supremacy through markets and ballots (Paris 2004; Zakaria 2003). Shock therapy, peacebuilding-style, undermines the construction of the very institutions that are instrumental for producing a stable peace.

In this chapter we offer an alternative explanation: peacebuilders have adopted strategies that have reinforced previously existing state–society relations—weak states characterized by patrimonial politics and skewed development.[2] Specifically, we develop a model of peacebuilding operations that helps explain why peacebuilders transfer only the ceremonies and symbols of the liberal-democratic state. The model, in brief, is as follows. We begin with the preferences of three key actors: peacebuilders (PBs), who want stability and liberalization; state elites (SEs) of the target country, who want to maintain their power; and subnational elites (SNEs), who want autonomy from the state and to maintain their power in the countryside. The ability of each actor to achieve its goals is dependent on the strategies and behavior of the other two. Peacebuilders need the cooperation of state and subnational elites if they are to maintain stability and implement their liberalizing programs. State elites are suspicious of peacebuilding reforms because they might usurp their power, yet they covet the resources offered by peacebuilders because they can be useful for maintaining their power; and they need local subnational elites and power brokers, who frequently gained considerable autonomy during the civil war, to acknowledge their rule. Subnational elites seek the resources provided by international actors to maintain their standing and autonomy, yet fear peacebuilding programs that might undermine their power at the local level and increase the state's control over the periphery.

Because peacebuilders, state elites, and subnational elites are in a situation of strategic interaction, where their ability to achieve their goals is dependent on the strategies of others, they will strategize and alter their policies depending on (what they believe) others (will) do.[3] Peacebuilders will have to adjust their policies and adapt their strategies to take into account their dependence on state elites, adjustments and adaptations that are likely to incorporate their preference for arrangements that safeguard their fundamental interests. State elites will have to acknowledge the legitimacy of peacebuilding reforms if they are to receive the stream of international resources.

Their strategic interactions will shape the peacebuilding agenda and hence the outcome of the peacebuilding process. For heuristic purposes, we argue that the logic of their strategic interactions—the game—can lead to one of four possible outcomes: *cooperative peacebuilding*: local elites accept and fully cooperate with the peacebuilding program; *compromised peacebuilding*: local elites and peacebuilders negotiate a peacebuilding program that reflects the desire of peacebuilders for stability and the legitimacy of peacebuilding and the desire of local elites to ensure that reforms do not threaten their power base; *captured peacebuilding*: state and local elites are able to redirect the distribution of assistance so that it is fully consistent with their interests; or *conflictive peacebuilding*: the threat or use of coercive tools by either international or domestic actors to achieve their objectives.

We argue that compromised peacebuilding is the most likely outcome because of the nature of the parties' preferences and constraints and because once they arrive at this result they have little incentive to defect. Compromised peacebuilding, with its allocation of roles and responsibilities to each of the parties, represents something of an implicit or tacit contract—a peacebuilder's contract. Peacebuilders recognize the interest, power and authority of local elites, although this may not be compatible with the objective of building a good peace. State elites acknowledge the legitimacy of the reforms proposed by peacebuilders, but are intent to minimize the possible risks to their fundamental interests. Peacebuilders and local elites pursue their collective interest in stability and symbolic peacebuilding, creating the appearance (and opening up the possibility) of change while leaving largely intact existing state–society relations.[4]

This model has several advantages over existing explanations for why peacebuilding fails to accomplish its stated goal of transformation and tends to reinforce the existing pattern of power relations. To begin, it brings "domestic politics" back into the explanation. Existing approaches tend to be systemic-centric, focusing on the international actors, treating domestic politics as "constraints," and thus failing to incorporate fully the preferences and strategies of local actors. Relatedly, by treating the interactions between external and local actors as game we are able to offer a model that is applicable to diverse regional settings and has leverage over divergent outcomes. Third, because we treat peacebuilding as a form of statebuilding, we are able to identify why the "degree of the state" is possibly strengthened (which may contribute to stability) but there is little transformation of the "kind of state." Fourth, our model provides not only an explanation for these post-conflict outcomes, but also insight into how international peacebuilders might change the terms of the contract to promote real, and not faux, transformation.[5]

This essay has three sections. The first section argues that peacebuilding is statebuilding, offers a distinction between the degree of the state and the kind of the state, and then discusses statebuilding in the post-colonial, post-conflict context, highlighting the patrimonial politics that characterize these states. The next section develops the peacebuilder's contract. We begin with a simple model in which there are two actors, peacebuilders and state elites, which eventually coordinate their actions around coopted peacebuilding. Afterwards we complicate the game by introducing a third actor—subnational elites—suggesting that it might lead to coopted peacebuilding between peacebuilders and state elites but captured peacebuilding between peacebuilders and subnational elites.

The subsequent section illustrates the utility of our model in Afghanistan and Tajikistan. Although these cases arrived at similar outcomes, they differ considerably with regard to the duration and nature of the war and the scope and intrusiveness of the peacebuilding project. Afghanistan is arguably one of the most intrusive, ambitious and well-funded missions ever and the international coalition clearly aims at building-up a modern democratic state from scratch, in a few years time, with the help of about 30,000 troops and annual aid of around $2.5 billion. By contrast, the mission in Tajikistan is very small in scope and much less intrusive. It was established in 1994 to monitor the ceasefire agreement between the Government of Tajikistan and the United Tajik Opposition. Following the signing by the parties of the 1997 general peace agreement, UNMOT's mandate was expanded to help monitor its implementation. The mission nevertheless helped to attract considerable flows of aid, which amounted to the single most important resource flow in Tajikistan. We conclude by speculating as to whether and how this contract might be changed so that the development of a more responsive and accountable state might be nurtured, whether compromised peacebuilding is such a disappointing outcome, and how compromised peacebuilding might be consistent with a reasonably successful outcome—putting into place an institutional framework that can promote a more deliberative, inclusive, and accountable state.

Peacebuilding and statebuilding

As can be expected with any recently invented concept, peacebuilding exhibits an impressive range of definitions. Yet underlying this diversity is a general agreement regarding what peacebuilding is not. It goes beyond the attempt to strengthen the prospects for internal peace and decrease the like-lihood of violent conflict. Instead, it involves an effort to eliminate the root causes of conflict, to promote the security of the individual, societal groups, and the state, and to nurture features that create the conditions for a stable peace. "Ultimately, peacebuilding aims at building: human security, a con-cept which includes democratic governance, human rights, rule of law, sus-tainable development, equitable access to resources, and environmental security."[6] This multidimensional and highly intrusive undertaking, involving a reconstruction of politics, economics, culture, and society, leaves no stone unturned.

Standing behind peacebuilding is statebuilding. The modern state "exists when there is a political apparatus (governmental institutions, such as a court, parliament, or congress, plus civil service officials), ruling over a given territory, whose authority is backed by a legal system and the capacity to use force to implement its policies" (Giddens 1993: 309). Statebuilding concerns how the modern state comes into existence, that is, how this process is accomplished. Most discussions of statebuilding generally attend to one of two elements. One concerns the specific instruments states use to control society. Attention is directed to the monopolization of the means of coercion and the development of a bureaucratic apparatus organized around rational-legal principles that have the capacity to regulate, control, and extract from society. The concern, then, is with the degree of the state.

The other dimension concerns how states and societies negotiate their relationship—that is, the kind of state. Attention is directed to the organizing principles that structure the state's rule over society. Two distinctions are particularly important for conceptualizing post-conflict statebuilding. One is between mediated and unmediated states. Mediated states exist when state elites rule through alliances with local notables. In this context, rule (or, more accurately, stability) is accomplished through indirect means as the state elite broker deals with and rule indirectly through local elites. Unmediated states exist when state institutions replace state elites in governing central features of the economy and society. In this context, state institutions are now more involved in providing public goods for local populations and state elites are no longer essential "middle men" (Waldner 1999: 2). The other distinction is between inclusionary and exclusionary regimes. Regimes can be distinguished according to whether or not they contain institutions that are designed to incorporate diverse views, hold the state accountable, and safeguard basic individual rights and liberties. Those that do are inclusionary; those that do not are exclusionary.

Because we are interested in post-conflict peacebuilding activities, operations that nearly always occur in the Third World, it is important to address what are the fundamental characteristics of the Third World state and the post-conflict politics that shape the statebuilding challenge. Although statebuilding exhibits tremendous variation depending on the global context, the economic structure, patterns of authority relations and political power, and elite networks, what distinguishes Third World statebuilding from Western statebuilding is the attempt to create centralized, legitimate, bureaucratic states in a post-colonial context. Colonialism had a profound effect on the Third World state. The colonial state was a creature of foreign forces and much of the internal apparatus, political system, and political economy was designed to protect the interests of foreign actors and those local elites that were given a cut. Consequently, the state was fundamentally alien to the society that it was charged with overseeing and controlling. The result, following Michael Mann's distinction, was that the colonial state was simultaneously strong and weak. Its infrastructural power was nonexistent, unable to mobilize or extract from society because it had little legitimacy. Its despotic power was high because of its authoritarian style (Mann 1984).

These characteristics of the colonial state frequently survived the transition to independence. Famously, Robert Jackson argued that many newly independent states were "quasi-states" because while they had juridical statehood they lacked empirical statehood (Jackson 1990). This lack of "empirical reality" led Third World governments to develop a Janus-faced survival strategy. They viewed the international system as containing a set of normative, political, economic, and security resources that might help them further their goal of regime survival. Sovereignty became a normative shield to guarantee their borders. During the Cold War they might play up to and off the superpowers to extract strategic rents. They might rely on the former colony or great power patrons for security assistance and survival in the last resort. These international resources proved crucial for domestic survival; because they ruled states that had little legitimacy and state capacity, the government was unable to undertake extractive measures such as taxation. Regime stability was produced by a narrow coalition and various forms of patrimonial politics. Toward this end, state elites engaged in the costly process of building and monitoring networks, distributing payoffs and perks to contenders, and providing some public goods to particularly important coalitions (especially in the urban areas).[7] To pay for these activities, they not only attempted to extract resources from the international environment but also to use the state as a private good, hence encouraging forms of corruption, and to create shadow networks and tolerate illicit economies.[8]

Post-conflict statebuilding is distinguished from "normal" statebuilding by the existence of a dual crisis of security and legitimacy. What makes post-conflict statebuilding post-conflict, obviously, is the prior existence of conflict. Indeed, post-conflict is frequently a misnomer for societies that are still experiencing periodic flashes of violence. Moreover, the history of violence and the continuing climate of fear mean that individuals and groups are unlikely to trust that the state will be an impartial force that can provide credible security guarantees. Until that happens, individuals will continue to seek security from alternative security organizations and militias will be unlikely to demobilize.

States after conflict also face a crisis of legitimacy. This is not terribly surprising. Domestic conflict largely erupts in illegitimate states and the subsequent conflict rarely invests the post-conflict state with legitimacy. The challenge, then, is to create public support and a modicum of legitimacy for the post-conflict institutions. Their effectiveness depends on it. The willingness of individuals to comply with the government's decisions depends on whether they believe it is legitimate. Moreover, the lack of legitimacy can contribute to the resumption of violence.

International peacebuilders are intervening in a post-colonial and post-conflict context as they attempt to socially engineer the post-conflict statebuilding process. Simon Chesterman defines international activities for statebuilding as "constructing or reconstructing institutions of governance capable of providing citizens with physical and economic security. This includes quasi-governmental activities such as electoral assistance, human rights and rule of law technical assistance, security sector reform, and certain forms of development assistance" (Chesterman 2004: 5). In our terms, peacebuilding is designed to enhance the degree and develop a particular kind of state. The state's effectiveness is defined by its ability to provide basic services and to deliver public goods. Its legitimacy (and effectiveness) is also related to the development of a particular kind of state, a liberal-democracy (Sens 2004; Paris 2004). Consequently, unlike European state formation, where there did not exist a hegemonic image of the ideal state, in the contemporary period the presumption is that modern states should have rule of law, democratic institutions, and market-driven development.[9]

The peacebuilder's contract

The concept of the peacebuilder's contract is intended to capture why peacebuilders begin with grand notions of transformation but nevertheless adopt strategies and strike implicit contracts with local elites that reinforce existing state-society relations. Before proceeding, a few words are required about the nature of our modeling exercise and its application to peacebuilding. The intent is to understand the origin and development of peacebuilding strategies in a range of post-conflict cases and examine some of the consequences of these strategies. The premise is that these strategies and the strategic interactions that unfold between the interveners and the intervened upon is an important but neglected explanation for the relative successes and failures of contemporary peacebuilding operations. Moreover, similar to other strategic approaches, we are interested in the "connection between what actors want, the environment in which they strive to further those interests, and the outcomes of this interaction" (Lake and Powell 1999: 20). Our model, therefore, seeks to identify the conditions that lead peacebuilders to adopt strategies that reinforce (or possibly even transform) existing arrangements. The goal, in other words, is to be able to understand the origin and development of peacebuilding strategies in a range of post-conflict cases and examine some of the consequences of these strategies.

We assume that the actors are unitary and goal-oriented. Although there is probably little controversy regarding the claim that actors are goal-oriented, potentially problematic is the notion that these actors are unitary. We readily acknowledge that this contrivance masks what invariably are important cleavages, which frequently derive from different conceptions of interests and alternative rank orderings of these preferences. Most international peacebuilding operations include an assortment of international actors, including UN peacekeepers, troop contributing countries, regional organizations such as the African Union and the European Union, international financial institutions such as the World Bank, and nongovernmental organizations such as Oxfam and World Vision International. State elites that are part of the post-conflict government also will evidence divisions. Not only can we expect all politicians to disagree on basic issues; these divisions might be greater in a post-conflict government where there frequently is a power-sharing arrangement between former combatants and shotgun coalitions that include rival politicians that represent distinct identity-based populations. Subnational elites also can have divergent interests, generated by distinct relationships to different socio-economic conditions and groupings. In addition, we assume that there is no overlapping relationship between state and subnational elites, whereas, in fact, subnational elites are frequently directly or indirectly represented in the post-conflict government. Finally, our model is elite-centric to the extent that we do not consider mass publics as a significant independent actor that needs to be considered as part of the equation. These simplifying assumptions are crucial to the modeling exercise and justified to the extent that they help us capture critical dynamics and divergent outcomes. Later, in fact, we will suggest that relaxing these assumptions does not weaken our analysis and observations, and possibly strengthens them.[10]

The ability of these goal-oriented actors to achieve their preferences is dependent on the strategic choices and behavior of others. Although not all strategic interactions will gravitate toward a focal point—indeed, in many games they do not—we are particularly interested in developing a model that can help us understand the underlying logic that might lead to an equilibrium outcome.

A final, critical comment about the setting: we assume that this game unfolds against the backdrop of a peace agreement that is accepted by the key parties on the ground; reflects the balance of political forces in the country at the time of the cessation of hostilities; and probably contains provisions that are designed to safeguard their power. We acknowledge that there is considerable variation in the domestic setting in any post-conflict process. Sometimes there is a stable peace agreement and at other times there is a peace agreement existing alongside a continuation of the fighting. Different backdrops, of course, will have quite different implications for the dynamic interactions between the actors. But we have to make choices in order to employ the model, and we assume that there is a peace treaty that represents a turning point from the conflict to the post-conflict setting. Still, violence is hardly a distant memory. Not only are there daily reminders; there also are patterns associated with a security dilemma, including, most importantly, the inability of foes to distinguish between behavior driven by lack of trust and behavior driven by predatory ambitions (Jervis and Snyder 1999; Kasfir 2003; Walter 2002). The simultaneous presence of a signed peace agreement and international actors signify that the parties have moved into a post-conflict stage and the peace accord typically includes "a set of mutually-agreed benchmarks to guide the process and that can be used to assess progress" (Goodhand and Sedra 2006: 5). Furthermore, we assume that the parties are generally committed to the implementation of the peace agreement. The parties might have signed the treaty for a variety of sincere and insincere reasons. They might have reached a hurting stalemate and concluded that because they cannot win through violence there is no rational alternative to a brokered deal. They might have decided to use the peace agreement to try to achieve through politics what they could not achieve through violence; in other words, the peace treaty does not signal the end of elite competition but rather a new phase. Consequently, we make no assumptions about the motives of the signatories but do assume that they are reasonably committed to their agreements. Although we do allow for the presence of spoilers who would prefer to fight than compromise, we assume that they do not have the political or military strength to act unilaterally to undermine the political process.

What they want: peacebuildings and local elites

Although peacebuilders (PBs) can have a variety of preferences and pre-ference ordering, in our model they have two critical preferences. They want to implement reforms that lead to a liberal peace. In other words, they want to deliver services and assistance that will create new institutions that (re) distribute political and economic power in a transparent and accountable way. However, they operate with limited resources and seek to minimize casualties. Hence, they desire, first and foremost, stability, and, secondarily, liberalization. Stability, or the absence of war and a stable partner in the capital, is an important precondition for the security of the peacebuilders and their ability to implement the liberalizing reforms. Consequently, peace-builders prioritize stability over the structural reforms that are posited to produce the kind of liberal peacebuilding they desire.

State elites (SEs) and subnational elites (SNEs) want to preserve their political power and ensure that the peace implementation process either enhances or does not harm their political and economic interests. As we have already argued, the political and economic survival of SEs depends on their ability to co-opt or deter challengers from the periphery; their complicity usually does not come cheaply, which means that they must finance their patronage system. SEs will thus try to balance the opportunities that peacebuilders offer with the threats that the implementation of liberal peacebuilding poses to their survival strategy.

SNEs generally want to maximize their power and their autonomy from the central government. In fact, the war might have strengthened their hand. A typical consequence of war and the collapse of state services (if they ever really existed) is that individuals and groups look beyond the state and toward their local communities and parallel organizations for their basic needs. Consequently, subnational elites can be a relative beneficiary from the conflict. In any event, they will want to make sure that they do not lose in any peace dividend or post-conflict statebuilding process. Like state elites, subnational elites will attempt to capture the resources offered by peace-builders while minimizing the costs that reforms might pose to their local power and autonomy vis-à-vis the central government.

The ability of peacebuilders, state elites, and subnational elites to achieve their preferences is dependent on the behavior, strategies, and perceived power of others. There are significant material and normative international constraints on peacebuilders. They are condemned to get results with limited resources, under high time pressure, and with minimal casualties. The international community has rarely spent lavishly on peacekeeping or peacebuilding exercises; indeed, the higher the projected cost the less likely is the UN Security Council to authorize the operation. Not only are peacebuilders expected to perform near miracles without requisite resources, but they are expected to do so with amazing speed because the international community suffers from attention deficit disorder and will quickly lose interest and patience. There also are normative constraints (Paris 2003). Indeed, peacekeepers and peacebuilders operate according to the principles of consent and are expected to negotiate with and gain the cooperation of the targets of their intervention in order to ensure that the intervened gain "ownership." In fact, the more enforcement mechanisms are needed to achieve the mandate, the greater are the costs of the intervention; and as the costs increase so, too, does the likelihood of the cessation of the peacebuilding operation. These constraints generate a strong desire by peacebuilders for security on the cheap. Consequently, local actors (SEs and/or SNEs) who are necessary for the production of stability will have a strengthened hand. Furthermore, the ability of peacebuilders to enact their liberalizing reforms is also highly dependent on the cooperation of local elites. Peacebuilding will succeed only if elites cooperate with a process that they are presumed to own.

The ability of state and subnational elites to achieve their preferences is dependent on the actions of peacebuilders and each other. The resources that peacebuilders can allocate, however limited, usually dwarf those of the state budget of the target country, and their allocation can have important consequences for the distribution of political and economic power.[11] Consequently, state elites will treat the international presence not only as a potential constraint but also as a potential opportunity. This is not a new development. During the age of imperialism local actors frequently attempted to attract international attention and resources in order to enhance their political position vis-à-vis local rivals, and during the Cold War state elites attempted to attract superpower support in order to garner strategic rents that they, in turn, could distribute domestically to bolster their political support.[12] Moreover, peacebuilders can confer legitimacy on local elites, choosing to treat some as important political powers or as agents of political communities, thus enhancing their bargaining power over rivals.[13] Yet in a situation of elite competition, what is viewed as a positive externality by one party is likely to be treated as a negative externality by another. Consequently, state elites will attempt to steer international peacebuilders in a direction that furthers their interests.

A simple game: peacebuilders and state elites

The game begins when the peacebuilders (PB) undertake a set of activities that can generate negative or positive externalities for populations in the country. PBs bring highly needed resources that can be life-saving in many instances and critical for rebuilding the country. PBs also can have goals that are diametrically opposed by local elites, especially when PBs encourage the pluralization of politics or enhance the position of rivals. Thus, externalities, in their intensity and in their sign, will differ depending on how they are viewed by distinct constituencies. Local elites can respond to these externalities in a variety of ways. At one extreme, they might intimidate, threaten or carry out violence against PBs. At the other extreme, they might actively cooperate with PBs, contributing manpower, resources, and time. It is beyond our task to delineate an exhaustive list of responses. Nor is it necessary. For our purposes here the crucial issue is whether local elites accept the peacebuilding reforms as presented or insist on a modification.

We posit four different kinds of outcomes: cooperative peacebuilding, co-opted peacebuilding, captured peacebuilding, and confrontational peacebuilding (see Table 2.1). If the SEs accept and support the peacebuilding program, then the game ends at cooperative peacebuilding. In this situation peacebuilders are able to design and implement their programs with the knowledge that they will receive the cooperation and assistance from local elites. More likely, however, local elites will attempt to alter the content and implementation of these programs so that they are consistent with their interests. If PBs accept these conditions, then the outcome is captured peacebuilding. Peacebuilders become little more than the agent of local elites and international resources are transferred from international to local actors, who have control over its allocation and use.[14]

It is doubtful, though, that peacebuilders will accept a situation in which they become the patron of a transitional government, especially one that comprises warlords and former combatants. Consequently, they are likely to present conditionality criteria that demand that local elites accept the legitimacy of local reforms in return for international support (Goodhand and Sedra 2006: 3). If state elites accept these conditions, then they and peacebuilders are engaged in what we call compromised peacebuilding: both peacebuilders and local elites have altered their policies and strategies in order to accommodate the preferences of the other.

There is the possibility, though, that peacebuilders and state elites are not able to reach a compromise, continue to resist the demands of the other, and begin to consider more coercive instruments. Although peacebuilders have

Table 2.1 Kinds of peacebuilding

Outcome	Description
Cooperative Peacebuilding	Unimpeded delivery of services and assistance leading to the creation of new institutions that distribute political and economic power to new actors.
Captured Peacebuilding	Local elites are able to shift peacebuilding programs and resources so that they are consistent with their interests.
Compromised Peacebuilding	Local elites and peacebuilders jointly determine assistance activities.
Confrontational Peacebuilding	Peacebuilders and local elites develop antagonistic and conflictive relations, leading to the suspension of assistance by peacebuilders and active resistance by local elites.

few coercive measures available to them, in rare circumstances they might threaten to go to the Security Council and ask for enforcement action or armed protection. More likely, peacebuilders will threaten either to curtail their activities or withdraw altogether. State elites might resist the incursions of peacebuilders or attempt to modify their policies by resorting to a range of coercive tactics, from intimidation to the threat and use of violence. In such a scenario, the game turns confrontational and possibly deadly. We name this outcome confrontational peacebuilding.

Given the preferences and constraints typically confronted by each actor, we argue that compromised peacebuilding is likely to be the equilibrium outcome. This is so because, in terms of preferences over outcomes, PBs prefer cooperative peacebuilding to compromised peacebuilding to conflictive peacebuilding to captured peacebuilding, and SEs prefer captured peacebuilding to compromised peacebuilding to conflictive peacebuilding to cooperative peacebuilding (see Table 2.2). Neither will be able to achieve its preferred outcome of either cooperative or captured peacebuilding (these are ordinal rankings); both would prefer conflictive peacebuilding to either captured or cooperative peacebuilding because it would distort (in the case of peacebuilders) if not threaten (in the case of state elites) their core interests. Compromised peacebuilding, therefore, becomes the equilibrium outcome because the parties have little incentive to defect.

There are various reasons why peacebuilders and state elites will be satisfied with this outcome. Peacebuilders achieve security alongside an acknowledgment of the legitimacy and desirability of reforms. They have developed a culture of principled pragmatism, ready to make compromises in the face of hard realities. They have an organizational interest in demonstrating success, especially once they have committed resources to the operation. Finally, they know the preference rankings of state elites and thus can anticipate that if they defect and attempt to revise the bargain then state elites are likely to resist. There are various reasons why state elites also will be satisfied with this outcome. They receive international resources that they can use to maintain their support at home. They receive international recognition of their political standing. Finally, they know the preference rankings of peacebuilders and thus can anticipate that if they defect and attempt to revise radically the bargain in their favor, peacebuilders might depart.

Table 2.2 Rank order of preferences of different actors for different outcomes

	Peacebuilders	*Target Government*	*Rural Elites*
4	Cooperative	Captured	Captured
3	Compromised	Compromised	Compromised
2	Confrontational	Confrontational	Confrontational
1	Captured	Cooperative	Cooperative

Compromised peacebuilding becomes something of a peacebuilder's con-tract—they have negotiated an arrangement in which each party has specific responsibilities and receives specific rewards. Peacebuilders agree to provide international resources and legitimacy for state elites in return for stability and acknowledgment by state elites of the legitimacy of peacebuilding reforms. Consequently, this contract reinforces the status quo even as it leaves open some possibility for reform. In other words, the reforms that do take place will unfold in a way that protects the interests of local elites. This outcome also can be seen as *symbolic* peacebuilding. In this way, it resembles what sociological institutionalists call "ceremonial conformity." The actor, or orga-nization, wants to maintain the stream of material and normative benefits required for its legitimacy and survival, but fears that full compliance will be too costly (Meyer and Rowan 1977: 50). Consequently, it adopts the myths and ceremonies of the organizational form, but maintains its existing practices (and in this way organizational form and practices become decoupled). It is symbolic or ceremonial peacebuilding in that the symbols of reform have been transferred and thus there is the surface appearance that there has been a transformation of the kind of state, that is, toward a liberal-democracy, even though the existing power relations have largely emerged unscathed. That said, symbols can matter. Once state elites have committed themselves to certain principles, these public commitments can be used by liberalizing elements at home and abroad to try and force them to keep their word. More-over, these symbols can encourage existing actors to reprioritize their inter-ests and develop new networks of associations that can, over time, build support for liberalization.

A more complicated game: subnational elites want their cut

It is now time to introduce some complexity into the model in order to increase its utility and reality. In most post-conflict settings subnational elites are critical to stability and thus their presence is likely to affect the outcome. Accordingly, let us now consider a second game, which is an extension of the first. Imagine that peacebuilders and state elites converge on a contract that is closer to the liberal agenda than it is to the status quo. Now assume that SEs propose this peacebuilding agenda to SNEs. If SNEs accept, the game ends with all actors agreeing on a cooperative peacebuilding agenda. However, subnational elites might very well fear that this arrangement will threaten their goals of preserving their power and maintaining their autonomy from the central government. Why? Peacebuilders are pressing reforms that are intended to pluralize power and recentralize the state. Consequently, subna-tional elites might respond by playing the spoiler or using their power to raise the cost of peacebuilding and threaten the regime's survival.[15] (Indeed, because frequently subnational elites are strengthened by a collapsed state, their bargaining leverage might be higher after the war than before.) In short, subnational elites are likely to resist an arrangement that might come at their expense. SEs now have two options. Fearing that subnational elites are about to gain relative power, they might strike out against the subnational elites. This is, however, extremely unlikely, because SEs in post-conflict setting are usually too weak to confront opposing elites without the consent or even support of PBs, and PBs will be extremely reluctant to become engaged in a new round of civil war. Because this first option is unlikely, SEs are likely to try to renegotiate the agenda with the peacebuilders in ways that better incorporate the preferences of the SNEs. In order to justify their desire to re-open negotiations, SEs might argue that at the present moment they do not possess the capacity to implement a liberal agenda, and that more patience and more resources are needed. If PBs accept these modifications, the game ends, and the outcome will be compromised peacebuilding.

There is another possibility. Upon realizing that SNEs may play the spoiler, SEs may try to directly engage them, hoping that subnational elites might accept the legitimacy of peacebuilding in exchange for resources and recognition from peacebuilders. While this is a theoretical possibility, it is highly unlikely because PBs are usually extremely unwilling to deal with subnational elites who lack democratic legitimacy and often have dubious wartime records, and fear the costs and the logistical challenges that accompany any effort to establish a robust presence in the provinces. However, if PBs decide to directly engage SNEs, the outcome may well be captured peacebuilding (see Table 2.2). There are several reasons why subnational elites might be able to achieve what state elites could not. To begin, in comparison to state elites, subnational elites might have greater bargaining leverage. Peacebuilders are increasingly and notoriously out of their depth the further they get from the capital city, tend to be more isolated and thus more dependent on subnational elites to provide security, and are more dependent on subnational elites to provide critical information and protection. Peacebuilders might be willing to be "captured" for what they believe are tactical reasons, betting that a bad agreement is better than no agreement and that it might be renegotiated at a later date. They also might not even know how captured they truly are, because the costs of monitoring programs in the provinces are so high.

In sum, our models suggest that given the resources, commitments, and preferences of the players, the most likely outcome—and the best that liberal peacebuilders usually can hope to achieve—is compromised peacebuilding. Cooperative peacebuilding is possible if and only if peacebuilders come in with tremendous resources and a strong commitment to liberalization. Even then, they will have to anticipate that local elites, both in the capital and in the countryside, will resist or attempt to change the peacebuilding program so that it more fully incorporates their preferences. In fact, we anticipate that captured peacebuilding, especially between subnational elites and peacebuilders, is more likely than cooperative peacebuilding. For these and other reasons, liberal peacebuilding is more likely to reproduce than to transform existing state–society relations and patrimonial politics.

Coopted and captured in Kabul and Dushanbe

We now illustrate our model in the cases of Afghanistan and Tajikistan. Both countries are difficult cases for peacebuilding. Both are landlocked, mountainous, and largely rural, least developed countries and both emerged from disastrous civil wars.[16] The civil war in Tajikistan resulted in 41,400 deaths between 1992 and 1998, while the war in Afghanistan claimed some 75,000 lives between 1989 and 2001 (Lacina and Gleditsch 2005). In terms of population size this means that roughly 7.1 out of 1,000 Tajik citizens died in battle between 1992 and 1998, while 2.4 out of 1,000 Afghan citizens died between 1989 and 2001, which places both wars among the bloodiest after 1945. The fault lines along ethnic, regional, and religious identities also complicated a peace process and post-conflict reconstruction project. They also differ in an important respect. Because of geopolitical circumstances, Afghanistan commanded considerable international attention; it experienced one of the most ambitious peacebuilding missions ever. The mission was well-manned, well-financed, equipped with a robust mandate, and intrusive. By contrast, the peacebuilding mission in Tajikistan was rather small, with a limited mandate, and less intrusive. Afghanistan did not necessarily fare better than Tajikistan, notwithstanding its relatively greater international support. In both cases, international actors entered with a broadly liberal agenda, proposing to reform the state, society, and economy in order to promote a durable peace.[17] Yet, in both cases, the result of the peacebuilding mission is, from the perspective of liberal peacebuilders, similarly disappointing. Although the strategic interactions between peacebuilders and local elites differed, both Afghanistan and Tajikistan traveled down a path of compromised peacebuilding as international peacebuilders traded stability for a more genuine commitment to liberal reforms, and state elites accepted the legitimacy of liberal reforms in return for a continuation of international assistance. Consequently, in both cases there was a modest increase in the degree of state while the kind of state had a liberal shell atop a mediated, exclusionary, and patrimonial state.[18]

Tajikistan

There are several features of Tajikistan's history that are important for understanding the challenges faced by peacebuilders. On the economic front, it was heavily agrarian, had been the least developed Soviet republic, and had been dependent on Moscow for 40 percent of its budget. On the political front, akin to other central Asian republics, Tajikistan had a hybrid political system that resulted from a Soviet state and party institutions that aspired to create a centralized rule that penetrated society down to the village level but nevertheless relied on informal middlemen and one particular regional grouping ("clan"), the Leninabad in northern Tajikistan. On the socio-cultural front there were very strong regional identities, due in part to the very mountainous terrain and poor infrastructure that hindered communication and strong ties between different regions.

The collapse of the Soviet Union in 1991 meant the end of its generous subsidies for the ruling Leninabadis, which, in turn, triggered a civil war. Although the war involved a clash of ideologies—communism and secularism versus Islamism; democracy/liberalism versus authoritarianism—the main divisions were between regionally based clans (Akiner 2001; Atkin 1999; Rubin 1998). The civil war brutalized the country, destroying infrastructure, reportedly killing 50,000 people, and leaving homeless hundreds of thousands (Akiner and Barnes 2001).

The international reaction to the war began in late 1992. In January 1993 the UN established the United Nations Mission of Observers in Tajikistan (UNMOT), a skeletal operation tasked with helping to coordinate humanitarian assistance. It would take another two years and a radical change in the region's strategic context before there would be further international action. What grabbed everyone's attention was the successful consolidation of the Pakistan-backed Taliban over large swathes of Afghanistan and the prospect that its influence, politics, and violence might spill over into Tajikistan. Alarmed by this possibility, in 1995 the UN and the CIS, with Russia as its driving force, increased their efforts to establish a political settlement. The UN undertook a fairly intensive shuttle diplomacy between Tajik leader Emomali Rakhmonov (leader of the Kulyob grouping) in Dushanbe and opposition leader Sayed Abdullo Nuri in Kabul that led to negotiations, but little else. In 1996 the fighting resumed.

On December 23, 1996, Rakhmonov and Nuri met in Moscow. This time they crafted a comprehensive agreement which laid the foundation for a peace treaty. After considerable international pressure and further internationally-sponsored negotiations, in June 1997 President Rakhmonov and the leader of the UTO, Nuri, signed the General Agreement on the Establishment of Peace and National Accord in Tajikistan. Among its more important features, the agreement called for: the creation of a Commission of National Reconciliation; the incorporation of UTO representatives into the government on the basis of a 30 percent quota; an end to the ban on UTO party activities; disarmament, demobilization and reintegration of UTO forces; and a general amnesty for all combatants.

To support the signed agreement and the post-conflict process, in June 2000 the United Nations disbanded UNMOT and created in its place the United Nations Tajikistan Office of Peacebuilding (UNTOP), which had a mandate to: provide the political framework and leadership for post-conflict peacebuilding activities of the United Nations; promote an integrated approach to the development and implementation of post-conflict peacebuilding programs; foster reconstruction, economic recovery, poverty alleviation, good governance, democracy and the rule of law; and organize the disarmament, demobilization and reintegration (DDR) program.[19] Although there were no explicit statements about the need to establish a liberal democracy in Dushanbe, the UN's mission included the standard checklist of activities that suggested this very goal.

In the wake of 9/11 and the US war against the Taliban, the peacebuilding mission in Tajikistan acquired a new strategic significance. UNTOP became the centerpiece of a booming peacebuilding industry, international non-governmental organizations (INGOs) flocked to Tajikistan and an impressive flow of money streamed into the country. Aid as a percentage of the central government's total expenditures climbed from 5 percent in 1993 to 27 percent in 2001 and then to a staggering 37 percent in 2004.[20] Official development assistance reached $240 million in 2004, compared with $180 million for the government's outlays. Aid, together with revenues from labor migration[21] and drug trafficking, became Tajikistan's blood and oxygen (International Organization of Migration 2003; Makarenko 2002).

What quickly emerged was compromised peacebuilding. President Rakhmonov had a clear preference for maintaining political power, ensuring stability throughout the region, and continuing the flow of international resources that was so critical for regime survival and stability. Toward that end, he cooperated with peacebuilders when there was a convergence of preferences, but when they did not converge he favored symbolic peacebuilding. He was not alone in his stated preference for stability over all other goals. All parties feared a resumption of hostilities (arguably exaggerated by Rakhmonov's regime in order to attract aid money and to ensure domestic compliance), and Rakhmonov's policy of stability was strongly supported by the population. Rakhmonov could play the "stability" card for political purposes, and during his national campaigns urged national reconciliation and portrayed himself as Tajikistan's best hope for stability.

The central government cooperated with the peacebuilding operation in various areas. It supported the DDR process, which, accordingly, was a relative success. A resource-starved government gladly outsourced welfare services in the subnational areas to an eager INGO community. The result was a major increase in basic goods as international actors became the major provider of food security, basic infrastructure, energy supply, education and health care in the countryside, especially in the former oppositional regions of Garm and Badakhshan.

There was little more than symbolic peacebuilding, though, when the preferences of state elites diverged from the international peacebuilding program. UNTOP attempted to promote the very idea of pluralizing politics and establishing a culture of dialogue and peaceful dissent. Toward that end, it initiated the Political Discussion Club (PDC) project, which brought "together representatives of central and local government, heads of political parties, citizens, NGOs, and representatives of private business and the independent mass media in sessions across the country. ... Topics for discussion rotate each year, and have included the themes of democratization, economic transition, security, local governance, and electoral laws and procedures."[22] All well and good but this arguably represented more ceremony than substance.

Tajikistan has no independent media, no robust political party system, no civil society outside of the fledgling and internationally-supported NGO community, and no meaningful institutions for local government.[23] Little wonder, then, that the PDC had difficulty "promoting political tolerance and dialogue." In a country without an independent media or even electricity in the rural areas, it is difficult to accept the conclusion that "coverage of discussions in local and national mass media, multiplied the effect of each session, increased the outreach in distant regions."[24]

There were various other reforms that were intended to increase public security, but in many cases they were undermined by the half-hearted and foot-dragging behavior of local elites. UNTOP instituted training seminars for state officials and community leaders on conflict prevention and resolution, but there is little evidence that such training was anything but pro forma and perfunctory. To promote the rule of law, UNTOP supported local capacity-building for law enforcement agencies, seeking to accelerate their reform, combat corruption, and increase professionalism. In the realm of human rights, a needs assessment mission of Office of the United Nations High Commissioner for Human Rights (OHCHR) concluded that "although Tajikistan was party to all major human rights conventions, it lacked national capacities in treaty reporting and had not established the necessary mechanism to implement its obligations."[25] As a remedy, it recommended that UNTOP assist in providing technical support in the area of treaty reporting and human rights education. Although it is quite possible that the primary obstacle toward improvement in this area is "technical," there is ample alternative evidence that it is fundamentally political.

The new government also demonstrated very little interest in promoting power-sharing or the pluralization of political power. There have been a series of elections—parliamentary and presidential elections in 2000 and a referendum in 2003 on whether Rakhmonov should be allowed to serve two consecutive seven-year terms—but they were hardly free or fair. Moreover, the government slowly reversed the key point of the peace agreement that had assured UTO 30 percent representation in the government. At the time of this writing, most of the key positions are occupied by loyal followers of President Rakhnov's home region of Kulyob. All of these reversals have been tolerated by the peacebuilders because Rakhmonov is viewed as a guarantor of stability in a country which appears to be vulnerable to internal cleavages and external destabilization. In fact, rather than using aid as a lever for greater democratization, aid has increased as democracy has become a more distant possibility.

Peacebuilding in Tajikistan has thus increased the degree, but not altered the kind, of state. Rakhmonov's regime has gained considerable strength (enough to rig two elections and a referendum) and successfully compromised or sidelined oppositional state elites. World Bank indicators reflect the institutionalization of one-party rule, patrimonial politics, and authoritarianism. The voice and accountability indicator, an aggregate measure of civil liberties, has declined since 2002, while indicators measuring government effectiveness have improved.[26]

The current political system in Tajikistan is characterized by highly entrenched patron–client networks supported by an increasingly coercive and arbitrary state apparatus. Governance is exercised mainly through informal channels. Civil society is weak and hardly existent beyond the village communities. Nevertheless, the institutional framework for democracy and market reforms is formally in place and Tajikistan's high dependence of international cooperation makes it—theoretically—more responsive to incentives for policy changes than, for example, isolationist Uzbekistan. In general, while there are important symbolic differences between the Tajikistan that was a Soviet republic and the sovereign state of Tajikistan, many of these differences are ceremonial and not substantive.

The international community has contributed to this outcome. It has generously funded a regime that is maintained more by "by raw power" than by "institutions" (Ottaway 2002). State elites have continuously renegotiated the peacebuilders contract in their favor, emphasizing stability over liberal reforms, and peacebuilders were willing to renegotiate because they, too, ranked stability over liberalization.

Afghanistan

When in 2001 international peacebuilders launched one of the most ambitious peacekeeping and peacebuilding operations ever, Afghanistan was a poor, highly fragmented country that had just emerged from more than two decades of disastrous wars. After the withdrawal of the Soviet Union in 1989, fighting continued among the various Mujahidin factions, eventually giving rise to a state of warlordism. The chaos and corruption that dominated post-Soviet Afghanistan in turn spawned the rise of the Taliban. After several years of further fighting, the Taliban laid claim to Afghanistan in fall 1996.

The possibility and desirability of an international peacebuilding in Afghanistan was the obvious result of the September 11th attacks on the United States and the American-led response the following month that successfully routed the Taliban government and Al-Qaeda forces. US forces supported heavily the Northern Alliance, a military-political coalition of various Afghan groups fighting against the Taliban. With extensive US military assistance, the Northern Alliance captured most of Afghanistan from the Taliban in early 2002. The defeat of the Taliban led to the broader debate about how both to promote a government that would join in the war against terrorism and to create the structural underpinning for a stable peace. While the former objective might have suggested something of a devil's bargain between the US and whomever emerged victorious in Kabul, the latter insisted on a broader peacebuilding operation. Although the victorious Northern Alliance, which represented mainly the Tajik and Uzbek population of Afghanistan, heavily influenced the new transitional authority, the international coalitional forces insisted on a broad coalition that would also represent the Pashtu population. In fall 2001, various representatives of influential Afghan groups under the auspices of the UN convened in Bonn, Germany, to discuss the future of the country.

Liberal peacebuilders confronted enormous challenges. After two decades of war, peacebuilders had to start from scratch and confronted considerable obstacles as they imagined beginning a statebuilding and peacebuilding project. Most infrastructure had been destroyed by the wars. The state, which barely existed even in the "golden age," was now decimated and had little capacity. The union of military forces that produced the victory could not mask the significant political cleavages that threatened to boil to the surface. The Taliban continued to exist and could play the spoiler. Most societal groups were mistrusting of any statebuilding process. Society was largely organized around regional, ethnic, and religious ties, and the subnational elites—large landowners, religious leaders, and Jihadi commanders—were content with a decentralized arrangement (Rubin 2002).

The emerging game between peacebuilders and state elites was influenced by a number of factors. To begin, peacebuilders were willing to make Afghanistan a flagship project; toward that end, they committed significant resources (manpower, soldiers, and money). Furthermore, the new state elites owed their positions to the victory over the Taliban and the subsequent peacebuilding operation; consequently, their preferences corresponded with those of the international peacebuilders. That said, they were in no great position to command anyone to do anything because the governing elites had little leverage over competing elites, especially outside Kabul. Regime survival, and presumably their physical survival, depended on whether they successfully accommodated their rivals. Finally, the US's focus on the war against terror led it to support individual warlords and local strongmen who, in its view, were instrumental for hunting down the Taliban and Al-Qaeda fighters; consequently, the US's preference of security over liberalization strengthened the power of those parties that opposed the creation of a liberal, democratic state. The weakness of state elites, the strength of subnational elites, and the ambiguous policies of the main peacebuilder, the US, explains why the peacebuilding game in Afghanistan veered down two different paths: cooperative peacebuilding between the new Afghan government and the peacebuilders, and captured peacebuilding between the subnational elites and peacebuilders.

The cornerstone of the political process emerged in the Bonn agreement of December 5, 2001. The agreement created an Afghan Interim Authority and a road map for political and economic prosperity. The agreement's explicit goal was to produce a state that would be democratic, efficient, rational, and limited, committed to Islamic values, social justice, and market-led growth, and contain a single army (Suhrke 2006). A major task of the Afghan Interim Authority was to convene an Emergency Loya Girga (Grand Assembly of Elders), which would select a transitional government until national elections for a permanent government.[27] Furthermore, while the agreement did contain transitional benchmarks and a timeframe, these were vague and disconnected from formal conditionalities. The reluctance to impose conditionalities owed to the international community's priority of stability and its fear that these conditionalities might exacerbate the already existing divisions within the government (Suhrke 2006). The agreement's vagueness and unwillingness to undertake a set of actions that might threaten stability was particularly evident regarding the militias and warlords. The agreement presented a "declaration of intent" but no details about the mechanisms for the transfer of authority, the composition of future state apparatus, or clear timelines (Suhrke et al. 2004a: 43). In marked contrast to elaborate and detailed political agenda, the vagueness of the language in the security protocols suggests that peacebuilders wanted to avoid getting caught up in a costly and dangerous struggle against subnational elites and thus chose to give the Northern Alliance maximum room for maneuver and politico-military freedom.

Because of its perceived importance to the new security agenda and the war against terrorism, the international community immediately provided support for the political process. In comparison to its funding for other operations, the international community was muscular and generous. Although its exact numbers have varied since late 2001, the US and NATO have deployed tens of thousands of troops to the country. In terms of aid, the relative generosity became apparent at the first donors conference in January 2002, when $4.5 billion was pledged for post-conflict reconstruction; at a subsequent donors conference in March 2004 in Berlin, there were pledges of $12 billion through 2007.

As outlined in the Bonn agreement, a Loya Jirga assembled in June 2002. The delegates were elected from 370 constituencies plus representatives from refugee groups, universities and religious elites, and the governors of all the provinces—mostly warlords. The results of the Loya Jirga were mixed: while major representatives of almost all Afghan groups agreed on the composition of the Transitional Authority, the actual negotiations were far from fair and transparent. Measured against previous deliberations, the Loya Jirga looked like a model of deliberation, but there was a general feeling that democracy was merely a façade as political power resided and decisions were taken elsewhere.

Presidential elections occurred on October 9, 2004, and Hamid Karzai, who had become the international community's critical partner, was elected with 55.4 percent of the vote. The elections were free, but the playing field was uneven, in part because Karzai enjoyed the undivided support of the international community (Gardish 2004). To complete the Bonn agreement, parliamentary elections occurred on September 18, 2005. The winners were warlords and women—reflecting the nature of the peacebuilders contract: subnational elites, warlords, and their followers gained the majority of seats in both the lower house and the provincial council (which elects the members of the upper house) but women, which the constitution guaranteed at least 25 percent of the seats in the lower house, actually won 28 percent of the seats.

Although Karzai and other reformers in the new government largely supported liberalization, the strong preferences of fairly autonomous regional elites for the status quo and the willingness of the international coalition to provide critical resources to them in exchange for an alliance against the remnants of the Taliban and Al-Qaeda propelled peacebuilders and the state elite toward compromised peacebuilding. Consequently, symbolic politics dominated many aspects of the government's reforms. For instance, in the area of judicial reform various government institutions contrived to outwit an array of poorly coordinated international donors by constructing an obfuscatory smoke-screen around the process of reform, and by cannily provoking competition between donor agencies, thus maximizing their benefits while hindering the implementation of real reforms (Bhatia et al. 2004; Goodhand and Sedra 2006).

The weakness of state elites and the strong position of subnational elites contributed to this outcome. President Karzai had to accommodate competing elites and prominent warlords because he lacked the means to crack down on them and did not wish to narrow further his ruling coalition. Specifically, because he could not crush his opposition, he tried to coopt or constrain them. Consider the cases of the warlords Rashid Dostum and Ismail Khan. Khan was initially encouraged to relinquish either his executive role as Governor of Herat, or his military role as Commander of 4th Army Corps (Giustozzi 2003). Subsequently, in 2004, Karzai successfully accommodated Khan in the Kabul-based central Government as Minister of Mines and Industry while stripping him of his executive authority as Governor in his home province (Dietl 2004). In 2003 Dostum was provided with the somewhat ceremonial role of Deputy Defense Minister and was granted executive powers as Karzai's "Special Envoy to the North."

Another favored mechanism for constraining the power of first-order warlords was the instrumentalization of second-order warlords against their first-order warlord patrons. Karzai, for instance, supported the second-tier warlord, Amanullah Khan of Shindand district, to militarily oppose Ismail Khan (Giustozzi 2006). This was conducted through the proxy of Gul Agha Shirzai, a powerful militia leader and subsequent Provincial Governor of Kandahar. Shirzai is a powerful strong-man associated with the monarchist network. Importantly, Amanullah was previously an ally of the Taliban. Karzai and his modernizers are instrumentalizing second-tier warlords with previous Taliban connections to weaken recalcitrant first-order warlords, using other first-order warlords as proxies.

The cooptation and inclusion of subnational elites and warlords not only limited the space for any substantive reforms but it also contributed to symbolic politics. Under pressure from international human-rights groups General Rashid Dostum, one of Afghanistan's most feared and powerful warlords, became a spokesperson for human rights. In May 2002, he issued a public rebuke to human-rights abusers within his militia; however, his message lost some of its power when he threatened to "kill" any abusers of human rights.[28] Similarly Hazrat Ali, the Pashtun warlord cum-Chief of Police of Nangahar, participated in the ritual of poppy eradication, (to "please the U.S. military"), while leaving untouched those poppy-fields that were not visible from the road.[29] Many analysts also have observed ritualized and empty disarmament as part of the demobilization, disarmament, and reintegration process (Suhrke et al. 2004). Only antiquated and worn-out weapons have been turned in. Commanders have sent only the most unfit and poorly trained militia fighters to the Afghan National Army. State ministries routinely and ritualistically speak in the discourse of western developmentalism, i.e., "conditionalities," "financial constraint," "fiduciary planning," but there is little evidence that rhetoric matches action. Peacebuilding, in short, is symbolic and nearly empty of substance.

While peacebuilders and state elites struck upon compromised peacebuilding, peacebuilders and subnational elites quickly veered down the path of captured peacebuilding—a result of a US that preferred routing the Taliban over liberalization and regional warlords who were willing to cooperate with the US's war on terror in return for resources and recognition that could strengthen their political power. In order to further its security interests, US officials and military planners attempted to "pick winners" that are on the "right" side in the war against terror and then give them with nearly unconditional support (Goodhand and Sedra 2006). This frequently necessitated military and monetary support of warlords and autonomous militias.

Although the US's decision to trade security for liberalization would complicate the policies of all other peacebuilders that were not ready to make such a bargain, even if the US had not made this bargain there are reasons to believe that peacebuilders would have been at a growing disadvantage because of their lack of knowledge the further they ventured from Kabul. But the double failure of ISAF to venture outside of Kabul and the US's bargain with the warlords meant that other peacebuilders would become captured.[30]

Most INGOs cannot help but interact with local strongmen in ways that deliver to them various benefits. They gain economically. INGOs rent offices, buildings, and storage facilities from them and their relatives, typically at prices far above local standards. They invite local strong-men to visit the headquarters of the INGOs, thus conferring on them greater legitimacy. In return, subnational elites respect the quid pro quo of the informal "contract." Local communities are exhorted to support and facilitate the work of the INGOs. Village leaders present a happy and welcoming face to INGO staff. Survey teams from the INGO are indulged. INGO offices, vehicles, and staff are physically secure, at least in the areas of the commanders' control.

Yet as security became more problematic INGOs became increasingly detached from local politics and more dependent on middle men and other indirect means for gathering information. The ominous security climate caused INGOs to build barriers between themselves and the local population, discouraging first-hand contact, which, in turn, led to a decline in the quality of their information a dependence on locals and information brokers for news, second-hand reports, and secondary (and recycled) data. INGO management retreated further into a comforting, hermetically-sealed, illusion of emails, donor reports, "performance appraisals" and day-to-day operational activity. Expatriate managers, residing in larger provincial centers, operating in an office environment of laptops, satellite phones, spreadsheet, log-frames and assisted by members of the "modern" English-speaking Afghan elite lacked the information or the will to change their relationship with local strongmen. They often did not realize how truly captured they were.

As predicted by our model, the development of captured peacebuilding between subnational elites and peacebuilders negatively affected the more cooperative contract between state elites and peacebuilders. It had two different ramifications. First, it decreased the incentives for state elites for cooperative peacebuilding and favored a compromised peacebuilding that more greatly favored stability over reforms. Because of the gathering strength of the warlords and other subnational elites, the new central government became more worried about its relative power and thus more interested in regime stability than liberalization. Second, this growing weakness of the state elite made them more insistent on rewriting the contract with the international peacebuilders. Consequently, the "paradox of weakness" was such as their relative power began to decline the more intense they became about regime stability and political power—and thus more insistent on rewriting the contract so that it more fully took into account their interest in regime stability.

In sum, several years of peacebuilding in Afghanistan have not furthered the establishment of a modern, democratic state. The government of Karzai became a close associate of peacebuilders. In turn, Karzai and the modernizers in the government have accepted in principle the legitimacy of liberal reforms. But the central state elite remain weak vis-à-vis the well-entrenched subnational elites. Warlords are circumspect about engaging in long-term, enduring contracts with the central state and prefer "spot" contracts, which provide opportunities for maneuver when international attention has waned (Suhrke 2006). This creates a self-sustaining dynamic of insecurity, which, in turn, makes Karzai and his reformer more indispensable as a partner for peacebuilders. Karzai and his government have been cautious not to alienate subnational elites. In some cases, the warlords have been temporarily "compromised." In other cases, warlords have come to de facto control power-ministries.[31] Decisive steps against the drug economy, widespread corruption or rent seeking by compromised members of subnational elite were avoided. State elites, who were in principle willing to engage in cooperative peacebuilding, are reluctant to implement those liberal reforms that might alienate subnational elites and endanger the fragile stability between state and subnational elites. Peacebuilders accepted these conditions because they viewed state elites as indispensable to stability, and did not want to risk a confrontation with subnational elites that might endanger domestic stability in Afghanistan and undermine the war on terrorism.

The current situation is captured by the big donor conference that occurred in London in 2006. The centerpiece of the conference was the discussion of the so-called Afghanistan Compact, a plan that was to guide international efforts in Afghanistan until 2011. Two features of this compact are particularly relevant to the peacebuilding contract. One, the phrases "sovereignty," financial "autonomy" and "Afghan ownership" litter the document. In other words, the compact is presenting a trustee relationship between the international community and the Afghan people—a pledge to help Afghanistan not only reclaim its sovereignty but also complete a successful liberalization project. The compact also acknowledged the destructive influence of militia leaders and warlords and the increasingly "criminalized" nature of the Afghan state. Although diplomatically worded, the document warns against their accommodation and stresses the need for increased mechanisms of accountability and enforcement to be imposed on such political entrepreneurs. However, it neither proposes any measures for addressing these concerns nor threatens to make future aid conditional on a different set of arrangements. However distasteful they might find this devil's compact, it nevertheless accurately reflects the US-led coalition's preference for security over liberalization.

Renegotiating the peacebuilder's contract?

Our model, in many respects, predicts that liberal peacebuilding has a chance only under very rare circumstances. Yet our model introduces an important but often overlooked reason why—strategic interaction—and also identifies some of the conditions that must be in place in order to improve the probabilities. It requires government elites who are willing to risk their political survival for the goal. It helps when SNEs are weak and cannot play spoiler. Peacebuilders can increase the odds when they are willing to truly commit to peacebuilding and willing to back up state elites that place themselves on the line. Because these facilitating conditions are unlikely in most circumstances, cooperative peacebuilding, and thus the liberal state, remains a distant possibility at best.

The problem, though, might be less with liberal peacebuilders than it is with the donors, funding agencies, and ultimately Western states, who do not give those in the field the time, money, and backing they need. In addition, the war against terrorism, as we visibly saw in the case of Afghanistan, has its occasional benefits but its more frequent costs. On the one hand, when the war against terrorism connects with the particular area of operation then Western states are likely to demonstrate more of a commitment to the operation. On the other hand, there might be a high price to be paid for this commitment, as Western states might allow their security interests to hijack their commitments to peacebuilding.[32] When security interests run at a fever pitch, then peacekeepers and peacebuilders might not mind being compromised or even captured so long as their security interests are fulfilled. Because liberal peacebuilders operate with one hand tied behind their back (or in some cases both hands), local actors have greater bargaining leverage and can promote their interests.

How might liberal peacebuilders better their hand? As we have already suggested, if they had more resources and power, their bargaining leverage would improve and presumably local elites would accept not only the symbols but also the substance of liberalization. Yet, there is always the possibility that the harder peacebuilders push and the more they demand, the more likely it is that local elites will resist and conflictive peacebuilding will result. There are no easy answers.

At the risk of gross rationalization, we are tempted to conclude that compromised peacebuilding might not be such a terrible result. Cooperative peacebuilding is unrealistic, captured peacebuilding might very well only inflame conflict dynamics, and confrontational peacebuilding would be a no-win situation. So, compromised peacebuilding does not look so bad given the alternatives. Even if local elites do little more than recognize the legitimacy of liberalization or accept the symbolic reforms, at the very least it creates new expectations and provides new benchmarks against which the performance of the central government and subnational elites can be judged. Symbols, as we said earlier, can matter. They can provide new focal points. They can become public commitments that even hypocritical reformers must take into account. They can be used by local and international reformers to continue to press for change.

Compromised peacebuilding also might be a normatively desirable outcome. Do peacebuilders truly know better? The underlying presumption of the model and many arguments in favor of liberal peacebuilding is that liberal peacebuilders are pure in motive and, in many respects, know what is best for the local population. Yet even if we grant, in a rather paternalistic gesture, that international actors are acting as public trustees, is there any evidence to suggest that they actually know how to socially engineer a liberal peace? Not really. At present, many peacebuilders escape their uncertainty by relying on general models that frequently are developed from their most recent experiences in the field.[33] But universal models can be a false sanctuary. The only way out is for peacebuilders to confess to a high degree of uncertainty—and actively incorporate local voices into the planning process. As Noah Feldman recently warned: "The high failure rate [of nation-building exercises] strongly supports the basic intuition that we do not know what we are doing—and one of the critical elements of any argument for autonomy is that people tend to know themselves, better than others how they ought best to live their lives" (Feldman 2004: 69).

Also, compromised peacebuilding, from the perspective of local elites and societal groups, might very well look normatively desirable because it provides greater opportunity for local voices to participate and to shape a process that is supposedly "owned" by them. We readily acknowledge that many local elites are not great democrats and are more interested in preserving their perks and power than in pluralizing politics (and in this respect are no different from politicians all over the world), but their presence does force otherwise steamrolling peacebuilders to go slow and adopt a more incremental approach.[34] Compromised peacebuilding, if done right, might be the best of all possible worlds.

If cooperative peacebuilding is going to be a normatively desirable outcome, then it must do more than simply be consistent with the preferences of local elites—it also must institutionalize a set of principles that might help create a more stable and mutually consensual outcome. Such principles might include a constitution that helps to distribute political power forces groups to negotiate and compromise with one another; deliberative mechanisms that force individuals to state their preferences in public (this publicity principle is likely to force individuals to discover and refer to more community-oriented values and interests in order to legitimate their preferences); and principles of representation which might or might not include elections in the days immediately following the establishment of a peacebuilding operation.[35] The object—and thus the measure of success—of peacebuilding must not be the establishment of values that only recently and barely obtain in many advanced democracies, but instead the creation of institutions that contain principles that compel individuals to consult, deliberate, and negotiate with one another as they decide what they consider to be the good life.

Notes

1 For statistical evaluations of their rates of success, see Doyle and Sambanis 2006, Fortna 2003; and Zürcher 2006.

2 See also the chapters of Roberts and Sisk in this volume, which both argue that electoral processes may, under some circumstances, reinforce rather than change existing social differences.

3 In this following discussion, we distinguish between state elites and subnational elites. We acknowledge that in many situations the two are virtually indistinguishable to the extent that subnational elites are part of the central government. However, we will insist on their differentiation in order to highlight that there are frequently (at least) two independent sets of elites in any country and that those outside the capital city often have independent powers that enable them to either block or frustrate any dreams of centralization by state elites. Finally, at times we will speak of local elites, a shorthand for a situation when state and subnational elites can, for analytical purposes, be treated as one.

4 Cooley 2005 advances an ambitious theory of hierarchy that offers potential insight into the relationship between peacebuilding and state–society relations. He observes two kinds of hierarchical governance structures, a U-form and an M-form, and argues that the latter "tends to institutionalize patrimonial institutions in peripheries" (57). Although we predict similar outcomes, we do not develop his argument as an alternative explanation for several reasons. First, it is not clear

whether the structure of peacebuilding operations conform to a U- or M-form. There is an argument that its centralizing characteristics tend to resemble the latter form yet this probability gives it more coherence than probably exists. Second, although his model takes into account the different actors that are part of each governance structure, there is little consideration of the interaction between the actors.

5 In their impressive book on peacekeeping, Doyle and Sambanis (2006) argue that the success of peacebuilding is a function of international capacity, local capacity and the level of hostility and war destruction. Our argument is consistent with theirs, but modifies it by examining the bargaining process between SEs and PBs, which is influenced by their capacities *and* their preferences.

6 Department of Foreign Affairs and International Trade and Canadian International Development Agency 2002. See Barnett et al. 2007, for a review of how different organizations use the term of peacebuilding.

7 Here is how one student of Soviet state formation characterized the 1920s:

> Personal networks originated in the prerevolutionary underground, but became better defined and more cohesive in the civil war. The major battle fronts of the civil war gave rise to informal groups of fighter organizers, who used their personal network ties to carry out territorial conquest and political consolidation. When hostilities finally ended, these wartime networks were not dismantled but adapted to the new challenges of the post-revolutionary regional administration. During the 1920s, center–regional relations were hampered by poorly developed bureaucratic lines and institutional incoherence. Consequently, the center was reconnected to the regions through personal network ties. In the regions, rival networks competed over access to and control over scarce organizational and material resources distributed by the center. Those networks that were most successful in that competition eventually came to dominate the administrative apparatus in their region. In the process, their network rivals in the region were either displaced or subsumed by these dominant networks.
>
> (Easter 2000: 12)

Easter's description of the post-civil war Soviet Union captures much of the "post-conflict" processes; the only important difference is that in the "new wars" these peripheral networks are sustained by shadow economic networks, thus giving them a fair bit of autonomy, power, and control.

8 For discussions of the post-colonial state, see Ayoob 1995; and Clapham 1996.

9 Akin to the post-communist experience,

> those making institutional choices thus face not only greater time constraints but also more intense international scrutiny. In contrast to previous episodes of statebuilding, international influence has not only become more acute, but it has had a profound effect on the very nature of statebuilding by changing the formal institutional requirements for becoming a full-fledged member of the international system.
>
> (Gryzmala-Busse and Luong 2002: 529–54).

10 A separate paper with Songying Fang, "The Game of Peacebuilding," upgrades the "heuristic" model into a full-blown formal model.

11 On this point, see Boyce 2002: 367.

12 For the case of imperialism, see Curtin 2000; and Robinson 1986. For Cold War see Clapham 1996 and Ayoob 1995.

13 On impact of aid, see Boyce 2002 and Terry 2002.

14 This situation is more likely in situations of extreme violence and instability, when peacekeepers and aid workers are dependent on local warlords, militias, and combatants in order to carry out their mandates and for access to populations at risk.

15 On spoilers see Stedman 1997. For a formal modeling of veto players, see Tsebelis 1991.

16 There is only scarce reliable economic data for Tajikistan and almost none for Afghanistan. Estimates published in the annual *CIA World Factbook* put the GDP per capita in purchasing power parity (PPP) in Afghanistan at 700 USD in 2003 (rank 221 in global comparison) and 800 USD in 2007 (rank 219 in global comparison). For Tajikistan, the PDP per capita in PPP was estimated to be 1,250 USD in 2003 (rank 196) and 1,300 USD in 2007 (rank 203). See Central Intelligence Agency (2007). CIA World Factbook. Available online at https://www.cia.gov/library/publications/the-world-factbook/index.html.

17 We treat these cases as illustrative and suggest that future research select on the critical variables in order to see whether and how a change in the preferences and constraints might lead to different outcomes.

18 There are, of course, various alternative explanations for these results, including the lack of coordination among the peacebuilders, which increased the autonomy of local elites and thus gave them the ability to escape any kinds of control mechanisms that might have been established; the American obsession with the war on terrorism; the American invasion of Iraq, which consumed the kinds of international military and financial assistance (and attention) that might otherwise have gone to Afghanistan.

19 UNTOP: http://www.untop.org/ (02/06/2006).

20 World Bank Development Indicators.

21 Business & Economics: Russia, Tajikistan Spar Over Illegal Labor Migration, 1/09/03. (http://www.eurasianet.org/departments/business/articles/eav010903.shtml 3.1.2004)

22 http://www.untop.org/ (02/06/2006)

23 See Bertelsmann Transformation Index BTI, country report Tajikistan 2006, http://www.bertelsmann-transformation-index.de/157.0.html?L=1 (2006/06/26)

24 Ibid.

25 http://www.untop.org/ (02/06/2006)

26 The figures are for Voice and Accountability: 2000: -1,76; 2002: -1,31; 2004: -1,35; for government effectiveness: 2000: -1,39; 2002: -1,13; 2004: -1,05. (Kaufmann et al. 2005).

27 Bonn, formally known as the "Agreement on Provisional Arrangements in Afghanistan Pending the Reestablishment of Permanent Government Institutions," was brokered by the four major Afghani factions. For discussions of the Loya Jirga, see Giustozzi 2004; Saba and Zakhilwal 2004; Thier 2004; and Thier and Chopra 2002. For a critical commentary, particularly the centralization of power in the hands of a few cliques, see International Crisis Group 2003 and Johnson and Jolyon 2004, Chapters 7 and 8.

28 *Christian Science Monitor,* May 9, 2002.

29 *Christian Science Monitor,* September 4, 2003.

30 The following section draws on Marc Theuss (Free U Berlin), Jan Koehler (Free U Berlin) and Christoph Zürcher's (Free U Berlin) field experiences and first hand accounts from rural regions in Afghanistan. Names and details are omitted in order to avoid endangering informants and organizations working in the field.

31 As *The Economist*, July 8, 2006, observed, the recent introduction of NATO and its preference for stability has altered what Karzai can hope to accomplish:

> This knowledge [NATO's strong preference for security and stability] no doubt underlies Mr Karzai's reluctance to upset the opium-cart. He seems resigned to ruling Afghanistan as it was ruled before the war descended:

through weak, centralized institutions and by issuing patronage to local strongmen. Last month [June 2006] Mr Karzai floated a plan to authorize pro-government militias in several southern provinences—in effect, rearming some of those disarmed in a $150 million UN programme. Some of their proposed commanders are unfit to hold a responsible post anywhere at all. But yet again, it is possible to see Mr Karzai's point: Kabul carries no clout at all in those places.

32 For a similar argument with respect to humanitarianism in Afghanistan, see Donini 2004.
33 In a report on Liberia and Sierra Leone, the International Crisis Group observes that peacebuilders possess an "operational checklist" that does not recognize the underlying political dynamics (ICG 2004).
34 For a related argument, see Barnett 2006.
35 These principles are republican, and not liberal, and are developed in Barnett 2006.

3 Understanding the "coordination problem" in postwar statebuilding

Roland Paris

A common critique of postwar statebuilding operations is that they suffer from a lack of coordination among the myriad international actors involved in these missions. Stories abound of international agencies duplicating efforts or even working at cross-purposes, sometimes with limited knowledge of each other's activities; and calls for improved coordination have become something of a mantra among scholars and practitioners of statebuilding.[1] But these oft-repeated calls may conceal as much as they reveal about the dilemmas of statebuilding. Like other mantras, this one offers soothing simplicity in the face of disturbing complexity. Lurking behind the organizational discontinuities of statebuilding are deeper disagreements and uncertainties about the means and ends of this enterprise, many of which are described in the other chapters of this volume. Getting statebuilding agencies to work smoothly together is, of course, a necessary condition for successful international action (however the goals of that action may be defined), but it is too easy to prescribe improved coordination as a remedy for the shortcomings and contradictions of statebuilding, which run much deeper.

Understanding the nature of the coordination problem—what it reveals, and what it hides—is a first step in this analysis. The second step is to explore the challenges of actually improving coordination among international statebuilders. Calls for greater coordination rarely delve into the details: Who will do the coordinating? How, when, and under what auspices? Just starting to answer these questions reveals the complexities of coordination. While there are compelling reasons to strengthen cooperation among the main international actors involved in statebuilding, there are also many pitfalls to avoid. Rather than conceiving of "more coordination" as an absolute good, this chapter argues that effective coordination requires striking a balance between competing imperatives, which are shaped by the characteristics of the environment and of the actors to be coordinated. Indeed, in the environment of statebuilding, there is a real risk that too little, too much, or the wrong type of coordination could do more harm than good. In making this argument, I draw upon organizational theory—in particular, the distinction between markets, hierarchies, and networks.[2]

Put differently, although the coordination problem is real, greater clarity is needed in both its diagnosis and treatment. Too often, unrelated problems are misdiagnosed as coordination failures because they manifest themselves, superficially, as disorderliness or ineffectiveness in the field, whereas in fact they reflect deeper frustrations, tensions, and uncertainties in the statebuilding enterprise. And too often, greater coordination is put forward as a remedy without considering the difficulties and risks of the treatment.

Thinking carefully about the coordination problem is timely, given initiatives now underway within the United Nations, including the recent establishment of a Peacebuilding Commission (PBC) that is designed to bring greater coherence to the myriad activities of statebuilding agencies, both inside and outside the UN. In its short existence, the Commission has launched an ambitious and innovative work plan, and hopes are high that it will fill what former UN Secretary-General Kofi Annan called a "gaping hole" in the institutional machinery for statebuilding: namely, the absence of a body to coordinate the alphabet soup of international actors involved in statebuilding missions. As we shall see, however, the design of the Commission makes heroic assumptions about the ability and willingness of independent agencies (whose goals often differ and conflict with each other) to embrace common, overarching strategies. While the Commission's design is well-suited to maintaining the flexibility and creativity of the international statebuilding network—and in this sense is sensitive to the distinctive characteristics and needs of this complex and "networked" policy domain—the Commission may be hobbled by its own lack of authority and leverage over key statebuilding agencies. It is a purely advisory body that has no independent decisionmaking authority, and even its recommendations depend on reaching full consensus among its members—all of which suggests that the Commission will have great difficulty reducing inter-organizational differences of approach and strategy.

Rising demand for better coordination

As the Cold War came to an end, a new brand of international peace operations emerged as the dominant security activity of the United Nations: missions aimed at helping war-torn countries make the transition from a fragile ceasefire to a stable peace, or what became known as post-conflict peacebuilding. Although this form of intervention was not unprecedented— the UN had stumbled into playing a similar role in the Congo during the early 1960s, when a mission designed to oversee the departure of Belgian colonial troops from the newly independent Congo got caught up in a civil war—post-conflict stabilization was a new area of focus for the world body in the period immediately following the Cold War.

As noted on Chapter 1, these missions were quite unlike the traditional peacekeeping operations that had been the UN's main security function during the Cold War, and which had typically involved monitoring ceasefires or neutral buffer zones between former combatants. Rather, peacebuilding now involved the implementation of multi-faceted peace agreements, which often included political and economic elements, in addition to a ceasefire. As then-Secretary-General Boutros Boutros-Ghali put it in 1992, the goal of peacebuilding was "to identify and support structures which will tend to strengthen and solidify peace in order to avoid a relapse into conflict."[3] This typically included monitoring or even administering post-conflict elections as well as other activities such as the demobilization of former fighters, reset-tlement of refugees, human-rights investigations, and economic reform. Furthermore, the UN shared these responsibilities with several other inter-national actors, including major regional organizations, international finan-cial institutions, national and international development agencies, and a host of international non-governmental organizations (NGOs).

With more agencies involved in performing a wider range of tasks than in earlier peace operations, coordination problems soon began to arise. In El Salvador, Mozambique and Cambodia, for example, the UN urged the governments of these countries to increase spending on peacebuilding-related programs, such as the re-integration of former combatants into civilian life, while the International Monetary Fund (IMF) pushed in the opposite direc-tion and demanded fiscal restraint.[4] Coordination problems also emerged between military and civilian actors, within the family of UN agencies, and between governmental and non-governmental actors, in most missions; and by 1995 the United Nations was recognizing such problems as serious.[5] The success of UN-led peace operations, wrote Boutros-Ghali in that year, depends on "cooperation and support of other players on the international stage: the Governments that constitute the United Nations membership, regional and non-governmental organizations, and the various funds, pro-grams, offices, and agencies of the United Nations system itself. If United Nations efforts are to succeed, the roles of the various players need to be carefully coordinated in an integrated approach to human security."[6]

These concerns led to sporadic efforts to improve coordination through devices such as ad hoc "Friends" groups, which brought together key gov-ernments to promote common approaches to specific missions, as well as country team thematic groups within the UN, and Special Representatives of the Secretary-General in the field. But the coordination problem actually became more difficult as time went on—for two reasons. First, peacebuilding missions became more complex in their functions and expansive in their aims, due in part to a recognition that a more comprehensive approach to peacebuilding was required in order to address the underlying sources of conflict in societies emerging from civil war. In the early years of the 1990s, peacebuilders tended to rush ahead with post-conflict elections, declare suc-cess and depart. This "quick and dirty" approach failed in Angola (where elections were a catalyst for renewed violence), Rwanda (where overly opti-mistic assumptions about the willingness of the parties to implement their peace settlement were shattered by genocide), and in Cambodia and Liberia (where elections yielded superficial democratization and a quick return to authoritarianism—and, in the case of Liberia, resurgent war).

Learning from the shortcomings of these missions, the UN and other international agencies began to shift their focus towards more far-reaching approaches to peacebuilding. This strategic reorientation was especially visible in the Bosnia operation, created in 1995 with the signing of the Dayton Accord. The post-Dayton mission was originally scheduled to last only one year (until the end of 1996) and in this sense reflected the prevailing "quick and dirty" approach that defined peacebuilding in the first half of the 1990s. But the need for a longer-term deployment in Bosnia quickly became apparent and the termination date was eliminated in order to give time for institution-building and economic reform to progress. By the late 1990s, new missions were being launched with broader mandates and authority: Kosovo, East Timor, and Sierra Leone. These operations had more expansive functions, and as a result peacebuilding became an even more complex and multi-faceted enterprise. This, in turn, increased the challenges (and importance) of achieving effective coordination.

The second complicating factor was the growing number and variety of international actors involved in peacebuilding. The 1990s saw a steady rise in regional and sub-regional organizations—as well as NGOs and private military companies—as important players in these missions.[7] Bosnia, in this respect, too, was a watershed. The post-Dayton mission was the first operation explicitly dividing core peacebuilding roles among multiple international actors, including the UN, NATO, EU, and OSCE. More generally, through the course of the 1990s, there was a movement away from UN-led missions and the greater reliance on lead states, ad hoc coalitions, and regional bodies to lead military and civilian functions, which contributed to the multiplication of peacebuilding actors. Simultaneously, a growing number of international agencies and national governments were creating specialized post-conflict and emergency response units, thus diffusing intervention capacity to a broader range of actors.[8]

By the early 2000s, there was a growing sense that an "immense coordination problem" existed within the international machinery for peacebuilding.[9] Efforts to implement "integrated mission" models in the field, beginning in Kosovo in 1999, were only partly successful.[10] Attempts to construct an institutional locus for peacebuilding within the UN itself also floundered,[11] and NGOs were coming under increasing criticism for their inability to coordinate amongst themselves.[12] What is more, the very proliferation of ad hoc coordination mechanisms appeared to be creating some confusion among peacebuilders in the field.[13]

In fact, problems of coordination existed at four inter-related levels: first, at the field level, between the various international actors (including governmental and non-governmental agencies) involved in statebuilding missions and domestic actors within the country itself, including government authorities; second, within the bureaucracies of the major donor governments, whose different departments and agencies often pursued different goals and activities within the same mission; third, within the UN system, where bureaucratic rivalries and turf-battles are legion; and fourth, at the head-quarters-level between all the major international statebuilding actors as well as the major governments supporting these actors.[14] In substantive terms, coordination involved bringing greater coherence to political, security, rule of law, human rights, and development activities of statebuilders at all four of these levels.

Perfect—or even near-perfect—coordination of these many statebuilding activities would be impossible. Indeed, I shall argue below that it would be undesirable. But major operational problems arising from a lack of coordination among statebuilding agencies have been well documented, giving rise to a growing body of reports and studies that reached the same conclusion: the hard nut of coordination had to be cracked. One 2004 study examined 336 peacebuilding projects sponsored by Germany, the Nether-lands, Norway and the UK and concluded that more than 55 percent of these projects had no link to any broader strategy for the country in which they were implemented, pointing to a "strategic deficit" in the design and conduct of peacebuilding missions.[15] Another report found that "diffuse planning and implementation of peacebuilding ... is extremely problematic and produces a greater chance of delay or failure."[16] In 2004, Cedric de Coning summar-ized what had emerged as a widely-held view among peacebuilding analysts and practitioners: "the lack of meaningful coordination among the peace-building agencies [is] a major cause of unsatisfactory performance."[17] It was in this context—in early 2005—that Kofi Annan described the insufficiency of coordination as a "gaping hole" in the UN's institutional machinery for peacebuilding.

When Annan made these remarks, there was growing support among UN member states to address the coordination issue. Several countries, including the United Kingdom, Canada, and the United States were already pursuing plans to develop more effective "whole-of-government" approaches to fragile states within their respective governments.[18] The High-Level Panel on Threats, Challenges and Change had also recently issued its report calling for the creation of a new body—the Peacebuilding Commission—"to monitor and pay close attention to countries at risk, ensure concerted action by donors, agencies, programs and financial institutions, and mobilize financial resources for sustainable peace."[19] Annan himself strongly supported the proposal for the PBC, as did many UN member states. This was, in fact, one of the few agenda items that achieved widespread support at the 2005 World Summit.[20]

The PBC—along with its Support Office (PBSO) and a dedicated Peace-building Fund—came into existence in 2006. As we shall see, their creation represented one of the most promising opportunities in recent years to improve coordination among statebuilding agencies within and outside the UN system. However, the degree to which a new body could "fix" the coordination problem would depend not only on how that body was designed, but also on the definition of the problem itself.

The coordination problem: a convenient catch-all?

There are compelling efficiency arguments for addressing the coordination problem among international statebuilders and for creating new mechanisms to foster more cooperation and coherence in the field. But there is also something peculiar about the number of operational problems that have been attributed to coordination failures, and the degree to which improved coordination is sometimes portrayed as a means of resolving these problems. In the light of deep uncertainties and disagreements that render postwar statebuilding such a complex (and sometimes controversial) exercise, the emphasis on improving coordination seems strangely anodyne and technocratic.

If we have learned anything in the past decade and a half—and by "we" I am referring primarily to the Western governments, organizations and specialists who support the international statebuilding machinery—it is that we know relatively little about how to transform war-torn countries into stable societies. The results of the missions undertaken to date have been mixed at best.[21] In some cases, such as Angola, Rwanda, Liberia, and East Timor, international efforts did not prevent a resumption of violence, with new conflicts erupting in these countries. In other cases, such as El Salvador and Nicaragua, peace prevails but the underlying socio-economic conditions that drove conflict remain largely unchanged. Elsewhere, including Bosnia, Kosovo, and Afghanistan, international deployments have arguably resulted in a seemingly permanent, quasi-imperial presence, which raises concerns about fostering excessive local dependence on international actors. All of these missions reveal the tremendous complexity and difficulty involved in building stable state institutions in war-torn states, particularly when this process is led by outsiders—problems that are further complicated when statebuilding takes place after external conquest, as in the case of Afghanistan and Iraq, and in the face of ongoing insurgencies. Major questions of strategy and legitimacy remain unanswered: What is the best combination of political and economic reforms in a post-conflict situation, and in what sequence? How can international actors play a statebuilding role without undermining the perceived legitimacy of the resulting institutions in the eyes of the local populace? Most fundamentally, how can a statebuilding process that took hundreds of years in most well-established liberal democracies be accelerated and achieved within a dramatically shorter time?

Indeed, lack of coordination in previous missions has resulted not only from obvious factors, such as the multitude of peacebuilding actors with overlapping or duplicative mandates, the time and money ("transaction costs") that coordination entails, competition for influence and visibility among some international peacebuilding agencies and their general unwillingness to sacrifice autonomy and independence.[22] More fundamentally, such problems also stem from the fact that many of these agencies have different approaches to postwar statebuilding and different philosophies, objectives and conceptions of how to create the conditions for stable and lasting peace in war-torn societies.[23] Such differences have been well-documented in many operations. In the case of Bosnia, for example, Bruce Jones, Elizabeth Cousens, and Susan Woodward each observed that lack of success in coordination stemmed from differing, even contradictory, policy goals of the international agencies and major powers involved in Bosnia.[24] While most international actors subscribe to the broad goals of transforming war-torn states into liberal market democracies, there is no universal agreement on what is required to achieve this goal, or how to achieve it under different circumstances.[25] Significant differences in approach also exist within individual agencies—including in the OSCE, where the democratization branch generally seeks to develop working relationships with local authorities, while the human-rights branch is tasked with responding to complaints *against* local authorities.[26] Discrepancies in strategic orientation can also give rise to concerns and disputes over the "politicization of humanitarian relief" in statebuilding missions.[27]

Discussions aimed at improving coordination have tended to overlook these substantive disagreements and to redefine them in procedural-technocratic terms: namely, as "coordination" problems. Undoubtedly, there have been genuine coordination problems, where actors share common objectives but fail to cooperate or work at cross-purposes because of insufficient information sharing. But there are also underlying substantive-philosophical differences which lead statebuilding agencies to pursue conflicting or incompatible strategies, and it follows that any response to such problems cannot be a purely procedural one.

Bureaucracies, in particular, have a propensity to deal with situations of complexity, novelty, and uncertainty by shifting these discussions into more familiar terrain: the realm of rules and procedures. This is true not just of bureaucracies, but of people in general. Social psychologists have shown that when people are faced with situations of uncertainty, they tend to fall back on habits and routines as a means of economizing on cognitive resources and coping with complexity.[28] But bureaucracies, which specialize in disaggregating administrative problems into manageable and repetitive tasks, have a particular tendency to revert to a procedural discourse in the face of uncertainty and ambiguity.[29] This is one aspect of what Max Weber first called the process of "rationalization" intrinsic to modern bureaucracies[30]—and it may help to explain how it was possible to achieve such widespread support for the creation of a Peacebuilding Commission at the 2005 World Summit, where other important agenda items were subject to paralyzing discord. Recasting the strategic disagreements over statebuilding as procedural problems apparently made it possible to reach near-universal agreement on specific measures to "strengthen" statebuilding through organizational reform.[31]

During the discussions that led up to the establishment of the PBC, even traditionally wary countries such as China chimed in with strong support for its creation: "China is favorably disposed toward the proposal for the establishment of a Peacebuilding Commission and believes that its main responsibility should be to help devise plans for the transition from conflict to post-conflict peacebuilding and to coordinate initiatives of the international community in this respect."[32] But the Chinese delegation pointedly avoided making any references to the more controversial substance of peacebuilding strategy, referring instead to such generalities "devising plans" and "coordinating initiatives." Even members of the customarily critical NGO community joined the chorus, supporting the establishment of the Commission, again in largely procedural terms, as an "institutional home for peacebuilding" that could "provide much-needed policy coherence and coordination within the UN system."[33]

However, there were potential costs to using the "coordination problem" as a catch-all for deeper disagreements and uncertainties over the strategy and purposes of peacebuilding. First, doing so could raise expectations about the degree to which procedural fixes are capable of reducing the inherent complexity of statebuilding or overcoming organizational conflicts rooted in the incompatible priorities and strategic orientations of statebuilding agencies, not just in their failure to communicate and coordinate. Second, defining the problem in this manner could deflect attention away from these deeper issues. Indeed, UN members spent a year wrangling over purely procedural aspects of the new PBC—its membership, structure, and so on—before the body was able to hold its first meeting. Perhaps such discussions were necessary, but they came with an opportunity cost: this time was not spent addressing substantive statebuilding strategies.

Interestingly, one of the few official statements that challenged the prevailing procedural discourse in this early period of the Commission's formation came not from a national delegation, but from the head of the UN bureaucracy itself: then-Secretary-General Kofi Annan. At the June 2006 launch of the Commission, Annan drew attention to the inherently political task of postwar reconstruction:

> [I]ncreased resources and improved coordination will not, in themselves, be enough to bring about lasting peace ... At times, the international community has approached peacebuilding as a largely technical exercise, involving knowledge and resources. The international community must not only understand local power dynamics, but also recognize that it is itself a political actor entering a political environment.[34]

These comments gently peeled back the procedural veneer of discussions on the Peacebuilding Commission, exposing the highly political—and contentious—core of the statebuilding enterprise that had been partially obscured by the emphasis on coordination.

The need for a balanced approach to coordination

Just as it is naive to blame coordination failures for a host of more complex problems, it is too easy to call for "stronger coordination" without understanding that not all types of coordination are well-suited to the circumstances and needs of statebuilding. Too much, too little, or the wrong type of coordination could do more harm than good. The challenge is to avoid these pitfalls and to devise coordination methods that are properly calibrated to the particular tasks and task-environments in question.

The starting point for this analysis is to recognize that the international statebuilding machinery is, at present, a loosely structured network of national governments and international governmental and non-governmental agencies. It is a "network" in the sense that statebuilding actors constitute a system that is neither purely a "market" in which individual actors pursue their individual goals with little sense of sharing common objectives, nor is it purely a "hierarchy" or a system of top-down or command management.

Networks are collections of actors who share common goals and engage in repeated, voluntary interactions in the pursuit of their shared goals. In the words of Walter W. Powell, transactions between networked actors "occur neither through discrete exchanges [as in the market] nor by administrative fiat [as in a hierarchy], but through networks of individuals engaged in reciprocal, preferential, mutually supportive actions."[35] The international statebuilding system is a network because its constituent members share information with each other, discuss common objectives, work together to achieve these objectives both at the headquarters-level and in the field, and use several formal and informal coordination mechanisms (outlined in the first section of this chapter). But it is a *loosely structured* network in that there is little joint planning for missions, patchy information sharing, inconsistent and often non-existent coordination, and no hierarchical command structure for the system as a whole.

When commentators or officials talk about the need for "improved coordination," they may mean different things. For some, improved coordination means moving towards a more hierarchical arrangement. Anja T. Kaspersen and Ole Jacob Sending, for example, have argued for "functional centralization" and a "fully integrated structure" for peacebuilding within the United Nations, in order to "reduce supply-driven programming and turf battles" and to "make it possible to implement a peacebuilding strategy that would draw effectively on the full spectrum of the tools and expertise of the UN system."[36] For others, such as Robert Ricigliano, improved coordination refers to international actors doing a better job of sharing information and subscribing to a broad set of common principles.[37] These are quite different visions of how to achieve better coordination. The former involves replacing the existing statebuilding network (at least the UN portion of this network) with a new hierarchy centered in the UN, whereas the latter eschews new hierarchies and seeks to make the network work more efficiently *as a network* through improved information sharing.

Both approaches have their advantages and disadvantages. Those who argue that the international statebuilding system should continue to operate as network, without the addition of new hierarchical elements, assume that better communication alone will yield a more coordinated "self-organizing" network of statebuilding actors. Greater communication is surely needed (not least to prevent the unintentional duplication of efforts) but can information sharing, alone, address strategic gaps and differences in approach to statebuilding? I doubt it. In fact, this is one of the principal scholarly criticisms of the various theories of network organization: they have neglected the role of power as an instigator of cooperation and have placed too high an expectation on consensus.[38] Achieving cooperation and coordination through networks cannot be taken for granted, even in networks whose members share a high level of trust and common goals.[39] Sometimes it is necessary to institute elements of top-down direction, such as a lead organization (or small group of lead organizations) to devise network-wide strategies and monitor the performance of network members.[40] Indeed, previous efforts to devise "integrated missions" within the UN were obstructed when "Agencies, Funds and Programs welcomed a greater say in the planning of UN peacekeeping operations but balked at the prospect of taking direction from them."[41]

On the other hand, moving toward centralization and hierarchy can also be problematic, for several reasons. First, as students of networks and network theory have pointed out, centralization has the potential to reduce policy innovation and experimentation by constraining the freedom of individual agencies and actors. The benefits of experimentation through decentralized organizational structures have long been recognized. Within the context of the American federal structure, Supreme Court Justice Louis D. Brandeis wrote in 1932 that US states serve as policy laboratories to "try novel social and economic experiments" that, if successful, could be replicated by others.[42] In a similar vein, when President Lyndon Johnson initiated his "War on Poverty" and a planning exercise to identify the most effective and least costly alternatives in achieving social-welfare goals, social scientists led by Donald T. Campbell called for an "experimental approach" to policy reform, or "an approach in which we try out new programs designed to cure specific social problems, in which we learn whether or not these programs are effective, and in which we retain, imitate, modify or discard them on the basis of apparent effectiveness."[43] In the circumstances of postwar statebuilding, the problems to be addressed are complex, there is no single obvious solution, and the stakes are very high—in short, there is a strong case for continued experimentation with alternative strategies.

Put slightly differently, centralized coordination has the potential to reduce the flexibility of constituent organizations in responding to shifting circumstances, which can be a serious disadvantage in rapidly changing and uncertain environments. "The rigid character of standardized procedures inherent in formal centralized structures," writes Donald Chisholm, "precludes adaptive responses to surprise, and the organizational system suffers accordingly."[44] Flexibility is most important in domains where surprises are likely and quick adaptation essential. Postwar statebuilding is an exceptionally unpredictable and uncertain enterprise, for three reasons: first, because these missions take place in volatile environments where there is a relatively high likelihood of violence, relative to conditions in other developing states; second, because these missions are multi-faceted and actions taken in one area—political, social or economic—have the potential to generate unforeseen results in other areas; and third, because international peacebuilding agencies have only limited knowledge of what is required to succeed in the ambitious task of stabilizing a fragile country after war. The ability of these agencies to adapt and react quickly to changing circumstances and surprises—including revising specific strategies that are producing unforeseen and undesirable effects—is a key to preventing small problems from swelling into crises that threaten the peace and the success of the mission. For this reason, rigid or overly bureaucratic forms of international coordination could reduce the overall effectiveness of statebuilding.

In addition, delegating strategic planning upwards to an international mechanism has the potential to result in de-contextualized "cookie cutter" approaches to statebuilding that do not adequately respond to the unique needs of individual societies emerging from war. Indeed, one of the most common recommendations in studies of peacebuilding—and criticisms of previous missions—is that strategies need to be carefully customized to local conditions, based on a deep analysis of the drivers of conflict within the society. A related criticism is that statebuilding missions have not been adequately accountable to the local populations they are affecting.[45] The more that peacebuilding strategies and mission plans are developed within an international coordination structure, the less latitude individual agencies may have to define their own policies—and, to the extent that individual agencies have already established accountability mechanisms of their own, these mechanisms may no longer be either adequate or relevant, because more of the key decisions on peacebuilding policy will be made by the *collectivity* of major peacebuilding actors involved in the mission, not by the individual agency. The formalization and centralization of any diffuse organizational system therefore runs the risk of reducing whatever public accountability previously existed within that system.[46] Reduced accountability is not inevitable—indeed, centralization involves the creation of a new locus of authority, which can itself be designed to operate according to norms and procedures of accountability. But the rationale for decentralization or delegation of authority normally includes the expectation that policies designed and implemented "closer" to the people affected by the policies will tend to be more responsive to these people's distinctive needs. This rationale is at the heart of decentralization arguments espoused by the "new public management" movement, which focuses on improving the responsiveness of governments to their "clients" or citizens.[47] It is also central to the concept of subsidiarity (most often in connection to the European Union's multi-level governance structure)[48] and in strategies of aid donors seeking to promote democratic decentralization in recipient developing countries.[49]

These observations suggest two broad conclusions. First, a healthy dose of skepticism is warranted when faced with boilerplate calls for more coordination. In each case it is worth asking: What specific type of coordination is advocated? How will this approach achieve tangible results? And how will it do so without stumbling into the pitfalls described above? Second, the challenge in statebuilding is not simply to "strengthen" coordination, as many observers suggest; rather, it is to develop coordination methods that are calibrated to the distinctive characteristics and requirements of statebuilding. On one hand, there are clear benefits to retaining the largely decentralized structure of the international statebuilding system. On the other hand, the statebuilding network as it is currently constituted has been incapable of effective "self-organizing" and is unlikely to do so merely by increasing the sharing of information or consultation among statebuilding actors. Some additional elements of hierarchy or central direction seem necessary to increase the problems of incoherence and inter-organizational conflict over goals, strategies and "turf" that have undermined previous missions. Adding new elements of top-down direction does not mean transforming the statebuilding network *into* a hierarchy, but rather, adding *elements* of hierarchy in order to address and at least partially resolving substantive disagreements over objectives and strategies without unduly squelching the flexibility and fluidity which remains a key strength of the decentralized statebuilding network. A balanced approach to improving coordination in statebuilding would thus entail retaining the predominantly network form of the existing system while (1) greatly increasing information-sharing and consultation, and (2) modestly strengthening the hierarchical features of the network.

As we shall see below, one of the goals of the new Peacebuilding Commission is to encourage international statebuilding agencies and national authorities to work together in planning new operations and devising integrated strategies for countries emerging from, or at risk of slipping into, violent conflict. Joint strategic planning is an excellent idea: it would bring different perspectives and priorities into the open, creating an opportunity to resolve these differences before they disrupt the flow and effectiveness of operations. But whether the Commission has been endowed with sufficient top-down authority or "hierarchy" to accomplish this goal—namely, to resolve key differences, to promote joint planning and (most importantly) to induce turf-conscious statebuilding agencies to work towards shared strategies—is questionable.

The Peacebuilding Commission: a preliminary assessment

At the time of this writing, any evaluation of the PBC must be preliminary, given that the body has existed for less than three years. However, it is possible to analyze the approach taken in the creation of the Commission, the direction in which the Commission has developed during its early period of operation, and the degree to which this new body elucidates and embodies the above-mentioned tensions and problems that accompany the "coordination problem" for statebuilding.

Following the September 2005 decision of the World Summit to endorse the creation of a Peacebuilding Commission, the UN General Assembly and the Security Council passed parallel resolutions in December setting out the elements of the Commission and the Peacebuilding Support Office.[50] According to these resolutions, the three main purposes of the Commission were:

1 To bring together all relevant actors to marshal resources and to advise on and propose integrated strategies for post-conflict peacebuilding and recovery;
2 To focus attention on the reconstruction and institution-building efforts necessary for recovery from conflict and to support the development of integrated strategies in order to lay the foundation for sustainable development; and
3 To provide recommendations and information to improve the coordination of all relevant actors within and outside the United Nations, to develop best practices, to help to ensure predictable financing for early recovery activities and to extend the period of attention given by the international community to post-conflict recovery.

In pursuit of these goals, the PBC would serve solely as an advisory body to the Security Council and the General Assembly. It would have no independent authority or decision-making power over other bodies. Further, its recommendations and advice would all be on the basis of consensus among the members of the PBC.

Membership of the main "organizational committee" of the Commission would include members of the Security Council, General Assembly, and Economic and Social Council, along with top troop-contributing countries and those providing the most funds to UN budgets, programs and agencies. In addition, the Commission would meet in "country specific" configurations to discuss particular cases. Such meetings will also include representatives of the country under consideration, key states in the region, major troop and financial contributors to the recovery effort, senior UN officials, and regional and international financial institutions "as may be relevant."

To support the Commission's work, a 15-person Peacebuilding Support Office (PBSO) would be established within the UN Secretariat. The office would focus on gathering information on financial resources and mission planning, evaluating progress towards meeting mission goals, and identifying best practices with respect to cross-cutting peacebuilding issues.[51]

In addition, the General Assembly and Security Council called for the creation of a standing Peacebuilding Fund to ensure "the immediate release of resources needed to launch peacebuilding activities and the availability of appropriate financing for recovery," to be financed by voluntary contributions from UN member states.[52]

Much of 2006 was taken up with organizational matters, including the selection and election of members of the Commission's Organizational Committee (see Box 3.1), the establishment of the Peacebuilding Support Office within the UN Secretariat,[53] and arrangements for the Peacebuilding Fund.[54]

The speeches made at the organizational committee's first formal meeting in June 2006 reflected the procedural discourse that dominated early discussions of, and in, the PBC. Most speakers offered vague endorsements of the general principle of improved coordination and then focused on administrative, not substantive, matters. The president of the UN General Assembly, for example, presented six specific recommendations to the members of the Peacebuilding Commission. All of them were procedural: involve local governments in the Commission's work; coordinate between the peacekeeping and post-conflict peacebuilding aspects of operations; recognize the critical role of the UN Economic and Social Council; appreciate the importance of annual debates on peacebuilding in the General Assembly; engage the international financial institutions; and make arrangements for dialogue with civil society.[55] These were all sensible suggestions, but they were mainly matters of housekeeping. Similarly, Denmark's Minister of Foreign Affairs, Per Stig Møller, noted that "Creating a new body whose main purposes is to bring together all relevant actors and to focus attention on reconstruction and institution-building efforts is an institutional innovation that will strengthen the United Nations and benefit its members."[56] But beyond celebrating "institutional innovation," it was unclear exactly how the PBC would strengthen either statebuilding or the UN.

Soon after this seemingly inauspicious start, however, the members of the Commission began to focus more directly on substantive issues—and they did so in innovative ways. Late in 2006, the first two country-specific

---

Box 3.1   Members of the Organization Committee of the Peacebuilding Commission (as of February 2008)

- From the Security Council: the "Permanent Five" (China, France, Russia, UK, and US) plus Belgium and South Africa.
- From ECOSOC: Angola, Brazil, Czech Republic, Guinea-Bissau, Luxembourg, Indonesia, and Sri Lanka.
- From the top ten financial contributors: Germany, Italy, Japan, the Netherlands, and Norway.
- From the top ten military and police contributors: Bangladesh, Ghana, India, Nigeria, and Pakistan.
- From the General Assembly: Burundi, Chile, Egypt, El Salvador, Fiji, Georgia, and Jamaica.

configurations of the Commission were created to examine peacebuilding challenges in Burundi and Sierra Leone. Each committee met twice: once in October and again in December.[57] Prior to the October meetings, the Peacebuilding Support Office prepared background papers on each country, identifying existing peacebuilding commitments and major challenges, and putting forward questions for discussion.[58] At each inaugural session, the governments of Burundi and Sierra Leone, respectively, were asked to make presentations on what they viewed as the "critical challenges to consolidating peace" in their countries. The meetings resulted in agreement on a few broadly-defined areas of focus for each country (for example, the key challenges identified in Burundi were promoting good governance, strengthening the rule of law and the security sector, and ensuring community recovery). Commissioners then asked both governments to develop plans for addressing these challenges and to report back in December at the next country-specific meetings, which they did. Commissioners also heard from NGO groups and representatives of other intergovernmental organizations including the IMF and World Bank. In addition, the Peacebuilding Fund was launched in October 2006.

In early 2007, members of the PBC began a series of "informal thematic discussions" on priority areas identified in the December meetings. A meeting on justice sector reform in Sierra Leone, for example, took place in February and included representatives from the national government (including the Chief Justice) and officials from other governments and international organizations directly involved in justice sector issues in the country (including the World Bank's country manager, the manager for the justice program in the British development agency, and the chief of the human rights and rule of law section of the UN's mission in Sierra Leone). Guest speakers with expertise on the country were also invited. Also in February 2007, a similar meeting was held on promoting "good governance" in Burundi. The following month, members of the country-specific committee on Sierra Leone visited the country and held meetings there with government officials, political parties, international organizations and civil-society representatives.

These informal discussions and country visits allowed a wider array of participants to be involved in the Commission's work than would be possible in the more formal meetings in New York. Ultimately, such discussions were intended to provide the information necessary to draw up "integrated peacebuilding strategies" for both Sierra Leone and Burundi. According to the then head of the Peacebuilding Support Office, Carolyn McAskie, the integrated strategies would take the form of an "agreement" between the country in question and the Commission, identifying the specific commitments undertaken by national and international authorities and "provid[ing] guidance to the various actors in how they can meet the broad goals of peacebuilding."[59] The idea of negotiating such a the framework seemed to be modeled on the "compact" negotiated between international donors and the Afghanistan government in early 2006, which set out objectives and commitments for that country's stabilization and development.

Also in February 2007, the PBC launched a Working Group on Lessons Learned, the goal of which was to draw conclusions on best practices from across peacebuilding missions and to become "the repository for peace-building advice within the UN."[60] Thus, between October 2006 and February 2007, work was launched on several fronts: operationalizing the Peacebuilding Fund, using formal meetings and informal gatherings to begin identifying priorities for peace consolidation in Sierra Leone and Burundi (the first two countries on the Commission's docket), and initiating a cross-cutting evaluation of good practices for statebuilding based on the experience of preceding years.

The Security Council and General Assembly reviewed for the work of the Peacebuilding Commission for the first time in the early months of 2007. These sessions were revealing for what was said—and for what was not said. In the half-year since the inaugural meeting of the Commission, the discourse had begun to shift from vague statements of support for the new body and toward calls for the Commission to quickly demonstrate "concrete results at the country level."

This emphasis on achieving results was prompted, in part, by concerns that the Commission had been spending too much time on procedural debates. Canada, Australia and New Zealand, for example, expressed disappointment at the "overemphasis placed on procedural matters by some members of the Commission at the expense of substantive peacebuilding issues."[61] The Ambassador from India also lamented how much time had been devoted to "housekeeping issues" and suggested that "we cannot continue indefinitely discussing preliminary issues such as reporting responsibilities, participation and operational matters to the detriment of the larger goal of assisting in the consolidation of peace in post-conflict societies," although he then devoted the remainder of his presentation to organizational issues,[62] as did several other delegations including the members of the Non-Aligned Movement.[63]

But even among those calling for more substantive progress and less procedural talk, it was not clear that there was common view of what, exactly, "progress" would entail. A recurring theme—arguably the leitmotif of the discussion in the Security Council—was the importance of developing integrated peacebuilding strategies along the lines set out by Carolyn McAskie, in order to provide a detailed "road map" for all actors in the field.[64] According to this perspective, the PBC could make a contribution by leading the task of identifying priorities and assigning responsibilities among the network of agencies and actors involved in statebuilding.

Indeed, defining priorities was precisely what the PBC was attempting to do. But it was one thing to agree on the importance of setting priorities, and another thing to agree on what the specific priorities should be—and yet another thing to corral the heterogeneous array of peacebuilding agencies to work towards these objectives. As the German Permanent Representative (speaking on behalf of the European Union) pointed out, "Defining priorities necessarily means making a selection among a huge number of possible areas of engagement."[65] Choosing priorities (and making them sufficiently precise to be meaningful) would therefore involve identifying some goals as primary, others as secondary, and perhaps ruling out others entirely. In a realm of conflicting visions of peacebuilding, this would be a demanding and contentious task. The German representative offered a few guidelines for making such decisions, including a recommendation that the Commission should focus on "areas that have a direct and traceable link to the causes of conflict."[66] But identifying root causes of a conflict is notoriously difficult and subject to radically different interpretations, including among major statebuilding actors.

In fact, a close reading of the Security Council and General Assembly debates of early 2007 revealed quite different visions of how to consolidate peace after conflict, which also reflected broader divisions within the network of international statebuilding agencies. For some UN delegations, such as France, the "most urgent challenges" involved institution-building, especially in such areas as the "rule of law, good governance, and security-sector reform."[67] For others, such as Guatemala, "building peace [was] not achieved only by preventing outbreaks of violence, nor by physical rebuilding, nor by establishing the legal basis for a State," but rather by going "far beyond that and support comprehensive changes that will eliminate practices of social, economic and political exclusion."[68] Reading these transcripts, one can imagine the nods of agreement on all sides for both of these statements—indeed, there are good reasons to believe that *both* institution-building and greater inclusiveness are valuable to the consolidation of peace. In the end, however, not all of these goals can be pursued with equal vigor. Establishing priorities requires, as the German representative indicated, "making a selection among a huge number of possible areas of engagement."

The only overt reference in these debates to the potential for disagreement over the purposes and strategies of peacebuilding came in a brief comment from the Chilean delegation: "We believe it is urgent to avoid *competing visions* that could weaken the work of the Peacebuilding Commission."[69] Rather than pursuing this line of analysis, however, the Chilean ambassador immediately reverted to more familiar (and presumably, more comfortable) procedural talk, calling for "action agreed between the General Assembly and the Security Council, as well as proper coordination with the Economic and Social Council."[70]

Working towards integrated peacebuilding strategies

For the remainder of 2007, the Commission's efforts to make a substantive contribution focused primarily on the negotiation and elaboration of integrated peacebuilding strategies (IPBS) for the first two countries on its docket, Burundi and Sierra Leone. The IPBS for Burundi, adopted in July 2007, set out broad objectives and "mutual engagements" between the government of

Burundi and the PBC.[71] The government of Burundi's commitments included a number of vague promises to advance democratic reforms, complete the implementation of the country's ceasefire agreement, pursue further efforts at disarmament, and improve Burundi's justice system. For its part, the PBC agreed to encourage "effective coordination" among international donors and peacebuilding agencies involved in the country, and to help with "the mobilization of resources to Burundi in support of its peacebuilding priorities." Similarly, the IPBS for Sierra Leone, adopted in December 2007, committed the government of that country to addressing the problem of youth unemployment, making the civil service as well as the justice and security sector more efficient and transparent, strengthening local-governance institutions and preparing for elections, and developing an energy strategy for the country.[72] As in Burundi, the PBC pledged to promote greater international coordination, to mobilize financial resources, and generally to support the efforts of the Sierra Leone government.

There was also widespread recognition of the need to monitor implementation of these IPBS agreements, including "qualitative and quantitative indicators to assess progress."[73] The first "monitoring and tracking mechanism" was created for the Burundi IPBS in November 2007, setting out a list of benchmarks and indicators that would make it possible to evaluate whether the goals of the IPBS were being accomplished over time.[74] The mechanism included an innovative, multi-layered process for reporting on progress. Working groups would monitor implementation of both the IPBS and the country's existing Poverty Reduction Strategy, feeding into higher level joint evaluations conducted by Burundi government officials and the PBC. This institutional design offered the hope of better coordination among international actors and ongoing participation and "ownership" of peacebuilding efforts by the national government.

Once again, however, process may have trumped substance. The review mechanism was institutionally innovative, but the substance of what would be reviewed was still vague. The IPBS itself suffered from a lack of clarity and ambition, and the specific "qualitative and quantitative indicators" that would be used to "track progress" were hazy—and in some instances trivial. For example, the Burundi government's broad commitment in the IPBS of "promoting good governance" which can mean virtually anything, was to be tracked according to a set of benchmarks and indicators that were nearly as broad and ambiguous: namely, the degree to which Burundi's "political environment" had become "conducive to the peaceful resolution of political conflict through the institutionalization of a culture and practice of dialogue," among other things.[75] To determine whether such an "environment" was being created, those responsible for monitoring progress would measure the "level of representation" of different societal groups "in the various frameworks for dialogue" as well as "progress toward respect for constitutional provisions related to power sharing arrangements (including gender) by the Government and all political actors." These indicators were both undemanding and vague—to the point that they verged on emptiness. Even the more substantive indicators listed in the tracking mechanism would depend on the seriousness and rigor of assessments performed, in part, by Burundi government officials who might have a vested interest in softening negative findings. Nor was it clear how the participants in the monitoring mechanism, or the PBC itself, would produce "effective coordination" among international actors in instances where these actors had differing perspectives or approaches to peacebuilding in Burundi.

Evaluation

The PBC clearly faces high and seemingly mounting expectations from the UN membership, which is calling for tangible progress and the articulation of detailed, integrated strategies. This is a tall order, given the existence of more profound differences on the goals and priorities of statebuilding than many UN members have been willing to directly acknowledge, at least in public. To its credit, the Commission and its small support staff have, in a very short time, developed a full work program—and integrated peacebuilding strategies have been articulated for Burundi and Sierra Leone. Furthermore, in December 2007, the Commission added Guinea-Bissau as the third country on its docket. But the truly difficult work remains to be done: namely, the task of translating vague objectives into substantive commitments and then encouraging a congeries of international actors, inside and outside the UN system, to work towards concrete and meaningful common strategies.

Can the Peacebuilding Commission accomplish this goal? One way of analyzing this question is to ask whether the Commission strikes the right balance as a coordination tool—namely, a balance between an overly rigid hierarchy and an under-organized network. In other words, can the Commission make the international peacebuilding and statebuilding system work more effectively and coherently as a still-decentralized but more "directed" network?

As a consensus-based advisory body, whose membership will include a broad range of peacebuilding actors, the Commission preserves the network form of the international statebuilding system intact, along with the principal virtue of this system: flexibility. In other words, the current plan does not create a rigid new hierarchy. Further, the design is unlikely to constrain experimentation with new and different approaches to peacebuilding; indeed, such experimentation (and cumulative learning) may be improved if the support office is able to perform its assigned task of providing the PBC with high-quality analyses of cross-cutting peacebuilding issues and reviewing the best practices of previous operations. On this point, much will depend on the quality of the analysis and analysts in the support office, the resources at their disposal, and the willingness of Commission members to consider alternative approaches to peacebuilding. However, the decision to finance the support office from the existing UN budget, rather than with new money, placed significant constraints on the size and resources of the office—and, by extension, on what the office could accomplish.

Including representatives from the host country (as well as the senior UN official in the field) in the country-specific meetings of the PBC should also help to focus discussions on the unique conditions and needs of particular societies. In the context of a fractured society emerging from war, ensuring a broad representation of domestic interests will be important—not only as a means of "customizing" peacebuilding strategies to local conditions, but also to enhance the accountability of the PBC and the broader peacebuilding system to the inhabitants of the host state. However, the role of civil-society organizations—including international NGOs as well as those within the host state itself—remains unclear. The authorizing resolutions "encourage" the Commission to "consult with civil society, non-governmental organizations, including women's organizations, and the private sector engaged in peacebuilding activities, as appropriate."[76] One of the strengths of the Commission's work to date—in its country-specific configurations—has been to foster discussions with local NGOs in Burundi and Sierra Leone and between these NGOs and their national governments. Ad hoc consultations have also taken place with international NGOs, but the Commission still seems reluctant to institutionalize such consultations as a routine part of its deliberations.[77]

The most critical question, however, is whether the Commission will be able to advance the goal of promoting meaningful and effective strategies for statebuilding. The Commission will offer little "added value" to the state-building system if it does not acknowledge and at least partially reconcile conflicting approaches and strategies for statebuilding. As previously noted, perfect coordination is both impossible and undesirable. But it is also unde-sirable—and a recipe for operational failure—to have different agencies work in opposing directions, as they have often done. If existing coordination problems were due only to communication failures, a better system for sharing information might be enough. But I have argued that the coordina-tion problem is not merely a communications issue. It reflects disagreements and uncertainties about how to "do" statebuilding.

Most states opted not to delve into these disagreements during the lead-up to the Commission's creation, but they and all Commission members will have to tackle these disagreements now that the body has been established, recognizing that such discussions will be difficult and potentially divisive. While the work on Burundi and Sierra Leone to date has drawn greater international attention to these two countries, the PBC appears to have set-tled on a relatively amorphus set of "priorities" for each country—and, as we have seen, the monitoring mechanism to track the implementation of these priorities in Burundi lacks specificity. Coordination is relatively easy if one avoids making tough choices between competing priorities, since most actors can claim to be contributing to the "common strategy" by continuing to do whatever it is that they are already doing. Devising strategies based on the lowest common denominator is also a recipe for inaction and ineffectiveness. Only by tackling directly the difficult tradeoffs and disagreements among the key actors, including the host government, will it be possible to address and reconcile competing perspectives on peacebuilding, which often masquerade as mere "coordination problems." Doing so is critical to improving the effectiveness of peacebuilding, particularly at a time when some observers are questioning the very legitimacy and viability of such missions.[78]

Unfortunately, much of the early ambition for the Peacebuilding Commission appeared to dissipate after the body came into being. The original idea of coordinating "all relevant actors within and outside the United Nations"[79] was, it seems, quickly replaced by a more modest vision of the Commission focusing on identifying programmatic gaps in existing operation, or specific issues or areas not receiving sufficient international attention, and marshaling resources to fill these gaps. One possible explanation for these scaled-back expectations may be that other parts of the UN bureaucracy, including the Department of Peacekeeping Operations (DPKO), had an interest in limiting the scope and influence of the new Peacebuilding Commission. Indeed, DPKO was already involved in its own effort to promote more integrated field operations during the "stabilization" or immediate post-conflict phase of a peacebuilding mission—thus implying that the Peacebuilding Commission should focus on post-conflict countries that had already achieved a substantial level of stability.[80] In fact, a primary motivation for the creation of the Commission was to focus on the longer-term requirements and coordination of international engagement in countries that might otherwise be suffering from diminishing international attention as time wore on. But the idea that a post-conflict period could be neatly (or even messily) divided up into distinct "phases," beginning with a "stabilization" phase, was itself misleading because planning for longer-term peacebuilding needs to be done during or shortly after the termination of a conflict. It is this moment when effective, coherent peacebuilding strategies are most urgently required—in addition to the short-term needs that understandably tend to attract more attention, such as the monitoring or enforcement of a fragile ceasefire. The extent to which bureaucratic jealousies may have constrained the role of the Commission is not clear, but the DPKO's capstone document for peace*keeping* (which, by definition, is the DPKO's bailiwick) offered surprisingly little room for the Peacebuilding Commission to contribute to strategic planning or high-level coordination of international peacebuilding actors, except in countries already deemed to be "stabilized."

Speculation about bureaucratic rivalries aside, the Commission's ability to achieve coordination has been profoundly hampered by its own lack of authority. It is only an advisory body, and any advice it offers must be based on a consensus of its members. If there is disagreement, even from a small number of members, the Commission cannot make recommendations. The result, thus far, has been the setting of lowest-common-denominator "priorities" that, as argued above, make few concrete demands of either the host governments or the array of international agencies involved in peacebuilding. Furthermore, even if the Commission were to make more substantive and pointed recommendations, it would have little capacity to ensure that these various agencies bring their activities into line with these recommendations. The Peacebuilding Support Office has similarly limited influence within the UN Secretariat itself. The PBSO has been empowered to "convene" elements of the UN system for strategic discussions of peacebuilding, but no other parts of the Secretariat are required to act on the outcomes of such discussions. When the Secretary-General's senior-level Policy Committee met in May 2007 to discuss the role of the PBSO, the most it would say was that decisions reached at strategy meetings convened by the PBSO would "normally have implications" for the participants and organizations involved in these discussions.[81] The phrase "normally have implications" was, like some of the benchmarks set out in the Burundi IPBS, so vague and noncommittal as to be almost meaningless.

In short, the problem of peacebuilding coordination—the "gaping hole" identified by Kofi Annan—remains largely unaddressed. The Commission appears to have little willingness or capacity to grapple directly with the problem of conflicting priorities and approaches to peacebuilding among the myriad international actors involved in these missions. Perhaps it had good reason to steer clear of such discussions, for reasons noted earlier: first, the PBC's decision rules requiring consensus decisions and, second, the Commission's purely advisory nature which limits its influence over peacebuilding agencies. Given these limitations, the approach of avoiding controversial matters—which could be paralyzing and pointless—can be viewed as entirely rational. But that is the problem. The PBC is largely a discussion forum with no executive management functions. Without some new measure of hierarchy within the loosely structured network of statebuilders, difficult discussions and difficult decisions are likely to be avoided in order to build and maintain a broad consensus. The result, in the worst-case scenario, could be meetings full of reassuring but empty rhetoric—not unlike the discourse surrounding the creation of the Peacebuilding Commission itself.

If the body is to offer more than a venue for information sharing, it will have to articulate positions that are widely, but not necessarily universally, accepted. It will also find ways of inducing statebuilding agencies to pursue shared objectives and implement integrated mission plans. There are no such mechanisms in the Commission as it is currently designed, but perhaps there could be in the future. If the internal politics of the UN preclude moving in this direction, alternative coordinating arrangements should be considered—including, if necessary, a more robust mechanism located outside the United Nations.

Conclusion

Whether through the Commission or some other mechanism, the coordination problem of peacebuilding will need to be addressed. The challenges of rehabilitating societies after war—and of creating functioning states in these societies—are large enough in themselves, and disorganization among the statebuilders unnecessarily multiplies the risk of operational failure. Yet, there is more to the coordination problem than meets the eye. Calls for greater coordination have become something of a mantra among practitioners and observers of statebuilding in recent years, and this mantra hides as much as it reveals. The record of statebuilding has been mixed, in part, because there is little agreement on what specific measures are required, in what sequence, and based in which priorities, in order to create the conditions for stable peace in war-torn societies. And there is little agreement not only because the myriad actors that comprise the international statebuilding machinery have different approaches and interests, but more fundamentally because the entire enterprise is so uncertain, complex, and politically sensitive.

Due in part to this complexity, it would not be desirable to establish a centralized, hierarchical coordination mechanism for peacebuilding—even if doing so were politically possible. But it is equally risky and unrealistic to expect the loose network of peacebuilding actors to remedy its coordination problems simply through information-sharing. The challenge, it seems, is to strike a balance between preserving the flexibility of the existing networked structure of the international peacebuilding system on one hand, and the requirement for some measure of hierarchy on the other. What is needed, in short, is a "directed" network that more effectively combines elements of hierarchy and decentralized autonomy.

The Peacebuilding Commission, as it is currently designed, does not strike that balance. It errs on the side of preserving the self-directed qualities of the existing peacebuilding network without introducing a capacity to make difficult choices between competing approaches and objectives. If anything, the debates surrounding the Commission—and the early work of the Commission itself—revealed a troubling propensity to fall back on procedural talk and other strategies that serve to avoid controversy rather than tackling more substantive problems at the heart of the peacebuilding enterprise.

Notes

1 For example, Olson and Gregorian 2007; Paris 2004; Smith 2004; Ricigliano 2003; Weinberger 2002; Sommers 2000; and Crocker et al.1999.
2 For other studies applying organizational theory to the problem of coordination in peace operations, see Lipson 2007a and Herrhausen 2007.
3 Boutros-Ghali 1992, p. 11.
4 On El Salvador see de Soto and del Castillo 1994; on Mozambique see Willet 1995; on Cambodia see UNRISD 1993.
5 For a review of major peacebuilding coordination problems during the 1990s, see Jones 2001.
6 Boutros-Ghali 1995, para. 81.
7 Jones 2003; and Bellamy and Williams 2005.
8 Jones 2001.
9 Fearon and Laitin 2004, p. 30.

10 Cutillo 2006.
11 Call 2005.
12 Cooley and Ron 2002; and Patey and Macnamara 2003.
13 Duggan 2004, p. 357.
14 On the multiple levels of coordination in peacebuilding, see de Coning 2007.
15 Smith 2004; see also Clingendael Institute 2005.
16 Dahrendorf 2003, p. 20.
17 de Coning 2004, p. 43.
18 Patrick and Brown 2007.
19 High Level Panel on Threats, Challenges and Change 2004, para. 225.
20 Other initiatives approved at the 2005 World Summit included an endorsement of
    the "Responsibility to Protect" principles; a condemnation of terrorism in all its
    forms; an agreement to establish a new Human Rights Council; and increased
    funding to humanitarian assistance. The summit, however, was widely viewed as a
    disappointment because of expectations for greater progress on poverty reduction
    policy and institutional reform of the UN itself—most notably, the Security
    Council—for which there was little agreement.
21 Paris 2004 and Doyle and Sambanis 2006.
22 Uvin 2002.
23 Miall 2007, p. 35.
24 Jones 2001; Cousens 2001; and Woodward 2002.
25 Paris 2004.
26 Jeong 2002, p. 9.
27 Donini 1996, p. vi.
28 Becker 2004, pp. 656–58.
29 Beetham 1996, p. 12 and March and Olsen 1989, p. 34.
30 Weber 1978.
31 On the tendency of organizations including the United Nations to respond to
    external pressures by promising reform, but not dealing directly with substantive
    issues, see Lipson 2007b.
32 Statement by Ambassador Zhang Yishan on Cluster II (Freedom from Fear) of
    the Secretary-General's Report, "In Larger Freedom: Towards Development,
    Security and Human Rights for All" at the Informal Thematic Consultations of
    General Assembly, New York, April 22, 2005, www.china-un.org/eng/xw/t192893.
    htm (accessed on October 5, 2006).
33 Statement by the NGO Working Group on Women, Peace and Security at the
    Informal General Assembly Civil Society Hearings, New York, June 24, 2005.
34 "Opening First Session of Peacebuilding Commission, Secretary-General Stresses
    Importance of National Ownership, Building Effective Public Institutions," UN
    document SG/SM/10533, PBC/2, June 23, 2006, www.un.org/News/Press/docs/
    2006/sgsm10533.doc.htm (accessed on October 5, 2006).
35 Powell 1990, p. 303.
36 Kaspersen and Sending 2005, p. 19.
37 Ricigliano 2003, p. 456. For similar arguments, see also de Coning 2004; and
    Roberts and Bradley 2005.
38 Klijn and Koppenjan 2000.
39 Tenbensel 2005, p. 281.
40 Alexander 1995, pp. 59–60.
41 Ahmed, Keating and Solinas 2007, p. 18.
42 *New State Ice Co. v. Liebmann*, 285 US 262, 311 (1932).
43 Campbell 1969, p. 409.
44 Chisholm 1989, p. 10.
45 Chandler 2005; Caplan 2005b; Beauvais 2001; and Chopra 2000.
46 Chisholm 1989, p. 200.

47 Vigoda 2002.

48 Føllesdal 1998; and Cooper 2006.

49 DFID 2002.

50 Security Council resolution 1645 (20 December 2005) and General Assembly resolution 60/180 (December 30, 2005).

51 General Assembly document A/60/694 (February 23, 2006), paras. 20–21.

52 Security Council resolution 1645 (December 20, 2005), para. 24; General Assembly resolution 60/180 (December 30, 2005), para. 24.

53 General Assembly resolution A/60/694 (February 23, 2006).

54 General Assembly resolution A/60/984 (August 22, 2006).

55 Statement by the President of the United Nations General Assembly, H.E. Mr. Jan Eliasson, at the Inaugural Meeting of the Peacebuilding Commission, New York, June 23, 2006, www.un.org/ga/president/60/speeches/060623.pdf (accessed on October 5, 2006).

56 Statement by the President of the Security Council, H.E. Dr. Per Stig Møller, Minister for Foreign Affairs of Denmark, at the Inaugural Meeting of the Peacebuilding Commission, New York, June 23, 2006, www.un.org/peace/peacebuilding/scpresident.pdf (accessed on October 5, 2006).

57 For summaries of these meetings, see Security Council document S/2006/1050 (December 26, 2006).

58 Peacebuilding Commission documents PBC/2/BUR/CRP.2 and PBC/2/SIL/CRP.1 (October 10, 2006).

59 "Statement by Ms. Carolyn McAskie, Assistant Secretary-General, PBSO," January 31, 2007, http://www.un.org/peace/peacebuilding/pdf/mcaskie31jan07.pdf.

60 Ibid.

61 Statement by Ms. Kirsty Graham, Deputy Permanent Representative of New Zealand, to the General Assembly on behalf of Canada, Australia and New Zealand, February 6, 2007.

62 Statement by H.E. Mr. Nirupam Sen, Permanent Representative of India, at the General Assembly, February 6, 2007.

63 Statement by H.E. Raymond Wolfe, Permanent Representative for Jamaica, to the General Assembly on behalf of the Non-Aligned Movement, February 6, 2007.

64 See, for example, interventions from the President of ECOSOC and from the representatives of Russia, Norway, the Netherlands, Sierra Leone, France, Belgium, Italy, Slovakia, Congo, South Africa, Indonesia, China, Germany (on behalf of the European Union), Japan, Canada, Croatia, Guatemala in the Security Council discussion. In fact, the importance of developing integrated peacebuilding strategies was mentioned no fewer than 48 times during the discussion. Security Council documents S/PV.5627 and S/PV.5627 (Resumption 1), January 31, 2007.

65 Statement by H.E. Mr. Thomas Mutussek, Permanent Representative of Germany, to the General Assembly on behalf of the European Union. February 6, 2007.

66 Ibid.

67 Security Council document S/PV.5627, p. 14.

68 Security Council document S/PV.5627 (Resumption 1), p. 11.

69 Ibid., p. 33, emphasis added.

70 Ibid.

71 UN document PBC1/BDI/4 (July 30, 2007).

72 UN document PBC2/SLE/1 (December 3, 2007).

73 UN document A/62/137-S/2007/458 (July 25, 2007), paras. 32 and 41. See also Mollett et al. 2007.

74 UN document PBC/2/BDI/4 (November 27, 2007). At the time of this writing, the monitoring and tracking mechanism for the Sierra Leone IPBS was still under development.

75 Ibid.

76 Ibid., para. 21.
77 In June 2007 the organizational committee of the Peacebuilding Commission issued provisional guidelines for the participation of civil society organizations in meetings of the Commission. See UN document PBC/1/OC/12 (June 4, 2007).
78 See, for example, Bain 2006; Chandler 2006; and Duffield 2001.
79 This language appeared in the authorizing resolutions for the Commission. See Security Council resolution 1645 (December 20, 2005) and General Assembly resolution 60/180 (December 30, 2005).
80 See Department of Peacekeeping Operations, "United Nations Peacekeeping Operations: Principles and Guidelines" (January 2008).
81 "Decisions of the Secretary-General—22 May 2007 Policy Committee Meeting," United Nations Interoffice Memorandum, Decision No. 2007/28.

Part II
Security

4 Foreign militaries, sustainable institutions, and postwar statebuilding

David M. Edelstein

Scholars and policymakers alike agree on the critical importance of providing security in post-conflict environments. Without security, the essential political, social, and economic tasks of statebuilding cannot be accomplished, yet in the wake of conflict, the local institutions necessary to provide this security are often lacking. Thus, foreign powers—either multilaterally under a United Nations mandate or individually—deploy their military forces to fill this void. This chapter examines the role of these foreign military forces in the process of post-conflict reconstruction and long-term, sustainable statebuilding. It asks under what conditions foreign military intervention is most likely to be an effective tool in the process of statebuilding.

Most of the chapter is devoted to examining two fundamental dilemmas that confront both the population of a state rebuilding in the wake of conflict and the foreign powers participating in that reconstruction. The first dilemma is the *duration dilemma*. Military forces may play an essential role in providing security, but the "welcome" afforded to those forces is likely to obsolesce over time as populations seek to regain full sovereign control over their territory. Facing this dilemma, military forces may face strong pressures to withdraw before indigenous security institutions have been fully established, or else they must be prepared to endure increasing resistance and resentment at their continuing presence.

The second dilemma is the *footprint dilemma*. Intervention forces vary both in the size of the presence and their degree of intrusiveness. A larger footprint may be better at fostering security, but may also introduce the risk of stimulating nationalist resistance against the foreign presence. A smaller footprint minimizes the risk of nationalist resistance but may also make it more difficult to sustain a secure and stable environment. Similarly, a less intrusive footprint may avoid alienating the population, but a more intrusive footprint may be better able to establish control over a divided and conflict-ridden society. Establishing the appropriate footprint—neither too large nor too small, neither too intrusive nor too passive—represents a significant challenge to military interveners.

Not all statebuilding military interventions suffer these dilemmas equally. After presenting the dilemmas, I consider what factors might make statebuilding military interventions either more or less susceptible to these dilemmas. I first differentiate between two different types of statebuilding interventions: military occupations and complex peacekeeping. Not surprisingly, unilateral military occupation forces that assume control through conquest are likely to see their welcome obsolesce more quickly and should expect more pronounced resistance to a large footprint. Conversely, UN-authorized forces that intervene with the consent of the population are welcome for longer and are generally able to sustain a more intrusive presence.

In addition to the type of intervention, the "threat environment" of the territory in question significantly affects the severity of the dilemmas. The logic of this argument is simple: to avoid either the duration dilemma or the footprint dilemma, foreign intervention forces must be viewed by the population as less of a threat than some other potential threat. After all, intervention forces are, in principle, deployed to provide security and protection. When a significant element within the population views the intervention forces themselves as the most immediate threat to its security and prospects for self-determination, then both the duration dilemma and the footprint dilemma are likely to be most acute. Even consensual multilateral interventions are likely to see their welcome obsolesce and their presence resented in an unpropitious threat environment.

Ultimately, though, the lesson of this chapter is that military force can aid in the process of statebuilding, but it cannot substitute for the political solution that is necessary for statebuilding to be successful. Put differently, military intervention may be necessary in some cases to build a stable, sustainable state, but it is usually not sufficient. The Kosovo case discussed below and in Jens Narten's chapter in this volume demonstrates how populations may value the protection offered by a military force while rejecting the abrogation of sovereignty by a UN administration. The pressures of the duration and footprint dilemmas are likely to persist as long as a political solution is absent. Only when a political solution is realized can the dilemmas of statebuilding military intervention be fully alleviated.

I conclude with policy recommendations for future statebuilding interventions. Certain factors may alleviate the duration and footprint dilemmas, but no statebuilding military intervention is completely immune from these dilemmas. Leaders contemplating the use of their military forces for statebuilding missions abroad must prepare to deal with these dilemmas, not deny their existence. At the end of the chapter, I also examine the geopolitics of military intervention for statebuilding purposes in the wake of the attacks of September 11, 2001.

The dilemmas of military intervention as a tool of statebuilding

Using military intervention as a tool of postwar statebuilding is challenging because such intervention can be both necessary and resented. Local populations may not welcome the infringement of their sovereignty by a foreign power, even on a temporary basis; and intervening powers often would rather expend their resources elsewhere or not at all. Potential interveners, therefore, must devise a strategy of intervention that allows them to accomplish their statebuilding goals but also to return sovereignty to the population before the resistance of the population or the intervening power's own impatience undermines the mission. More concretely, military intervention for the purpose of statebuilding poses the following two dilemmas.

Dilemma #1: the duration dilemma

Foreign military forces can serve to deter the reemergence of conflict in the wake of civil wars while also preventing opportunistic foreign powers from exploiting the weakness of a post-conflict society. For this reason, intervening forces may initially be welcomed by the population of a war-torn society, but this welcome is likely to diminish over time: hence, the problem of the "obsolescing welcome." In particular, national groups that are accustomed to governing themselves may bridle at living under the control of foreign political and military organizations. As resistance to the foreign presence rises, a dilemma emerges: military forces remain essential for maintaining security in the post-conflict society, but the population grows increasingly weary of the military intervention. Intervening powers may be forced into a choice between ending an intervention prematurely or prolonging an increasingly unpopular intervention. This dilemma typically emerges in three stages.

In the initial stage, intervening powers tend to enjoy a "honeymoon period" during which the population adjusts to postwar reality and sizes up the foreign presence that has undertaken the reconstruction mission. During these periods, foreign forces typically establish their goals and attempt to convince the population to accept their presence without resistance. Even in postwar Iraq, insurgent violence against the US-led occupation did not begin immediately; it emerged only after it was evident that the coalition was not going to be able to provide post-conflict security.

In the second stage, the honeymoon period comes to an end, and the population (or often different segments of the population) makes decisions about whether or not to embrace or reject the intervening foreign forces. How the population responds may depend not only on whether the foreign forces are providing valuable security, but also on the credibility of the intervening powers' pledges to return sovereignty to the population in a timely manner. The willingness of the population to tolerate the foreign military presence, in other words, is shaped by its perceptions of the benefits (security or otherwise) of that presence.

Finally, in the third stage, intervening powers face the duration dilemma. Statebuilding is an ambitious and time consuming enterprise. Populations dissatisfied and impatient with the progress in these missions may turn to various forms of resistance, ranging from violent insurgency to election boycotts or labor strikes. If this resistance grows strong enough, foreign powers will confront an unwelcome choice between either withdrawing forces prematurely or prolonging an unwelcome military presence that may only grow more costly and less effective. If the forces withdraw too soon before stability and security is ensured, then the prospects for conflict reemerging will increase. If the forces stay too long, however, then the resistance of the population is only likely to grow, making it more difficult to create a stable and secure environment conducive to effective statebuilding.[1]

The duration dilemma also impacts the domestic politics of the intervening country. Foreign military interventions are often expensive, both in terms of lives and money. As a statebuilding mission becomes longer and more expensive, domestic audiences in intervening countries are likely to question the wisdom of continuing the mission. At the same time, however, ending the mission too soon may result in wasted resources if stability fails to take hold in the target state. The pressures of the duration dilemma, then, originate not only in the country in which the intervention is taking place, but also in the countries doing the intervening.

To illustrate the two horns of the duration dilemma, consider the experiences of the United Nations in East Timor and Kosovo. These cases illustrate not only the difficulty of managing this dilemma, but also the important relationship between military intervention forces and the political aspects of statebuilding. Military forces, it seems, cannot sustain their welcome in the absence of genuine progress toward returning sovereignty to the local population.

The UN operation in Kosovo began shortly before the intervention in East Timor. Although the pretexts for the interventions differed—the UN came into Kosovo on the heels of NATO's war against Serbia whereas the UN was ultimately invited to intervene in East Timor—they still represent the most ambitious statebuilding operations undertaken by the United Nations to date and the experiences of statebuilding in the two still make for a useful comparison. In East Timor, the United Nations Security Council authorized the formation of the International Force for East Timor (INTERFET) in UN Security Council Resolution 1264 on September 15, 1999. By September 20, the first elements of an Australian-led multinational force consisting of 12,000 troops began to arrive in East Timor with the task of restoring peace and security in East Timor following a tumultuous vote on independence.

In late October, the Security Council approved the formation of the United Nations Transitional Administration in East Timor (UNTAET), which was to facilitate the transition of East Timor from Indonesian sovereignty to independence. When the final elements of the Indonesian government withdrew at the end of October, the UN remained as the interim holder of authority over East Timor. In March 2001, UNTAET announced that the elections for the first East Timorese representative assembly would be held on August 30, exactly two years from the popular consultation on independence. Finally, on May 20, 2002, the Democratic Republic of East Timor was officially promulgated with the long-time East Timorese leader Xanana Gusmao as the first East Timorese president. Though a small UN security force—the United Nations Mission in Support of East Timor (UNMISET)—remained in East Timor for three years after independence was officially declared, the primary UN statebuilding mission in East Timor had come to an end.[2]

From its inception, all parties involved understood that the United Nations presence in East Timor was meant to be a transitional one leading to independence.[3] With the military force in East Timor operating under UN auspices, the East Timorese had little reason to fear that they might be permanently denied their sovereignty by an imperial power. As Anthony Goldstone summarizes, "[T]he vast majority of East Timorese living in the territory regarded the UN intervention as essentially benign, at worst as an uncomfortable interregnum that was the necessary precursor to independence" (Goldstone 2004: 84). By making this end goal of independence perfectly clear to the East Timorese population, the United Nations was able to avoid much of the unrest that afflicts other foreign statebuilding operations.

UNTAET did, however, encounter criticism at the perceived slow pace of the operation and the lack of involvement by the local population.[4] Leaders of the most significant Timorese political organization, the National Council of Timorese Resistance (CNRT), called for disobedience against the United Nations and contemplated a unilateral declaration of independence (Chopra 2000: 34). Recognizing these signs of growing disaffection as early as November 1999, Sergio Vieira de Mello, the Transitional Administrator, supported the creation of "a participatory, inclusive process that involves the Timorese, their representatives, in particular the CNRT, which has a pre-eminent role to play in decision-making."[5] Vieira de Mello agreed in April 2000 to the appointment of East Timorese deputies to the regional administrations under international control (Chesterman 2004: 137). Nevertheless, these initiatives were insufficient in the eyes of some local leaders. In May, CNRT Vice President and Nobel Peace Prize laureate Jose Ramos-Horta asked Kofi Annan to remove all UN district administrators by August and to fix a date for the UN's departure (Chopra 2002: 33). According to Ramos-Horta, "There was a sense of frustration, a lack of faith in UNTAET. This was because of their inability to involve the East Timorese, their inability to come forward with a roadmap, a plan. We saw time going by and no Timorese administration, no civil servants being recruited, no jobs being created."[6] In a manner similar to Jens Narten's description of the situation in Kosovo in Chapter 11 of this volume, the initial lack of local ownership in East Timor placed significant pressures on the UN mission.

Even in the case of East Timor where the intervention was welcomed by most of the population and Indonesia acceded to the intervention the UN had begun to wear out its welcome within only a year of its arrival. As the honeymoon period came to an end, Vieira de Mello noted that the population now sensed that, "UNTAET is on a separate path from the East Timorese."[7]

In December 2000, Timorese Cabinet members complained that they were being "used as a justification for the delays and the confusion in a process which is outside our control. The East Timorese Cabinet members are caricatures of ministers in a government of a banana republic. They had no power, no duties, no resources to function adequately."[8] In his New Year's speech for 2001, Timorese leader Xanana Gusmao called for the political empowerment of Timorese and a relatively quick end to the international administration of East Timor.[9] UNTAET responded by continuing to turn more authority in the country over to local Timorese in an effort to assure the population that its self-determination goals would be met.[10]

Ultimately, the United Nations mission in East Timor ushered East Timor out of the control of Indonesia and into its current status as a legitimate, sovereign nation. Although East Timor is hardly a prosperous society today (in fact, it is one of the world's poorest countries) and has been racked by periodic violence and political instability in recent years, the UN's accomplishments in East Timor must be weighed relative to the alternatives. Without the Australian-led military intervention, uncontrolled militia violence in East Timor could have led to a much larger conflict. The United Nations facilitated democratic elections in East Timor, assisted in the management of a large-scale internal refugee problem, and maintained security during East Timor's transition to independence. Further, the UN was able to accomplish these goals in less than three years – and, importantly, before East Timorese dissatisfaction with the continuing international presence grew to the point of rebellion against the international presence.

Even as the United Nations enjoyed certain successes in East Timor, however, the outbreak of riots in East Timor in May 2006 and the political instability that followed have raised the question of whether the United Nations did, in fact, leave East Timor too soon. The prospect that the United Nations drew down its presence in East Timor too quickly poses one horn of the duration dilemma. Withdrawing forces quickly has the advantage of placating nationalist populations, but it introduces the danger of recurring instability if forces leave prematurely. In fact, Jose Ramos-Horta has admitted, "For the immediate future, we need a special police force … that is a rapid-reaction force to stop riots, hooligans, looting."[11] And former UN Secretary-General Kofi Annan has understandably asked, "There has been a sense that we tend to leave conflict areas too soon … We've been in Cyprus for ages, we've been in Bosnia, Kosovo. Why do we often try to leave other areas after two or three years?"[12]

Annan's question is a good one, but the case of Kosovo illustrates precisely the difficulties of more prolonged United Nations-sponsored security missions. Longer missions may be able to prevent the recurrence of violence, but they also invite impatience among nationalist populations that long for independence. Without progress toward a political statebuilding solution, impatience among the local population is likely to grow. Unlike the case of East Timor where the government of Indonesia ultimately agreed to the UN mission, the UN and NATO mission in Kosovo was preceded by NATO air strikes against Serbia beginning in March 1999, after negotiations failed to resolve the status of Kosovo within the Federal Republic of Yugoslavia (FRY). On June 3, following more than two months of intense NATO bombing, Yugoslav President Slobodan Milosevic capitulated to NATO's demands to withdraw Serbian troops from Kosovo. The defeat of Serbia, however, left unresolved important questions about the ultimate status of Kosovo as either an independent country or an autonomous state within Yugoslavia.

This issue was initially addressed in United Nations Security Council Resolution 1244 of June 10, 1999, which called for the establishment of an international civil presence in Kosovo under the control of a special representative of the United Nations Secretary-General. The UN presence was charged with facilitating the political, economic, and social reconstruction of Kosovo. Most controversially, UNSCR 1244 simultaneously recognized the continuing territorial integrity of the FRY while also assigning the civil administration the task of: "Promoting the establishment, pending a final settlement, of substantial autonomy and self-government in Kosovo." As commentator Timothy Garton Ash correctly observed, UNSCR 1244—the product of a divided UN Security Council in which Russia strenuously opposed independence for Kosovo—simultaneously called for "virginity and motherhood."[13] One could not reinforce the territorial integrity of the FRY while at the same time granting that Kosovo was entitled to "substantial autonomy and self-government."

By the end of July, the United Nations had essentially seized sovereignty over Kosovo with all legislative and executive authority claimed by UNMIK. The first UNMIK regulation proclaimed that "[a]ll legislative and executive authority with respect to Kosovo, including the administration of the judiciary, is vested in UNMIK and is exercised by the Special Representative of the Secretary General."[14] The administration created in Kosovo was composed of the United Nations Mission in Kosovo (UNMIK) together with a NATO-led Kosovo Force (KFOR).[15]

KFOR faced a number of security challenges when it first began its work in Kosovo. Violence between Kosovar Albanians and the remaining Serb population (as well as the minority Roma population) remained a dangerous possibility. Despite an agreement to demobilize, the Kosovo Liberation Army continued to operate throughout the province. An estimated one million Kosovar Albanians had been displaced before and during the war, and, after the war, many Kosovar Serbs were forced to leave their homes in Kosovo.

In December 1999, UNMIK took its first valuable step toward allowing Kosovar Albanians to govern themselves. An agreement between three Kosovar Albanian leaders—Hashim Thaci, Ibrahim Rugova, and Rexhep Qosja—and UNMIK created Kosovo–UNMIK Joint Interim Administrative Structures and an Interim Administrative Council (Caplan 2005a:

99). These shadow institutions would, for the first time since UNMIK had assumed control over the territory, enable indigenous input into governance decisions.[16]

Shortly thereafter, however, the UN's honeymoon in Kosovo came to an end. While many Kosovars continued to value the protection offered to them by the KFOR troops, they resented the denial of sovereignty that attended the UNMIK mission. Kosovo was subsequently plagued by sporadic violence and increasing Kosovar Albanian impatience with the unwillingness of the United Nations to allow Kosovo to gain full independence. In an effort to alleviate this pressure, progress was made in the direction of self-rule. In October 2000, municipal elections were held, and a year later Kosovars elected their first regional assembly in nearly a decade. In March 2002, Provisional Institutions of Self-Government were created as yet another step toward autonomy.

Michael Steiner, a German who took over as the Special Representative of the Secretary-General in Kosovo in February 2002, initiated a significant step toward the consideration of Kosovo's ultimate status.[17] In April 2002, he introduced an idea that would come to be known as "standards before status."[18] The "standards before status" policy held out the promise of independence for Kosovo, but only if Kosovo could achieve lofty benchmarks. It was not the simple grant of independence that many Kosovar Albanians desired. In March 2004, demonstrations against the perceived lack of progress toward independence turned into riots as nationalist Albanians directed their violence against not only Serbs, but also against symbols of the UNMIK presence, including the UN's iconic white vehicles.[19] By the time the riots ended, 19 were dead, over 900 were injured, hundreds of homes, public buildings, and churches were destroyed, and 4,500 people were displaced.

The riots again raised question about the progress that had been made in Kosovo as well as the inability of KFOR to deal effectively with the riots. In response, the Secretary-General dispatched Kai Eide as a special envoy to investigate the situation in Kosovo. As James Traub wrote in the *New York Times*, by this point "Kosovars were sullen because they were sick and tired of international tutelage."[20] Soren Jessen-Petersen, the then-Special Representative of the Secretary-General in Kosovo, remarked: "There was a sense after the March riots [in 2004] that we had to accelerate the process and simplify standards implementation, not to reward violence but because to keep this place in limbo for much longer would be rather risky."[21]

In October 2005, Eide presented a report to the Secretary-General affirming that Kosovo has made sufficient progress on the standards that negotiations on final status should begin. The decision to move toward final status negotiations was less a recognition of extensive progress in Kosovo than an acknowledgment that UN policy had been troubled from the start.[22] Progress toward a sustainable long-term political solution in Kosovo was slow. Serbia, with the vocal support of Russia on the United Nations Security

Council, continued to resist any move toward an independent Kosovo and feared for the safety of the small Serb minority within Kosovo. Kosovar Albanians, meanwhile, indicated that they would settle for nothing less than full independence.

The international intervention into Kosovo succeeded in stopping the ethnically-motivated warfare that was being perpetrated by Belgrade in Kosovo. For this, KFOR deserves much credit. Unfortunately, the verdict for the postwar statebuilding mission in Kosovo is less positive. As Simon Chesterman concludes, "Kosovo was stillborn as a political entity. As long as its final status remains undecided, its political development will continue to be undermined by uncertainty" (Chesterman 2004: 226). Many years after the war in Kosovo ended, ethnic tensions persist and the international presence in Kosovo has become a semi-permanent fixture in Kosovar society.[23] Eide, writing in 2004, was even more critical: "The international community in Kososo is today seen by Kosovo Albanians as having gone from opening the way to now standing in the way. It is seen by Kosovo Serbs as having gone from securing the return of so many to being unable to ensure the return of so few."[24]

Thus, the cases of East Timor and Kosovo help to illustrate the two horns of the duration dilemma. In East Timor, the UN mission ended before intense resistance built up against the UN presence. Arguably, however, the UN left too soon. Prolonging the mission may have facilitated more stability in East Timorese society, but at the risk of East Timorese resistance and resistance. In Kosovo, on the other hand, the UN and KFOR missions continue, but the prolonged UN presence, in particular, generated considerable resistance among the Kosovar Albanian population. As I will explore in greater detail below, while NATO's KFOR may have offered valuable protection, its civilian counterpart—UNMIK—was seen as an impediment to the ultimate goal of national self-determination. An earlier withdrawal from Kosovo may have alleviated some of this pressure, but at the considerable risk of a resurgence of ethnically-motivated violence. Both cases illustrate that progress toward political self-determination is a necessary condition for foreign military forces to remain welcome within post-conflict societies. The dilemma for future forces, therefore, is to devise strategies for maintaining an intervention that is sufficiently prolonged to provide security for statebuilding, without precipitating widespread resistance from nationalists.

In particular, in order to avoid the duration dilemma, foreign military forces engaged in statebuilding should ensure that three tasks are accomplished before withdrawing. First, there must be a local government prepared to assume the basic tasks of governance with the support of a substantial segment of the population. Returning power to an incapable government will simply undermine the initial purpose of the intervention. Second, the security of the post-intervention state must be largely assured. The training of local forces is often a lengthy and complicated process, so it may be incumbent on foreign forces to continue to provide security even after the intervention has concluded.[25] Third, foreign powers must establish support mechanisms for the post-intervention state. Statebuilding missions do not end when the intervention itself has formally concluded. To be successful, intervening states must develop means of continuing outside assistance to the rebuilt state without seeming overbearing or overly intrusive. The difficult challenge confronting intervening powers is to accomplish these three tasks in a timely manner, withdrawing neither before these goals have been reached nor too long after the tasks have been completed.

Dilemma #2: the footprint dilemma

The second dilemma that confronts statebuilding intervention forces involves the footprint of the intervention. The footprint refers to not only the number of intervention forces, but also to their degree of intrusiveness within the domestic affairs of the host state.

In many contexts, foreign military forces may need to be large and intrusive in order to establish security in post-conflict (or continuing conflict) societies. If local groups continue to fight each other, intervention forces may need to employ aggressive tactics to ensure that the process of reconstruction can proceed. More troops with a more assertive mandate may have beneficial security effects. But, as noted above, such assertiveness may also accelerate nationalist resistance to the presence of foreign military forces. When an intervention force is smaller and more passive, then the force is likely to encounter less resistance but also likely to accomplish less toward the goal of statebuilding. A large, less intrusive force may be effective at training local forces to take over the intervention, but the force will be less effective in fighting any resistance that is present to the foreign presence. A small force that is highly intrusive is perhaps a model force for counterinsurgency operations, but to be effective, such a force needs to be capably trained in counterinsurgency tactics. Smaller forces must efficiently accomplish their goals, or their limited size may undermine their ability to successfully assist in the process of statebuilding. In short, achieving the appropriate footprint underlines the dilemma that larger and more intrusive forces may promise greater success, but at the risk of greater resistance, whereas smaller, less intrusive forces lower the probability of resistance, but also make it more difficult for an intervening power to accomplish its goals.

Figure 4.1 summarizes the dilemmas of statebuilding through military intervention. It illustrates the benefits and risks of different footprints of intervention forces, and also reveals how these different footprints interact with the duration dilemma. Certain footprints are more likely to encounter the duration dilemma than others. More than anything else, the table conveys the sense in which these two dilemmas are true dilemmas: any choice made by the intervening power has both significant potential benefits and risks.

		Intrusiveness of Intervention Forces	
		Low	*High*
Size of Intervention Forces	*Small*	Benefit: Low resentment; May be able to intervene to resolve acute cases Risk: Difficult to accomplish ambitious goals Duration: Sustainable at low costs but with limited results	Benefit: Potentially effective counterinsurgency force Risk: Smaller force may lack capability to control large country Duration: Prone to duration dilemma as intrusive force generates resentment among population
	Large	Benefit: Well-suited to training indigenous security forces Risk: Lacks capability to defeat any emerging insurgency Duration: Large force generates impatience among intervening country	Benefit: May allow fuller control over target country Risk: High costs and high probability of resentment against perceived occupation Duration: Most prone to duration dilemmas as both population and intervening power grow tired of perceived occupation

Figure 4.1 Dilemmas of statebuilding intervention

As with the duration dilemma, the footprint dilemma is also affected by domestic and international politics. Missions with large footprints must find support from domestic publics in both the host and intervening countries. In multilateral missions, a critical mass of countries must dedicate their forces to the mission in order for it to succeed. For a more intrusive footprint, as well, international actors must agree on rules of engagement and be willing to accept the casualties that may result from a more intrusive footprint.

To demonstrate the dynamics of the footprint dilemma, consider the post-September 11th interventions in Afghanistan and Iraq. The US-led invasion of Afghanistan began in October 2001. Many Afghans initially welcomed the invading forces with the hope that the US would end the tyranny of the Taliban and evict the foreigners that the Taliban had invited into the country (Barfield 2004: 290). In December 2001, a conference of leading Afghan politicians agreed to form an interim authority with a chairman who would govern Afghanistan until an Emergency Loya Jirga could be convened within six months. The Emergency Loya Jirga would, in turn, be charged with constructing a transitional administration that would hold power until a separate Constitutional Loya Jirga could be held within eighteen months of the Emergency Loya Jirga.

Annex I of the Bonn Agreement also requested the assistance of the United Nations in authorizing an International Security Assistance Force

(ISAF), which would help maintain security in Afghanistan and provide assistance in the training of a new Afghan military.[26] In the spring of 2002, the ISAF began its operations with eighteen participating countries and five thousand troops under British command. ISAF was separate from the US-led coalition invasion force that continued to fight remnants of the Taliban regime and Al-Qaeda within Afghanistan.

In October 2003, the United Nations authorized the extension of the ISAF mission beyond its previously limited mandate for Kabul. ISAF has subsequently expanded its military security mission to more of Afghanistan as well as its participation in Provincial Reconstruction Teams (PRTs) to assist in reconstruction and security efforts.[27] By December 2003, however, 13 of Afghanistan's 32 provinces were still judged to be unsafe for UN humanitarian personnel (Goodson 2004: 15).

After several delays due to concerns over security, Afghanistan's first democratic presidential elections were held in October 2004. Karzai garnered the support of approximately 55 percent of the Afghan electorate and was victorious in 21 of Afghanistan's 34 provinces. In September 2005, the first parliamentary elections were peacefully held after yet more delays due to security concerns. Meanwhile, ISAF continued its operations both around Kabul and through the Provincial Reconstruction Teams, although locating the resources to support these operations has become a growing problem (Goodson 2005: 90). A resurgence of the Taliban in southern Afghanistan and the inability of the central Afghan government to exert authority beyond the capital has raised increasing concern about the long-term prospects for the Afghan state.

In Afghanistan, the United States and its allies opted for a relatively light footprint with approximately 22,000 US troops and 20,000 NATO ISAF troops in the country.[28] Rather than creating a comprehensive occupation authority with deployed military forces that attempted to control the entire country, the US and its allies focused its efforts on Kabul and on fighting remaining Taliban elements in the southern part of the country. The Afghan government remains weak as regional warlords exert their authority outside of any central control. Efforts to curtail the trade of heroin out of Afghanistan have largely failed, and the illicit drug trade continues to comprise 40 percent of the total Afghan economy (Goodhand 2004: 163). Only with the introduction of PRTs in 2003 has ISAF made any concerted effort to aid in the reconstruction of Afghanistan's remote provinces. While the PRTs have had some success in rebuilding at the local level, it remains unclear whether they will facilitate the national integration of Afghanistan. The Afghan National Army, with only approximately 50,000 troops by October 2007, remains weak with regional militias mostly providing security.[29]

By not completely occupying Afghanistan, intervention forces have avoided many of the familiar problems of occupation.[30] The building of a strong, central Afghan state would have required a comprehensive occupation—a much heavier footprint—that ultimately would have had to rely on greater coercion, particularly of the regional warlords. The long-term consequences of a lighter footprint strategy, however, may be dangerous.[31] If conflict does erupt among the regional provinces of Afghanistan or if the Taliban remains resurgent in the remote parts of the country, then this strategy may only make futile efforts at effective statebuilding in Afghanistan.[32]

In comparison with Afghanistan, consider the case of Iraq. Thus far, the statebuilding mission in Iraq has encountered considerable difficulty and violence, which is not surprising given the difficulties locating a sustainable political solution in Iraq. While Saddam Hussein has been displaced, one consequence of the invasion has been a costly insurgency that has not yet been suppressed. To be clear, some parts of Iraq, in particular in the northern Kurdish region, have been relatively peaceful and have taken steps toward rebuilding social, political, and economic institutions, but in the rest of the country, displaced Sunnis Arabs have been concerned about whether their minority rights will be protected within a democracy run by the majority Shiite population. Within both the Sunni and Shi'a communities, internal divisions have further impeded efforts at consolidating the Iraqi state.

In the case of Iraq, the United States has relied heavily on a strategy of coercion to facilitate the building of political, economic, and social institutions. Upon its arrival in Iraq, the United States made several critical errors that made the tasks of occupation more difficult.[33] Most notably, the US decided to disband the Iraqi army, letting loose thousands of disgruntled soldiers (Packer 2005: 195). Further, Washington underestimated the tasks confronting US forces. Secretary Rumsfeld infamously dismissed the initial looting after the invasion, "Freedom's untidy, and free people are free to make mistakes and commit crimes and do bad things. They're also free to live their lives and do wonderful things. And that's what's going to happen here."[34]

The United States and its allies have employed a larger footprint in Iraq than in Afghanistan, but this footprint has been incapable of defeating the anti-occupation insurgency. In turn, the unsuccessful effort to squash the insurgency through coercion has only produced more opposition to the occupation as Iraqis increasingly question American motives in Iraq. Many have argued that the United States needed to deploy even more troops to Iraq. More troops may, in fact, have aided in creating initial security, but it is likely that nationalist Iraqis would have grown even more impatient with a larger and more intrusive US footprint in Iraq. As Larry Diamond, who participated in the Coalition Provisional Authority, laments, "At every step, the United States and its allies would underestimate the force of Iraqi nationalism" (Diamond 2005: 38).

In sum, the cases of Afghanistan and Iraq illustrate the two sides of the footprint dilemma. In Afghanistan, a relatively light footprint has to some extent avoided provoking nationalist resistance, but at the cost of limited central control over Afghanistan's more remote provinces. In Iraq, the US-led coalition has attempted to be more assertive in taking control over the country, but the visible and intrusive presence has generated costly resistance that has made the tasks of postwar statebuilding more difficult. As with the duration dilemma, the challenge of the footprint dilemma is to get the presence "just right": too small a footprint may make it difficult to create stability; too large a footprint invites nationalist resistance at the presence of an occupying power. Overwhelming force may be able to achieve success through coercion, but coercion is a costly strategy for both the intervening forces and the population.

How can the footprint dilemma be solved? Successfully managing this dilemma requires finding a narrow and elusive sweet spot. Forces must be large enough to control any violence within the territory, but not so large that they are perceived as an overbearing occupier. The forces must be intrusive enough to disrupt any destabilizing insurgency, but not so intrusive that they only generate more resistance to the intervention and rebuilding of society. Ultimately, resolution of the footprint dilemma depends, like the duration dilemma, on progress in the development of stable, sustainable political institutions acceptable to the variety of groups within a society. The appropriate footprint for a particular intervention is a product of the dangers within that society. Those dangers, in turn, are most likely to be relieved by a political agreements to build up a stable, sustainable state. Given this, it is hardly surprising that statebuilding by military force has historically proven so difficult.

How are these two dilemmas related? If an intervening force faces one dilemma, do they necessarily face the other? Figure 4.1 illustrates the challenges of military intervention for the purposes of statebuilding. Effective interventions must find a small and elusive intersection among the right size, duration, and intrusiveness of the military force. Intervening forces may be able to avoid the duration dilemma, but to do so may invite the footprint dilemma. That is, the duration dilemma may best be avoided by eschewing a large military presence in the post-conflict territory. With a light presence, the population may become less impatient with the presence of the foreign forces, but it may become more difficult to establish stability and security. The case of Afghanistan perhaps best illustrates a case in which intervening forces are not confronted by a duration dilemma, but the lighter footprint has made it difficult to create strong central authority in Afghanistan. In the next section, I examine ways in which intervening powers may be able to avoid these dilemmas.

Why some interventions are more susceptible than others

The interventions in East Timor, Kosovo, Afghanistan, and Iraq all have different characteristics that make them more or less susceptible to the two dilemmas described above. None of them is immune to either the duration or footprint dilemma, but they are not all affected equally. The UN mission in East Timor experienced pressures to end its intervention, but not nearly as strong pressures as the UN mission in Kosovo faced. And neither East Timor nor Kosovo witnessed the anti-occupation insurgency that has engulfed Iraq.

Afghanistan, meanwhile, has largely avoided the duration dilemma but only by embracing the footprint dilemma. Ideally, intervening powers are able to maintain a sufficient footprint for a long enough period of time to provide stability and security until local institutions can be rebuilt. The severity of either the duration or the footprint dilemma is measured by the pressure that intervening powers feel either to withdraw their troops prematurely or to reduce the footprint of their forces to an insufficient size.

In this section, I identify factors that affect the degree to which interventions suffer from these dilemmas. First, I note different characteristics of the intervention itself—the context of the intervention and the composition of the intervention force. Second, I argue that the threat environment of the territory in which the intervention is taking place—whether the territory faces internal, external, or no threats to its stability—critically affects how acute either the duration or the footprint dilemma is in any statebuilding intervention.

Type of intervention: military occupation vs. complex peacekeeping

Statebuilding interventions take many different forms, but two of the most common are military occupations and complex peacekeeping. Two critical characteristics—whether the intervention is consensual or adversarial and whether the forces are under the auspices of the United Nations—define these two different types and explain why occupations are generally more susceptible to the two dilemmas outlined above.

First, military occupations are adversarial statebuilding missions if they are undertaken in the aftermath of conquest. Post-conquest occupations usually lack the approval of any international body, and occupations are often (though not always) viewed as an illegitimate usurpation of the occupied population's sovereignty. The best-known occupations include the occupations of Japan and Germany after World War II. More recently, the United States led an occupation of Iraq following the invasion and conquest of that country in 2003. Historically, military occupations have tended to fail more often than succeed (Edelstein 2004, 2008). That is, they fail to stabilize the territory subject to occupation in a timely manner, at a cost acceptable to neither the intervening power nor the population of the territory.

Occupations have succeeded only in rare and unusual circumstances when the occupied population is willing to suspend or set aside its nationalist impulses and accept a prolonged denial of self-government. Most notably, in the aftermath of World War II, the populations of western Germany and Japan did little to resist occupation, presumably because they recognized that the US-led occupation would simultaneously assist in their reconstruction and provide protection from a looming Soviet threat. In most cases, however, including contemporary Iraq, occupied populations see little value in occupation and resist the presence of foreign troops. Any welcome that might have greeted US troops as they arrived in Baghdad quickly faded away as the security situation in Iraq quickly deteriorated as the occupation ensued

(Hashim 2006). In the face of the insurgency, the occupying powers in Iraq have been confronted by both the duration dilemma and the footprint dilemma.

A second form of statebuilding military intervention is carried out in a more consensual manner, typically under the auspices of the United Nations. The most ambitious UN sponsored statebuilding missions have assumed the role of de facto sovereign powers in the territories that they control. These complex peacekeeping missions differ from traditional military occupations in several important ways. Most significantly, the imprimatur of the United Nations appears to grant them legitimacy in the eyes of both the international community and the population of the territory that they control. The involvement of the UN, therefore, slows the rate at which a population becomes impatient with a foreign military presence and makes that population more willing to accept a larger and more intrusive footprint.

The threat environment: external vs. internal threats

The threat environment of the post-conflict territory is also relevant. By "threat environment," I mean whether the primary threats to the safety, security, and survival of the territory and its population arise from potential predatory external powers or from internal ethnic, religious, or national divisions.

Ethnic, religious, or national divisions within a post-conflict society will tend to accelerate the obsolescence of any welcome as it is unlikely that all the various groups within a divided society will trust the foreign military force to protect them. In addition, internal divisions make disgruntled segments of a population less receptive to an intrusive military force. Foreign military forces are essential to statebuilding precisely because they provide security, so perceptions that such forces are, in fact, a threat will undermine any welcome these forces receive. Of course, in some cases, foreign troops may be able to play an invaluable security role in societies that are wrought by internal divisions. If all sides accept that the presence of foreign troops is valuable because it prevents the resurgence of violence, then the welcome may persist. The difficult challenge for military forces, however, is to appear as if they are not providing preferential treatment to any particular group within a divided society (Betts 1994).

Alternatively, the presence of a commonly perceived external threat to the post-conflict society slows the obsolescence of any welcome and makes a larger footprint more acceptable. When such a threat is present, the population is more likely to value the protection offered by foreign military forces. As suggested above, Soviet-sponsored communism was seen as such a threat from which US forces could protect western Germany and Japan after World War II. Thus, adversarial military occupation was made tolerable to the population by the presence of an external threat from which the occupying powers could provide protection. Post-conflict societies are willing to defer their nationalist demands for sovereignty if the presence of foreign troops prevents others states from acting in predatory ways. When such a threat is absent, the value of foreign military forces will diminish in the eyes of the population.

To illustrate the logic of this argument, consider again the cases discussed above. Iraq has been the least successful of the statebuilding missions discussed. In Iraq, there is no external threat that is seen by the entire population as a greater threat to Iraqi sovereignty than the occupying power itself. While some Iraqi Sunnis and the United States may see Iran as a significant external threat, other groups, including many of the Iraqi Shia, are less fearful of Iran. Alternatively, al-Qaeda might pose such an external threat to Iraq. The effort of the United States in the spring and summer of 2007 to "awaken" moderate Sunni tribes in al-Anbar province in opposition to the al-Qaeda presence is an indication that al-Qaeda might constitute such an external threat. The question with al-Qaeda, however, is whether or not its presence in Iraq is substantial enough to sustain cooperation between the Sunni moderates and the United States, or those moderates will turn on the United States when and if al-Qaeda in Iraq is defeated. As a consequence of the absence of a clear commonly shared external threat, the United States and its allies have encountered both the duration dilemma and the footprint dilemma. Ironically, the former head of the Coalition Provisional Administration, Paul Bremer, has now retrospectively recognized this key difference between the occupations of western Germany and Japan after World War II and the occupation of Iraq: "The vast majority of Iraqis were delighted to have Saddam and his henchmen thrown out, but few were happy to find a foreign, non-Muslim army occupying their country. And ... with the Soviet Red Army occupying eastern Germany and Japan's northern offshore islands, the countries we had defeated in World War II had a strong motive to cooperate with us—nobody wanted the American Army replaced by the Red Army" (Bremer 2006: 37). A significant percentage of the Iraqi population has seen little value in the current occupation and has rejected its continuing presence. Although a case could be made that Iran is such an external threat to Iraqi sovereignty, it is not clear that a majority of the Iraqi populations views Iran as a greater threat to self-determination than the occupation itself.[35]

The greater threat to the future stability and coherence of the Iraqi state is an internal one. Iraq is a deeply divided society between the Shiite, Sunni Arab, and Kurdish populations.[36] Such divisions, especially politically-charged ones, are unlikely to produce agreement on one primary external threat to the country's security. Instead, as they are divided internally, these groups are likely to see different allies and adversaries beyond the state's borders. Early in the occupation, many Iraqis did believe that the internal threat warranted a continuation of the occupation. In a November 2003 poll conducted by the US Department of State's Office of Research, 66 percent of Iraqis responded that continuing insurgent attacks indicated that coalition forces needed to remain in place in Iraq.[37] It was, however, the objections of the other 34 percent of the population that has made the statebuilding occupation of Iraq so difficult. Asked in November 2005, most Iraqis saw their life improving, but 50 per cent maintained that the US-led invasion of Iraq in 2003 was a mistake.[38] Not surprisingly, the Kurds, who lack many allies in the region, have been most receptive to the US presence in Iraq while the Sunni Arab and Shi'a communities have been less receptive. The lack of an external threat—and the presence of an internal threat—have exacerbated the duration dilemma by making both withdrawal and continued occupation unattractive. Further, the internal threats to Iraq's security and the perception that the United States favors the Shiite majority have made it difficult for the US to consider an even larger footprint in Iraq, even though such a footprint might more effectively establish security.

In Afghanistan, there is no commonly shared external threat that would lead the Afghan people to embrace a heavier footprint in the form of foreign military occupation. There are, however, internal divisions that would have complicated any effort at comprehensive military occupation. Thus, it is fortunate that a more comprehensive occupation of Afghanistan was not attempted. Such an occupation would likely have generated an acute duration dilemma of either prolonging a costly and difficult comprehensive occupation or withdrawing forces before essential statebuilding tasks were accomplished. The downside of the lighter footprint adopted in Afghanistan, however, is that any attempt at centralized statebuilding in Afghanistan is unlikely to succeed with the danger of increasing instability at the margins of the Afghan state.

In comparison to Iraq and Afghanistan, the threat environment in East Timor suggested that the two dilemmas of intervention might be less severe. The East Timorese population mostly agreed on the external threat posed by Indonesia, and it welcomed the intervention by the United Nations.[39] Seventy-eight percent of the East Timorese population voted for independence from Indonesia and were left helpless by the violence that followed the referendum on August 30, 1999. Thus, the East Timorese were willing to suppress their strong nationalist feelings in the short term if the United Nations could offer them protection from the external threat posed by Indonesia and pro-Indonesia militias.[40]

Not only was there an initial external threat, but the sense of threat was exacerbated by the vulnerability of East Timor. East Timor was decimated by the violence preceding and immediately following the popular consultation. A *Washington Post* article in May 2002 described post-conflict East Timor as an "unimaginable apocalyptic ruin."[41] As much as 70 per cent of East Timorese infrastructure was destroyed by the end of the September 1999 militia rampages (Candio and Bleiker 2001: 64). More than 75 per cent of East Timor's nearly 900,000 residents were displaced by the violence. The United Nations promised assistance in rebuilding from that ruin in a way that the East Timorese could not have done on their own.[42] When the UN arrived in East Timor, it found a population that was seeking protection and desperately needed help in rebuilding its society. Nevertheless, although the duration dilemma was certainly less severe in East Timor, the UN did not completely avoid pressure from the population, leading to the perhaps premature withdrawal of UN forces. In the end, the credible promise of East Timorese self-determination lessened the pressure on the UN from either the duration or the footprint dilemmas.

Finally, there is the case of Kosovo, where there were the differences in public opinion regarding the NATO presence as opposed to the UN presence. While NATO entered Kosovo to provide security in the wake of conflict with Serbia and has been generally effective at doing so, the UN has been responsible for the challenging political dimensions of statebuilding. The method in which this political and military aspects mission has been divided among different external actors allows us to disaggregate the views of people within Kosovo with regard to this mission. Unsurprisingly, KFOR has been far more popular than UNMIK among the Kosovar population.[43] Since November 2002, the percentage of the population satisfied with KFOR has consistently been over 80 per cent, making it along with the Kosovo Police Service the most population main institution within Kosovo. UNMIK, on the other hand, received the lowest satisfaction scores with less than 40 per cent satisfied and going as low as approximately 20 per cent. As expected, Kosovars seemed to appreciate the security that KFOR provided against a potentially revanchist Serbia, but they also longed for the sovereignty that they believed UNMIK was withholding.[44] Leading Kosovar Albanian Ibrahim Rugova proclaimed, "I am for straightforward, formal recognition of Kosovo, better now, when KFOR and UNMIK are here. Today or tomorrow—for me, better today."[45] Sadik Halitjaha, president of the Association of War Veterans of the KLA, expressed in September 2002, "I never thought that we'd come to the stage of protesting against [UNMIK]. We never thought we would say goodbye by throwing stones at them, and we hope we don't have to."[46] As Bajram Redenica, executive director of the Society of War Invalids of the Kosovo Liberation Army, lamented in September 2004, "This isn't what we fought for, to be half-free."[47] Indeed, one lesson that emerges out of Kosovo is, while populations clearly value protection, they are able to disentangle their desire for protection and their desire for self-determination

Statebuilding and the global war on terror

Statebuilding through military force faces yet another dilemma in the aftermath of the terrorist attacks on the United States of September 11, 2001. In both Afghanistan and Iraq, the United States led military invasions nominally aimed at both rooting out terrorist networks and fostering statebuilding. As both cases have made clear, however, these two goals are not necessarily mutually reinforcing. An ongoing anti-terrorist campaign layered on top of a statebuilding effort, or vice versa, may only complicate efforts to build effective state institutions. In Afghanistan, the priority put on rooting out Taliban and al-Qaeda elements remaining in the country has often relegated the tasks of statebuilding to secondary status. In Iraq, the on-going counterinsurgency campaign has often worked at cross-purposes to the goal of rebuilding a functional Iraqi state. Intrusive and violent military campaigns aimed at terrorist groups impose significant collateral damage on villages and towns struggling to reemerge from conflict. Further complicating the task of statebuilding military interventions in the post-9/11 world is the potentially multilateral nature of these missions. While the United States may prioritize fighting transnational terrorism over the objectives of state-building, others states may view statebuilding as the more important priority. Such differences may ultimately undermine the coherence of any coalition constructed to carry out statebuilding operations in the future, even in set-tings that are considerably less hostile and controversial than Iraq and Afghanistan.

As the United States and its allies face the prospect of future statebuilding in the shadow of the war on terror, their leaders need to be conscious of all these dilemmas. When the goals of fighting terrorism undermine statebuilding goals, how can these two sets of objectives be reconciled, especially when ineffective statebuilding might only encourage future terrorism? In this sense, the United States and other statebuilding actors would be well-advised to pursue a long term strategy that focuses on effective statebuilding as a means of reducing the incentives for people to join terrorist groups. Unfortunately, domestic political pressures as well as the threat posed by radical terrorist groups often pressure leaders to prioritize the immediate targeting of terrorist groups over the more fundamental goals of building effective and legitimate states.

Conclusion and policy implications

While multilateralism and the consent of the population are certainly critical to slowing the obsolescence of any welcome afforded to foreign military forces, they cannot fully explain the variation in the reception that foreign forces receive. Instead, I have argued that the threat environment of the post-conflict society adds to our understanding of the reception that foreign forces receive. Foreign forces will have difficulty maintaining a prolonged presence in internally divided societies, while those forces will receive more of a welcome in societies that face a widely perceived external threat. Ultimately, the dilem-mas of foreign military intervention for statebuilding can only be resolved through political, not military, means.

This argument generates five critical policy implications.

First, while UN endorsement is certainly beneficial, UN missions are by no means immune from the dilemmas described in this chapter.

Second, the rate at which the welcome afforded to foreign troops obsolesces can be slowed by credible signals that sovereignty will, indeed, be returned to the population of the post-conflict society. The continuing presence of military forces must be combined with political strategies that alleviate the concerns of the population that they will not regain control over their territory.

Third, in the end, leaders confronting the duration dilemma may be better off prolonging their stay rather than leaving prematurely. A longer-lasting presence will usually have a better chance of preventing a resurgence of violence that could undo any benefits gained from the initial intervention. What makes this a real dilemma, however, is that such long-term commitments are unlikely to be easy in the face of mounting costs and increasing domestic pressure in the intervening countries themselves. What is best for the rebuilding territory may not always be seen as best by the intervening countries.

Fourth, the footprint dilemma might best be avoided by prioritizing the training of local security forces that can supplant external intervention forces. Thus, states that are likely to be involved in such interventions, such as the United States, should prepare themselves better for the difficult challenge of training local forces that can replace foreign forces. A larger local footprint both legitimizes the domestic security forces and demonstrates that the new state can provide for its own security. Creating these forces, however, requires more than just training them to use weapons and to fight insurgency. To be effective, these forces must constitute legitimate institutions under civilian authority.[48]

Fifth, and perhaps most importantly, intervening powers must recognize the limits to what military force can achieve in the context of a statebuilding mission. Military force can be an important tool that aids in the process of finding a political solution, but ultimately it is only the political solution itself that can resolve the dilemmas described in this chapter.

Notes

1 Barbara Walter argues that a credible commitment from a foreign force is a significant cause of successful peace settlements. My argument diverges from Walter's in two ways. First, Walter confines her argument to civil wars whereas my analysis addresses situations of international war as well. One would expect a foreign force to be less successful at maintaining peace when it is an invading force. Second, as Walter admits, the commitment of foreign forces is only effective after the parties involved in conflict have agreed to the terms of the peace. In cases of foreign intervention, the intervening forces may be party to the peace agreement. See Walter 2002.

2 On the need for UNMISET, see Gorjao 2002: 323. On UNMISET in general, see Ishizuka 2003. On the continuing security threats facing East Timor including potential internal divisions, see Smith 2004. On tension between Christians and Muslims in East Timor, see "In East Timor, A Crucible of Tolerance," *Washington Post*, June 8, 2000, p. A23.

3 On the importance of a clear end goal, see Chesterman 2004: 135.

4 Jarat Chopra, who served as Head of the Office of District Administration for UNTAET, offers a critical appraisal of the UN's effort to devolve responsibility to the Timorese. Chopra advocates for "participatory intervention," which would better incorporate local decision makers into the administration of an international occupation. See Chopra 2002: 94–95, 989; and Chopra and Hohe 2004. For another critique of the UN performance incorporating East Timorese into governance, see Goldstone 2004. Goldstone maintains that UNTAET was more concerned with achieving short-term humanitarian goals than with achieving long-term stability and capacity. See also Smith 2002: 55; and Suhrke 2001: 13.

5 Briefing by Ian Martin, Sergio Vieira de Mello, and Xanana Gusmao, November 11, 1999. Available at www.un.org/peace/etimor/DR/br191199.htm. For more on Timorization, see Dunn 2003: 372.

6 "Bungled UN Aid Operation Slows East Timor's Recovery," *Guardian*, August 30, 2000, p. 13.

7 Speech by Vieira de Mello, June 2, 2000 (quoted in Suhrke 2001: 16).

8 Quoted in Chesterman 2004: 140.

9 For Gusmao's speech, see http://www.pcug.org.au/~wildwood/JanNewYear.htm.

10 In reality, even the East Timorese leaders recognized that they would need considerable assistance during their transition to independence. See Cotton 1999: 245–46.

11 "East Timor: U.N.-Led Police Force Needed," Associated Press, June 8, 2006.

12 "East Timor Commanding World's Attention," Associated Press, June 8, 2006.

13 See Timothy Garton Ash, "Anarchy and Madness," *New York Review of Books*, February 10, 2000, p. 48.

14 UNMIK Regulation 1999/1 (July 25, 1999), On the Authority of the Interim Administration in Kosovo.

15 The tasks of UNMIK were further divided into four "pillars:" an interim civil administration (under the control of the special representative of the United Nations Secretary-General), a humanitarian affairs pillar (led by the United Nations High Commissioner for Refugees), a pillar for reconstruction (led by the European Union), and a pillar for institution building (coordinated by the Organization for Security and Cooperation in Europe). For a discussion of the composition of UNMIK, see O'Neill 2002.

16 The creation of the Joint Interim Administrative Structures co-opted many Albanian leaders into the UN-led reconstruction project. See Yannis 2001: 39.

17 For Steiner's review of his time in Kosovo, see Steiner 2003.

18 More than a year later, Steiner presented benchmarks in eight specific areas that Kosovo needed to address: functioning democratic institutions, rule of law, freedom of movement, returns and reintegration, economy, property rights, dialogue with Belgrade, and the form and function of the Kosovo Protection Corps. For a discussion of "standards before status," see Caplan 2005: 216–17.

19 For more on the riots, see International Crisis Group 2004a.

20 James Traub, "Making Sense of the Mission," *New York Times Magazine*, April 11, 2004, p. 32.

21 Quoted in Jonathan Steele, "If Kosovo is Left in Limbo, It will be a Victory for Milosevic," *Guardian*, April 22, 2005, p. 26.

22 Kosovar Albanian leaders signalled a willingness to move forward toward independence on their own if UNMIK did not accelerate the process of independence. As moderate Kosovo Albanian leader Bajram Rexhepi indicated, "We don't want to undertake unilateral decisions ... but we shall be forced to do that and have moral justification for this move if the international community hesitates." Quoted in *Collapse in Kosovo*: 5. Ibrahim Rugova, Kosovo's president, similarly said, "We are drafting our own constitution, as is our right, and in due time it will be presented to the parliament, which will either vote on it or send it for a referendum." Quoted in "Kosovo's Draft Constitution Widens Serbia Gulf," *Financial Times*, May 16, 2005, p. 2.

23 Further, the possibility exists of conflict between Kosovar Albanians and UNMIK. See Yannis 2004: 77.

24 Kai Eide, "Report on the Situation in Kosovo," November 30, 2004, S/2004/932

25 On the difficulties of training local militaries and the complications involved with the use of private military contractors, see Avant's chapter in this volume.

26 United Nations Security Council resolution 1383 of December 6 endorsed the Bonn Agreement, and UN Security Council resolution 1386 of December 20 authorized the formation of the International Security Assistance Force. On December 22,

Hamid Karzai, an ethnic Pashtun, was sworn in as the chairman of the Afghan interim authority. For UNSC 1383, see: http://daccessdds.un.org/doc/UNDOC/GEN/N01/681/09/PDF/N0168109.pdf?OpenElement. For UNSC 1386, see http://daccessdds.un.org/doc/UNDOC/GEN/N01/708/55/PDF/N0170855.pdf?OpenElement.

27 Previously, there had been great reluctance to moving ISAF operations beyond the area of Kabul. See Goodson 2003: 95. On the Provincial Reconstruction Teams, see Dziedzic and Seidl 2005.

28 Contra Suhrke, and Barnett and Zürcher, in this same volume, I contend that the international military footprint in Afghanistan has been small by almost any standard. Effective counterinsurgency may require a ratio as low as 20:1. The ratio of population to intervention forces is around 739:1, compared, for example, with a ratio of approximately 180:1 in Iraq. In addition, coalition forces in Afghanistan have largely ceded control of the outer provinces of Afghanistan to local warlords. See Quinvlivan 1995.

29 On the development of the army, see Jalali 2002.

30 For lessons learned from Afghanistan from the perspective of the first postwar US ambassador to Afghanistan, see Khalilzad 2005.

31 On the dangers of relying on warlords in Afghanistan, see Gannon 2004; and Suhrke et al. 2004. On the decaying security situation, see Jones 2006; and Rashid 2006.

32 Generally, on the effort to rebuild Afghanistan in comparative perspective, see Marten 2004.

33 Larry Diamond identifies three key strategic mistakes made by the United States: dissolving the Iraqi army, de-Baathification, and creating a formal occupation with no clear end date. (Diamond 2004: 294).

34 Rumsfeld and General Richard Myers Press Briefing, April 11, 2003. Transcript available at: http://www.defenselink.mil/transcripts/2003/tr20030411-secdef0090.html.

35 On the concern of some moderate Shiites about the influence of Iran, see Diamond 2005: 122–23.

36 The population of Iraq is roughly 60 percent Shiite, 25 percent Sunni Arab, and 15 percent Kurdish.

37 US Department of State, Office of Research, "Iraqis Say Coalition Troops are Vital Now, but Prefer Handoff to Own Security Forces," January 6, 2004, p. 3.

38 Oxford Research International, "National Survey of Iraq," November 2005. Available at: http://news.bbc.co.uk/1/shared/bsp/hi/pdfs/12_12_05_iraq_data.pdf.

39 On the population's general acceptance of the UN mandate in East Timor, see Martin and Mayer-Rieckh 2005: 136.

40 On the welcome afforded to the United Nations in East Timor, see Chopra 2000: 28.

41 "Saved from Ruin: The Reincarnation of East Timor," *Washington Post*, May 19, 2002, p. A1.

42 On the challenges of reconstruction in East Timor, see "Ruined East Timor Awaits a Miracle," *New York Times*, April 22, 2000, p. A1.

43 Even the Kosovar population has been split on this question. Albanians have tended to see KFOR as a liberating force, while Serbs have seen it as an occupying force. See Yannis 2001: 36.

44 For the public opinion data, see UNDP Kosovo, "Fast Facts on Kosovo, Early Warning Report #12," January 2006.

45 "Albanians Rejoice in Their March to Freedom," *Independent* (London), October 30, 2000, p. 13.

46 "UN Welcome Wearing Thin," *Pittsburgh Post-Gazette*, September 22, 2002, p. A10. See also, "Angry Kosovars Call on 'Colonial' UN Occupying Force to Leave," *Observer*, October 19, 2003, p. 21.

47 Quoted in "Even in Eager Kosovo, Nation-Building Stalls," *Christian Science Monitor*, September 22, 2004, p. 1.

48 On military training, see Avant in this volume.

5 Making peacemakers out of spoilers

International organizations, private military training, and statebuilding after war

Deborah Avant*

Effective security forces are a crucial element of successful statebuilding. The security forces most conducive to statebuilding are those with basic capabilities that are also responsive to political leadership and operate in accordance with broad international professional norms. Creating security forces in which all three of these elements work together is particularly important in countries emerging from war. Incapable security institutions undermine immediate prospects for order. Capable security institutions without political control risk coups. Capable security institutions that operate outside international norms can breed resentment and the resumption of conflict.

Though economic arguments often see state institutions as a product of "market failure"—the reverse is also true. The turn toward markets for goods that should be (or have been) provided by the government is also often a product of "state failure."[1] Organized violence is often considered the quintessential governmental service—but even that can be found on the marketplace, particularly in the current era (Avant 2005; Singer 2003). The growth of a vast range of military and security services for purchase in the last 20 years provides a new tool for statebuilders and there has been an increasing tendency by both transitional states and the international community to contract with private security companies (PSCs) for training security forces, military and police, to both shore up forces during conflict and reshape them in its wake.

PSCs pose dilemmas to would be statebuilders, though. While they are hailed by some as an avenue to fix broken security institutions in the face of a shortage of western troops (or will) and thus a tool for peacebuilding, they are derided by others as an option that increases the chance for opportunism: generating spoilers or otherwise offering incentives for intervening states, non-state actors and domestic groups to evade institutional processes that foster effective security institutions (Reno 1999; Shearer 1998). In many cases the short term capabilities that PSCs offer have exacerbated the difficulties of creating effective and democratic institutions in the longer term. There have been instances, however, where the PSC capabilities have been incorporated into a long term statebuilding project.

Policy solutions to manage this dilemma require a better understanding of what factors lead to variation in outcomes associated with private training. Under what conditions does the turn toward markets provide a useful tool for statebuilding rather than setting states on a vicious cycle of breakdown and decay? I argue that involvement by international organizations can be one important factor explaining this variation. I explore the mechanisms through which international organizations (IOs) can facilitate the statebuilding benefits of private training and evade the costs, both logically and then in two case studies: Croatia, where PSCs operated with the benefit of IO oversight, and Sierra Leone, where they did not. These cases are not selected to test the hypothesis that IOs can tame the use of PSCs for statebuilding, but to demonstrate its plausibility and establish support for the causal pathways by which such taming can occur.

Private security, statebuilding dilemmas and IO mediation

When state security organizations are broken or ill-formed, the market can offer security tools that are more effective in the short run. For a variety of reasons too complex to adequately address here (decline of super-power patrons, democratization efforts, illicit transnational flows of goods and services, and interventions to topple rogue governments, among others), the problem of repressive states that many worried about during the Cold War has been replaced by the problem of disorder. Weak or failed states that can neither fend off attacks nor generate internal order have been linked to chronic under-development, civil war, transnational crime, and terrorism. While western states (and the international community they are often associated with) are concerned with disorder, this concern is not matched by willingness to commit forces. Beginning in the 1990s and continuing after 9/11, there have been consistent complaints that the "international community" either does not intervene (Rwanda, Sudan) or intervenes with forces that are not numerous enough to accomplish their mission (Kosovo, Afghanistan), not capable enough to accomplish their mission (Sierra Leone), or both (Democratic Republic of the Congo). Even the US-led action in Iraq has been plagued by complaints about inadequate numbers of forces. In these situations PSCs can bolster or substitute for western forces to provide raw security capabilities—one ingredient necessary for building a state after conflict.

Stable security institutions depend, though, not only on military capacity but capacity that operates through political processes and values seen as legitimate.[2] At a minimum forces need to have elements of each of these: moderate capacities, under coordinated (if not centralized) political control with some modicum of respect for the population they serve. The key to the impact of PSCs on statebuilding is not only its short term effectiveness but also how the use of private forces impacts the unfolding of political processes and social norms through which force is allocated. Capable security instruments can undermine statebuilding if they make possible the use of force for individual or sub-group gains. While the efforts of western troops are not impervious to this dynamic, private forces are more likely to feed into opportunism. By their very nature, the flexibility of private forces can more easily be taken advantage of for private gain. As demonstrated in the literature on "warlords," the potential for these forces to compete with state forces or aid parallel forces often exacerbates state decay (Reno 1998). In some cases, however, this potential is avoided and the short-run capacity that PSCs provide is employed to build security institutions for the state.

I examine the impact of market security options on statebuilding efforts by focusing on how it impacts the micro-institutional setting that shapes strategic action. The most consistent feature of private security is that it changes who controls force and by which processes. This interruption of a broken process offers the prospect of a different (and potentially better) foundation for statebuilding. Often this change is sorely needed in post-conflict environments. Whether it is used to harness force for collective purposes that the population views as legitimate or as simply a more effective method for reaching individual aims that promises no improvement in governing institutions, however, depends not only on whether those empowered by the new market options are successful, but also on whether they pay attention to long-run goals rather than (or in addition to) short-run personal goals, and whether they support moves toward professional standards for security personnel that link the effectiveness of force to abiding by greater collective values. Thus, it is not only important to pay attention to the market forces themselves—private security companies and private financiers of security—but also the constraints (or absence thereof) that inform their use.

Norms and professional standards within the international community are one particularly promising source of constraints for democratic statebuilding because of their focus on principles and processes that have yielded such governance systems in much of the western world. International organizations have tools with which they can encourage attention to these norms and standards: education, financial incentives, and conditionality. By coordinating attention around particular norms and inducing attention to them among both private and governmental actors, IOs could be a potent means for discouraging the opportunism often associated with the use of PSC.

Others have argued that IOs can enhance democratization (Pevehouse 2002, Powell 1996; Pridham 1994; Pridham 1995). Pevehouse (2002) finds that joining democratically dense regional IOs is positively associated with consolidating democracy and hypothesizes a variety of mechanisms by which this occurs. More recently, Mansfield and Pevehouse have argued that transitional states often choose to join IOs when they embark upon democratization because the organization can inhibit leader's incentives to roll back democratic reforms; thus joining IOs is a way for leaders to commit to the democratization agenda (Mansfield and Pevehouse 2006: 137–67). Building on these insights, but seeking a clearer view of the causal processes through which IOs influence statebuilding and democratization, I rely on process tracing in two case studies where PSCs trained militaries in countries emerging from war.

Both Sierra Leone and Croatia employed PSCs during and after conflict to train their military forces. In each case, it is widely agreed that PSCs provided important security capabilities. In Sierra Leone, these capabilities fell prey to opportunistic action that eroded statebuilding efforts, while in Croatia they were harnessed to a slow but successful statebuilding effort. Careful analysis of these two cases demonstrates the importance of IOs for this outcome.

PSC training in Sierra Leone directly contributed to processes that inhibited statebuilding in many of the ways suggested by the literature on rentier states and warlordism. The use of PSCs both allowed civilians to hijack the military for non-democratic purposes and enhanced security institutions that did not have strong ties to the state—the kind of parallel forces that are most tempted to opportunistic action. Thus, while private training efforts in Sierra Leone were beneficial in generating short-run capacities, these capabilities were used by more than one group within the transitional state for counterveiling purposes. With no larger international body to impose conditionality on the leadership, forces were used in a way that inhibited the prospects for long run statebuilding and democratization.

The Croatian case demonstrates, however, that democratically dense regional IOs—particularly NATO and its Partnership for Peace (PfP) program—provided an important framework which ameliorated many of the potential drawbacks of private training. The PfP worked not so much to constrain PSCs (though it did this too) but to both inform and constrain the clients of private security (the government) and students (military personnel) and even international financiers. The PfP informed the fledgling government and military personnel about proper behavior, induced them to behave properly by rewarding proper behavior, and funneled resources through the state in a way that dissuaded opportunism all of which encouraged participation in emerging political processes even as PSCs performed the training. The information, inducements, and dissuasion were tightly coupled to reinforce behavior among a wide variety of actors: civilian leaders, the military, PSCs, opposition parties, and international partners.

Aside from generating support for the propositions that IOs can both aid democratic statebuilding and harness the benefits of using PSCs and guard against the costs, this comparison yields insights about why this is the case. First, because effective security institutions rely on a mix of capabilities, political controls, and social controls, it is important that information and incentives work together. An IO can provide such coordinating mechanisms. Second, once members of an IO have agreed on a program to encourage effective security institutions, that program can also restrain unilateral efforts by donor states that might undermine the program. Third, it is the mix of informing civilian and military leaders about proper behavior, providing inducements for proper behavior on the part of both civilians and the military and providing sanctions (often in the way of frozen inducements) that makes democratically dense regional IOs useful tools for encouraging effective security institutions. When ideas about what is best for statebuilding are reinforced by rewards for behaving in a consistent way and both are perceived to create more capable institutions, the prospects for statebuilding are greater. Fourth, while the received wisdom is that the two building blocks for security institutions are civilian control and military capability, these cases (along with many others) demonstrate that these are not sufficient. Capable security institutions can be hijacked by civilians operating outside of proper channels as well as by lack of civilian control. By issuing costs for inappropriate action to civilian leaders as well as the military, IO conditionality can curb this tendency.

Finally, these insights suggest that the institutional nesting of NATO and the PfP with a variety of other international organizations into a global network was an important feature of their impact. Regional organizations unconnected (or more loosely connected) with this global network may not have the same effect. Market security options are most likely to be harnessed for statebuilding efforts if they focus on organizations tied to the state, if coordinated effort outside the state can punish and reward the civilian leadership, and if military forces (and others) believe that "proper" behavior is also more "effective." Though there may be other ways to do this, globally networked IOs are clearly a promising source of coordinated effort.

Sierra Leone: contracts for private training and failed statebuilding

Sierra Leone was widely recognized as the paradigmatic weak state in the 1990s (Reno 1999). During colonial rule the British obtained stability in the least costly manner by relying on local chiefs for governance which led to competing centers of power and a system by which the state bureaucracy was used to manipulate resources and undercut challenges (Migdal 1988: 129; Reno 1997). The state became quite prominent—with a large bureaucracy and authoritarian strategies—but popular loyalty remained tied to the local chiefs. This proved a fertile environment for nepotism, cronyism, and corruption. Though large, state bureaucracies were neither strong nor effective (Allen 1978; Migdal 1988: 129–39; Reno 1999).

Sierra Leone's rulers bought loyalty in a variety of ways and the country's diamond deposits played an important role as a revenue source. President Siaka Stevens (in office 1967–85) used diamond mines both as a source of revenue for payoffs and then as a source for payoffs themselves. Before leaving office, he bestowed the ultimate benefit upon his cronies: control of the diamond industry and its exemption from taxation (Reno 1999: 228). This left his successors with only limited ability to supply either state services or patronage and invited a succession of rebellion and coups (Hirsch 2001).[3]

By late 1994/early 1995, the government—now headed by Valentine Strasser—was on the ropes. Its finance minister estimated that although

70 percent of state revenues were going to fight the rebels, the regime was still losing ground. In 1995 the rebels attacked (and ended production at) two diamond mines that provided significant state revenues and then drove toward the capital (Howe 1998; Reno 1997). Strasser's strategies to manage the escalating crisis only worsened the situation (Reno 1997; Venter 1995). The RSLMF was a poor force. The officer was largely ceremonial—part of the patronage system—and troops were not well trained (Douglass 1999: 178; Musah 2000: 81). Also, as the financial situation worsened and wages were not forthcoming, its soldiers were not only ineffective but unruly. They were induced to serve with supplies of marijuana and rum, which led to accidents, poor performance, bad behavior among the civilian population (particularly rape and looting), and a tendency to flee when they met the RUF on the battlefield (Musah 2000: 86; Venter 1995). Finally, as more and more conscripts were sent to the field without pay, rumors of collusion with the rebels (at least in the pursuit of loot) surfaced. These "sobels"—soldiers by day, rebels by night—undermined state control and security in Sierra Leone (Douglass 1999; Howe 1998, 2001; Venter 1995).

Contracts for private security

In early 1995, Strasser turned to the international market for help. He first hired a British firm, Gurkha Security Guards (GSG). Fifty-eight Gurkhas and three European managers arrived in January to train Sierra Leone Special Forces and officer cadets (Vines 1999). On 24 February, though, members of the company and a platoon of RSLMF came in contact with the RUF while on a reconnaissance mission. At least 21 (including several GSG personnel) were killed (Ripley 1997; Vines 1999). GSG sent replacements but refused to perform a more active role or to engage in operations with the RSLMF, as Strasser requested, and were subsequently fired (Douglass 1999: 179; Venter 1995; Vines 1999: 129).

In March, Strasser turned to a second company, Executive Outcomes (EO) from South Africa, and got the capacity he wanted.[4] Branch Energy (a mining company working in Sierra Leone) negotiated a contract between EO and the government by which EO would provide 150–200 soldiers (fully equipped with helicopter support) to support, train, and aid the RSLMF in their war against the RUF (Douglass 1999: 180). The bill was to be $2 million per month, but the company issued credit to the government, agreeing to be paid with 50 percent of the tax revenues from the Sierra Rutile mine once it was re-opened. EO's deputy commander, Colonel Andy Brown, was set up in an office directly below Sierra Leone's defense staff chief, Brigadier Maada-Bio, and the government delegated significant authority to EO over training, logistics, and command and control of Sierra Leone's forces.

EO arranged for an intensive three-week training cycle (for 120 soldiers at a time) at a RSLMF base just east of the capital, emphasizing basic skills, tactics, discipline, and procedures (Venter 1995).[5] They also established intelligence and effective radio communications. "EO intelligence operators identified possible informants, isolated them, trained them, and supplied them with communications equipment" (Howe 1998: 316). EO handled logistics for the operations in which they participated, employed a doctor on board one of the MI-17 troop-carrying helicopter gunships on all ground operations, and had two casualty evacuation aircraft available (Venter 1995). Though they saw their prime mission as training the RSLMF, EO director Lafras Liutingh admitted that his forces reacted "with vigor" when under attack (ibid.).

Just a month after their arrival, EO led the RSLMF on a counteroffensive. They assumed operation control, provided intelligence information, and accompanied units on operations. Under EO's leadership, the RSLMF drove the rebels away from the capital and caused hundreds of rebel deaths. EO then continued to work for the government with the goals of clearing the rebels from the diamond areas (in the Kono district) and destroying the RUF headquarters. But as it moved away from the capital, the RSLMF, even under EO's direction, was less effective; it failed to coordinate with EO and soldiers often fled when faced with RUF ambushes. In the east, however EO found another resource in the local militias. These forces knew the terrain, had an incentive to fight the RUF to protect their families, and became a good source of intelligence. The Kamajoisia or Kamajors, an ethnic Mende group from the southeast of the country, were particularly useful. EO trained the Kamajors in counter-insurgency, supplied them with weapons, and gained much from their local knowledge (Howe 1998: 316–17). The Kamajors helped retake the Kono district and remained as a force to be reckoned with (along with private forces at the actual mines—taken on by Lifeguard Security) while EO and the RSLMF moved on to destroy the RUF's base (Douglass 1999: 184).[6]

Under EO's tutelage, the Kamajors became a significant regional defense force but were still beholden to local rather than national authority. As the civil militias gained recognition for their success, the RSLMF grew suspicious of Strasser and his control of the army weakened. When Strasser announced (in late 1995) that elections would be held the following year, there were rumors of collaboration between the army and the rebels to stop the election and mount a coup (Douglass 1999: 183–85; Musah 2000: 90). Strasser was further weakened when EO (having not been paid) threatened to leave—awkward timing given the threat of a coup (Douglass 1999: 184). Despite an agreement with EO in December, Strasser was overthrown by his defense chief in January, whereupon the RUF announced a ceasefire, agreeing to talk with the new leader.[7] Even disregarding speculation that EO was involved in the coup, the company did not step aside as the coup was launched but continued to work on its contract—in effect aiding the coup effort.

When, despite efforts to frustrate them, elections were held in February 1996, the newly elected President Kabbah reportedly did not even learn of the contract with EO until April (ibid.: 186). In the ensuing months, Kabbah did manage to secure a rebel ceasefire and open peace talks, but tensions between the RSLMF and the militia groups heightened and broke out into clashes on several occasions. When Kabbah (in response to rumors of coup planning) purged the army and cut its budget in half in September, these tensions increased and it was the Kamajors that struck "with devastating effect" (ibid.) against renewed RUF attacks in the fall while the army operated virtually unto itself in large parts of the country (ibid.: 185).[8]

The rebels did sign a peace accord on November 30, 1996. One of their conditions, though, was that all foreign military presence, including EO, should leave the country.[9] EO withdrew according to the terms of the peace accord in January 1997 (Douglass 1999: 187). When Kabbah took steps to solidify security in the wake of EO's departure, tensions between the army and the civil militias complicated his task. He appointed Chief Norman (a public advocate of the Kamajors) the Deputy Minister of Defense.[10] Chief Norman then reorganized and formalized several militias into the Civil Defense Force (CDF) of Sierra Leone (Douglass 1999: 185; Musah 2000: 94–95; Spearin 2001: 12).[11] Norman's public disrespect for the RSLMF heightened tensions between the government and the army. Kabbah also signed a "Status of Forces Agreement" with Nigeria in March 1997, arranging for Nigeria to provide military and security assistance for the Sierra Leone government.[12] The steps were for naught, however, as army associates of the coup plotters from September (led by Major Johnny Paul Koroma) overthrew the Kabbah regime and Kabbah himself fled to Guinea in May 1997 (Douglass 1999: 188–89; Musah 2000: 95–96). The plotters justified their actions by referring to Kabbah's marginalization of the army (ibid.). Koroma and his cronies, however, also had connections with the rebels. The RUF aligned itself with the new junta, and senior members of the RUF were appointed to positions in the administration (Douglass 1999: 188–89.)

As chaos again took hold in Sierra Leone, the Economic Community of West African States (ECOWAS) sent in Cease-fire Monitoring Group (ECOMOG) peacekeepers (primarily Nigerians) to maintain law and order and, eventually, to reverse the coup (ibid.: 188; Hirsh 2001: 146). Control of the country was then split between the new junta, which controlled the capital, the Nigerian force, which held the Lungi airport, the Kamajors and civil militia groups, which controlled most of the country's interior. PSCs were still present—not working for the government but protecting the mines. A ground operation to retake the capital by the Nigerians was unsuccessful and resulted in further destabilization—including the closing of some mines.

In July, exiled President Kabbah turned to another PSC—Sandline International—to help him retake power.[13] Sandline's role was to train and equip 40,000 Kamajor militia, plan a strategy for (and coordinate) the assault on Freetown, provide arms, ammunition, transportation, and food for the assault coalition, coordinate with the 20,000 ECOMOG troops in control of the Lungi Airport, and provide air support and intelligence gathering

(Douglass 1999: 190; Musah 2000: 98;). The financing for Sandline's work was heavily reliant on the private sector. Jupiter Mining Company and its owner/representative Rakesh Saxena paid for a Sandline representative to travel to Sierra Leone in July and assess the Kamajors' needs and promised to underwrite the costs of personnel and equipment in return for concessions from the restored government (Douglass 1999: 190).

Planning for this contingency continued through the fall as Kabbah and his international supporters negotiated with Koroma's government (ibid: 191).[14] During this time, the Kamajors undertook some operations and Sandline, International acquired LifeGuard Security (the former EO-owned security company in charge of guarding mines in Sierra Ruptile and Kono) (ibid.). In December 1997/January 1998 the operation began in earnest. Kabbah's forces quickly moved on initial areas in Bo and Kenema and then ECOMOG launched an offensive on Freetown (Douglass 1999: 189).[15] Despite assorted mishaps with the financing and delivery of equipment and services, forces friendly to Kabbah continued to make progress and he was returned to power in March 1998.[16]

By April, though, "a stalemate seemed to have developed, with the RUF and its allies settling in the alluvial diamond areas, their rear secured by the Liberian border and supported by Charles Taylor's government in Liberia" (Douglass 1999: 193). The civil war continued to drag on and in 1999 the rebels again occupied Freetown. Nigeria, the UK, and the US pressed for new negotiations, which resulted in the controversial Lome peace agreement in July 1999 and the deployment of a UN mission peacekeeping (UNAMSIL).[17] The RUF did not abide by the agreement and even seized UN peacekeepers as hostages in May 2000. A British intervention in June and enhancements to the UN mission stabilized the situation and made slow progress toward peace. In January 2002, President Kabbah declared the civil war over; elections were held the following May, and a process of truth and reconciliation began.[18]

British training efforts since 2002

After 2002, efforts to create effective security institutions fell to the British, who had deployed some 1,500 elite troops in May 2000 to strengthen government forces. British efforts continued with the deployment of International Military Advice and Training Teams (IMATT) to train Sierra Leonean military forces.[19] In addition to the British forces, the UN mission in Sierra Leone (UNAMSIL), the OAU and ECOWAS, the EU and the US joined numerous NGOs and monitoring groups working to promote democratization in the country. The aim was to reduce the size of the army to a more affordable size while also upgrading its capabilities along with creating other strong institutions including a civilian bureaucracy and police to maintain internal security.[20]

The British efforts at training Sierra Leone's forces focused on human rights and were relatively more successful inducing a level of professionalism in the forces (Riley 2006).[21] Even proponents of that training, however, worried that these professional soldiers might not prevent opportunistic action by civilian leaders. Of particular worry was the fact that quick elections in 2002 led many of the traditional Chieftains who had long held power in Sierra Leone to be returned to office. Many of these Chiefs have been accused of using diamond taxes for personal gain rather than public goods and many assert that their exclusionary governing style was responsible for alienating the population in ways that led to the civil war in the first place (Hanlon 2005).

Furthermore, even after many civil defense forces were officially disbanded and the Kamajor's one-time leader Sam Hinga Norman was indicted by a war-crimes tribunal, the Kamajors retained a semblance of organizational readiness (Grant 2005). Indeed, though many former members of the RUF were reintegrated through the DDR process in Sierra Leone, most former members of the CDF were not interested in reintegration because they saw themselves as only fighting to defend their villages.[22] The power of the local chiefs and the continued capacity of these forces, of course, may also be linked. Also, the reintegration process was faulted for not offering real opportunities; and many of the young men who were demobilized remained unemployed. Unemployed young men are often easy targets for recruitment into parallel or rebel forces.

Thus, while progress was made and the last UN peacekeepers were withdrawn in December 2005, much remained to be done. Many of the difficulties exacerbated by contracts with PSCs have remained issues even as Sierra Leone's government turned to Western states for help.

Contracts for private security and statebuilding in Sierra Leone

Overall, the participation of PSCs under contract with the government of Sierra Leone enhanced the state's short-term security capacities but did not provide a platform for effective statebuilding. Though different PSCs performed differently, it is clear that EO enhanced the government's security in the short run. The company led the effort to free the capital from rebel assault, to free the diamond mines from rebel control, and to attack the RUF headquarters. Sandline's overall effect is more disputed, but it, too, has been deemed indispensable to Kabbah's return to power by many observers.

Both EO and Sandline (and their advocates) have also argued that the companies hired professionals, behaved professionally and as such increased the chance that force would be seen as legitimate. There are many who support their claims and provide evidence that the personnel each company fielded did behave appropriately in Sierra Leone—much more in line with international norms governing armed conflict than the forces they operated with and against.[23]

The contracts with PSCs, however, were not guided by overarching principles and did not include such long-term goals as training in human rights or democratic control of the military. More importantly, they exacerbated the diffusion of control over force. Simply hiring PSC in the first place enhanced the power of international commercial interests given that both companies were affiliated with diamond-mining companies. In Sandline's contract, this link was explicit, given that payment came directly from Jupiter Mining Company owner, Rakesh Saxena. Also, their security capacities led the companies to become political players in their own right. EO's experience is particularly demonstrative of this impact. In the lead-up to the coup, EO was in a position either to dissuade or to encourage the coup by promising to leave (or not to leave). In effect, the company supported the plotters by refusing to tie its continued work in the country to Strasser's regime.

In their execution of their contracts, both companies also empowered new domestic interests—those within, and tied to, the civil militias. This choice generated political power for the civil militias that Sierra Leone's leaders had to contend with. Given that these were just the social forces that had complicated the state's consolidation in the first place, this effect did not bode well for statebuilding efforts. The civil militias became, in effect, parallel forces without clear ties to the state. The tensions between this parallel force and the army were in some instances directly responsible for territory falling back into rebel hands.

When training was taken over by British IMATT teams, the training of Sierra Leone's army was improved. Without hurdles to the prospects for opportunism by civilian leaders, however, it is unclear that the professional training of the army will be enough.

Croatia: contracts for private training and successful statebuilding

Croatia was a new state in the 1990s, born of Yugoslavia's disintegration. The Yugoslav elections of 1990 brought the Croatian Democratic Community (HDZ) under Franjo Tudjman to power. Also in 1990, constitutional changes made Croatia a de jure nation-state.[24] In April, Croatia simultaneously formed the Assembly of the National Guard (ZNG) within the framework of the police forces and halted the enlistment of Croats in the Yugoslav Army (YPA). When a referendum in May resoundingly expressed Croatians' desire for independence, the Republic of Croatia declared its independence from Yugoslavia and simultaneously began a statebuilding process and a war.[25]

Initially, local militias nominally coordinated by the ZNG structure fought against both YPA troops and Serb paramilitary forces. The Croatians were handily defeated—some argue by design as Tudjman wanted Croatia to be seen as a victim of Serb abuses so that members of the international community would recognize the legitimacy of its claims to independence (Woodward 1995: 171, footnote 69, 463).[26] By 1992, though, the international community had begun to recognize Croatian independence and it behooved

Tudjman to enhance the effectiveness of his armed forces. He began this with the creation of the Croatian Armed Forces (Hrvatska Vojska, HV) (Vankovska 2002: 6; Woodward 1995: 146–47). The force was designed to reflect the Croatia that Tudjman envisioned: party leaders occupied prominent military positions and its ultra-nationalist perspective opened the way for extremist elements (Irvine 1997).

Despite efforts at consolidation, in 1994 the HV had poor leadership, an unprofessional organizational structure (where some forces reported directly to the President and the Minister of Defense) and poor morale and skill. Some officers were reportedly foreign soldiers of fortune, and troops were both poorly disciplined and poorly supplied (Zunec 1996: 221). According to one analyst, "the HV would not be able to wage the offensive operations necessary to liberate its territory and crush the Serbian (Croatian Serbs) insurgency" (ibid.: 222). Meanwhile, territorial losses also led opposition leaders to challenge Tudjman's rule.

Contracts for private security

It was at this point that Croatia turned to Virginia-based Military Professional Resources Incorporated (MPRI) for help. In March the Minister of Defense, Gojko Susak, requested permission from the US government to negotiate with MPRI for various services.[27] In September MPRI President Carl Vuono and Defense Minister Susak signed two contracts. The first, for long-range management, was begun in January 1995, headed by retired Major General John Sewell and designed to help Croatia strategically restructure its defense department (Shearer 1998: 58; Singer 2003: 125). The second, for assistance in the democratic transition, provided for "military education and training of staff officers and uncommissioned [sic] officers of the Croatian army" (Alborghetti 1995). MPRI sent a 15-man team headed by retired major general Richard Griffitts to run this program.

MPRI's official training in the DTAP consisted of 14-week sessions with courses in physical training, education management, instructor training, topography, logistics, military service (international military law), leadership, military management (including analyses of historical battles and lessons), and first aid. The materials used were translated textbooks identical to those used at US professional military education institutions (Goulet 1998). The first officers graduated in April 1995 (Goulet 1998).[28]

The exact nature of MPRI's work for the Croatian government is disputed. Some have claimed the company went well beyond its contract to offer scenario planning, advice on arms purchases, or even command on the battlefield. Without going into the details of these arguments, it is clear that at the very least the contract had significant political effects. It signaled US support for the Croatian government, enhanced the power of both Susak and Tudjman, and boosted morale in the Croatian Army in ways that had both domestic and international benefits even before any change in the capacity of the HV.[29]

The PfP framework

Regardless of the intent behind the contract, NATO and its PfP provided a blueprint for both defense planning and democratization of armed forces that informed MPRI's behavior. From its inception, NATO was not simply an alliance but a security management institution—designed to deal with external threats and also to foster trust and understanding among its members.[30] The liberal-democratic values of NATO led to a set of practices that addressed both external threats and the potential for mistrust and misunderstanding among its members. These practices were successful and provided a model for defense institutions. After the Cold War's end, NATO countries established the North Atlantic Cooperation Council to bring together NATO countries and Central and Eastern European countries to discuss issues of common concern. The Partnership for Peace grew out of this focus on practical bilateral programs between individual NATO countries and its new partners.[31] Many transitional states in Central and Eastern Europe sought this model because of its perceived success, its association with a community of democratic states, or both. NATO countries designed their efforts to socialize transitional states by emphasizing the links between proper democratic behavior and military effectiveness, and the importance of both for full participation in the community of democratic states.[32]

The PfP framework embedded cooperative defense relations in the existing web of democratically dense European institutions—making specific reference to the European Community and the Council of Europe as well as CSCE, NATO, and many of its specific programs.[33] The PfP draws from the principles on which this web of European institutions is based, with both general commitments and specific options for partners (and prospective partners).[34] The menu of options includes a range of defense activities from air defense through defense planning through peacekeeping, military education, training, doctrine, and logistics.[35] All, however, require attention to the general principles including effectiveness criteria such as harmonization and interoperability, as well as normative criteria such as commitment to democratic control of forces and respect for human rights.

The services Croatia purchased from MPRI were designed specifically for the purpose of moving Croatian forces closer to participation in NATO's PfP.[36] The Democracy Transition Assistance Program (DTAP) was meant to democratize the military and reorganize its troop structure to ensure that Croatia would meet the standards for entry to the PfP. The defense reorganization and strategic planning contract also sought to restructure Croatian defense planning in concert with PfP guidelines. Furthermore, Croatia's commitment to ready its forces for the PfP made Croatia eligible to purchase military training in the midst of an UN arms embargo on the former Yugoslavia.

Even if preparation for the PfP was only a rationale through which Croatia was able to purchase military advice in the midst of an arms embargo, this rationale nonetheless shaped the advice Croatia received. The PfP influenced the context in which military advising took place and provided standard practices to be taught. It stipulated appropriate and inappropriate behavior, and was linked to a wide range of incentives and sanctions in both international institutions and bilateral relationships.

Croatian behavior during MPRI training

There were several prominent incidents or policies in the initial period of MPRI's training that called into question its democratizing effects. The two offensives shortly after MPRI's arrival were not only successful, but also brutal. In both operations, the HV engaged in an ethnic-cleansing campaign despite little resistance. The latter was, until the war in Kosovo, "easily the largest single instance of 'ethnic cleansing' of the Yugoslav war" (Danner 1998).[37] Human-rights violations included extrajudicial executions, torture, rape, a massive program of systematic house destruction, and forcible expulsions.[38]

MPRI expressed regret at these incidents, but did not suspend its training efforts. Instead, one official claimed that the behavior of the Croatian troops demonstrated their need for democratic assistance.[39] Neither did the US government freeze the contract between MPRI and Croatia—it also cited the potential benefits of the training for long-term democratization in Croatia as well as the need to maintain US influence in that country.[40]

Some of MPRI's work to transform the Croatian Army also fed into controversial Croatian policies. Efforts to root out communist "dead-wood" played into the HDZ's platform to create an ethnically pure army. Many of the officers with experience were also officers who had served in the YPA. Though it was not intentional, MPRI nonetheless allowed and even facilitated this non-democratic feature of the HDZ's plans as part of a "democratic" restructuring of the force. Also, MPRI's contract with the government was undertaken without the required parliamentary oversight (Vankovska 2002: 25). Even the budgetary category for MPRI's contract (intellectual services) evaded discussion of the contracts as military or defense related expenditures.[41]

After Operation Storm and the subsequent Dayton Accords, Croatia made some progress toward statebuilding. In 1997, the IMF granted the country $486 million credit over the next three years and the Fund's statement praised Croatia for its efforts in reform despite regional military conflict.[42] The IMF's move gave a boost to the Croatian Democratic Party, and Tudjman was re-elected in 1997.[43] On May 27, 1998, the US Ambassador to Croatia, William Montgomery, praised Croatia for its efforts at improving its military with the assistance of MPRI.[44] The country also changed its laws in 1998 to make torture and ill-treatment, as defined in the Convention Against Torture and Other Cruel, Inhuman or Degrading Treatment of Punishment, a criminal offense.[45]

Under Tudjman, however, democratization was halting. Even though the country changed its laws to make possible the criminal prosecution of torture, it refused to investigate the atrocities alleged in Operation Storm.[46] Tudjman's hard-line nationalism led him to resist many Western initiatives. He made it difficult for Serbian refugees to return to their homes and played an obstructionist role vis-à-vis Western efforts in Bosnia. Also, cronyism within the HDZ led to money going to the party elite rather than to more deserving others. Though Tudjman managed to keep inflation down, he resisted sweeping economic reforms because they threatened his political support (Kuhner 1999). More pertinent to the military's behavior, he also refused to turn over evidence and war-crimes suspects to the international war-crimes tribunal. This resistance had costs. Croatia's failure to help with the war-crimes issue led international financial institutions to cut off relations. "Under HDZ rule, Croatia was prevented from joining NATO's Partnership for Peace program, from gaining an Association Agreement with the EU, from receiving assistance under the PHARE program, and even from becoming a member of the World Trade Organization (WTO) or the Central European Free Trade Agreement (CEFTA)" (Fisher 2000).

Even during this time, US Department of Defense reports to Congress pointed to a gradual increase in the integration of the Croatian military with international professional values.[47] Writing for the PfP consortium, Rudocar Vukadinovic and Lidiji Cehulic suggest that there were advocates of democratic standards, respect for human rights, and greater democratic control over the armed forces within the Army in the late 1990s. Although they point out that these advocates were "labeled by the Croatian leadership as national traitors, dilettantes, devils, 'sheep,' 'goose,' and so on," their presence, alone, is evidence for the impact of the training program on interrupting Tudjman and the HDZ's hold on the military (Vukadinovic and Cehulic 2001: 70). International standards for military professionalism began to take root in Croatia in the 1990s as the result of MPRI's training.

Stronger evidence for the impact of training emerged after Tudjman's death in 1999. The opposition defeated the HDZ in the January 2000 election and a peaceful transfer of power to the coalition yielded a new president, Stipe Mesic. At that time Washington promised to increase foreign aid to Croatia (from $12 to $20 million) and to push for Croatia to become part of NATO's PfP (Drogin 2000). Under Mesic, the Croatian government made some significant and tough decisions with regard to its military that reflected attention to the principles of democratic civilian control and human rights. In September 2000 Mesic fired seven generals who criticized the government's crack-down on war criminals.[48] In July 2001 the Croatian parliament decided to cooperate with the Hague war crimes tribunal and to extradite two Croatian generals—Ante Gotovina and Rahim Ademi—who were indicted for war crimes.[49]

Though Mesic's reform capacities were hindered by an awkward constitutional structure that placed opponents in key government posts, the US noted improvements in democratic practices and military reform.[50] Croatia joined the PfP program in 2001, signaling its commitment to the Charter of the United Nations and the principles of the universal Declaration on Human Rights as well as to facilitating transparency in national defense planning, ensuring democratic control of the armed forces, maintaining capability and readiness, developing cooperative military relations with NATO countries, and developing forces better able to operate with NATO forces.[51] Croatia began to participate in the highest level of military–military exchanges with the US outside the NATO structure.[52] Gradually MPRI's work in Croatia expanded to include an Army Readiness Training Program (CARTS) and then, after Croatia's admission to the PfP program in 2001, assistance and support in implementing that program's requirements.[53] MPRI is happy to take credit for helping Croatia to design and implement the military reforms, and members of the US government back their claims.

Contracts for security and statebuilding in Croatia

In Croatia, the participation of PSCs enhanced the state's security capacities, inserted professional security personnel and changed who controlled force. In this case, the increased capacity, professional personnel, and political change led to improved state institutions.

Even without arguing that MPRI had a significant effect on the operational capacity of Croatian troops during Operation Storm, most agree that the government's contract with MPRI improved the capacity of the Croatian forces. Although there are some who criticize MPRI's approach to training the Croatian army on purely functional grounds, on balance most observers agree that the Croatian military is significantly better and that Croatia's security has been enhanced by its contract with MPRI.[54] According to one source, "the Croatians are the premier fighting force in Southern Europe," due to their training from MPRI; according to another, with MPRI's help, "the Croatians can do anything."[55] Tonino Picula, Croatia's former Foreign Minister, claims that MPRI's aid was significant in helping Croatia achieve its rightful independence.[56] Even critics of MPRI's training concede that it had effects on the defense establishment.[57] Due to both its impact on morale (evidence that the US was on its side) and its long-term reformulations of the defense department and the structure of the forces, the contract is hailed as enhancing the abilities of the Croatian armed forces.[58] As American defense officials claim: the "results speak for themselves."[59]

The impact of MPRI's contract also changed the balance of political power over force in Croatia. It accorded more power to one portion of the government—Tudjman and the HDZ—less power to the parliament, and skirted constitutional procedures. MPRI's training also aided the HDZ by bringing political benefits to the party, and gave justification to the HDZ's platform by facilitating the removal of communist officers, which played into Tudjman's plans for an ethnically-based army in Croatia. Furthermore, the contract enhanced the leverage of the US government. By freezing the contract, the US could damage Tudjman's credibility. MPRI, with a strong commercial interest in keeping the US happy, emphasized its attention to the US government's goals in its contract with Croatia.

As critics have pointed out, many of these political changes were undemocratic (Vankovska 2002: 20). They also opened the way for international interests (particularly American ones) to be represented in Croatia. But these political changes consolidated rather than diffused control over violence. Before the contract, there was little control—on anyone's part—over the use of violence in the country. Furthermore, even though the contract opened the way for US influence over the use of force, US influence operated through the Croatian government rather than independently. Thus contracts with MPRI did not lead to the diffusion of power over violence the way they did in other cases, such as Sierra Leone. This was true for international actors (the US had no direct access to Croatian forces) as well as for domestic actors (MPRI did not work with sub-state forces but instead worked to integrate forces into the Croatian army). Though it restricted direct exercise of power over violence by international actors or domestic actors outside the state, this structure, somewhat paradoxically, also gave international actors a central point of leverage within the Croatian government and made it easier to encourage the Croatian military and government to attend to collective (rather than individual) goals.

The government's contract with MPRI also enhanced the Croatian army's integration with professional values. The ethnic-cleansing campaign undertaken after Operation Storm did not reflect attention to military professionalism, and some have claimed that units of the HV trained by MPRI took part in ethnic-cleansing campaigns.[60] That very serious episode aside, however, there has been a long-term trend towards acceptance of international professional values by the Croatian military. The speed at which reforms were undertaken in the wake of Tudjman's death indicates that international standards for military professionalism have taken root in Croatia.

The overarching web of institutions and the PfP framework were important at several points in this contracting story. First, the justification for the US to license MPRI's contract with Croatia in 1994, when the country was under an arms embargo, was the argument that the contract would speed democratization. This justification led to the inclusion in the contract of courses and training that focused specifically on appropriate professional behavior and international law as it applied to military personnel. These training units, common in US professional military education, taught about the system of democratic civil–military relations (at least as it exists in the US) and used case studies and other methods to teach appropriate military responses to difficult situations. Similar to courses taught in US military academies, they did not simply preach the acceptance of civilian control of the military and appreciation of human rights, but demonstrated how these principles are related to military effectiveness. Even though there were pressing and immediate security concerns in Croatia, the training program focused on long-term institution building.

Furthermore, the PfP framework both provided a standard for military institutions as part of a democratic state, and also offered carrots (increased US funding) and sticks (freezing of training) that the US (and other international actors) could use to encourage the Croatian military and government to focus on long-term professional development in the military in addition to their short-term security goals. The Croatian government had reason to abide by the PfP terms, even if only instrumentally.

A significant number of Croatian military personnel were educated on the basis of these principles in classes. Partly because of the cachet of American training, partly because of the lure of the PfP program, education by MPRI also enhanced the individual careers of those in the Croatian military who participated.[61] The reorganization of the Croatian Defense Department further reinforced these policies. Finally, the promises (and then delivery) of US financing for continued military reform have further reinforced the standards for military professionalism in Croatia. The long-term aims of the training and the fact that the contracts were sustained over several years also gave more time for these effects to be felt. By introducing new values, connecting them with effective military performance, and promising military aid for continued changes, the participation of MPRI in training the Croatian military has nudged improvements in the professionalism of the force.

The participation of PSCs under contract with the Croatian government improved security, changed who controlled force (and through which process), and improved the integration of force with international values. It is unclear that Croatia would have started down this path without the private option. The contract between MPRI and Croatia was a way around the international embargo in the Balkans, which had made sending US troops to train the Croatian forces very difficult. The contract proved crucial to Tudjman's consolidation of political power and to the ability of Croatia to expel Serbian forces from its territory, and allowed for the beginning of a process of statebuilding in Croatia. The ultimate result in Croatia, however, has been a more capable force that is also responsive to political institutions and professional norms. This is a testament not to MPRI, per se, but to its use within NATO's PfP program, which required an extended training program and issued significant external incentives for Croatian political and military leaders to work toward international standard of military professionalism. This high conditionality—along with some lucky junctures—led private advice and training to enhance long-term control over force in Croatia.[62]

Comparisons and conclusions

There are a number of differences between these two cases. Croatia had been part of a relatively functional state, while Sierra Leone had no such history. Also, the conflict in Sierra Leone had a different logic and the rebel forces fought differently than in Croatia. Finally, Croatia's factor endowments and economic situation was much more conducive to statebuilding than Sierra Leone's. Statebuilding in Sierra Leone, then, presented more hurdles at the outset.

Regardless, these cases do reveal that market-based security can influence statebuilding in very different ways. In both instances, PSCs offered new capacities, increased professionalism (relative to poor state forces) and a changed political dynamic. In Sierra Leone, the new capacities diffused control over force and made it easier for capacities to be used for sub-group goals. In Croatia, however, the new capacities centralized control over force in a way that enhanced the potential for statebuilding and democratization. At the very least, this analysis demonstrates that, rather than assuming that the market for force will either aid or undermine international efforts to promote statebuilding and democracy, analysts would be well served by investigating the conditions likely to lead to one or the other outcome.

I have suggested that institutional factors contributed to these differences. While the use of market options empowered new international and domestic actors in each case, different actors were empowered in the two instances. In Sierra Leone, it was international commercial firms, PSCs themselves, and eventually sub-state forces. In Croatia, by contrast, the use of market forces empowered states, state-based organizations (the US and NATO), and the emerging state (Tudjman and his party). While market forces worked to centralize control of force in Croatia, they exacerbated the diffusion of control in Sierra Leone. Further, the contracts in Croatia were justified by (and operated under) a clear international framework designed to both inform and encourage institutional development in transitional states, whereas no such framework existed in the case of Sierra Leone. The framework of the PfP program offered many tools with which to leash market forces to long-term collective goals—and the progress that Croatian forces have made can be linked directly to those tools. Absent these tools in Sierra Leone, there was not a coordinating mechanism to inform the variety of actors involved about what might be best to include in a contract, let alone to induce these actors to make choices that would contribute to Sierra Leone's long-term institutional development.

One might argue that the difference between these two experiences can be explained by some difference between the companies or what they did. For instance, one might argue that MPRI is a more professional company and its employees are less prone to opportunistic behavior than EO or Sandline, or that MPRI's contract in Croatia was for training while EO and Sandline's was for more direct participation. In fact, however, as the discussion of Sierra Leone demonstrates, it was not the individual behavior of EO and Sandline employees was the issue. Also, there is widespread speculation that MPRI did, in fact, participate more heavily in the planning and implementation of Operation Storm than it has claimed. MPRI's contract with Croatia did have within it attention to civilian control of the military, human rights, and other professional norms, but this was because it was ostensibly designed to prepare Croatia for the PfP program.

Some also claim that MPRI worked much more closely with the US government than did EO with the South African government, or Sandline with the British government. This is true. The US has a regulatory structure that neither South Africa (at the time) nor Britain share. This regulatory framework, however, did not prevent MPRI from siding at times with the Croatian government against the demands of officials in the Pentagon. As one Pentagon official put it, "the contract was a tool with which MPRI could resist compliance with shifts in US policy. Contracts are rigid tools for fluid environments."[63] The PfP framework, however, provided boundaries that MPRI had a harder time evading. Finally, MPRI has engaged in a number of training efforts with states involved in, or emerging from, conflict such as Colombia and Iraq that have not resulted in similar successes. Though I do not have the space to go into the details of these instances here, the relative success of MPRI's efforts in Croatia and Bosnia stand in sharp contrast to what are widely regarded as failures in Colombia and Iraq.

Security institutions are a key component of statebuilding. To contribute to statebuilding, these institutions must be effective, abide by political controls, and operate within the bounds of acceptable behavior. PSCs provide a tool for generating more effective forces in transitional states. Because they operate outside of what are often regarded as corrupt state institutions, they also redistribute political power in ways that may be beneficial for long-term change. The dilemma, however, is that this tool can be hijacked in ways that make statebuilding harder rather than easier—by diffusing control over force and/or allowing force to be used for private or sub-group purposes. Though any military training is subject to hijacking, the market forces involved in contracting with PSCs exacerbates these difficulties.

I have examined international organizations as a potential framework by which such hijacking can be evaded. The two cases examined in this chapter reveal that IOs can simultaneously inform the fledgling government and military personnel about proper behavior, induce them to behave properly by rewarding proper behavior, and funnel resources through the state in a way that dissuades opportunism. My analysis is similar to those who have examined the way in which international institutions are socializing states in Europe, though it focuses greater attention on the tight coupling between information, inducements, and dissuasion (Checkel 2005). IOs can thus be instruments that coordinate the interests of powerful states and provide tools with which actors in less powerful states can be persuaded to cooperate (Hurrell 2005). They are most successful in influencing security institutions, however, when they link perceived effectiveness and proper behavior.

Europe, of course, is the quintessential "democratically dense regional IO network." Can the insights here be of use to other regions? Or, as Keohane puts it, is it possible to do peacebuilding in bad neighborhoods (Keohane 2003)? It may be harder to build states in bad neighborhoods, but the analysis here suggests that features that coordinate international preferences by translating broad normative commitments into specific blueprints for action, centralize (rather than diffuse) control over force within a territory, and coordinate carrots and sticks for civilian and military personnel will work towards statebuilding. This may seem like a tall order, but the fact that institutions in Europe exist offers the prospect of extending portions of the existing framework. In that context, suggestions for a "global NATO" provide not only the promise of increased capacity for international action, but also the potential for staying power rather than simply triage.[64]

Finally, efforts at statebuilding in the 1990s seemed difficult at the time, but look comparatively easy in retrospect—particularly when contrasted with efforts in the post 9/11 world. Cooperation between western states has been strained as some have seen the US as acting in unilateral ways. As Astril Suhrke's chapter in this volume demonstrates, US efforts to fight the "war on terrorism" in the short run have often hampered efforts to create the stable states that promise to reduce breeding grounds for terror in the long term. These post 9/11 and post-Iraq strains may generate more resistance to cooperating within a global web of institutions. At the same time, institutions that enhance global coordination are even more important when preferences among the powerful diverge and when short-term goals threaten to undermine long-term security.

Notes

* The author thanks Alex Cooley, Kim Marten, and the participants and directors of the Research Partnership on Postwar Statebuilding for comments on previous drafts.
1 Sometime this failure (real or perceived) is in particular issues areas – such as schools or prisons. Other times it is more fundamental.
2 For discussion of rational legal authority, see Gerth and Mills 1978: 299. See also the discussion in Barnett and Finnemore 1999; and Barnett 2001: 59.
3 The RUF had grown in the 1980s sponsored by Liberian warlord, Charles Taylor and filled with young men who had few other options. See Abdullah 1998.
4 Abdullah 1998.
5 Three groups of 120 were trained in the first three months.
6 The RUF headquarters was attacked in October 1996.
7 There was some speculation that EO aided Bio's coup because Bio's brother, Steven, was partner in Soruss – a Belorussian company that leased aircraft to EO.
8 The RUF believed that EO was the reason for the Kamajor success.
9 The Adibjan Peace Accord.
10 Norman had a long history in Sierra Leone – though initially as a part of the RSLMF. He was a participant in the first post-independence coup that unseated Siaka Stevens after his APC party had defeated the SLPP in the 1967 general elections. See Musah 2000: 81.
11 The CDF was to coordinate five different militia groups: the Kamajors in the South, the Gbethis in the center, the Donzos in the East, the Kapras in the West, and the Tamaboros in the North. The coordination effort has been less than successful. Much of the training that EO (and to a lesser degree, Sandline) accomplished was with the Kamajors.

12 The Status of Forces Agreement Between the Government of the Federal Republic of Nigeria and the Republic of Sierra Leone, Lagos, March 7, 1997, cited in Musah 2000: 93.

13 Purportedly at the suggestion of British High Commissioner Peter Penfold. Ibid, p. 189; Musah 2000: 98.

14 It appeared as if agreement was reached in late October, but it fell apart over details in November.

15 Four other major factions, with the Kamajors make up the CDF: the Gbethis in the center, the Donzos in the East, the Kapras in the West, and the Tamaboros in the North. Efforts to transform these into a single force by Deputy Defense Minister Sam Hinga-Norman have not been successful. "Sierra Leone: Managing Uncertainty," ICG Africa Report, No. 35, October 24, 2001, p. 5.

16 Just why these arms were impounded is unclear. Alex Vines suggests that Kabbah had changed his mind about purchasing the weapons. See Vines 1999: 65. Douglass suggests that they were impounded on the basis of questions about their legality given the UN arms embargo. See Douglass 1999: 192.

17 See Hirsh, "War in Sierra Leone;" and "Sierra Leone: Time for a New Political and Military Strategy," ICG Report, April 11, 2001.

18 See "Sierra Leone's Truth and Reconciliation Commission: A Fresh Start?" ICG Report, December 20, 2002.

19 Human Rights Watch, World Report 2003: Africa/Sierra Leone.

20 British Foreign and Commonwealth office, "Security Sector: Africa" available at http://www.fco.gov.uk.

21 See also Human Rights Watch, World Report 2003: Africa/Sierra Leone.

22 UN Office for Coordination of Humanitarian Affairs, "Sierra Leone: Disarmament and Rehabilitation completed after five years," IRIN News Brief, February 4, 2004.

23 See for instance, Bergner 2003.

24 See Zunec 1996: 217.
   See also Tatalovic 1996.

25 For the international politics of Yugoslavia's disintegration and how it affected the extremism of each of the republics, see Woodward 2002.

26 See also Vankovska 2002: 6.

27 This is disputed. According to Roger Cohen, Croatia asked the US for help and the US referred the Croats to MPRI. See Roger Cohen "US Cooling Ties with Croatia After Winking at its Buildup," *New York Times*, October 28, 1995, p. A1. See also Gaul 1998: 1.

28 Ed Soyster claims a six-person assessment team was sent in November 1994. Also in November Joe Kruzal made a trip to Croatia offering some limited mil-mil contacts and a token IMET ($65,000) program. When Croatia (in January 1995) announced that it wanted the UN out by March 1995, the US withdrew the mil-mil contact and the IMET but, "someone in State with some vision decided that we needed to maintain contract with them and saw the long range benefits to DTAP." Email correspondence, March 23, 2000.

29 For more on the speculation about MPRI's actual behavior, see Avant 2005, ch. 3.

30 See Alexandra Gheciu, *NATO in the "New Europe": The Politics of International Socialization After the Cold War* (Stanford: Stanford University Press, 2005).

31 See http://www.nato.int/issues/partnership_evolution/index.html; and Goldgeier 1999: ch. 2.

32 See the general discussion of socialization in Europe in Checkel 2005.

33 See, for instance, NATO Ministerial Communique. 1991. "Partnership with the Countries of Central and Eastern Europe," Statement issued by the North Atlantic Council Meeting in Ministerial Session, Copenhagen, 6–7 June. http://www.nato.int/docu/comm/49–95/c910607d.htm.

34 http://www.nato.int/issues/pfp/pfp.htm.

35 See activities for 1997–98. http://www.nato.int/pfp/docu/d990625a.htm.
36 PfP was designed as a stepping stone to NATO. See NATO, "Partnership for Peace: Framework Document," January 1994. Available at http://www.nato.int/docu/comm/49–95/c940110b.htm.
37 "Croatia: Impunity for the Storm," Amnesty International Report 1998, available at http://web.amnesty.org/library/print/ENGEUR640041998.
38 Ibid.
39 Background interview with MPRI employee, January 1999.
40 See Holbrooke 1999: 73.
41 Other problematic expenditures for weapons and the Bosnian war were handled in the same way.
42 "Croatian government welcomes IMF Credit," *Agence France Presse*, March 14, 1997.
43 Hedges 1997.
44 Montgomery's speech is available at http://www.usembassy.hr/speeches/980527.htm (4/1/02).
45 "Croatia: Statistics and laws alone will not end torture and ill-treatment," Amnesty International News Service, AI Index: EUR 64/09/98.
46 Ibid.
47 The Foreign Military Training Report FY 1999 and 2000 claimed "Along those lines, IMET Funds have fostered appreciation among Croatian military officers for the proper role of the armed forces in a democracy." See *Foreign Military Training and DOD Engagement Activities of Interest, Vol. I*, Joint Report to Congress, March 1, 2000, Ch. III, European Region, p. 5.
48 Associated Press, "Generals Criticize war crimes crackdown," *St. John's Telegraph*, September 30, 2000: 16.
49 Obradovic 2001.
50 Drazen Budisa, the party that posed Mesic's key opposition for the presidency, was given the post of Defense Minister (Vankovska 2002: 31).
51 "Partnership for Peace: Framework Document," NATO Headquarters, Brussels, January 10–11, 1994, available at http://www.nato.int/docu/comm/49–95/c940110b.htm.
52 Interview with John Erath, Pentagon Croatian Desk Officer, April 16, 2002.
53 http://www.mpri.com/subchannels/int_europe.html.
54 Interview with former NATO Special Assistant, June 1999; interview with State Department staff, June 2000; interview with Pentagon staff, April 2002.
55 Interviews with officials at the State Department, Defense Department and Joint Staff, June 1999 and April 2002.
56 "A Nation Resolved to Overcome Its Tough Heritage," *International Special Reports – Croatia*, March 10, 2002 available at http://www.internationalspecialreports.com/europe/01/croatia/anationresolved.html.
57 Vankovska 2002: 20–21.
58 Indeed, the State Department credits MPRI with significant effect on the Croatian military. Interview with State Department Official, April 2002.
59 Interviews with Pentagon and State Department officials, April 2002.
60 One site of atrocities in southwestern Bosnia, Mrkonjic Grad, where the bodies of 185 Serb civilians were found, was alleged to have been the location of atrocities committed by a Croatian Army Unit that had been trained by MPRI. William Norman Grigg, "Selective 'Justice' Turns Blind Eye to Croatian Atrocities." http://thenewamerican.com/tna/1997/vol3no21/vol3no21_croatian.htm.
61 Interview with Ed Soyster, MPRI, April 2002; interview with Pentagon official, March 2002; interview with State Department official, March 2002.
62 For the term "high conditionality" and another positive view of its effects, see Cooley 2003. See also Pevehouse 2002.
63 Interview with Pentagon official, April 2002.
64 See Daalder and Goldgeier 2006.

Part III

Political economy

6 Trajectories of accumulation through war and peace

Christopher Cramer

Statebuilding in war to peace transitions has economic dimensions.[1] The service-delivery dimension of states depends on the existence of productive assets in order to generate revenues needed to sustain functioning institutions, including financing security, the judiciary, electoral bodies, and the monopoly of violence. The transformation dimension of states requires the development of institutions that help to produce sustained economic expansion and structural change. These include institutions to manage and enforce the reconfiguration of property rights during protracted processes of social transformation, as well as institutions to encourage the acquisition of technology and to foster innovation, to mediate conflicts of interest, and to manage the distribution of the fruits of peace, recovery, and growth in ways that sustain or develop political legitimacy.[2]

However, there is still too little known about the complex economic consequences of and influences on war to peace transitions and postwar statebuilding experiences. The political-economy literature on recent (post-Cold War) post-conflict reconstruction moments has been largely biased towards macroeconomic and aid debates, in some of which evaluative short cuts have been taken in the terms and assumptions of analysis (how success or failure are defined, what is understood by "good policy," what datasets are deemed sufficiently robust, etc.).[3] Further, there is a common assumption that war is exclusively "development in reverse" (World Bank 2003), or that war retards development and development retards war, despite evidence that this assumption is flawed. This assumption corresponds to the equally widespread imagery of the "blank slate" inherited by postwar societies.

Instead, this essay recommends that researchers and policymakers focus more than they have done on the real economy of wartime and its implications. What is significant about statebuilding challenges in postwar conditions is that economic activities have taken particular forms through war, or through phases of a "peace–war–peace continuum" (Richards 2005). Postwar statebuilding challenges, therefore, include not only those features of accumulation before the war that might have contributed to the processes leading to war, but also those challenges thrown up by the actual patterns of change that have taken place in a war economy and by the fact that many features of war economies are carried over into the peacebuilding period. These may be sources of either opportunity or threat for statebuilding and peacebuilding efforts.

The main aims of this chapter are to contribute to the literature on the political economy of postwar statebuilding by developing the idea of "trajectories of accumulation" through war and peace;[4] to discuss some examples of these trajectories; and to relate these to dilemmas of (and policy implications for) war to peace transitions. The main examples are drawn from Mozambique and Afghanistan but other cases, including Angola, Lebanon, and Bosnia and Hercegovina, are also used.

The challenge is to develop policies and institutions that consolidate those dimensions of the peace–war–peace economy with greatest potential to contribute to longer-run structural change, economic development, and statebuilding. In terms of Hirschman's (1977) distinction between the passions and the interests, the task is to investigate how to forge institutions that help create such a distinction in political economy environments typically characterized more by "passionate interests" (Cramer 2006a). My main argument is that there is a tension between the assumptions of liberal peace statebuilding (as, for example, reflected in the World Bank's *Breaking the Conflict Trap*) and the transformation of primitive wartime accumulation into structural change and a sustained momentum of reinvestment.

The following section explores the ways in which war economies carry over into peacetime and influence the challenges of statebuilding. Then this discussion is linked to orthodox economic policy prescriptions and ideas of statebuilding through the examples of markets for Afghan raisins and Mozambican cashew nuts. Next, the paper examines the main contours of the economic dimension of the "triple transition," i.e. market oriented reforms linked to foreign aid, with a particular focus on fiscal and trade policy and privatization.

Trajectories of accumulation, revenue tussles and statebuilding dilemmas

In all wars, beyond the destruction caused by indiscriminate and selective violence, many people survive and some thrive economically. The different individuals and groups who do relatively well out of war and its aftermath may or may not form the foundations of postwar economic reconstruction. In Mozambique, for example, a number of types of entrepreneur succeeded in the war economy. Some were traders (e.g., those supplying basic food and consumer goods to the countryside or those bringing imported foodstuffs from Swaziland and South Africa into the besieged capital, Maputo, and its large population of foreign-aid workers). Some were military officials: there is evidence of military officials during the war siphoning off equipment and re-selling it in the Southern African region (and towards the end of the war also selling it to opposition Renamo forces) or, in the case of military fuel supplies, onto the black market in Maputo (Fauvet and Mosse 2003: 249–50). Some were money changers (usually Mozambicans from Asian communities). Others were farmers.

Indeed, it is important not to conjure up an idea of a homogeneous class of war entrepreneurs or, indeed, of a coherent, united postwar capitalist class. If the interests of a range of Mozambicans in war do not necessarily make of them a single class, this is even more obviously true of Afghanistan. For example, Giustozzi (2006) traces the variations in the organization of business, power, and violence across different regions of Afghanistan. He distinguishes between warlord-controlled businesses and factionally aligned businesses, and stresses that many of the warlords who have engaged in business retain important local political power. And he introduces greater subtlety (2005: 9) by suggesting that non-state military-political actors are split "into different types, rather than unifying them under the single label of 'warlords.'"

Despite this variety, wealth appropriation and creation during war and the transition to peace is not random. Both states and individuals (or groups of individuals) capture surpluses from production and exchange, and use those surpluses in the service of various goals that include the accumulation of wealth and of political power, legitimacy, military security, and capability to resolve conflicts and provide other services. States, meanwhile, mobilize resources through various mechanisms, but especially through direct and indirect taxation, inflationary finance, receipts from resource and other rents, bribery, and so on. Individuals and economic enterprises have historically appropriated surpluses and accumulated wealth through a number of mechanisms, including slavery, rent, and the successful organization of competitive capitalist production and exchange. In each case, accumulation is shaped by opportunities and incentives and by constraints. These in turn are affected by political conditions; that is, by existing institutions, by the political settlements that sustain those institutions, and by changes in the political settlement. Thus, who are the dominant accumulators and how in the main they accumulate depend on politics, institutions, and policy. The "who" and the "how" can change over time, giving rise to evolving patterns or trajectories of accumulation.

Mozambique provides an example of trajectories of accumulation through colonialism, independence, war, and post-conflict reconstruction. There were substantial changes both in who accumulated and in how, through the second half of the twentieth century and the beginning of the twenty-first. The principal shifts were from colonialism (during which the economy was particularly marked by plantation agriculture, infrastructural services linking the Southern African region to the world economy, and the provision of migrant wage labor to South African mines) to independence; a post-independence period characterized by nationalization and a state-led industrialization strategy and by overlapping forms of war economy; and thence to a postwar society characterized by market deregulation, privatization, massive foreign-aid inflows, and a revival of foreign investment.[5]

Across this whole period, political upheavals and policy experiments helped to forge a national bourgeoisie and to delimit the extent to which Mozambican entrepreneurs were likely to contribute to longer run processes of structural change, diversification and economic development. At independence, there was virtually no such class at all. The state, through both aggressive and defensive nationalization, took control of many productive assets and enterprises. Through experience in political positions and through relative success in the economy that evolved through conditions of war and in response to the failures of state-led industrialization, a number of people accumulated the assets and wherewithal to succeed economically. Towards the end of the war and then more rapidly after the war, thanks especially to a sweeping privatization program, many Mozambicans then took ownership and management stakes in a large number of enterprises. At the same time, a number of foreign investors took advantage of the opening of the economy.

War in Mozambique amounted to more than "development in reverse" and, in rural areas, a "retreat into subsistence." As one researcher put it: "Far from retreating into a subsistence economy ... the war and crisis heightened the need for the poorer peasantry to sell their labour to obtain cash to buy food and other rural wage goods" (Wuyts 2003:147) and the process of socio-economic differentiation in the Mozambican countryside accelerated. While many such people lived in desperate conditions through the war, others began to do relatively well. Among them were former settlers and military commanders who got control over land, more and more with state support. As O'Laughlin (1996:32) put it: "the war resolved their labour recruitment problems." There may have been little technological innovation during the Mozambican war. However, a range of people laid the basis of political and economic strength from which they were able to launch post-war entrepreneurial careers. Something similar has been evident in Afghanistan, where landowners leasing out their land to poppy growers and people with the capital to invest in and organize the heroin business have accumulated, while others have become increasingly indebted and less self-sufficient (Goodhand 2004).

The configurations of such a war economy and the experiences, political clout, and interests of people who benefit from it present important challenges, and at times difficult choices, for postwar reconstruction and state-building initiatives. It helps, therefore, to highlight the main features of such war economies.[6]

In war economies there are often activities characterized by heightened risk, increased barriers to entry and, as a corollary, potentially high returns.[7] Such activities may include production of food and trade in consumer goods (clothes, food, batteries, kerosene, etc.) or smuggling illicit goods across borders. Depending on the degree of shortages and on government policies, there are often also opportunities for illegal arbitrage, for example, in foreign-exchange transactions. Second, barriers to entry into various activities are not just a function of risk but also of coercion or local monopolies of force. Where there is no clear monopoly of force, however, there are niches (by activity or location) where one group will exercise a monopoly (over reselling military fuel, over cross-border consumer goods trade, over heroin exports, etc.).[8]

These are the conditions that generate what might be termed "war rents." Rather than a developmental or economic vacuum, what often evolves in war is a form of what Chingono (1996) called (specifically in the Mozambican context) a "vicious market fundamentalism" characterized by ruthless exploitation of workers, the coercive establishment and protection of monopoly control over production or trade, and substantial profits. Much of this activity may look very like what classical political economists referred to as "primitive accumulation," a phase of accumulation of wealth (or appropriation of surpluses) through largely non-economic and usually coercive means. Where primitive accumulation has played this foundational role in the spread of capitalism, it has always only done so because of the support and/or control of states.

Peacetime sharply rearranges the incentives and conditions of accumulation, especially if it is accompanied by far-reaching economic policy reforms. Yet there is rarely a pure break between war and peace. Postwar Mozambique has experienced episodes of violent confrontations, a rising trend of urban violence, and high-profile assassinations relating to the allegedly corrupt outcomes of financial-sector liberalization. Putatively postwar Afghanistan and Iraq have been extremely violent. Urban violence in postwar El Salvador has been at notoriously high levels. More generally, many argue that the war/peace distinction is a misleading one, best replaced by the notion of a "continuum" (Bourgois 2004; Richards 2005: 5). Indeed, political and economic interests and agendas pursued through war are typically carried over into peacetime.

In these conditions, there are protracted tussles between state and non-state agents over access to revenue streams from resources and productive (and exchange) activities. These tussles characterize most societies; however, they are often especially intense in the wake of violent conflicts. One among a number of reasons is that states often lose the ability to command access to goods and services through inflationary "war taxes" and, therefore, need to generate alternative techniques of resource mobilization; yet simultaneously postwar states are typically constrained by macroeconomic imbalances and the need to restrain inflation. It makes a difference whether a centralized bureaucratic state more or less survived through war (e.g., in Mozambique) or whether a more fragmented system of regulating clientelist politics replaced such a state (e.g., Sierra Leone).[9]

Nonetheless, some existing activities come under threat in a war to peace transition while new opportunities arise. There are often changes in the balance and distribution of force, even if not complete, which affect barriers to entry in certain activities. Where roadblocks and landmines are removed, for example, barriers to transport, trade, and farming are lowered. Where an effective state and international accountability operate, then barriers to abusive methods of accumulation, including labor coercion, or to illicit economic activities may be higher. And the conditions of accumulation change with peacetime policy reforms, including trade and industrial policy and fiscal policy. However, the conditions of accumulation, the choice and implementation of policy and the distribution of force are all contested in war to peace transitions.

The other side of changing conditions for private accumulation is that those who have secured material wealth and political position during wars influence the reach and character of postwar states. In other words, all four of the sources of power that Mann (1993) identifies are contested in war to peace transitions: military, political, ideological, and economic. State and non-state actors struggle to wrest control over each of these sources of power. "Postwar" Afghan warlords have not only fought each other over control of trade routes, they have meanwhile had "few incentives for engaging with the embryonic central state" (Goodhand 2004: 61). Angolan diamond-mining companies and their private-security contractors have resisted efforts to cede authority to local police (see below for more on this example). This is why postwar statebuilding cannot be reduced to a technical exercise.[10]

In principle, the fact of wartime economic activity and in some cases dynamism could provide a boon to postwar statebuilding. Continued economic activity in peacetime, coupled with the common boost to activity from peace, easier and safer mobility, landmine clearance, and a reallocation of the labor force, can reinforce the legitimacy of a state presiding over a new political settlement, as well as generating the economic growth and revenue sources that are fundamental to statebuilding.[11] In Mozambique most, and in Afghanistan some, of the economic beneficiaries of war have shown an interest in peace. In much of Mozambique one of the most obvious outcomes has been the improvement in conditions of mobility: the removal of roadblocks may have reduced (but not eliminated) the scope for ad hoc privatized taxation but has increased the returns to internal trade. In Afghanistan the situation is far more complex in that there are parts of the country where, after the removal of the Taliban, there were fewer roadblocks but there are others where there has been a return to pre-Taliban days of fragmented sovereignty affecting transport. In both countries there has been substantial investment in construction, with significant employment creation (or switching) effects as well. If the majority of people whose postwar economic advantages owe much to wartime roles in the state or to close connections to the state and if the state continues to be dominated by the same political forces, then there is less chance that there will be any threat to a project of statebuilding.

However, economic interests and statebuilding interests do not necessarily coincide nicely in the transition from war to peace. The example of diamond mining in Angola shows that a trajectory of accumulation from war into peace can threaten prospects for growing political legitimacy of the state, but at the same time reinforce a political equilibrium. Arguably, something similar has happened in Bosnia, where a political equilibrium in peacetime endures, more fragile than in Angola, yet its basis in parceling out assets on ethno-nationalist lines undermines the prospects for central statebuilding and more inclusive growth. There is, then, a tension between peace and state-building. This tension creates a dilemma for supporters of statebuilding: whether to prioritize stability and hope for a gradual improvement in the reach of the state, or to insist on statebuilding even where this may threaten the political settlement underpinning peace.

The tensions of peace–war–peace economies can be acute. In places like Afghanistan and Lebanon, some individuals and groups (warlords, militias, war profiteers, military commanders turned economic entrepreneurs, etc.) have been fairly successful in resisting the demands of the central state.[12] This can involve straightforwardly resisting taxation. It can also involve resisting the governance principles of a state seeking international legitimacy. And it can involve resisting the political project of statebuilding if there is an enduring alternative project of sovereignty (even locally).[13] If sources of wealth built up during war and carried over into peace lie in international networks and commodity chains that do not depend on state support (infrastructure, subsidized market access, security, assistance in meeting phytosanitary conditions internationally, etc.) and may actively be linked to oppositional political projects, then there will be little support for state-building where it might be perceived as a threat to continued activity. This would apply to those national and international interests involved in Con-golese resource exploitation, and to Afghan and Latin American producers of and traders in illicit commodities.

More prosaically but just as importantly, one source of wartime accumulation is often the ability to mobilize cheap labor without conforming to regulations of pay and conditions. Statebuilding may involve efforts to extend such reg-ulation—in the interests of domestic legitimacy, "broad-based" growth, and/ or membership of international bodies such as the International Labour Organization (ILO). Yet many entrepreneurs may well try to re-create wartime labor relations. Yet again, Angolan diamond mining provides a striking example. Informal, garimpeiro miners are deemed illegal but mining com-panies depend on them: the companies exercise considerable power over these miners, essentially using the withholding of licenses to blackmail them into working for the companies on their terms.

These tensions—which differ considerably from Angola to Afghanistan, Lebanon to Mozambique, and Democratic Republic of Congo to Central America—create dilemmas of statebuilding. Should economic activities be encouraged/accepted because they generate employment and because they may involve channeling passions into interests (pace Hirschman, 1977), even if accepting them means foregoing human rights, compliance with ILO and other international standards, and tax revenue? Or should states and inter-national agencies supporting statebuilding flex their powers more assertively, in which case they may risk undermining some economic activities and livelihoods or they may risk undermining the political settlement achieved in a peace deal? Arguably, quite often in such situations peace endures and this kind of dilemma is not fully resolved: the outcome is one of some economic growth but with limited human development or "trickle down" yet with peace and a surviving political equilibrium.

Another difficult choice is whether or not to launch an assault on illicit commodity production, such as narcotics, when this production supports many rural people's livelihoods. An alternative might be to promote a massive investment in alternative sources of work, income, and foreign exchange. But this involves huge risks—of crop failure, weak prices, etc.—and also may run aground on inadequate international commitment or on political threats to international involvement. Further, it is risky to hold out a promise of "alternative livelihoods" from licit commodity production and trade if there is not the will or power internationally to overcome the use of non-tariff barriers to market access, which has been widespread in recent years (UNCTAD 2006).

One dimension of these dilemmas is that the statebuilding project in conditions where powerful economic interests have endured from the war into the peacetime economy may require credible threats of force from the central state. This in turn requires a substantial investment in military power. Of course, in some contexts, arguably especially those where there has been an outright military victory, as in Angola, a strong state with an effective military force may well reinforce the perpetuation of wartime accumulation strategies. However, the Angolan example partly underlines the ungainliness of some concepts of statebuilding and state capacity: while not performing many of the commonly expected functions of a legitimate state, the Angolan state could hardly be called weak. Perhaps it is the apogee of that recent coinage (Prunier and Gisselquist 2003) the "successfully failed state." The dilemma here is whether to shore up the state's monopoly of force or to pursue a more rapid peace dividend from disarmament and a shrinking military budget.[14] Failure effectively to assert the monopoly of central force can of course lead to situations like that in Southern Afghanistan in 2006, where, as Human Rights Watch (2006) put it: "An explosive combination of resurgent Taliban forces, record-high drug production, ineffective local governance, and re-armed warlords is threatening the well-being and rights of hundreds of thousands of ordinary people in Afghanistan and, increasingly, across the border in Pakistan."

What this particular example shows is that the dilemmas of statebuilding are acutely dependent not just on national politics or aid policy and resource flows, but also on regional interests and international politics. There are difficult choices involved if reinforcing one statebuilding project (in Afghanistan or Somalia) runs counter to the interests of another statebuilding project (Pakistan or Ethiopia).

Some of the other dilemmas linked to trajectories of accumulation from war into peace are a function of policy preferences internationally and their consequences for political equilibrium, desirable governance outcomes, economic growth, and the fiscal foundations of statebuilding. Arguably, the choices for policymakers are more difficult—in a context of the trajectories of accumulation and tussles over resource mobilization—than is typically acknowledged in international institutions generating policy advice. However, just as more generally there has been some movement toward acknowledging the counter-orthodox experiences of successfully industrializing economies, so too there are examples of increasing awareness in international organizations of the need for more nuanced analysis of local contexts. Two examples to build on are the IMF recognition that "undesirable" trade taxes may prove more acceptable than the textbook alternative in the early postwar period and the Independent Evaluation Group's emphasis on the need for the World Bank to "internalize political analysis in strategy design and implementation" (IEG 2006: 22).[15]

The nuts and raisins of statebuilding

One example of the challenges that arise in post-conflict statebuilding is in the markets for processed commodities for export. There can be no hope of statebuilding without efforts to secure a rapid rise in export revenue. Export earnings are a basis of reducing "aid dependency" and of getting access to imported goods and inputs, as well as providing employment and profits and generating fiscal revenue whether through trade taxes or income tax. Most low-income countries emerging from violent conflict will rely on primary commodity exports and there is often some scope for vertical diversification, structural change, higher domestic value addition and less market volatility through processing primary commodities before export. The key to successful export of primary commodities and their processed derivatives (for example, shelled and roasted cashews in Mozambique or dried and packaged raisins in Afghanistan) lies in securing a reliable supply of high-quality primary inputs. Otherwise, it is difficult to meet demanding phyto-sanitary requirements and quality preferences in international markets. Raisins in Afghanistan and cashews in Mozambique are two examples of processed commodities that have been leading exports in the past but that have suffered during protracted violent conflict.

There are constraints throughout the chain, from production to international market sales, for Afghan raisins (Lister et al. 2004). These constraints include poor irrigation, proliferating informal taxes, the risk of consignments being hijacked, obsolete and/or dilapidated processing plants (there used to be an estimated 31 but few survived the war), and poor transport infrastructure. Further, the regulatory environment is ineffective and there are few channels of access to commercial credit for market participants other than those who have come out of years of war with privileged access to finance.

The story of Mozambique's cashew-nut sector has been told many times (Cramer 1999; McMillan et al. 2002; Pitcher 2002) but there are similarities with the Afghan raisin market. Processing factories were, by the end of the war, in a parlous condition. Production of raw nuts was blighted by elderly, often diseased trees, poor handling of the harvest, conflicting interests, and an incoherent policy and regulatory environment. The World Bank insisted on radical liberalization mainly via a sharp reduction on the export tax on raw, unprocessed nuts. The effect has been a more or less comprehensive collapse of the processing industry and a failure to achieve more than moderate reconstruction of raw-nut production.

The raisin example is one of several illustrations of the way that post-conflict markets operate in Afghanistan. Lister and Pain (2004) argue that plans for reconstruction "have been premised on economic growth created by the rejuvenation of 'collapsed' markets, driven by the private sector and organized within the 'free' market. The key concerns of policy making have centered on the need to create a light regulatory state to promote private sector growth." They go on to argue that this approach strips the market of its wider dimensions and that the way markets actually function has a "negative effect on political governance and 'statebuilding'" because of close links between businesses and politicians. In other words, a vision of liberal market reconstruction is actually helping to promote a profoundly illiberal reproduction of the war economy, with substantially inequalizing outcomes.[16] They recommend "more, rather than less active state intervention" to ensure wider opportunities to participate in markets and to allow for wider distribution of the benefits of growth. There is, then, a contradiction at present and a difficult choice for policymakers: indeed, a choice that has in Afghanistan become more politically difficult as time has gone on, as an agricultural sector distinct from and forming a viable alternative to the opium economy has become an increasingly distant possibility and lack of international investment in rural infrastructure has become more dramatic (Rashid 2006). The dilemma in rural Afghanistan, for donors, has been whether to throw more resources into rural-development projects or to wait in hope of the security situation improving.

Something similar characterizes postwar Mozambique. During the country's privatization program in the 1990s, for example, an ideological commitment to rapid and sweeping privatization, combined with market deregulation, produced what were from the perspective of the ideas underpinning the reforms perverse effects. The government steered a course between external ideologues of privatization and its own entanglement in the trajectories of power and accumulation. In doing so, it offered subsidies to Mozambicans buying privatized enterprises, in the form of accepting deferred, late or sometimes missing payment installments. But these subsidies were not allocated according to any criteria of productive strategy, increasing the scope for essentially clientelist allocation of these subsidies (or what Amsden 2001 calls "intermediate assets").

So the typical policy ideas informing international support for postwar economic reform and statebuilding easily generate contradictory outcomes.

These in turn generate dilemmas. Should donors and lenders encourage more state intervention rather than less? But if they were to do this, it would require a greater commitment to raising the fiscal capacity underpinning intervening states. And how is it possible to discern effective interventions, a priori, from wasteful interventions?

However, the dilemmas are more acute. Introducing greater transparency and other accoutrements of good governance might lead to a withdrawal of investment by some of the people involved in a given sector, or to a weakening of the coalition of interests underpinning an uneasy peace. Further, the choice policymakers face is not straightforwardly between promoting the correction of market failures and ignoring them. Rather, the dilemma ought to be how to find ways to support a state that creates the kind of market failure that have positively supported economic development historically. More starkly, the choice is not between subsidies and no subsidies, for example, but between subsidies that promote productivity improvements, employment, and other benefits, and those that do not. It can even be a choice between identifying genuinely wasteful corruption and accepting that some corruption is "value enhancing."[17] In the Afghan context, for example, it is not about breaking the hold over markets of warlords or faction-affiliated businessmen but about forging a coalition around this kind of imperfect market structure that might more effectively promote productivity enhancement such as grading procedures, simplified tax structures, and investments in irrigation.

For example, Giustozzi (2006) argues that a window of opportunity to control strongmen after 2001 was missed and that in the "pax mafiosa" that has resulted, the key to peace and statebuilding and development may be "to recognize the role played by the strongmen in the economy, remove the uncertainty about their fate and offer selective incentives to invest in long-term businesses, in order to speed up their conversion from 'robber barons' to legitimate magnates" (ibid.: 86). This would sharpen another dilemma common to many experiences of postwar statebuilding: the choice between justice and security or indeed between justice and development. For "such an option would rule out any concept of 'transitional justice' in Afghanistan, which would target many if not all the leading strongmen" (ibid.: 86).

The dilemma for policymakers becomes a problem of accepting that for the sake of peace, stability, and progressive change deals may have to be struck, or allowed to be struck, that confound expectations of good governance and good policy.[18] A parallel example is the international treatment of the heroin market in Burma/Myanmar. McCoy (1999: 130) suggests that as states expand they often leave peripheries "poorly integrated into a central apparatus still struggling to take form. In these mountain and maritime fringes, weak state control can provide an opening for men of prowess—pirates, bandits, warlords, or ethnic chiefs—to mediate between the center and its margins ... [who are] a manifestation of an ongoing, incomplete process of state formation" rather than an index of state failure. Specifically, the "weak Burmese state, like its early-modern antecedents, has been forced to engage the reality of such powerful outlaws as both threat and asset. To counter Khun Sa's modern army, the SLORC was forced to harness the illicit border trade for hard currency to buy arms. When this center–periphery synergy had crushed his revolt, Rangoon then transformed Khun Sa ... into a national financier, using his illicit assets and overseas Chinese connections to promote economic growth" (ibid.: 160). In a world where, as McCoy argues, "major powers are struggling to build a world order upon shared principles" (ibid.: 161), this kind of coopting of outlaws is anathema.[19] However, it is also extremely common in a variety of forms, not just in Burma but in Afghanistan, Mozambique and many other places (see also the chapters by Roberts, and Suhrke, respectively in this volume).

Does neoliberal economic policy raise transition costs?

Standard approaches to the economic dimensions of war to peace transitions in recent years have encouraged stabilization and liberalization policies, which have shaped the outcomes of such transitions (Cramer 2006a). These policies are encouraged under the influence of the benchmark of an ideal-typical efficient market economy in an ideal-typical Weberian state. They are often drawn up by external advisors and funding agencies in a way that implies a "blank slate" in countries emerging from violent conflict. However, deregulation, market liberalization and orthodox economic policies may generate dangers for peace-building operations, as Paris (2004) among others, points out.[20] The contradictions of economic policies driven by faith in the liberal peace project but having consequences that may undermine peace and statebuilding therefore generate difficult choices for policymakers.

The dangers associated with orthodox economic policies in post-conflict reconstruction episodes include the possibility that austere monetary and fiscal policy may weaken living standards for many people and provoke political unrest or, at least, reduce recruitment costs for "spoilers" of the peace process; and the possibility that resources reallocated through liberalization (e.g., through privatization) are captured by ethnic or other special interest groups that may then, presumably, reproduce patterns of "horizontal inequality" (Stewart 2000) or "categorical inequality" (Tilly 1999), which in turn may raise the risk of a return to war. These resources may also be captured by the people who were the principal economic beneficiaries of the war economy: an outcome that may to varying degrees reproduce the characteristics and conditions of a war economy and that may or may not represent an "investment in peace." These outcomes challenge the expectations that flow from the liberal interpretation of war. According to this tradition—from Tom Paine and Richard Cobden through to the World Trade Organization and Thomas Friedman—political and economic liberalization remove the obstacles to a natural social condition of peacefulness (Howard 1978).

Stabilization and liberalization may thus compromise peace, recovery, and statebuilding through different mechanisms.[21] They may fail to stimulate the rapid economic growth they are designed to promote. They may facilitate growth that is not "broad-based" or "inclusionary." They may sharpen inequalities. They may have contradictory effects on unemployment and labor markets. They may reinforce a country's dependence on a narrow range of primary commodities. Through all these effects they may undermine the expansion of the revenue foundation of statebuilding. Further, they may weaken the state's capacity to regulate so-called shadow economies, while privatization may as easily provoke asset-stripping and the entrenched power of interests opposed to a broader-based project of state formation as encourage productive investment, employment, and tax-generating output.

Privatization

Three dimensions of standard postwar economic reforms may be highlighted: privatization, taxation/fiscal policy, and trade policy. Privatization may be expected to liberate enterprise from the shackles of bureaucracy and the confused objectives often identified in state-owned enterprises. If privatization releases entrepreneurial adventure and confers on managers more efficient incentives, it may then lead to new investment, expanding output and rising productivity, and employment. These effects are not only desirable in themselves but also for the contribution that enterprise growth and employment make to government revenue.

However, privatization has often had extremely uneven and typically mixed consequences. For example, financial liberalization and bank privatization in postwar countries including Cambodia and Mozambique has generated greater corruption rather than less, has failed to produce mechanisms for directing credit to potentially progressive domestic capitalists, and has led to substantial fiscal burdens rather than adding to the fiscal capacity for institution building.[22] Privatization in postwar contexts may also aggravate the potential for productive enterprises to be captured by those who have accumulated wealth and power during war. Privatization is thus an important influence on trajectories of accumulation through war and into peace. Two examples highlight this risk and introduce the significance of such trajectories.

First, privatization in Bosnia shows how the expectations of textbook economics can be confounded by the passionate interests at play in postwar transitional societies. Pugh (2005) argues that privatization and the shrinking public realm in Bosnia, driven by "raids on the public sphere from interveners equipped with a neoliberal agenda of political economy as part of a civilizing mission to introduce a 'liberal peace'" (p. 450), have occasioned a crisis of "public squalor and private affluence" (quoting Galbraith). Ten years after the Dayton peace accord GDP per capita was only 50 percent of the average for South-East Europe and less than 50 percent of its pre-war level. Receipts from privatization have been "temporary, irregular, and low." An extension of a postwar amnesty to cover "economic crimes" "enabled thousands ... to safeguard their wartime gains and to consolidate their economic control. Telecommunications and energy were divided along ethno-party lines … Command and influence in the peacetime political economy could then be exerted on the public space through clientelism, rentier fraud, corporatism and capture of privatization processes" (ibid.: 450–51).

Second, in Angola since the end of the war and in at least a partial spirit of economic reform and privatization, diamond mining and many associated (commercial) security functions have been handed over to private-sector interests—both diamond-mining companies and private security firms. Marques (2006) shows how diamond mining in Cuango (in Lunda Norte Province) is dominated by enterprises with close ties to the government and by individuals who have moved into this activity from government and military experience. He also shows how the private security firms (e.g., Teleservice, described by a police official as "a company of generals") often have greater powers than state institutions such as the local police (see also Deborah Avant's chapter in this volume). In this environment, human-rights abuses are rife. Effectively, in Cuango and throughout the Lundas in northern Angola, many characteristics of the war economy—slave labor, brutal treatment of poor people, weak regulation of lucrative activities—have carried over into a peacetime economy characterized by at least lip service to multi-party politics and market-oriented economic reform.

Fiscal policy

Both the service-delivery functions and the transformation functions of states are costly to create and maintain, probably especially so in countries emerging from violent conflict. Until recently, the literature on the economics of post-conflict reconstruction paid little attention to questions of resource mobilization, especially to fiscal policy. However, there has been an increasing emphasis on this challenge.[23] Improving institutional capacity and ensuring a rising revenue stream must be a minimum condition of postwar statebuilding. Further, there is a widespread argument, drawing on Tilly's (1992) analysis of early modern European state formation, that states are unlikely to develop legitimacy unless they are pressed to forge a "tax-mediated social contract" (Moore and Putzel 2000). From this perspective, emphasizing postwar fiscal policy, politics, and institutions may be an important dimension of sustainable statebuilding.

Addison and McGillivray (2006) have argued that although donors stress liberalization and privatization rather than fiscal policy, fiscal policy is actually more important. Fiscal policy, they argue, is at the heart of postwar demands for changes in tax incidence and expenditure policy. The IMF has tried to learn largely technical lessons for rebuilding fiscal institutions in post-conflict environments. Reviewing advice to a number of countries from the Fund's Fiscal Affairs Department, Gupta et al. (2004) argue that there was often a trade-off between short-term revenue mobilization efforts and tax efficiency: "In some instances, taxes that were less than desirable from an efficiency point of view were recommended, given the limited options available for generating revenues" (Gupta et al. 2004: 12), including the "necessary evil" of export taxes.

Most of these contributions have in mind fiscal policy for a service delivery state. If the goal is a transformational state as well as a service delivery state, the challenges of resource mobilization and fiscal policy are even greater. Possible trade-offs and dilemmas include the following: first, there may be a difficult choice between pursuing trade liberalization on grounds of "good policy" and securing revenue to deliver services, shape economic policy and patterns of production, and to build institutions; second, there may be a choice between pursuing other policies common to orthodox post-conflict policy reforms, such as sweeping privatization and financial sector liberalization, and securing revenues to underpin statebuilding (see above); third, and by contrast, pursuing less orthodox fiscal policy risks provoking the evasive tactics of informality and illegality, which themselves often help perpetuate a lack of structural change in the economy and undermine state legitimacy and hegemony.

Trade policy

Trade liberalization is a common feature of post-conflict (and other) economic reforms. The key feature of trade liberalization is drastically to simplify and reduce trade taxes. Export taxes should be reduced or removed. There should be a reduction in both the levels of import tariffs and the number of different levels of tariff. Exchange rates should be encouraged to float. Non-tariff barriers to imports should also be scrapped. One mechanism for such reforms is the Economic Partnership Agreement (EPA) model, developed in the European Union to replace previous provisions for preferential access from African, Caribbean and Pacific (ACP) countries to the European market. Arguing that preferential access failed to generate development, the EU proposes mutual trade opening agreements with ACP countries, including Angola, Mozambique, and other postwar countries.[24]

The dilemma for policymakers is that this kind of orthodox trade policy may undermine prospects for improving governance, state capacity, and service delivery, let alone any more ambitious goals of trade and industrial policy in service of structural change.[25] For proponents of trade liberalization typically advocate replacing trade taxes with indirect taxes such as value added tax (VAT) or general sales taxes, which are anticipated to generate compensatory revenue streams. Yet, IMF research has shown that in low-income countries—and post-conflict countries are commonly low-income countries—typically the revenue lost from trade liberalization is not fully recovered by the introduction, itself costly, of these indirect taxes (Baunsgaard and Keen 2005). By contrast, Di John (2006) argues that gradual trade liberalization in Uganda and the shift over time from export taxes to import taxes were crucial to maintaining fiscal revenues while the political and administrative challenges of introducing new tax instruments were addressed. Indeed: "The case against rapid tariff reduction as a means for maintaining and increasing fiscal resources, a key element in state consolidation and state-building, is one of the main lessons in the political economy of the Ugandan postwar reconstruction" (ibid.: 17).

Further, orthodox trade policy may undermine the scope for states to implement a trade and industrial policy designed to accelerate diversification and structural change. Given that no country has successfully industrialized without trade and industrial policies that have involved protection and exemptions, the pursuit of orthodoxy might not only undermine post-conflict statebuilding but it might also represent what Chang (2002), following Friedrich List, calls "kicking away the ladder."

To Addison's recommendations for further improvements in transparency in international trade and investment and for a dismantling of rich country protection against developing country exports, this essay adds the recommendation that greater attention should be paid to the design of more active export promotion policies in such countries. On the one hand this would involve a more creative use of WTO provisions for phased introduction in low-income countries of liberalization. On the other hand, there may be a case for adding special provisions, in international trade negotiations, for countries that have experienced violent conflict. This does not escape the fact that trade policy and protectionism have often been misguided and ineffective; it does, however, acknowledge that this has often not been the case. Instead of relying too heavily on special provisions and exemptions, an alternative is to build on some of the momentum behind support for more earmarked "aid for trade" and to make this a priority for postwar economies. This involves support for the supply side, raising trade capacity in institutions, investing in infrastructure geared towards exports, and so on. However, this aid needs to allow for selectivity in trade policy (UNCTAD 2006), building on the creeping recognition that non-orthodox policies may be effective (World Bank 2005b).

Conclusion

Postwar statebuilding involves crafting institutions and policies that can help to channel trajectories of accumulation towards a sustained momentum of economic development and structural change, which in turn will provide a basis for greater (and more remunerative) employment opportunities and for a deepening revenue base for the state.

However, it is unreasonable to expect any such process of postwar statebuilding in low- and middle-income countries to take form rapidly. Historically, statebuilding has been a protracted and conflictual process. Moreover, it is probably unreasonable to impose a sequencing of institutional, political and economic developments that was not achieved in the early state formation and capitalist development of the industrialized nations. The goals of "good governance" are undoubtedly desirable. However, they have not historically been prerequisites of successful statebuilding and economic development. Meanwhile, this essay has argued that it is unreasonable to expect economic growth and structural change to unfold on the basis of neo-liberal economic policies and the "light state."

Acknowledging this may be one foundation for policymakers to reconsider approaches to postwar statebuilding dilemmas. The basic recommendation must be for international actors committed to supporting postwar state-building to shelve their commitment to short-run implementation of neo-liberal economic policies and the good governance agenda, while still holding onto the longer-run goals of improved governance. The history of state formation and successful capitalist development is a history of states intervening effectively to promote national capitalists who are competitive internationally, whether pursuing "Ricardian" or "Kaldorian" strategies (Schwarz 1994).[26] The history of successful postwar reconstructions is a history of managed integration into the world economy and state support for infrastructural expansion and institutional change (Cramer 2006; Foner 1988; Marglin and Schor 1990; Milward 1992). In trade, fiscal and other policy fields, if pragmatism among international policy advisors were to trump ideological commitment to neo-liberalism and normative commitment to shared values, some of these dilemmas might more easily be overcome. The overall argument of this essay is that development agencies have made a rod for their own back by hitching aid to ahistorical orthodox economic policies.

Postwar economic policy needs to build at the very least on the acknowledgment that fiscal expediency outweighs orthodox ideals (Gupta et al. 2004), for example, to encourage trade taxes rather than seeking to remove them or reduce them to a bare minimum. This would have to go hand in hand with a focused commitment to improving state control over customs duties and trade taxes, for the importance of building the fiscal foundations of a state cannot be over-emphasized. Rubin (2006) points out that only 5.4 percent of non-drug GDP in Afghanistan is raised in fiscal revenue, lower than any other country with data. This suggests that support for postwar statebuilding since 9/11 may run foul of another dilemma: whether to put the regeneration or development of fiscal capacity first or to take the shortcuts of pursuing international security objectives first while bankrolling the shell of a technocratic "showcase" state. However, weak taxation is the context in which governance worsens rather than improves in war to peace transitions, as there is no fiscal foundation for the state to support services or even to engage effectively in factional politics, and the incentives to corruption increase correspondingly.

Finally, policymakers internationally can only hope to help in postwar statebuilding if they appreciate the trajectories of state resource mobilization and private accumulation that have developed historically and that have taken new directions through war and through war to peace transitions. Otherwise, naïve policy advice can further entrench the formation of classes (and states) reproducing themselves by farming rents from resources or illicit markets. However, the recommendations made here also generate their own difficult choices. Ditching global and ahistorical models of good governance and good economic policy exposes international policymakers or advisors to other risks. For the challenge is to identify, in a particular country, which policies may realistically encourage greater fiscal capacity, greater long-run productive expansion, and so on, where there can be no guarantee that this will work. And these advisors, and lenders, will also be exposed to their own taxpayers' scrutiny, for the policy approach recommended here acknowledges that there will be an accountability asymmetry. Western donor governments are accountable to their electorates for aid spending, while they may be supporting political and economic policy compromises overseas, in the interests of statebuilding and development, which cannot match domestic expectations.

Posed as a dilemma, one possibility is that pursuing a goal of statebuilding in war to peace transitions that is consistent with common international norms of "good economic policy" and "good governance" may actually restrict the scope for the development of states that more closely approximate historical experiences of state development. The difficult choice would be whether to abandon or compromise principles, assumptions, and ideals inherent in these norms for the sake of more effective development or whether to stick to the principles while risking the creation of perpetually stalled state development. Posed as a contradiction, there is arguably a tension between the kind of path of state development envisaged in typical international visions of war to peace transitions and the historical evidence on how successful states have actually developed.[27]

The question of what kind of state is to be built has in some ways changed since 9/11. This is partly reflected in the concern with spillover effects from weak or failed states, or with "international public bads." Arguably, one effect—in some regions—has been to intensify a dilemma for international actors: whether to invest in the slow process of helping to design local institutions compatible with specific historical and political contexts and to help forge strategies of economic development likely to allow a country over time to finance its own statebuilding costs; or whether to hot-wire a political settlement or set of institutions most likely to protect international actors against these international public bads. The evidence from cases such as Afghanistan and Somalia appears to be that some international actors have favored the latter course. And the evidence so far suggests it is not wholly successful.

Notes

1 This essay adopts the definition of statebuilding used across the contributions to the RPPS project: "The creation or strengthening of effective and legitimate governmental institutions within a bounded territory."

2 On the significance of this symbiosis in historical experiences of state formation and development see Tilly (1992) and Schwartz's (1994) emphasis on the "guns, lawyers and merchants" nexus at the heart of the global political economy.

3 See Kriger's (2003) argument that the war to peace literature is dominated by assumptions that are subjective, arbitrary, and externally made. This literature has also, arguably, paid too little attention to the longer-term history of post-conflict reconstruction and statebuilding (Caplan and Pouligny 2005; Cramer 2006a).

4 The phrase "trajectories of accumulation" refers to developments over time in the rates and forms of accumulation of wealth and the patterns in who accumulates.

5 Trajectories of accumulation have regional dimensions too. Virtanen and Ehren-preis (2007) summarize the way that Mozambique's insertion into South Africa's regional political economy has changed: from being characterized by migrant labor flows and transport links to being organized around spatial development initiatives including "mega-project" industrial investments such as Mozal's alu-minium smelter plant located by Maputo's port and contributing a mere 0.4 percent of revenue as tax to the Mozambican state.

6 One earlier example of changes in the patterns of accumulation (who and how) was the American South, where conditions of accumulation shifted from a society based on slavery and plantations, through the Civil War, and into the fraught period of Reconstruction and its aftermath. War and Reconstruction drastically rearranged incentives, opportunities, and institutions underpinning the southern economy. The political struggles over Reconstruction reforms, both between North and South and within each, were reflected in institutional developments that shaped economic development in the South in the latter part of the nine-teenth century (Ochiltree 2004). There were many opportunities in the South after the war, just as there were many ruined fortunes; the two, indeed, went hand in hand. The notorious carpetbaggers flocked south (many of them former soldiers in the Union army) and took advantage of commercial or speculative opportu-nities. They often benefited from state support for the infrastructural expansion that was at the heart of the uneven postwar southern boom (Klein 1968).

7 The distribution of economic risk in wartime, and of investment, in reality varies between sectors and regions, depending on the intensity of conflict, the char-acteristics of particular sectors, and the distribution of fragmented sovereignty. This affects both domestic investors and foreign investors. For example, high returns could be made by foreign oil companies with very little direct risk throughout the war in Angola.

8 On the spatial distribution of violence and control in civil wars, see Kalyvas (2006).

9 See Allen (1995) for a model of different types of politics and trajectories of political systems through decolonization, political experiment, and structural adjustment in Sub-Saharan Africa, and for a critique of efforts to fit all African political histories into a single explanatory model.

10 Ghani et al.'s (2005) statebuilding model recommends the calibration of a "sovereignty index," against which the "sovereignty gap" may be measured and then addressed through a series of efforts to support the ten core functions of a state that they identify, efforts that are then expected to roll out in a "virtuous cycle."

11 For assessments of the—often elusive—peace dividend across a range of country and regional contexts see Gleditsch et al. (1996) and Brömmelhörster (2000).

12 On Lebanon see Picard 2000.

13 On contested reconstruction in Lebanon after the 2006 conflict with Israel see Biedermann 2007.

14 In Haiti, for example, which has some analogies with a postwar society, the World Bank IEG points out that a number of donors regard the lack of effective political

analysis as a reason for the "dangerous neglect by the donor community of the need to provide adequate resources for dealing with the current security problems" (IEG 2006: 20).

15 Neither instance of Bretton Woods Institutions adaptability, however, goes so far as to acknowledge Amsden's (2007) argument that during the "first American empire" (i.e., before 1979) laissez-faire meant "do it your way,", i.e., so long as developing countries were not swayed by communism they had considerable room for policy experiment. The scope for such experiment nowadays is arguably far more restricted, though it is not wholly absent.

16 On the tendency since 2001 in Afghanistan towards market concentration, see also Giustozzi (2006).

17 See Khan 2002.

18 For critiques of the good governance agenda and its assumptions see Rodrik 2003; and Khan 2004.

19 McCoy's argument is particularly relevant in a context where donor countries "are threatening to limit their aid if narcotics production is not curbed quickly, regardless of its economic effects. The U.S. Congress 'fenced' part of this year's aid disbursement, pending certification by President Bush that Afghanistan was cooperating with U.S. counternarcotics policies" (Rubin 2006: 32).

20 "Orthodoxy" is sometimes referred to, in development economics, in terms of the Washington Consensus and/or the shift since the 1990s towards a greater role for institutions reflected in the idea of a Post-Washington Consensus.

21 On Central America see Boyce 1996; Carbonnier 2002; and Pearce 1999.

22 See Addison et al. 2001 on Cambodia and Mozambique; Fauvet and Mosse 2003 on the banking scandals in Mozambique; and Hanlon and Smart 2006 on the failure of initiatives to support horticultural export projects in Manica Province in Mozambique.

23 See, for example, O'Donnell 2005.

24 See Cramer 2006b; and Goodison and Stoneman 2005.

25 See, for example, Chang and Grabel 2004.

26 Put simply, a Ricardian strategy accepts static comparative advantage and is likely to emphasize primary commodity exports while a Kaldorian strategy will aim to create comparative and competitive advantage, emphasizing production and export of manufactured goods with greater scope for increasing returns to scale and learning by doing effects.

27 Two of the main intellectual sources of recent statebuilding ideas—Stiglitz's (1998) development of the idea of a Post-Washington Consensus derived from his work on asymmetric information generating market failures and Fearon and Laitin's (2004) arguments in favor of neo-trusteeship based on the production of international "public bads"—imply the role of the state is restricted to correcting market failures. However, states have developed by other routes and through the performance of other functions, including war-making, the mobilization of nationalism, and indeed the development of specific market failures that have supported economic development. For a critique of the Post-Washington Consensus, see Fine et al. (2001).

7 The superficiality of statebuilding in Cambodia

Patronage and clientelism as enduring forms of politics

David Roberts

This chapter is concerned with whether large-scale statebuilding interventions have an impact on democratizing state polities much beyond their metropolitan centers. It reviews the effectiveness of statebuilding in Cambodia vis-à-vis its impact on aspects of the political and social organization of metropolitan elites and rural masses, and finds that, after nearly two decades, political change in both sectors has been superficial and remains operationalized and dominated by informal, socially-ruled systems of patronage and clientelism, rather than determined by impartial, independent and impersonal institutions associated with the democratic prerogative explicit in statebuilding and democratization. The chapter discusses how comprehending political activities is complicated by the appearance of democracy disguising the functioning of political and social institutions. There are, I argue, superficial political institutions in the metropolis of Phnom Penh that are nominally democratic, but which, on closer scrutiny, are political husks. They are less meaningful democratic institutions concerned with the rule of law and the separation of powers, for instance, than they are labeled buildings. Furthermore, rural areas seem even less susceptible to democratization than the metropolis, especially where "new" systems render people temporarily or permanently less secure than the pre-democratic means of social organization. The chapter proposes that statebuilding in Cambodia has been of limited impact in terms of its implicit and explicit democratization agenda.

The roots of this "failure to launch" and lack of susceptibility to democratic conversion are also to be found in many other countries undergoing externally-assisted statebuilding. This suggests that we can make some broad generalizations about likely outcomes of postwar statebuilding and therefore the approaches we might take. The essay concludes by arguing that providing more than the basic pluralization and electoral systems to non-democratic systems would ultimately be ineffective and therefore wasteful. Furthermore, since indigenous polities adapt and reject elements of democracy they find useful or meaningless, hybrid plural-indigenous systems are the most likely, and in some respects the most desirable, outcome. These should be encouraged, I argue, because they allow specific political evolution best suited to local experiences and capacities. This approach would also reduce the risks and perceptions of "democentricity" and imperious intent. It may also result in statebuilding being conducted more economically and with fewer indigenous and endogenous challenges.

The first section of this chapter introduces the subject matter and debate. The second section discusses the literature on political elitism and common social patronage. The third section describes Cambodia before the recent period of externally-driven statebuilding. The fourth section examines the statebuilding intervention conceptually and practically, focusing on the specific areas of political and social institution building. The fifth section examines Cambodia in the aftermath of the exercise and discusses and explains the lack of democratization in specific areas of elite and social activity. The final section presents some concluding generalizations and recommendations relating to postwar statebuilding interventions.

Context

Statebuilding is being finessed from an ad hoc and little-understood issue that emerged from the embers of the Cold War, to a multi-dimensional, complex and coordinated concept that might be consistently applied to the many parts of the world that seek the best strategy for political and economic development after conflicts have been ended (Jeong 2005: 83–86). Whilst these conflicts have many and various causes and manifestations, their conclusion entails the shared objective of identifying a direction, through domestic and international policy choices, that will maximize the longer-term benefits of peace and development for the greatest number. This nominally involves departure from pre-democratic practices, toward practices associated with Western democratic functioning and values. Currently, although there is still resistance to the choice and application of democracy and capitalism for post-conflict development from some quarters, that model is the dominant tool of political organization with the least incredulity and the most arguments in its favor as a determinant of internal peace and international harmony.[1] Democracy may not represent the "end of history," but many would consider that it represents "progress." Implicit and explicit in this belief is the notion that whatever systems of political organization predate democratic statebuilding, the introduction of democracy and capitalism would benefit a significant majority over the long run (Jeong 2005: 83–86).

Statebuilding enterprises face a variety of similarities and dissimilarities when they are pursued in states emerging from conflict and seeking peace. There may be extant competing parties within the state, or there may be a single-party state facing challenges from national citizens outside its political border. The polities of the host states may seem keen to embrace liberalism, or there may be entrenched elite opposition to such change. They may be secular, or theocratically determined. Power-sharing as a compromise solution might be acceptable to the elites, or single-party/person absolutism may be the prevalent view of authority and legitimacy. At grass-roots level, there may be popular acceptance of the legitimacy of the interveners, or there may be reluctance based on, for example, mistrust of an international body or some of its components. The intentions and benefits of such interventions may be well-understood and invited, or there may be incomprehension and ignorance coupled with perceptions of or actual disadvantage attached to internationally-driven transformation. More normally, statebuilding initiatives face a combination of resistance and acceptance, and this dualism tends to be reflected and mixed at mass and elite levels, and may shift over the duration of the operation.

However, two characteristics that are common to many states emerging from conflict are poverty and elite entrenchment. Poverty may have been caused primarily by long wars; pre-existing economic hardship; catastrophes such as floods, droughts or famines; market variables and vulnerabilities such as mono-crop dependency; internal corruption perverting just resource distribution; specific aid policy (such as withholding resources); or other factors. Poverty may also have had its roots in colonial expropriation. The second characteristic—elite entrenchment and, with it, internal illegitimacy for some portion of a population—may be a product of historical experiences deriving from Royal Court authority; it may stem from Monarchic and Court parentage (copied behavior); or it might have been drawn from or enhanced by perspectives of the "right" of the state to enjoy certain benefits, replicated from the authoritarian days of colonialism. Normally, however, democracy is not in place and the legitimacy of elite authority is contested.

These two characteristics are rarely disconnected. The state in many poor countries has only limited social legitimacy traditionally and, in some cases, contemporaneously, because citizens' early experience of state interventions was often linked to taxes and conscription, rather than beneficence and protection. In terms of basic needs supply, the state did not provide and locally-organized provision grew as customary practice. This practice is commonplace globally in the form of common social patronage (CSP). Few expected a social contract from the mistrusted, corrupt and exploitative state, and the state had little intention of providing one. This is one of the core reasons families in many poor countries see kin provision as their responsibility and indeed duty, and have no expectation that the state should be involved in these relationships (Bayart 1993; McCloud 1995: 284). Both groups—elite and mass—in such poor countries have routinely viewed employment in the state—and the state's role—as a means to personal profit more than public good. State employees often joined for personal benefit, and those that did not often viewed such employment with hostility or mistrust. Thus, statebuilding in its most recent manifestation is often confronted with multi-causal partial development and associated high levels of poverty, conjoined with socio-political systems that do not routinely recognize fundamental tenets of the liberal social contract or the necessary conceptual elements of political liberalism outlined above. Indeed, quite different forms of social organization at the grass-roots and elite levels nearly always set the stage for a statebuilding project. Do large-scale statebuilding interventions change this, or, after the external statebuilders depart at strategically identified points, do they have only a limited and superficial impact? The following section introduces and discusses how these situations are affected by statebuilding.

Political elitism, patronage, and clientelism

Elitism has been largely diluted in Europe since the decline of absolute monarchs and since authority and legitimacy have been constitutionally determined. Scruton defined elites as that group of people in a particular polity and society "who are in a position to view themselves ... as chosen, either by others or by nature, to govern" (Scruton 1982: 143). This privileged position can be a result of a variety of factors, some of which confer legitimacy on elites, but they can also be determined by domination and violence, through coups for example. Many revolutionary leaders in the developing world, such as Jomo Kenyatta in Kenya and Julius Nyerere in Tanzania, gained their legitimacy as dominant elites from successfully challenging imperial rule. However, many others have effected appointment by means less agreeable to a population, such as Emperor Bokassa of the Central African Republic. Yet others have elite authority and legitimacy by divine association from the cosmos; Chinese emperors and Cambodian kings are examples of such phenomena.

McCargo expands the conceptualization of elite governance further when he refers to elite governance being "the prerogative of a narrow set of interlocking elite interests." These may coexist with formal "democratic" structures and institutions, but in practice, McCargo notes, "they often have to reflect entrenched bureaucratic economic and military interests," adding that "the dividing line between the public and private sectors can be extremely blurred" (McCargo 1998: 126). This characterization makes clear that very few elite leaders have absolute control over the populations, but instead often create systems of elite patronage and clientelist personal networks within the narrow decision-making cartel.

But a fundamental characteristic of elite power is the regularity with which it resists change and threats from within and without. Such resistance often involves using the state apparatus like the police and army, as well as paramilitary organizations associated with a specific personality or party, often in the pay of the hegemonic master or group. It is this resistance to change and the instruments of its entrenchment that are addressed in this chapter on Cambodia, which demonstrates both the superficiality and ineffectiveness of external intervention in internal vested elite interests. Although leaders of all political parties, including in western democracies, would most likely prefer to stay in positions of power, elites in countries prone to statebuilding interventions tend to exist in polities devoid of routinized, constitutionally-determined power transfers, and lack a culture that institutionalizes such change as legitimate and necessary. Since the desire to remain is unlikely to change, it is reasonable to expect more vigorous defense of the hegemonic status quo during some statebuilding operations, particularly those that "threaten" power sharing or power transfers. Patronage is thus routine behavior, and is important when considering attempts at pluralization.

This concept, of vertical power linkages of patronage and clientelism, also finds expression in routine life in very poor societies, but is much less visible to the unpracticed observer. This is important to the second element of this chapter as it relates to common social patronage at the mass (rather than elite) level. Eisenstadt and Roniger characterize this form of patronage and clientelism as "not a distinct type of social organization, but different modes of structuring the flow of resources and of interpersonal interaction and exchange in society: different modes of generalized exchange" (Eisenstadt and Roniger 1984: 164). I refer to its broad use in everyday life as common social patronage. This entails "a set of expectations and preferences ... cast in the idioms of patronage, assistance, consideration, and helpfulness. They apply to employment, tenancy, charity, feast giving and the conduct of daily social encounter" (Scott 1985: 185). In quite general terms, Scott talked of the

> Everyday forms of peasant resistance—the prosaic but constant struggle between the peasantry and those who seek to extract labor, food, taxes, rents and interest from them. [Such activities] have certain features in common. They require little or no coordination or planning; they make use of implicit understandings and informal networks; they often represent a form of individual self-help; they typically avoid any direct, symbolic confrontation with authority.
>
> (Ibid. 184–85; see also Elson 1997)

Randall and Theobald note that the large numbers of people who live routinely at "the margin of subsistence" are so often "driven below this margin by the vicissitudes of their existence: flood, drought, diseases, sickness, death, violence and intimidation by outsiders. ... " (Randall and Theobald 1985: 52; see also Roberts 2005, 2006). Common social patronage is essential to counter such crises, and it is crucial to note that emerging democracy does not, and cannot, provide in such circumstances. In such conditions, the rule of law is meaningless and useless. Where the family or local community (kin and extended kin) cannot or will not intervene to ameliorate severe conditions, and when the state and the market do not provide, vulnerable people often turn to a more powerful individual such as their landlord, or a village chief, or a wealthy businessperson. These relationships may compensate for the absence of important or essential human security provision. However, they do not do so in the regulated, transparent democratic sense at the grassroots level, where priorities are often decided by a non-elected "official" linked to a particular identity or other such grouping.

The poverty of the state itself and its attitude towards the people within its boundaries are major contributing factors to these relationships and the conditions that sustain them. As a consequence, in some parts of the world it is the family's moral obligation and responsibility to sustain their poor and vulnerable, not the state's. Concomitantly, the state would not expect demands for such provision (Pak et al. 2005; McCloud 1995: 40). Such expectations reflect pre-state social functionality and remind us that the state is a quite recent, artificial, and socially constructed intervention in human organization.

These two practices, of elite entrenchment sustained through complex and shifting networks of personal alliances sustained through state funds, and CSP as the central means of subsistence sustenance, are common throughout statebuilding scenarios. The following sections examine the extent to which they were transformed by statebuilding, by comparing conditions in Cambodia before and after statebuilding intervention.

Cambodia before statebuilding

Cambodia and Asia more broadly share a long history and recent practice of absolutism and elitism. No Khmer leader since independence, whether regal, communist, republican or former peasant, has accepted without resistance a challenge to the absolutism of their authority (Chandler 1993b). Absolutism, derived from cosmological traditions predating Angkorean domestic organization, has been a core element of authority and legitimacy in Cambodia. In short, entrenched elitism in Cambodia largely followed the general model outlined in the preceding literature. It was sustained by deep and wide personal networks of elite patronage and clientelism, remote and largely disconnected from broad civil society, which drew on localized forms of CSP for self-sustenance and which was legitimated by the absence of sufficient state-sponsored support to ameliorate the ravages of Pol Potism and international economic isolation in the period preceding United Nations statebuilding intervention. In turn this autonomous civil independence reinforced traditional antipathy and hostility towards the organs of state, creating a vacuum of mistrust and inertia between state and society originating in the past but predominant in the period immediately preceding the deployment of the UN Transitional Authority in Cambodia (UNTAC) in 1992.[2] Whilst this discussion has been fairly general in terms of CSP, I turn to the specific issue of local rule of law practices.

Rule of law as social organization

Despite French colonial intervention, the notion of the rule of law has had limited meaning in Cambodia. Instead, status, patrons, and hierarchies frequently have acted as systems of dispute management. But in addition to this, outside the capital, the notion of ownership of land—a central element of most societies' security concerns—is not managed through the rule of national laws. The very notion of "entitlement" in many pre-capitalist and democratic societies is difficult, because, in general, a combination of limited Royal Court/elite influence over the peripheries, limited pressure on land availability, nomadic lifestyles, and subsistence rather than profit production, meant that contest and conflict for and over land did not reach the more advanced stages visible in many advanced economies around the world (McCloud 1995: 40; Osborne 1997: 35–53; Tambiah 1977). Partly for these reasons, and partly because state apparatus intervened less in the pre-colonial era, land entitlement was often not routinized or regulated through formal law.

Cambodia's case is more complex: the Khmer Rouge period resulted in forced migration from cities to the countryside, and from one area of the countryside to others. This well-documented disarray and confusion was further aggravated when, after the Khmer Rouge were routed, people sought both to reunite their dislocated families and to return to original dwellings and communities that had, in many cases, been torn apart. Where they could not, they sometimes settled in previously occupied, recently vacated lots. The government allowed public use of state-owned land for free in some areas with few challenges.[3] If a piece of land had been more or less settled for a period of "X" years, the village chief recognized the "right" of the occupants to remain in situ. Challenges to that claim would normally go to the village chief or to the monks for arbitration.[4] Even in the pre-democratic period, the notion of taking a claim or challenge outside the village-community was frowned upon, not least because it became complex, less personal, and, in the case of legal arbitration and intervention, unaffordable for villages.

The State of Cambodia (SoC) introduced changes in 1989, but these were more concerned with house ownership, rather than land entitlement, in response to the Khmer Rouge's disastrous displacement policies.[5] Coupled to this, because foreign direct investment was all but non-existent, pressure on land resources was not complicated by powerful, wealthy foreign companies vying for cheap land. This ambiguity in resource and conflict management was also reflected in personal disputes. Vickery contends that "for the rural 80–90 percent of the Cambodian people, arbitrary justice, sudden violent death, [and] political oppression ... were common facts of life" long before the war and revolution of the 1970s and the Pol Pot time that followed (Vickery 1984: 17). Ovesen et al. also note the absence of local peaceful mediation in general. They specifically remark that "to the extent that con-flicts stem from contrary opinions, it follows that one opinion is perforce more correct than the other; and the one who holds the incorrect opinion will have lost face ... [Cambodians'] 'cultural heritage' offers no way out of a humiliating ... or ... difficult situation" (Ovesen et al. 1996: 42). Necessary arbitration often and normally came from sources such as the village chief, his designates, or the monks. It was specific (local) rather than general (national), and personal rather than impersonal; and although mediation failing at this level could be referred to provincial level courts, this was less common partly because of the costs and partly because of the prevailing mistrust of working outside personal networks. Such were conditions in Cambodia before UNTAC's arrival.

The Paris Peace Agreement and UNTAC

Cambodia is arguably the earliest modern example of postwar statebuilding, although it was not then recognized as such. Terminology had not yet been developed that adequately reflected the current concept of statebuilding. Terms such as "multi-dimensional" and "second generation operations" were used, but the conceptualization of statebuilding did not develop more clearly until later (Mackinlay et al. 1993). However, large-scale administrative "trusteeship," a wide and varied mandate with domestic and international consent and political authority, and national-level elections and constitution building are now all recognized elements of contemporary statebuilding.[6]

This chapter is specifically concerned with the adoption and impact of key elements of political democracy in government and civil society that were inserted into Khmer society through early statebuilding. It is not directly concerned with the other elements of the operation, nor is it concerned with "lessons learned" for "peacekeeping." These have already been addressed, with varying quality, in many other works (Brown and Timberman 1998; Brown and Zasloff 1998; Findlay 1995; Heder and Ledgerwood 1996; Heininger 1994; Roberts 2001). Rather, this chapter provides a long range assessment of deep and meaningful change pursuant to statebuilding interventions. It is concerned with the extent of the "take-up" of particular democratic mechanisms and institutions that were explicit and implicit in the ambitions of the Paris Peace Agreements (PPA) of 1991.[7] UNTAC remains politically, logistically, and militarily the largest and most comprehensive Chapter VI peace operation in the UN's history. But conceptually, it is significant for its role as a vessel for the communication and emplacement of ideals of democratic statebuilding contained in the PPA framing document, which itself was determined mainly by international actors and their priorities (Mysliwiecz 1988; Kiernan 1993; Haas 1991). In other words, the PPA was created as a means of resolving an international superpower conflict first, which would create conditions for the ending of the Cambodian civil war, after which democratic elections could create a power-sharing arrangement arrived at through multiparty elections.

In statebuilding terms, the UN acted as a vehicle to create a pluralist political framework to resolve elite conflict, with elections to legitimate elite authority. The outcome would allow Cambodia to be governed peacefully with broad consent. In short, citizens were to be protected as they are in the West from the potential and real abuse of the state through a separation of powers and by ensuring that the nation would have the right and ability to select and deselect governments through a fair and open process. These efforts had mixed results.

Impact on elitism

UNTAC's astonishing success in bringing off the May 1993 elections was one of its most important achievements. A staggering 89.56 percent of those eligible to vote turned out to the polls. In the 14 months after main deployment and before the polls opened, the Khmer Rouge had withdrawn its cooperation the month before the election; refugee repatriation had been hampered by land shortages; the landmines situation had been severely underestimated; and demobilization and disarmament of the main four groups had barely been touched. In addition, security was poor outside the capital. It is all the more remarkable, in these circumstances, that the defining aspect of the operation was barely marred by political violence, although there were numerous allegations of voting and vote-counting improprieties.

Despite these remarkable achievements, the application of democratic process had a limited impact beyond the polling week. That is, the event could be called democratic by dint of the presence of polling sites, invisible ink, electoral observers, electoral computers, and mass participation. However, traditional political practices resumed when the results were known and, according to some, had continued throughout the electoral process.[8] The impact of the election, beyond the physical manifestation of polling, was negligible to the domestic elite. When the election result relegated the entrenched elite to second place, they simply resisted it with political and military muscle in a number of well-documented ways (Roberts 2001: 104–50). No serious elite transformation occurred, despite the dominant CPP being defeated by the Royalist returnees known as FUNCINPEC. This disequilibrium, or asymmetrical power arrangement, persists at the time of this writing.

The technical winner and the loser "shared" power in a 50–50 ratio, with Prince Norodom Ranariddh of FUNCINPEC being named "First Prime Minister" and the runner-up, Hun Sen, being named "second Prime Minister." But few were in any doubt who held the reins of power, and a key characteristic of the next four years was the "Second" PM's refusal to hand over power to the "First" PM, a relationship which ultimately resulted in the two leaders going briefly to war in Phnom Penh in July 1997. This antipathetic relationship forged in the Paris Agreements for superpower interests and implemented through compulsory elections, destabilized the years between the UN elections and the "coup." In that period, the practice of government was subsumed to internal political struggles and security declined dramatically in the provinces and the metropolis. The power-sharing formula was anticipated by external interests as a method of including the main political competitors, but the original conflict over legitimacy had not been addressed. Accordingly, the war of the 1980s continued by political means through the 1990s in a political setting incapable of resolving irreconcilable differences regarding absolute authority. The atmosphere of danger was palpable in the months preceding the 1997 confrontation. Rather than democratic statebuilding puncturing the Khmer practices of elite domination and absolutism, the new practices of "democracy" were subsumed to elite dominion and traditional practice. The result was that democratization was a patina, more honored in nomenclature than in substantial political practice; a case of form before function. This outcome reflects the observations of various structuralists and critics of the notion that democracy can be readily transposed onto systems such as Cambodia's and the many others that share such structural similarities.[9]

This elite conflict was simultaneously replicated in administrative and government structures. The *Daily Telegraph* commented that enforced power-sharing appeared "to be designed to encourage power struggles."[10] To reflect the 50–50 divisions of prime-ministerial power, the apparatus of state was also divided up between the contenders, not for the public good but for personal empowerment and party gain. Ashley rightly notes that:

> Rather than depoliticizing a one-party state (controlled by the CPP), power-sharing ... created two separate and competing party states operating within every ministry, province, military command and police commissariat. Instead of working with their counterparts from the other party, officials from the prime ministers' level down conducted business with their party clients and colleagues. [This has] served to weaken the state by building and reinforcing parallel structures of personal and party authority, operating both within and outside the state. Hierarchical patron-client networks ... have expanded and subsumed the formal state structure.
>
> (In Brown and Timberman 1998: 55;
> see also Vickery 1993)

Such structures have persisted over time and in many cases have become more complex in various administrative sub-divisions from Phnom Penh throughout the principalities (Roberts 2001).[11] The branches of government that are normally separated in western democracies were and remain interconnected in Cambodia through personal loyalties, business connections, rent seeking, and other alliances. These structures' connectivity and persistence in Khmer politics were exacerbated more than diminished by the introduction of democratic pluralism and power-sharing. Pluralization multiplied the number of clients to be rewarded for political loyalty, resulting in state resources (normally used for rewards) being divvied up amongst four parties' members, rather than just the one of the single party days. Furthermore, newly-enfranchised civil servants and party members also expanded by a factor of at least two, aggravating yet further the demand for patronage and the theft of the state's resources to provide it. For instance, a FUNCINPEC official stated that "the price list quoted by FUNCINPEC officials for jobs in the administration ranges from 200 USD to 3,000 USD, depending on how good the position will be for extracting bribes."[12] In short, the networks that sustained one main individual in the single-party system expanded and were replicated to support the pluralized competition in ways far from democratic. Whilst these attitudes may seem unfamiliar to outsiders, they are seen as quite "normal" to most Cambodians.

It is more widely accepted now (although such a claim was far less popular in the 1990s) that optimal political security and stability had been achieved through a superficial charade of pluralism investing the dominant hegemon with ultimate control. Hun Sen "shared" power with an acquiescent "coalition" partner (Prince Ranariddh) who initially accepted the limits of what he could autonomously achieve. His party followers also recognized the limits this structure placed on their own aspirations. After Ranariddh, the "First" Prime Minister, left Cambodia in July 1997, he was replaced by the pragmatic Ung Huot. Ung Huot declared that the secret to a peaceful and stable coalition rested in submission. He remarked that he and Hun Sen

> Very rarely meet. We have little need to. We have stability and co-operation. He is a good leader and I intend to continue this coalition. [Unlike Ranariddh,] I work with Hun Sen and there is peace and stability. We will not think of political power in the same way as we have done. And the price [of violence] will not be so high to pay. Political competition will not be the same, because in a coalition, everyone can win.[13]

The nature of absolutism in the CPP elite may have been inspired originally by the dictates and structures of the socialist single party state, or by Hun Sen's search for legitimacy through his adaptation to "peasant-King," or by much older hierarchical and patronage structures. Either way, absolutism did not permit surrender to the consequences of the actual election outcome. Resistance from elite political culture impeded the challenge of democratic transition. This applies equally to the challenger. Ranariddh's objectives were less motivated by a desire for adherence to western democratic principles, and more by a desire to undermine the CPP's position in order to create for himself a degree of power which would not be characteristic of democratic values (Heder 1995).

This contest should not be confused with democracy: the struggle was never framed in the politics of accommodation and democratic power-sharing. Such "rules" were tolerated by the CPP and exploited by FUN-CINPEC. But at the heart of the struggle lay differing claims to legitimacy and no accepted means of resolving this dispute. The war of the 1980s, although clearly aggravated and prolonged by external interests, was about the right to rule, and, according to Hun Sen, Ranariddh's right was demolished by his association with the Khmer Rouge and his comfortable exile during the harsh years of internationally-imposed isolation. For Ranariddh, the issue was of entitlement and association with the Royal throne of his father and his aspirations for regal ascendancy, in contrast with Hun Sen's peasant status. Power-sharing, democracy, and coalition cooperation were not terms through which this dispute could ever be resolved. The system diluted Hun Sen's hold on sovereign power and forced him to work harder to sustain his dominion, whilst Ranariddh's challenge was too weak to succeed. The multiparty framework only allowed a competitive and insoluble dysfunctional power-sharing arrangement to fester. These conditions led to the "coup" of July 1997, in which the challenge to legitimate leadership was settled by force of arms.[14] This approach to state-building, rather than instilling a shift from confrontation to mutual power-sharing, instead created conditions that destabilized the country's fragile political order.

To manage these ongoing tensions, after the 1997 "coup," Khmers added an upper house to the lower chamber established in 1993. Superficially, this seems like a positive advance on democratic systems of conflict management and political organization. A closer examination reveals different motives. The creation of this un-elected chamber in Cambodia during October and November 1998 represented two positive achievements in the Cambodian context (Brown and TImberman 1998: 55). First, it allowed the second party, FUNCINPEC, to form part of a coalition on some of its own terms, rather than being a more subordinate partner in a unicameral system dominated by its CPP opposition. This then reduced internal government political confrontation.

Second, the creation of the Senate also permitted, to a greater degree than would have been possible under a single lower house (the National Assembly), the continuation of more traditional aspects of Cambodian politics, by creating extra positions that perform the task of redistributing wealth through patronage and clientelism. FUNCINPEC members are again claimed to have said that "the Senate was a cash bonanza ... One senator bought his seat for $100,000."[15] This in turn could be used to preserve political power bases supporting or sustaining either major political party. In effect, it resolved the issue of an increased number of politicians chasing the relatively constant number of beneficial and profitable political posts in the old system. The political transition from a single-party state to a competitive multi-party system still requires that the economic interests of the elite be upheld; but it also strains the capacity of a nation's resource base to fulfill such expectations. Increasing the number of government positions, which traditionally come with privileges and rewards for loyalty, accommodated the increased demand for such positions commensurate with an expanded polity. It also ameliorated the consequences of political defeat or marginalization, and the conflict quite frequently attendant upon this.

It should not be confused with a step forward for democracy. Its purpose was the political and financial servicing of the elite and its clients, rather than the furthering of open government on meritocratic terms for the benefit of the population as a whole. However, in the Cambodian context, the provision of the Senate was expedient and appropriate. Political stability, which in

Cambodia is constructed more in terms of elite absolutism rather than democratic ideals, is a necessary precursor to socio-economic development and the evolution of a political democracy. This is a contentious position, which speaks to a wider debate regarding the primacy of democracy and the rule of law before development, or vice versa.

Impact on common social patronage and social organization

In broad terms, institutional statebuilding's greatest influence in Cambodia has been on social participation in electoral practices. Rath claimed that as a result of democratization in Cambodia since 1993, democracy offered the poorest people "a chance to be heard: before democracy, most people were ignored."[16] Furthermore, he argued, "politicians now need support," a reference to the pre-1993, pre-democracy single-party system devoid of mechanisms to which politicians had to respond. Ying concurred, noting that while in the countryside, "people know nothing of [and are] very confused about democracy," they recognized "the existence of a plurality" meaning that "politicians now needed their vote" in national level elections.[17] The democratic electoral system has both enfranchised the people and allowed them to be heard, and this has caused politicians running for high office to respond to public demands, at least prior to polling day. Democracy is making people "optimistic" because it provides them with "full peace, travel where they want, exporting clothes, tourism ... The political system contributes to this growth."[18]

There are no doubts that democracy has indeed brought many benefits to some people in Cambodia since 1993; and the cities—primarily Phnom Penh—have developed massively in terms of public provision and private wealth. Ending the international proxy element to Cambodia's internal struggles paved the way both for the UN and democratization, as well as for huge foreign investment and development. The noisy, brightly-lit, 24-hour-electrified Phnom Penh of today is a far cry from the near-silent, blacked-out city of 1991. Major roads are paved and signposted and traffic discipline is tighter, although to some it may not appear so; restaurants are cleaner and moto-dup taxi drivers have better machines and charge a lot more. And in a further reflection of positively changing times, tuk-tuks have arrived as well.[19] The media in Phnom Penh has flourished, the polity has evolved into a bicameral system with an expensive Senate building in the capital, and anti-corruption is a recent "buzzword" amongst the elite.[20] But as government spokesperson Khieu Kanharith once noted, "Phnom Penh is not Cambodia."[21] Many others have recognized that the capital's economic bright lights may blind some observers to the grass-roots level, where a different set of people and their needs encounter the new democratic systems and find them sometimes at odds with the old ways.[22] The following section examines the introduction of the rule of law to land ownership—a key security issue—in the predominantly rural society.

Impact of rule of law on social organization

The inception of democracy into a post-conflict scenario normally entails the provision of the rule of law. When this happens is less the point than what happens as a result. The constitution of 1993 provided for the usual political developments associated with the rule of law, but land legislation took some years to get to. Whilst little of substance regarding land law altered in the wake of the UN's intervention, significant land legislation under the democratization rubric took effect ten years later in 2003. Land reform reflecting the rule of law and private land property rights enshrined in formal documentation is a new process for most Cambodians.

Before UNTAC began statebuilding in accordance with the PPA's blueprint, land claims, and disputes were more often than not worked through informally under the previous non-democratic system via a village chief's interpretation of events, a monk's mediation or a provincial court's binding and relatively inexpensive verdict. The introduction of the rule of law and democracy has accelerated significantly the rise of a legal system akin to those in the US and Europe. In Cambodia, this is unaffordable for the majority of poor people, most of who are without substantial state or private legal aid interventions. Urs and Hwang agreed that land ownership was not eased by legal land entitlement; indeed, it was made more complex and with more challenges which cost more money or draught animals because land disputes and allocation were no longer the responsibility of a village chief.[23]

But Urs also noted that democratic processes related to land contest and ownership have been "indigenized" by Khmers to suit their needs. This is less the case where external parties are involved such as large business interests (which also, like may other places, make land unaffordable for local people), but more the case when the contest is local. It is within the remit and "right" of an arbitrator like a village chief to operate outside of "due process" as long as this approach had not been rejected or excluded by the contestants. Thus, a dispute would be kept out of court to prevent lawyers or their representatives coming from Phnom Penh and taking the draught animals as fees.[24] Ying concurred: using the village chief and monks was inevitably cheaper than going to the provincial level (to challenge a village chief's verdict) or private lawyers. The former consumed much time, the latter much money (there are no "formal" courts below provincial level; they reflect French colonial provision). Further undermining the whole system is the routine practice of corruption, nepotism, and cronyism: "traditions" related to a political culture that sees government and state as intrusive vehicles of exploitation and theft that will take many decades to erode.[25]

Rath believes that the application of the democratic rule of law model to land issues has aggravated landlessness.[26] He is not alone. Andreasson notes that throughout recent history the general concept of "property rights necessarily generate violent, and oftentimes lethal, processes of dispossession ... [because advocates] ... fail to consider societal power asymmetries impeding the ability of property rights to protect the interest of the weak and the marginalized." Western-determined statebuilding, then, has the ability to "play a pivotal role in this process of systematic marginalization and immiseration of people beyond its 'civilizational' boundaries."[27] In other words, statebuilding's democratization program entails formalizing the informal in the crucial arena of land entitlement at a cost unaffordable to the poorest, who remain most vulnerable. One result of this process is the disempowerment and impoverishment of people vulnerable to powerful, rapacious economic interests—including both state and private interests.

Conclusion

Statebuilding is a hugely ambitious project; even with the best will in the world it can be inadvertently counterproductive and unnecessarily rigid. It is accused of being imperialist in intent or nature, or as "development patronage."[28] And it certainly mirrors the development debate about how "we" should develop "them," which in turn reflects a diluted notion of the racist superiority of colonialism and imperialism. But it seems to contain the seed of something useful if less uncritically and unrelentingly considered and offered.

The democratic approach has worked quite well for many Western states, but it ignores basic differences and makes assumptions about its eligibility and propriety for parts of the world that did not simultaneously produce democracies for very obvious, sound reasons of historical trajectories of political and social evolution. One size cannot fit all. It is no coincidence that many of the states "we" are to "rebuild" share historical trajectories and experiences in terms of economic and political development. Many also share practical contemporary forms of social and elite organization analogous with the Cambodian model; this, too, is no coincidence. For this reason, it is judicious to expect that future statebuilding operations will, where accepted, have a superficial impact on very resilient indigenous societies and polities. And where change breeches the extant social fabric, it will probably also introduce conflict without providing accessible conflict resolution systems for the poorest and most vulnerable to modern economic practices.

Cambodia shows us that "enforcing" democracy can create paradoxical tensions and dilemmas when merged uncritically with systems that have arisen in response to quite different historical experiences. On the one hand, we might seek to democratically develop the rule of law at all levels as an expectation. But on the other, Hyung-Gon Paul Yoo suggests that the "promotion of the rule of law and civil society at the cost of and toward the elimination of patron-client politics would be a grave mistake."[29] Thus, a core dilemma appears to be that universalizing democracy may create some of the very social conflicts it is intended to manage or allay.[30]

A second dilemma lies in how to define and describe, beyond the confines of Eurocentricity, the polities of the "new" states we "build." The rather rigid consideration of "Other" polities is most evident in the way we describe states undergoing attempted transformations. "They" are ascribed versions or degrees of democracy, denying indigenous capacity and identity. Such states have been represented in a variety of ways, as partial democracies, semi-democratic, and so on. Zakaria called them "illiberal democracies" (Zakaria 1997: 27). However, "illiberal democracies" might alternatively be described as "hybrid" polities, loosely defined as pre-democratic systems that absorb, through the process of statebuilding, indigenously acceptable elements of the democratization process whilst retaining indigenous mechanisms of socio-legal and political organization derived from their own historical experiences, which are considered more appropriate than those offered by externally-provided democratization programs. Accordingly, "our" aspirations and strategies in peacebuilding and statebuilding should alter to reflect this realization. This is not to say Western intervention is entirely inappropriate. But it should be carefully reconsidered in the light of findings such as these.

An approach that allows the debate to move away from this problem of symbiosis and "syncrecity"—the linguistic, theoretical, and practical problem of trying to conjoin democratic systems with other political systems—is to consider such hybrid polities within a range of different terms. "Hybridity" also begins to help define and identify what it is that is being created in various polities in response to statebuilding exercises and indigenous responses.[31] Zakaria's terminology—and that of many others—reveals this problem to be one of "demo-centricity," or political "Otherness"; like saying "non-white" when referring to people of color whose skin is black. Thus: the democentric labels "illiberal" and "partially democratic" define the "other"— the "non-democratic" in relation to the dominant model (democracy). Scholars to date have developed the term "consolidated democracy," but this is also democentric and relies on regimes meeting "all the procedural criteria of democracy and in which [everyone] ... adhere[s] to democratic rules of the game" (Gill 2000: 235). Instead, other terms and approaches are preferable. Different terms might include plural-indigenous systems or indigenocracies, when a single-party system or no functioning state–society relationship has existed before. These are political systems that combine indigenously approved elements of incoming democratic practice (with pluralism as the point of departure) with enduring indigenous systems.

Statebuilding, then, could be based on smaller-scale interventions, less ideologically compelled. It could offer expertise in elections as a means of trying to resolve elite legitimacy problems, where such support was actively condoned. But beyond technical contributions, it needs to accept, not tolerate, different practices that may not be of a democratic form. This approach contrasts with convention, and the dichotomy between the two is reflected to a degree in Sørensen's "Liberalism of Restraint" versus "Liberalism of Imposition" (Sørensen 2006: 267). In less complex terms, this chapter recommends a variation on the current approach to statebuilding that seeks to "kick-start" pluralism in states coming out of conflict (where host parties agree to this, and many do in order to move from war to peace) by supporting national and local level multi-party elections (assuming there is indigenous competition to rule and agreement for elections). However, it should not seek to impose rigidly all the elements of western democracies that have developed along their own specific historical trajectories.

It seems quite reasonable and clear to maintain that the clothes have to fit. People must be able to relate to the functioning of democracy and what it provides, but if their own conditions make this impossible, or if the democracy in question is superficial, the effort will be wasted. Political systems evolve in conjunction with many other factors, and this complex miasma of historical developments varies between states and regions. It is essential to match a statebuilding agenda to field conditions, even if they may be distasteful (or not understood). People are unlikely to adopt a system that is less appropriate and meaningful to them than one they are already using (Migdal 1974; Migdal et al. 1994). If it disadvantages them, there would be no reason to adapt to it, where political and human development are measured primarily in terms of short-term dynamics. Julius Nyerere reminds us that

> the machinery through which a government stays close to the people and the people close to their government will differ according to the history, the demographic distribution, the traditional culture (or cultures), and the prevailing international and economic environment in which it has to operate.
>
> (In Lumumba-Kasongo 2005: 11–12).[32]

Similarly, Inoguchi argues that "democracy must stem from, and serve, local conditions" (Inoguchi et al. 1998: 1), and McCloud confirms the importance of "restating political and social behavior in terms that are meaningful within the indigenous cultural context [to ensure] the growth and functioning of local institutions" (McCloud 1995: 15). It would be imperiously arrogant to assume that indigenous institutions have no value or meaning; they have arisen with no more or less indigenous legitimacy than the flawed and problematic Western systems (ibid.).

If global governance and "good government" regimes are to persist as extensions of liberal orthodoxy and political globalization, and it seems that they are set to do this for the foreseeable future, then they can be modified to be less politically dictatorial. Indeed, the emphasis seems to be on rebuilding states such that they conform to global governance norms, at the expense of indigenous viability. They may then also address indigenous efficacy rather than emphasizing compliance with international norms. Statebuilding does not have to try to replicate European practice, which would fail inevitably in any case. Indeed, it should not attempt this because doing so creates or aggravates dysfunctionalism and interrupts indigenous processes and may in fact prolong instability where it misunderstands or ignores indigenous roots of conflict. This was the case in Cambodia. One may reasonably argue that all that has developed to date could have been achieved without statebuilding and with only the removal of the international embargo (freeing up international development and investment). Hun Sen was in charge then as now; members of political parties continue to die at the hands of political counterparts; and the institutions of democracy are present but their processes and the values that underpin them are largely absent. The elections have achieved little in the short term that has not occurred in the long term, and what political accommodation amongst elites has occurred (such as the Senate) has come about as a result of Cambodian political entrepreneurship, not statebuilding design.

If we assume that political parties see power-sharing as more desirable than continuing fighting, then elections can, however, act as a jump-start mechanism. But statebuilding does not have to elaborate on this, and given the problems of transition and structures, it should only be encouraged with most careful thought and the inclusion of indigenous elites' interests. Such a minimalist approach I term "reef theory." To encourage the development of healthy sea life in dying waters, an alien object such as a decommissioned ship is introduced to the sea floor. This provides a basic "building block" around which native sea life coalesces and flourishes. The intervention is minimal and facilitates indigenous development without further intrusion, resulting in a life system appropriate to the context in which its interactions are important. The proposed model of statebuilding seeks the same approach and outcome: the insertion of a basic building block in the form of national and local elections, with the result that, devoid of further intervention, an indigenous system appropriate to social needs flourishes in relation to the historical experiences and contemporary conditions that have arisen. The likelihood of harm is diminished in relation to the size, scale, and nature of the intervention and what emerges relates to domestic needs and may then become self-sustaining in its own setting (Anderson 1999). It is vital not to push too hard with tools that have been designed elsewhere; the results in Cambodia were waste and superficiality, as well as later conflict and long running tension and hostility obstructing and limiting indigenous economic, social, and political development. This approach needs patience and above all trust and acceptance of "Other" ways of being. Without this, the contemporary imperious design runs the risk of creating similar problems that the last round of European meddling caused.

With these qualifications in mind, however, there are additional means by which the statebuilding process might make for a smoother transition, enhance elites' local legitimacy, and accord with wider global governance regimes, whilst simultaneously enhancing local basic human security. Working on the assumption that societies must accept anointed elites to prevent the outbreak of renewed fighting, for example, this social acceptance can be reinforced by additional social (as distinct from political) statebuilding prerogatives. To enhance local state–citizen stability and create a durable framework for further peaceful evolution towards prosperity, external funding, instituted through the organs of state, may be directed at creating basic human security and social consent. Channeling such funding into basic social security—for example in providing critical health care to vulnerable infants—would send an important message to the electorate regarding the role of the state. This might in turn legitimate the state and, in its turn, the statebuilding process. Furthermore, this would connect new states and their governments to extant global governance regimes, rendering more effective the idea of the liberal peace. In short, a retraction of political determinism could be accompanied by the enhancement of essential social provision designed to prevent unnecessary deaths and cement authority and legitimacy.

However, while this more indigenously empathetic approach is not merely culturally appropriate but pragmatically necessary, and while it may also answer the demands of some of democratization's critics, the post-9/11 environment may not sustain such an attitude. It may, indeed, be quite antithetical to demands that have emerged in response to difference and "Otherness." The "War on Terror" conducted mainly from the US demonstrates an oversimplification of complexity on the part of foreign policy makers, an attitude that does not bode well for the recommendations offered above. It also continues the pattern of uncompromising language (democentricity; terrorism) and a refusal to see legitimacy in difference. "Terrorists" attack because they "hate" US freedom and democracy; this shallow and regrettable perception denies the very possibility that someone— anyone—else may not see things the American way. Indeed, the uncompromising stance of non-negotiation with "terrorists"—the term is fraught with subjectivity—remains predominant, despite the successful outcome that has come from the British and US governments talking with the IRA in Northern Ireland. This is only one more example of dogma in peacebuilding.

In the light of this trend, it is difficult to see how a practice such as common social patronage—just one example of indigenous political activities— could be tolerated because it is "corrupt" in an era where difference is treated with disdain rather than respect and tolerance. But cultural diversity and indigenous political practices will persist in spite of the attack on New York's twin towers and the US reaction. On one hand, the self-legitimizing global project of democratization increasingly becomes less self-critical and less aware of indigenous evolutions which maintain a superficial veneer of democracy (periodic elections, etc.). But on the other hand, these indigenous evolutions continue, and they practice quite different systems right under our very noses. Perhaps, in some respects, we should be thankful for this.

Notes

1 Challenges have been mounted from various perspectives and include Burbach et al. 1997; Idris 1998; Thomson 2000, ch. 10; and Young 1994.

2 Interview with Kimchoeun Pak, Research Associate, Netra Eng, Research Associate, and Sedara Kim, Research Fellow, Cambodia Development Resource Institute, Phnom Penh, July 12, 2006; Ledgerwood 2002; Ovesen et al. 1996. 84; interview with Sophoan Ruth, US Agency for International Development (USAID), US Embassy, Phnom Penh, June 30, 2006; Roberts 2002; interview with Bendarom Ying, Senior Programme Officer, International Republican Institute (IRI), Phnom Penh, July 7, 2006.

3 Interview with Ying 2006. Currently, government, ministers, and private enterprise with attendant resettlement disputes are expropriating such land.

4 Interview with Henry Hwang, Attorney Advisor, Public Interest Legal Advocacy Project, Phnom Penh, July 6, 2006; interview with Rath 2006; interview with Tara Urs, Khmer Institute for Democracy, Phnom Penh, July 6, 2006.

5 Interview with Ruth 2006.

6 Junne and Verkoren 2005.

7 "The Agreement on a Comprehensive Political Settlement of the Cambodia Conflict, and Agreement concerning the Sovereignty, Independence, Territorial Integrity and Inviolability, Neutrality and National Unity of Cambodia, With a Declaration on the Rehabilitation and Reconstruction of Cambodia and the Final Act of the Paris Conference on Cambodia," Paris, October 23, 1991. London: HMSO Treaty Series, No. 111, 1991. (The Agreement).

8 Various Khmer actors, mainly from Hun Sen's Cambodian People's Party (CPP), were accused of harassment and intimidation. See Findlay 1995; Heder and Ledgerwood 1996; Roberts 1996; and Roberts 2001.

9 Bratton and van de Walle 1997; Bunce 2000; Carothers 2002; and Diamond et al. 1999.

10 *Daily Telegraph*, September 27, 1993.

11 Pak et al. 2005.

12 *The Nation*, February 12, 1994; interview with Lao Mong Hay, January 6, 1998, Phnom Penh. See also Brown and Timberman 1998: 54.

13 Interview with Ung Huot, January 8, 1998, Council of Ministers, Phnom Penh.

14 The notion of a coup has long been laid at Hun Sen's door. This is a facile explanation that ignores Ranariddh's role in illegal arms dealing and party-aggravated provocations. The war of words was followed by the inevitable armed clash.

15 *Phnom Penh Post*, vol. 8, no. 9, April 30–May 13, 1999: 3.

16 Interview with Ruth 2006.

17 Interview with Ying 2006.

18 Interview with Ruth 2006.

19 Tuk-tuks are cheap, covered passenger vehicles used routinely in Thailand to convey people more comfortably and safely than "moto-dups," which are small pillion-style motorbikes. Tuk-tuks are often more expensive, indicating economic changes at street level.

20 Kitschelt 2000.; Roberts 2001, 202.

21 *Cambodia Daily*, September 19, 1998: 6; and Pak et al. 2005; 6.

22 Lizée 2000; Rath 2006; and Roberts 2001.

23 Interview with Hwang 2006; interview with Urs 2006.

24 Interview with Hwang 2006; interview with Urs 2006. Draught animals are costly and essential items of rural cultivation and transport.

25 Bayart 1993; Rodney 1973; Tambiah 1977; interview with Ying 2006.

26 Interview with Ruth 2006; see also Andreasson 2006: 9.

27 Andreasson 2006: 3–4.

28 Tegegn 1997: 4. Chandler (2006) describes the system as "Empire in Denial," while Ignatieff (2003) calls it "Empire Lite."

29 Hyung-Gon 2003: 37.

30 Ibid.
31 The terms "hybrid" and "hybridity" arose in this work and were discussed with the research associates at the CDRI, who had also proposed, quite independent of this work, the same terms. Both parties appear to have arrived at these propositions independently, but both also seem to agree on their utility.
32 Whilst this argument parallels those of other contributors to the debate, it should also be borne in mind that Nyerere used these arguments to justify his particular form of single-party, semi-authoritarian rule in Tanzania. He is not without his critics.

Part IV
Institutional design

8 Postwar constitution building

Opportunities and challenges

Kirsti Samuels

In a postwar environment, the transition from a society governed by violence to one governed by rules and institutions, and most importantly, by a supreme law that is intended to bind all members of the society including the most powerful, is a fundamental challenge. The always present risk is that statebuilding will result in cosmetic change, and create weak, unstable or even criminal state structures (e.g., Haiti, Liberia or East Timor). As Amos Sawyer (Former President of Liberia) says, "The state we produced turned out to be a criminal state, legitimized by elections."[1] However, initiating changes in political and institutional culture, and building and rebuilding institutions, are some of the most difficult aspects of any societal transformation—requiring changes in behavior, expectations and norms. These sorts of societal changes require long-term strategies involving large segments of society and extensive education and sensitivity campaigns as well as dialogue and consensus building within society.

Constitution building[2] can provide a key opportunity to shape the institutional and governance framework, and opens the door to important societal dialogue. Until recently, constitutional theory had tended to focus on constitutions in stable political contexts or after victory rather than the role and relevance of constitutions during periods of political change and uncertainty. Some constitutions evolved incrementally through generations of practice and negotiations (such as the UK) and largely represent the status quo. Others were drafted after times of upheaval, revolution or renewal. These, such as the French or American constitutions, were aspirational documents aiming to put in place a new order, once one side had won. Constitutions made during or after civil conflict nowadays, however, generally emerge from a stalemate, or a compromise aiming to end the violence, when neither side is able to secure victory and the parties are pressured to consider negotiation and compromise.

A realist approach to constitutions in political theory views constitutions as a reflection of the balance of power at the time of drafting, and thus does not consider them to have any particular role as agents of change or in transitions (Lijphart 1984).[3] The idealist perspective recognizes their foundational role, considering them to provide a break with the old regime and to act as the foundation of the new political order (Ackerman 1992; Ackerman 1989). However, "transitional constitutionalism" best recognizes the multi-faced role such constitutions can play in postwar settings. As Ruti Tietel points out, constitutionalism is "inextricably enmeshed in transformative politics": it both codifies the prevailing consensus, and also transforms it (Tietel 1997: 2075). Constitutions in times of political change have frequently included deliberate transformative agendas. In Germany and Japan, for instance, the constitutions were conceived and designed to transform a particular tendency, particularly illiberal tendencies (such as the rejection of political tendency towards military nationalism in Japan, and the attempt to restrict the popular support for and expression of fascism in Germany). Thus, constitution building can be seen as a process and a forum for negotiation in environments of conflict, and can play a role in constructing the political transition, as well as shaping the institutions of state.

Until the last few years the literature on postwar constitutions was surprisingly sparse. The issue has mainly caught the attention of academics in the last few years following the constitution making processes in Afghanistan and Iraq (Bastian and Luckham 2003:1; Rubin 2004). However, some lessons can be drawn from the earlier literature focusing on transitions from authoritarian rule, post-colonial transitions, and post-Soviet transitions, as such transitions have many features in common with postwar states.[4] Moreover, recent case studies commissioned by the International Peace Academy[5] and International IDEA[6] provide a useful basis to begin drawing lessons from evolving experience in this field.

This chapter draws some tentative conclusions about the impact of process, substance choices, political dynamics, and the implementation challenges facing constitution building in the postwar context. It finds that participatory and inclusive constitution building, in particular, can provide a forum and process for the negotiation of divisive issues in postwar societies, and it can bring fragmented elements of a state together to think about a future vision of the state and to build a road map on how to get there. Constitution building can also provide basic democratic education to the population, and ensure that the governance structure has legitimacy and local ownership.

At the same time, it recognizes that such constitutional processes face difficult challenges. If a constitution building process is undertaken poorly, through an exclusionary, provocative or inflammatory process, by entrenching divisive governance choices in the constitution, or without commitment to implementing the document once adopted, constitution building can undermine the creation of sustainable peace and a legitimate state. It can result in disillusionment and bitterness in the population if the consultations are not genuine, if the resulting constitution is not representative, or if the constitution is never implemented. It can exacerbate conflict if unfair or divisive provisions are adopted that privilege certain groups over others. Moreover, the challenges are stark in the postwar context, as the process seeks often irreconcilable goals: to end or prevent a return to violence in the immediate situation, as well as to create a normative framework for the long-term peaceful governance of the state. In the postwar context, the competing interests and compromises faced are heightened, and can easily undermine a fragile democracy, or result in a return to conflict.

Some strategies can be implemented to minimize the inherent tensions in a postwar constitution building, including supporting longer time-frames between the negotiation of peace agreements and constitutions, and ensuring that a broad range of local actors can draw on knowledge of comparative experiences with respect to both process and governance options. The international community should also commit sufficient aid to supporting inclusive and participatory processes with long enough time-frames to allow proper dialogue and consensus building, as well as to support follow-through strategies to implement the constitution. In addition, the international community, and particularly the regional actors, should take a more proactive approach to requiring that any new government act in accordance with its constitutional obligations. One of the benchmarks in the international community's relationship with a postwar transitional government could be the expectation that the government will abide by the constitution negotiated as part of the transition.

The impact of process

It is increasingly recognized that how constitutions are made, particularly following civil conflict or authoritarian rule, impacts on the resulting state and its transition to democracy. The primary issues that arise are who will be involved in negotiating the constitution, and how the constitution will be drafted and adopted. Increasingly, these issues form the content of an initial agreement between warring parties, often in a peace agreement or interim constitution. The tension between the aim of achieving the cessation of conflict and creating a legitimate democratic state is particularly acute here, as pragmatic considerations and political limitations may dramatically reduce the options available in that negotiation.

In recent years, the international community has begun to recognize that constitution-making involves more than merely drafting a constitution. At one time, it was acceptable to have a few lawyers in a room draft a constitution for a country. It is now at least recognized that drafting a legitimate constitution that reflects the hopes and fears of the population involves a process of consultation and participation, and hence that constitution-making requires a process. There have been a range of different approaches to making constitutions; however, the trend is towards recognition of the importance of inclusive and participatory processes in constitution-making. This reflects a perception that the people must be included in the search for solutions to conflict rather than it being a division of the spoils between factions, and that consultation and participation increases the perceived legitimacy of the constitution.

Elite roundtables

Until the last few decades, constitutions were negotiated and drafted by elites, representing primarily "elite bargains." Elite negotiated transitions in the form of roundtables have formed the basis of the transition from civil conflict in Spain and a number of the countries in Latin America. The post-Soviet transitions in Eastern Europe were also based on elite roundtable negotiations (some of which took place after conflict and others to avoid conflict). These agreements varied both in the extent to which they incorporated compromises or restrictions on the issues that were open to decision by democratic processes after the transition, and the extent of inclusiveness and representativeness of the process.

The research into pacted[7] democratic transitions in Latin American and Southern Europe (which were entered into either to facilitate a postwar transition or to prevent conflict following the fall of an authoritarian government)[8] can provide interesting insights into the impact of elite processes, which can inform our understanding of the value of broader inclusion. Such pacts represent the extreme end of the spectrum of elite negotiated transitions, involving a small number of elite participants, and seeking to impose long-term power divisions, restrict the policy agenda, and limit government accountability to the broader population.[9] The Latin American experience of such pacts has turned out to be largely negative in the longer term. While the pacted democracies in Venezuela, Colombia, and Brazil did survive the authoritarianism in the 1960s and 1970s, they did so at "serious costs in terms of social and economic equity," and they empowered "already powerful actors for whom promoting democracy may not be a priority."[10]

The experience in Spain, however, was largely positive; the pacts relied upon in that postwar post-authoritarian transition resulted in a consolidated stable democracy (Encarnación 2005: 182). Omar Encarnacio Encarnación maintains that the key difference between the two outcomes was who participated in the bargaining cartel (ibid.: 182). In Venezuela, Colombia, and Brazil, the pact-making was secretive with a few powerful actors including the outgoing regime, whereas in Spain the bargaining group included practically the whole ideological spectrum. Spain adopted many different forms of pacts: a secret pact between Franco's democratic opposition that set up the democratic transition based on a series of compromises, followed after the elections of 1977 by policy-making pacts such as the Moncloa pact which addressed economic reform, salary regulation, and extensive redistributive policies (ibid.: 187–92). Although the agreements in Spain instituted policy limitations, it seems that they did so in a way that was representative of the major interests in society, which supports the proposition that inclusion and representativeness is a key factor for success.

National conferences

An alternative to the roundtable elite negotiated transitions has been the more inclusive (and often more participatory) national conferences held in

Francophone Africa since 1989. These national conferences were primarily used to achieve political liberalization and transition from authoritarian regimes.[11] The early experience with the national conferences in Africa was positive. In Benin, Congo and Niger they achieved political liberation as well as managing a gradual regime transition, and they doubled as constitution-making conferences. In later cases, the conventions were not able to institute regime change against the wishes of those in power, however, and remained controlled by the authoritarian regimes.[12] Nonetheless, on the whole, those processes allowed a broad and inclusive participation (involving representatives from key political and civic groups), and are thought to have helped create some consensus in society over the way forward by encouraging national debate and developing a plan for the county's political future.

Participatory constitution-making processes

A new trend of participatory constitution-making processes has emerged in the last few decades (e.g., Uganda, Colombia, Guatemala, South Africa, and Rwanda). These processes developed in countries undertaking constitution-making largely without international involvement, and in highly divided or postwar societies. They have since been used as inspiration in other circumstances (e.g., Kenya, Afghanistan). Such processes have involved extensive education programs as well as consultation and discussion. They have encouraged national debate and allowed representatives from key political and civic groups to discuss and develop a plan for the counties' political future, with a focus on attempting to create a basic consensus.

In Uganda, for instance, the constitution was developed through a highly participatory process which took nine years to complete. A constitutional commission was appointed and charged with the duty of gathering information from the people regarding the form of governance they preferred, analyzing the views gathered and preparing a draft constitution. An extensive civic education campaign, involving 86 district seminars and educational forums in all 813 sub-counties, was followed by a process of collecting oral and written testimony. The commission analyzed 25,547 written memoranda and ultimately produced a draft constitution. It was initially anticipated that the draft would be taken before the National Resistance Council and the National Resistance Army (an unelected body) for confirmation. However, ultimately the commission recommended that it be adopted by a representative elected Constituent Assembly of 284 delegates, in line with the opinions of the majority of the population they had been consulting.

This process was particularly successful as a mechanism of inclusion after many years of conflict. It included all levels of the population which was important not least because one of the reasons for the conflict had been the over-centralization of power and undemocratic practices. It also created a break with the old regime's unilateral and imposed constitution. The new constitution was adopted at referendum with a very high positive vote. It continued to have strong support eight years later. A study of the attitude of Ugandans showed that 80 percent believe that their constitution "expresses the values and aspirations of the Ugandan people" and 74 percent believe that "People should abide by what was written in the constitution whether they agree with what was written or not" (Moehler 2006).

South Africa is considered an example of best practice in participatory constitution-making. Agreement on the process was part of the peace negotiations between 1991 and 1994. The interim constitution (1993) set out 34 principles on which the constitution would be based. The constitution was to be drafted by an elected Constituent Assembly (400 members elected by proportional representation) that would solicit the views of the people. The draft was then to be considered by the Constitutional Court to ensure that it was consistent with the 34 principles. The Constituent Assembly rolled out an extensive public information campaign. The educational effort included a media and advertising campaign using newspapers, radio and television, billboards, and the sides of buses; an assembly newspaper with a circulation of 160,000; cartoons; a Web site; and public meetings—together these efforts reached an estimated 73 percent of the population. From 1994 through 1996, the Constitutional Assembly received two million submissions from individuals, advocacy groups, professional associations, and other interests. The submissions were collated into reports, noting the convergence of ideas and agreements as well as contentious issues and ideas for addressing them.

One of the remarkable features of this process was the level of consensus achieved, in the highly charged environment of a country that many feared would dissolve into civil war. At the time the constitution-making process was being undertaken, clashes and political violence were ongoing, leading to many deaths, and there was a large disparity in the proportion of seats held by the parties—with the ANC at almost 64 percent, the NP a little over 20 percent, the IFP almost 10 percent, and the remaining four parties comprising the remaining 6 percent of the seats. Nonetheless, the Constitutional Assembly was able to crystallize a largely (although not entirely) consensual approach. This success was due both to the flexibility of the major players who were committed to seeking "win-win" agreements and to the design of the negotiating structures that generated workable proposals.

The value of process

A review of the literature and a range of case studies[13] suggest that in the best-case scenario, a participatory or representative constitution-building process can provide a forum for the negotiation of solutions to the divisive or contested issues that led to violence, it can play a reconciliation and healing role through societal dialogue, and it can support sustainable peace by forging a consensus vision of the future of the state. It can also provide basic democratic education to the population, and ensure that the governance structure has legitimacy and reflects the hopes and aspirations of the people.

Impact of process on perceived legitimacy

Extensive participation and consultation certainly brought about public support for the Rwanda constitution, as it did in South Africa and Uganda. In contrast, the people strongly rejected the constitutions in Nigeria and Bahrain which were not at all participatory—they were imposed rather than made by the people. As Hart points out, "Where conflict is essentially over governance by, and respect for, a diversity of people and peoples, those people and peoples must be heard in the process of constitution making" (Hart 2001: 160). Power is not "solely an inter-elite matter, and limited to purely geo-ethnic and institutional aspects;" for sustainable peace the governance framework will have to be more inclusive and "build up broader stakes of participation in the peace process" (Adekanye 1998: 29, 32–33).

Despite the potential benefits, there are number of potential risks that require careful management when dealing with participation and consultation. The constitution-making process itself may be divisive rather than unifying, especially if it is undertaken in an inflammatory or provocative way. For instance, the bill of rights constitutional process in Canada acted as a process of escalation rather than conflict resolution (Hart 2001: 161). Moreover, a national dialogue too soon after the end of the war may undermine the fragile peace by entrenching divisions and hostility before any of the peace dividends can help stabilize the situation.

The inclusion of certain armed factions, leaders who have committed human-rights abuses, or hardened spoilers can also undermine the legitimacy or effectiveness of an interim agreement. This is one of the difficult compromises however. As Lakhdar Brahimi, one of the UN's most experienced negotiators, maintains, irrespective of questions of broader representativeness and fairness, agreements to end conflicts must constitute a realistic workable compromise between the major powerful actors.[14] "If you have a shaky agreement then your difficulty is to prevent the fighting from recurring, which makes your statebuilding work much more difficult."[15]

Impact of process on constitutional provisions

The cases of Kenya, Guatemala, and Colombia emphasize that a participatory process can have a substantial impact on the content of the document produced. The broad participatory process in Kenya resulted in the inclusion of provisions addressing issues of social and economic justice, as well as issues of corruption and the failure of political elites to act responsibly. In Colombia and Guatemala the participatory and inclusive process resulted in strongly reforming constitutions which expressly provided rights to groups that had not up to then gained political protection or recognition.

In contrast, constitutions written and imposed by one faction or one dominant interest have tended to be biased towards that interest or to undermine some aspect of democracy. For instance, the 1980 Pinochet constitution in

Chile sought to entrench military control and exclude the left from political power. It resulted in years of oppressive dictatorship. The 1990 Fiji constitution explicitly sought to entrench military and indigenous Fijian power and has been the source of increasing tensions. Similarly, Nigeria and Bahrain's current constitutions were documents imposed by authoritarian bodies and include substantially undemocratic provisions.

In this respect as well, a difficult tension arises since the use of more participatory and inclusive processes tends to broaden the constitutional agenda and is more likely to result in constitutions that threaten established power structures. Predictably, such structures often react by undermining the constitutions, amending them, preventing their adoption, or preventing their enforcement. This undermines constitution-making's key peacebuilding benefit—creation of a social contract—and can result in disappointment and disillusionment in the political process, as seen for instance in the aftermath of the processes in Colombia and Guatemala. As Neil Kritz points out:

> While powerful elite factions will play a major role in any postwar constitution making process, it is essential to reduce their monopolization of that process, and to avoid a final constitution that simply reflects division of the spoils between such factions. If the constitution and the process of its adoption are to play a role in transforming society, then constraints on such monopoly of power need to be built into the process.
>
> (Kritz 2003: 3)

Thus, careful balancing of elite interests with broader inclusion and participation will be a key challenge in the design of a constitution-building process.

The impact of governance choices

The governance choices and institutions adopted in a constitution will evidently play an important role in shaping the future of the state. A new constitution seeks both to create new democratic institutions and to assure their protection in the longer term. However, unless these are carefully designed and implemented, democratic institutions can foment conflict in sharply divided societies (Stewart and O'Sullivan 1998; Bastien and Luckham 2003: 1; Lake and Rothchild 1998: 345). Although an appropriate governance framework may not always result in stable states, a poor governance framework will undermine the sustainability of the peace. It can exacerbate fault lines in society, entrench conflict-generating electoral or governance models, or provide a basis for contest of the government. In Haiti, for instance, the 1987 Constitution continues to undermine sustainable peace. The majoritarian structure has encouraged tyranny of the majority and reinforced Haiti's winner-takes-all political culture. Uncertainty in the constitutional provisions regarding elections has also provided a flash point for violence following the 2000 elections, the results of which were contested by the opposition. Moreover, the dissolution of the army was never constitutionally ratified and contributes to the ongoing instability and to former army members' sense of frustrated entitlement.

As Vivienne Hart emphasizes, in postwar situations, constitutions can be used to "recognize, include, give voice to, equalize, or advantage, and to exclude, silence, or stigmatize people and peoples" (Hart 2001: 156). Many constitutional choices are made with little comparative understanding of how such provisions have played out in other developing contexts, or are adopted because they seem to provide what is required to secure the peace in the short term, without proper consideration of what is required for longer-term peace and stability.

Power-sharing and long-term instability

One of the primary governance choices in postwar environments is how to share power between the various factions, ethnic or confessional groups. The search for institutional structures that encourage moderate behavior is a crucial aspect of devising governance structures in postwar environments and it is widely viewed as a key to preventing the return to conflict. The pure majoritarian democratic model is generally considered unsuited to conflict-prone and highly-divided societies (Lijphart 1999: 33). As the Carnegie Commission on Preventing Deadly Conflict points out:

> In societies with deep ethnic divisions and little experience with demo-cratic government and the rule of law, strict majoritarian democracy can be self-defeating. Where ethnic identities are strong and national identity weak, populations may vote largely on ethnic lines. Domination by one ethnic group can lead to a tyranny of the majority.
>
> (Carnegie Commission on Preventing Deadly Conflict 1997: 100)

Incentives in the form of power-sharing structures and electoral rules have been promoted to shape democracy and to address divisions and encourage moderation. The focus of the power-sharing debate has been on the relative desirability of variations of two versions of power-sharing: consociational and integrative governance models. Consociationalism involves power-sharing between cooperative but autonomous groups,[16] whereas integrative govern-ance aims to transcend group differences by encouraging groups to cooperate around common political goals.[17] However, in many ways this terminological and technical distinction is not very helpful, as in reality most power-sharing models integrate elements of both.

There is a relatively widely-held view that in the short term, at least, power-sharing devices are useful in bringing violence to an end. In postwar settings, a power-sharing model is often the only option that will bring the parties to the table and stop the violence—in South Africa, for instance, interim power-sharing structures played an essential role in peace negotiations.

Nicholas Sambanis has pointed out, however, that power-sharing approaches will not succeed where the assumption that the security dilemma of various ethnic groups underlies the conflict is incorrect and the conflict is due to "the 'predatory' goals of their leaders" (Sambanis 2000: 441). Similarly, Spears argues that the consociational view that inclusion will lead to an end to violence does "not probe deeply enough into how much inclusion and what kind of inclusion will end the violence" (Spears 2002: 123).[18]

In any event, the short-term usefulness and impact of power-sharing devices should be distinguished from their medium- to long-term impact. Despite their evident value in terminating conflicts, power-sharing devices appear to have less positive impacts in the longer term. One important criticism of power-sharing structures that they rely on formalized divisions of power along identity or ethnic lines, and that they may have the perverse effect of entrenching the ethnic and divisive positions that have fueled the conflict (Rothchild 2002: 118). Their rigidity prevents the fostering of reconciliation and a broader national identity. In Sisk's view, power-sharing leads to stalemates and "cold peace" "in which the parties do not continue to employ violence but neither have they embarked on a serious process of reconciliation" (Sisk 2003: 140).[19]

The case studies commissioned for the International Peace Academy largely support the theory that such agreements, which are often fundamental to ending the violence, may have destabilizing impacts in the medium term, and may even contribute to entrenching and reinforcing divisions and perceptions of rivalry and threat in the society. In addition, these agreements open the way for a multitude of ongoing disagreements over how the power sharing is interpreted and carried out. Moderate leaders that have agreed to participate in power-sharing arrangements are too often undermined by more extreme factions that decry compromises or conciliatory actions as "selling out" and governments have been repeatedly immobilized by the clauses intended to ensure moderation and consensus. In Lebanon, for instance, the government was often paralyzed by the decision-making system. In Fiji, it resulted in ongoing court battles and growing tension, occasional violence between the ethnic Fijian and Indo-Fijian communities, and ultimately another coup.

Thus, although governments of national unity and power-sharing models have successfully maintained peaceful relations in highly-divided societies in Europe,[20] in countries coming out of conflict in less developed environments such models have been less successful so far. The situation in Northern Ireland is currently a hopeful example of potential complex power sharing being implemented, but it is in a relatively developed country and it remains to be seen how it will evolve over the years.

One issue of particular concern is the apparent trend of radicalization of politics following power-sharing agreements. While all societies investigated in the cases already had long-standing deep divisions, these appeared to become even more entrenched during the power-sharing phase. More moderate leaders that had agreed to participate in power-sharing agreements were easily undermined by more extreme members of the party that pointed to compromises or conciliatory actions as "selling out."

For instance, in Fiji and Bosnia there has been a distinct increase in support for more extreme parties over more moderate parties since the adoption of power-sharing structures. In Bosnia, the only significant party with a cross national ideology is the Social Democratic Party, but even it has largely mono-ethnic support among Bosnien Muslims. In Fiji, even though power sharing is not formally ethnically-based, elections have favored more radical nationalist and ethnically based parties. No new cross-ethnic parties have been created since implementation of the Fijian constitution, and those that previously existed have split into their constituent parts. Even in Lebanon, which has relied on power sharing along confessional lines for close to a hundred years, the Taif agreement was only partially implemented and divisions remain as strong as ever.

Thus, paradoxically, although such agreements may be the only route to agreement during the peace-negotiation stage, in the longer term they are susceptible to deadlock and collapse, and risk both entrenching and radicalizing underlying divisions.

Electoral design and unpredictable outcomes

The timing and design of elections have also raised difficult issues in the postwar context, from entrenching the warring parties and the conflict-producing divisions, to favoring radical parties over more moderate ones through the unpredictable outcome of electoral design. There is increasing international pressure on states emerging from conflict to adopt participatory democratic governance structures.[21] It is thought that the adoption of democracy can assist in the resolution of the struggle for power by providing an internationally accepted standard of who is entitled to govern based on an open and fair competition for power through a popular vote. It is also generally assumed that democratic governance decreases the likelihood of a return to civil conflict (this is known as the "domestic democratic peace" theory[22] to differentiate it from the democratic peace theory that concerns international wars).

This theory relies on the assumption that conflict-mediating structures and increased opportunities for participation will encourage peaceful resolution of conflicts (Bastian and Luckham 2003: 15).[23] Despite the fact that transitions between regimes (in any direction) have been shown to be highly destabilizing and conflict prone,[24] democracy is considered the best governance structure for long-term conflict cessation. The evidence suggests that in established democracies, ethnopolitical groups are more likely to protest than rebel, minimizing internal violence (Gurr 2000: 162),[25] and that autocracies are less stable (that is, more prone to regime change) than democracies (Hegre et al. 2001: 42).[26] As Hegre and Ellingsen argue: "The most reliable path to stable domestic peace in the long run is to democratize as much as possible" (Hegre et al. 2001: 44).

However, there are no simple and universal relationships between democracy, peace and development. Democratic institutions are not enough to prevent conflict and can foment it in sharply divided societies (Paris 2004). In some instances, redesigning democratic institutions to reduce conflict may actually accentuate it (Stewart and O'Sullivan 1998). Democratization "can also become the tool of powerful economic interests, reinforce societal inequalities, penalize minorities, awaken dormant conflicts, and fail in practice to broaden popular participation in government" (Bastian and Luckham 2003: 1).[27] Some have concluded that it is inclusive government, rather than democratic government, that best prevents conflict (Stewart and O'Sullivan 1998).

Elections are one of the key elements of democratic governance, although it is increasingly recognized that rule of law is another fundamental component and that elections on their own are far from sufficient. Nonetheless, in the postwar context, as the chapter by Timothy Sisk in this volume illustrates, elections themselves are often highly divisive and can easily undermine the chance of building a sustainable democracy (Reilly 2003: 176). The question of elections is thus beset by dilemmas. It is recognized that early elections increase division and can entrench the warring parties as the dominant political players. However, late elections can entrench the compromise interim solution and may fail to achieve any opening up of political space to broader participation.

There have been substantial attempts to design electoral models that "promote moderate voices over extremist ones, and to facilitate intra-group as well as inter-group competition" (ibid.: 176, 179.) The aim is to use the electoral process to transform the structure of competition for political power. A major tension arises, however, between whether to accept that elections will amount to, at best, a snapshot census on ethnicity, or whether it is worth attempting to reconfigure political divisions and encourage moderation through electoral models.

Incentives and electoral rules have long been used to shape democracy. Kleisthenes, credited with having created democracy in the 6th century BC, required that his elected Tribes (which took turns governing) be structured to include members from the three main geographic divisions in Ancient Greece: the city, the coast, and the plain. The structure worked against regional cleavage and encouraged moderate governance (Herodotus 1910).

The literature has also debated the merits of different electoral models in postwar contexts. Detailed and increasingly complex electoral provisions are becoming more common in postwar constitutions. However, using electoral design in an attempt to engineer certain outcomes, such as moderation or intra-ethnic compromise, is not a straightforward proposition, and may in practice result in the opposite outcome. One of the major debates has focused on which electoral models are best able to ensure the required moderation and representativeness. A key area of contention between proportional (PR) and preferential models[28] is over the extent to which they ensure moderation. The PR model, as Horowitz points out, places the focus on post-electoral coalitions, which in his view "no doubt entail compromise over the division of cabinet portfolios, but typically not compromise over divisive inter-ethnic issues." It does not require candidate parties and coalitions to attract votes across group lines (Horowitz 2002: 20, 22).

There is no doubt that PR models in postwar countries often act as a census on ethnicity or confessional grouping, although where these models are used without religious or ethnic quotas, they may at least allow for the society to evolve and to focus on new issues such as education or health. One interesting example that Stewart and O'Sullivan considered was the impact of constitutional engineering in Sri Lanka in the 1970s and 1980s. They argued that the adoption of the PR system created incentives for the creation of a Muslim regional party which gathered support through anti-Tamil rhetoric:

> The Sri Lankan experience indicates that even when institutional structuring does in fact produce the intended outcomes supposedly conducive to ethnic accommodation, these multi-ethnic coalitions of commitment— the supposed guarantees of ethnic accommodation—may not only be insufficient to promote peace, but can even be recipes for further conflict.
> (Stewart and O'Sullivan 1998: 23–26)

Preferential systems have also been promoted in civil conflict states. However, these should be approached with caution. A striking finding to emerge from the IPA case studies was that the results of preferential voting models— such as Alternative Vote (AV) or Single Transferable Vote (STV)—were hard to anticipate, and in some cases the system perversely funneled votes to the more radical parties, undermining accommodation and moderation. The AV model can also play out in unexpected ways if moderate parties are eliminated in early rounds, redistributing preferences towards the more extreme parties. As Fraenkel points out in relation to Fiji, "the AV system could serve, not as a vehicle for inter-ethnic compromise, but as a means of cohering a politically fragmented ethnic group around an extremist position" (Fraenkel 2001: 15). In Fiji, it was initially hoped the AV system would lead to the development of multi-racial parties or foster deals among moderate parties. However, even the small proportion of open AV seats seemed not to deliver moderate outcomes. In the 1999 elections, a more radical party won a majority of seats although it only had 33 percent of first choice support. In the 2001 elections, the electoral system funneled votes towards more radical parties, while parties that had explicitly endorsed the idea of cross ethnic cooperation during the constitution making process fared very poorly.

Similarly, Northern Ireland adopted multi-member district STV and the model had an unpredictable outcome in comparison with typical list proportional representation. Republika Srpska in Bosnia experimented with AV for the 2000 presidential elections. This system resulted in a decisive victory for the hard-line Serb candidate, as Bosnian Muslims refused to cross ethnic boundaries and instead gave their second preference to Bosniac parties that had no hope of winning, rather than supporting moderate Serb parties. Moreover, the AV model proved to be a get-out-the-vote strategy for the hard-line Serb parties, who claimed that the electoral changes were designed to undermine them. This campaign tactic seemingly resulted in increased voter support as Serb voters realized the aim of the electoral changes and sought to defeat them.

In the cases considered, neither PR nor preferential systems were shown to encourage moderation. PR often acted as a census on the ethnic or confessional divide and entrenched it, and preferential systems acted unpredictability and sometimes even funneled more votes towards the more extreme parties than they would have obtained under PR. In the postwar statebuilding context, the challenge may therefore be to select an electoral system that will have the least likelihood of encouraging extremism and entrenching division, and care must be taken in considering how the electoral systems will play out in the particular circumstances of a given country.

The impact of political dynamics

When considering the impact of constitution building, it is of key importance to recognize that despite the value of adopting a good process and choosing appropriate governance options, much of the overall impact of the constitutional process and the constitutional design will be determined by political dynamics, the individuals involved, and the country's historical and geopolitical context. This reflects the inherently political nature of constitution building, and the recognition that constitutional reform involves a raw competition for power between the various stakeholders in the state. Some of these dynamics can be illustrated through the cases of South Africa, Northern Ireland, and Lebanon.

South Africa

The case of South Africa provides an example of how the political and military context, the personalities of individuals, strategic compromises, and careful encouragement and pressure from the international community, can play an important role in shaping the resulting constitution. Early negotiations on the constitutional processes focused on the need for the ANC resistance movement and armed groups in KwaZulu-Natal to cease hostilities.[29] The National Peace Accord signed in September 1991 sought to put in place five strategies to mitigate conflict: an agreement on general principles of democracy; codes of conduct for political parties and organizations; an agreement of general principles for the armed forces; codes of conduct for the police in particular; and measures to facilitate socio-economic reconstruction and development. Nonetheless, as Paul Graham points out, "between 15 and 20 thousand people did die in village massacres, attacks on individuals, attacks on commuter systems, and in direct battle between various self-defence units of young people and the police." An uprising of white militia was defused following a pitched battle in the Bophutatswana homeland capital, election bombs exploded in Johannesburg, and there were serious threats of post-election uprisings in KwaZulu-Natal.[30]

The fears of much of the minority white population of being swamped, discriminated against, or being legislated into an inferior position, were key drivers in shaping the process and governance choices. Partly, this situation was managed through a foundation of 34 constitutional principles agreed by negotiation which could not be modified by the elected constituent assembly and would be certified by the newly formed constitutional court. These principles were used in some ways to defer further deliberation of deal breaking issues. One of the principles, in particular, was a last-minute deal with the right wing, which provided that some form of self-determination would be explored for groups (predominantly the white constituency) if "there is substantial proven support within the community concerned for such a form of self-determination."[31] This ultimately has not materialized but the option to try was fundamental to breaking deadlock and moving forward.

However, as negotiations proceeded, the difficulties continued. Ultimately, a compromise solution including a series of sunset clauses (clauses with fixed expiration periods) was agreed to. These provided for national unity in the executive at all levels and for continuity of decision making and the civil service, which ensured that the white minority retained some entrenched power until such provisions lapsed. As Paul Graham points out:

> The sunset clause arrangement demonstrated a fine willingness to understand the fears of the white majority and a hard headed commitment to the demands of the black majority. This pragmatism of the majority, and its ability to defer its gratification based on a belief that a non-racial and democratic future would prove to be morally unassailable and economically and culturally attractive even to those who were presently most resistant to change has largely proved to be a correct approach.[32]

He also emphasizes that perhaps this solution could only have been heard "when uttered by someone with the political, military and personal credentials of a Joe Slovo."[33] In essence, those compromises prevented a slide into further conflict and ensured that the National Party remained in a government of national unity, at least until two years after the election when it opted to leave the government.

Another fundamental compromise was the amnesty for past acts, which has shaped the constitution and the future of South Africa. It was inserted in the closing days of the negotiation on the insistence of the South African armed forces. The armed forces made it known that unless this element was inserted they would turn to violence. Hence, a complete amnesty was provided, "in respect of acts, omissions and offences associated with political objectives and committed in the course of the conflicts of the past."[34] At the same time, negotiations with the Inkatha Freedom Party (IFP) were ongoing, in an attempt to bring that party into the process and to stop the incipient civil war. Pressure and coaxing by local church-based and international actors ultimately persuaded the Inkatha Freedom Party to participate in the elections four days before they were held. This resulted in the IFP being included in the government of national unity, and ultimately brought the violence to an end. The depth of Mandela's commitment to a compromise approach was seen in his appointing the leader of the IFP as acting president during his absences.

Northern Ireland

The case of Northern Ireland highlights the relevance of timing, the changing attitude of key leaders, and the role of key international players. Coming after numerous broken agreements, the Good Friday, or Belfast, Agreement was first negotiated at a time when the Republican movement was seeking an alternative to the Provisional IRA's "long war." The UK and Irish governments sought to capture the possibility by making a joint declaration in December 1993, which provided that if the Provisional IRA ended its campaign of violence, Sinn Fein would be included in negotiations on a new political future for Northern Ireland. This compromise, despite a series of set-backs in the interim, ultimately set the stage for the 1998 Good Friday Agreement negotiations, and the most recent amendments to it.

Adrian Guelke highlights the influence of other negotiated processes on bringing the parties to the table: "If violent conflicts as intractable as those in South Africa and Israel/Palestine could be resolved through negotiations, surely, so the argument went, the politicians in Britain and Ireland had a duty to initiate negotiations on the Irish Question."[35] This focus on inclusivity and sustaining the paramilitary ceasefires on both sides of the sectarian divide influenced the choices adopted in the agreement. In particular, it shaped both the governance structure and the electoral rules, which aimed to ensure the success of small Loyalist political parties linked to the major Loyalist paramilitary organizations.[36]

The UK's support for the principle that any durable government in Northern Ireland should have the support of majorities in both communities, which they had attempted to implement from 1972, also played a major role in shaping the choice of power-sharing under which all four main parties were able to nominate members of the Executive. As a further example of the importance of timing, while the situation seemed dire at the time the case study was written, it currently seems hopeful. Following the St Andrews Agreement of October 2006 and the March 2007 elections, the Democratic Unionist Party and Sinn Fein have formed a government which thus far seems to be functioning.

Lebanon

The case of Lebanon highlights the influence of a state's constitutional history in shaping the choices made. Negotiations for ending the war had begun as early as 1976, but the Taif Agreement was reached only in 1989, in talks encouraged by both the US and Saudi Arabia. The Taif Agreement eliminated the ratio of 6:5 seats in favor of Christians in parliament, which had been put in place under French rule, in favor of equal representation for Christians and Muslims. However, it retained the fundamental premise of Lebanese governance: that the management of inter-group tensions should be based on confessional representation. This model was already in place during the 1861–1914 period and was adopted by the French in 1926–27. Power sharing along confessional lines was part of the unwritten National Pact of 1943 which provided for the sharing of power between a Christian President and a Sunni Prime Minister. A similar approach was adopted in the Taif Agreement, despite Lebanon's experience that such a model was vulnerable to government paralysis in times of tension or disagreement. It was perceived as the only model able to bring all the parties to the table and prevent arguments of unfairness. This model was strongly shaped by the perception of the politicians involved in the negotiations that the best form of governance for Lebanon was, as Paul Salem puts it, "a set of traditional confessional leaders, with traditional patron-client relations with their communities, that can assemble in Parliament and form governments in order to share the spoils of government and cooperate on policy and decision making."[37]

Lessons learned

It is evident that much will turn on local and international actors: their commitment to developing a genuine and honest process, their motivations and strategies and the expertise they have at their disposal. A challenge for the participants in constitution-building processes has been the need to create a vision of purpose that is greater than short-term politics. While in South Africa, for instance, the leaders were able to move beyond the immediate crisis through statesmanship and vision, in Kenya short-term politics dominated the process resulting in a highly divisive and politicized process and a constitution that was ultimately rejected at referendum.

Moreover, the degree to which the constitutional process is enmeshed with the peace process, as it was in the three examples cited above, has shaped the compromises and governance choices. Although some compromises seem inevitable, the degree to which they can be balanced with a greater future vision for the country, rather than merely represent a division of spoils, is a key factor in the outcomes. Some strategies may reduce these key risks. South Africa, for instance, adopted a staged transition process with increasingly participatory steps ranging from a broadly inclusive initial convention to a constitutional convention that involved drafting by a democratically elected body and ratification by the constitutional court. An advantage of a staged process is that a transition can be made from early agreements, which focus more on what is required for immediate cessation of the conflict, to more representative and participatory discussions of what sort of state the people want over the longer term. Nonetheless, unless the timing between the initial agreement and the drafting of the constitution is sufficiently long, or certain issues are delayed through sunset clauses or interim agreements, the processes may not allow sufficient time for divisive issues to be addressed, or for new political elites to challenge the dominant actors from the conflict. Another option is to adopt an interim constitution with a long but limited time-frame (e.g., ten years) with built-in review phases, which might create a political space for new ideas and leaders to emerge.

The challenge of implementation

The implementation stage, which begins directly after the constitution is adopted and continues indefinitively, is the most important element of constitution-building, since a constitution without implementation is no more than a piece of paper. This of course requires the creation of machinery of rule of law, as well as education, training, legislating, creating administrative decisions, and so forth.

Implementation is the most difficult and least well understood phase of constitution-building. The practical outcomes of any constitution always involve a complex interaction between formal and informal institutions and processes, and the historical and cultural environment. Evidently, any attempt to change basic system rules in society through constitutional or institutional reform faces considerable implementation challenges, including path-dependency, political transaction costs, and inertia. In postwar contexts, this can be compounded by problems of weak rule of law, rapacious elites, lack of political will, inadequacy of funds to create the institutions or train those required, and lack of international community follow-through after the adoption of the constitution.

Constitutional reform alone will not overcome long-entrenched informal and institutional practices unless there is substantial domestic support for the changes (Adekanye 1998: 16; Bratton and van de Walle 1997: 130; Spears 2002: 130). This is a fundamental challenge, and to some degree it depends on the constitution-building process and whether societal dialogue and consensus-building is successful in creating sufficiently broad support for the vision in the constitution and the changes it entails. At the same time, the postwar context offers a window of opportunity to implement substantial governance changes through constitutional reform, for instance though the inclusion of human rights provisions. However, such provisions are the most likely to threaten the ruling power holders, who tend to resist their implementation.

In some cases, the judiciary has played an important role in moderating a winner's conduct by imposing limits on the decisions that a government may take and enforcing the constitution (Issacharoff 2004). As Klug suggests:

The resolution of extreme political differences often involves mutual compromise, but always seems to foreclose on alternative visions. Judicial decision-making—and by implication democratic constitutionalism—does not foreclose on alternative options, but rather provides a mechanism through which space for alternative approaches and visions, within a set of bounded alternatives, is continually retained.

(Klug 2000)

This "judicially enforced constitutionalism" has been highlighted in the case of the Bosnian Constitutional Court and the South African Constitutional Court. In South Africa, the legal system was already well established and the appointment of lawyers with impeccable anti-apartheid credentials certainly played a role in ensuring the quality of judgments (ibid.: 179). In Bosnia, the presence on the court of a number of experienced foreign judges selected by the President of the European Court of Justice has played a role in ensuring the court adopts a democracy-protecting stance.[38] Nonetheless, the role of the judiciary can be undermined by a lack of independence, low capacity, and a lack of established culture of rule of law, all of which often characterize the postwar environment.

Another strategy to increase the incentives for the ruling elite to implement a new constitution would be through explicit regional and international recognition of the importance of respecting and implementing constitutions in the creation of peaceful and stable states. Ashraf Ghani, the former finance minister in the Afghan transitional government, emphasizes the role the international community can play in statebuilding based on a double compact, that is "a compact between rulers and their people and a compact between the government and the international community. And this must be framed in a context of a series of achievable benchmarks" (Ghani 2005). One of the benchmarks could be the expectation that domestic government will abide by the Constitution negotiated as part of the transition.

International monitoring of elections is already widely accepted. Other influences can derive from the requirements for joining economic organizations, or the use of aid policy conditionality. In Europe, EU pressure and joining standards are considered to have played an important role in shaping the post-communist eastern European states and encouraging the adoption of human-rights standards (Ottaway 1994).[39] The African Union (AU) has also adopted principles rejecting unconstitutional changes of government on that continent.[40] Accordingly, the international community could take a more proactive approach to ensuring that any new government acts in accordance with its constitutional obligations. This is particularly important given the inherent weaknesses of new institutions during a statebuilding transition, which can substantially undermine the quality of the democracy that emerges.

Recommendations

Constitution-building can play an important role in shaping the governance and political transition in postwar statebuilding. However, ensuring that such a process supports the establishment a peaceful and legitimate state is a challenge that requires careful balancing of the compromises needed to maintain the peace and the involvement of the people in deciding the future of their country. Some strategies that can be implemented to minimize the inherent tensions in a postwar constitution-building exercise include supporting longer time-frames between the negotiation of peace agreements and constitutions, and ensuring that a broad range of local actors can draw on knowledge of comparative experiences with respect to both process and governance options.

The international community should also commit sufficient aid to supporting inclusive and participatory processes including proper dialogue and consensus-building, keeping in mind that such processes are not simple drafting exercises but must contribute to a legitimate and sustained peace. If domestic, geopolitical or international pressures prevent the adoption of a sufficiently long time-frame to undertake a participatory process, or if insecurity and the possible return to conflict require compromises that prevent such a process, the international community should recommend that a participatory constitution building process be delayed, and support the drafting of an interim arrangement instead. It is essential not to squander the potential of a participatory constitution-making: once disappointed, the population is likely to become disillusioned and bitter.

Finally, the implementation of constitutions in postwar and developing countries require greater attention. Additional research into how to design constitutions that recognize the realities of postwar environments (for instance, weak rule of law and limited resources) is required. However, the international community should approach assistance to constitution-building with a clear understanding that its support should not end when the constitution is adopted. Moreover, there should be greater emphasis by the international community and regional bodies on the importance of implementing constitutional agreements after they are negotiated. One of the benchmarks in the international community's relationship with a postwar transitional government could be the expectation that the government will abide by its constitution in the ensuing period.

Notes

1 Interview with Amos Sawyer (New York, March 28, 2005).
2 For the purposes of this essay, a constitution is defined as a system which establishes the fundamental rules and principles by which a state is governed. The

constitution can be unwritten, or can be codified in one or more documents, including a peace agreement. This essay uses the term constitution making to refer to the process of making a constitution which begins with the decision to review or renew a constitution and includes dialogues and consultations, the negotiation of the provisions, the drafting, and the adoption of the constitution. Constitution building is used to refer to a broader time frame that includes the pre-constitution making phase (setting the scene), and the post-constitution-making phase (implementation and enforcement). A more detailed discussion of the cycle of constitution building is undertaken in an upcoming International IDEA policy paper.

3 See also O'Donnell et al. 1986.

4 Even though there is likely to be less physical destruction in the case of a transition from an authoritarian regime, it still involves many key features of postwar states, such as a devastated infrastructure, destroyed institutions, a lack of professional and bureaucratic capacity, an inflammatory and violent political culture, and a traumatized and highly divided society.

5 The case studies were produced by external consultants for an expert meeting of IPA in 2005 (Bosnia and Herzegovina, Fiji, Lebanon, Northern Ireland, South Africa, and Uganda) evaluating the medium-term impact that constitutional choices had on statebuilding and return to conflict in those countries. They are available at www.ipacademy.org.

6 See Samuels 2005. The 12 case studies were prepared for International IDEA by the following experts: Afghanistan case study: Carolyn McCool; Bahrain case study: Mohamoud Awil; Chile case study: Esteban Montes and Tomás Vial; Colombia case study: Iván Marulanda; East Timor case study: Randall Garrison; Fiji case study: Jill Cottrell and Yash Ghai; Guatemala case study: Roddy Brett and Antonio Delgado; Hungary case study: Andrea Mezei; Indonesia case study: Edward Schneier; Kenya case study: Jill Cottrell and Yash Ghai; Nigeria case study: John Simpkins; Rwanda case study: Priscilla Ankut.

7 A political pact is defined as "An explicit, but not always publicly explicated or justified agreement among a select set of actors which seek to define (or better to redefine) rules governing the exercise of power on the basis of mutual guarantees for the vital interests of those entering into it." See O'Donnell et al. 1986: 37.

8 See Kirchheimer 1969.

9 O'Donnell et al. 1986: 38. The pacts consisted of an agreement among a set of actors on the rules governing the exercise of power on the basis of mutual guarantee of their vital interests. For example, the Punto Fijo pact in Venezuela incorporated a worker–employer agreement and a "Government of National Unity" power-sharing agreement.

10 O'Donnell and Schmitter anticipated this very concern by noting that because pacts are typically negotiated by "established and often highly oligarchical" groups, "they tend to reduce competitiveness as well as conflict; they seek to limit accountability to wider publics; they attempt to control the agenda of policy concerns; and they deliberately distort the principle of citizen equality" (ibid.: 42).

11 For a general discussion of such conferences see Harris and Reilly 1998.

12 As Joseph points out, they were undermined in Cameroon, "physically intimidated in Togo, and rendered chaotic and impotent through a Byzantine combination of concession and retractions in Zaire" (Joseph 1999: 366, 375).

13 See, for example, the case studies commissioned by International IDEA, reviewed in Samuels 2005.

14 In his view, the agreement in Afghanistan suffered from "the original sin" that not all the parties were included (particularly the Taliban). Interview of Mr. Brahimi by Kirsti Samuels, UN Headquarters, New York, January 6, 2005.

15 Ibid.

16 The consociational model proposes to divide power between competing groups in society independently of the electoral process through a governance arrangement that includes all political leaders in a grand coalition. Arend Lijphart, the leading proponent of consociational power sharing has identified essential elements to the model: 1) a grand coalition between political leaders, such that all of the significant ethnic communities of society are included in the government; 2) the existence of a system of mutual veto to allow sub-groups in society to block political decisions affecting their vital interests; 3) proportional access to state resources and proportional representation in the government and public service of all segments of society; and 4) segmental autonomy permitting each segment to be self-governing to some extent, particularly with respect to matters that are of exclusive concern to it. See for example, Lijhart 1977; Lijphart 1985; Lijphart 1999.

17 I adopt terminology from Luckham et al. 2003: 45. Integrative governance aims to encourage cross-cutting coalitions that transcend communal cleavages. Thus integrative power sharing will tend to rely on non-ethnically-based decentralization, recourse to power sharing based on electoral models such as proportional representation or alternative preference voting but not based on ethnic groupings, and strong minority rights. Bastian and Luckham identify seven mechanisms that can ameliorate majoritarian democracy and can be designed with an integrative intention: 1) strong constitutionally guaranteed human rights protections; 2) affirmative action measures to achieve ethnic balance or reverse the legacies of discrimination; 3) recourse to alternative electoral models which are more representational, including Proportional Representation or the Single Transferable Vote; 4) geographical decentralization of power including different forms of administrative devolution, federalism and confederalism; 5) corporate decentralization which accords representatives of groups vetoes over policies impacting on the group or gives the group particular rights; 6) professional and autonomous state bureaucracies which can act as a protection against the arbitrary use of power by governments; 7) civilian control over a non partisan army and police. (Bastian and Luckham 2003: 50).

18 Considering Sierra Leone, Angola and Rwanda, see 125, 126.

19 Pointing out that the return to violence in Angola, Cyprus, Lebanon, Sierra Leone, and Sudan were the result of broken power-sharing agreements.

20 For example, Switzerland, Netherlands, and Belgium.

21 See the range of Security Council resolutions calling for democratic resolution of conflict and elections. See also Lijphart 2002: 38.

22 See, for example, Davenport 1996 and Krain and Myers 1997.

23 See also Gurr 2000: 153.

24 Snyder establishes that "a country's first steps towards democracy spur the development of nationalism and heighten the risk of international war and internal ethnic conflict" (Snyder 2000: 352). But according to Gurr the outcome of such transitions are variable: transitions in the postcommunist states led to increased rebellion, whereas transitions in the developing world generally led to a decline in rebellion (Gurr 2000: 162). Note that his analysis does not differentiate between nations emerging from civil conflict and those emerging from other authoritarian situations.

25 The Polity data set was used to compared data on ethnopolitical conflict in four categories of nations in 1985–98: 27 old democracies, 33 new democracies established between 1980 and 1994, 32 transitional regimes (mixture of autocratic and democratic features or had attempted a transition to democracy after 1970 and had not consolidated), and 26 autocracies.

26 See also Davenport 2005.

27 See also Lake and Rothchild 1998: 345.

28 In First Past the Post (FPTP) the candidate with the most votes (not necessarily a majority) in a single-member constituency wins the election. Block Vote (BV) takes place in multi-member districts and voters have as many votes as there are seats to be filled. The Alternative Vote (AV) model aims to encourage moderation and cooperation. Electors rank the parties in order of preference in single member districts and votes are allocated through these preferences until a winner emerges. Single Transferable Vote (STV) is a preferential system with multi-member districts, it produces largely proportional results but aims to encourage party appeals beyond ethnic or communitarian groups. Under a party list Proportional Representation (PR) model, elections are held in multi-member districts where each party presents a list of candidates. Electors vote for a party rather than a candidate and the proportion of votes a party receives determines in the number of seats it holds in parliament.

29 IPA South Africa Case Study, p. 5.

30 Ibid.

31 Ibid. 10–11.

32 Ibid, p. 7.

33 Ibid, p. 7.

34 Ibid, pp. 19–20.

35 Ibid.

36 Ibid, pp. 19–20.

37 Ibid.

38 In Bosnia the nine member court has four members who are selected by the Federation House of Representatives and two members selected by the Republika Srpska National Assembly. To prevent ethnic deadlock in adjudication, the remaining three members of the court must be non-citizens, are selected by the President of the European Court of Human Rights "after consultation with the Presidency," and cannot be citizens of any neighboring country. Two international judges sit on the East Timor Court of Appeal.

39 See also Papagianni 2003.

40 See the Constitutive Act of the African Union, 2002.

9 Pathways of the political

Electoral processes after civil war

Timothy D. Sisk

Most civil wars today end in negotiated settlements, and in most instances an essential part of such agreements are provisions that outline a defined political pathway through which a transitional process to consolidate peace is to unfold. These transition paths often feature the formation of interim governments, sometimes create constitution-making processes, and, at some point, envisage an electoral process to imbue postwar governance with popular legitimacy.[1] This chapter argues that the political pathway of transition and especially the initial, postwar electoral process matters significantly for statebuilding over the long-term. The transition sequences and institutional choices made in war-settlement negotiations often determine the nature and timing of initial postwar elections; in turn, these initial electoral processes deeply affect the nature of the state that emerges for years to follow. In sum, elections are the principal means by which war-terminating peace agreements are democratically legitimated by the affected population, and the outcomes of elections determine initial control of state institutions by either affirming existing patterns of power or ushering in new elites and by re-arranging state–society relations.

Generally, those electoral processes that are broadly inclusive and that pair proportionality with accountability have the best chance of creating the legitimacy needed for effective postwar governance because they create the conditions for mutually empowering state–society relations. When states have the support of their societies, they can more effectively act to address social challenges (such as providing security or facilitating development), thereby strengthening society's capacity to effectively participate in governance (Migdal et al. 1994). Employing a perspective of path dependence—that is, focusing on the antecedent events that lead up to initial postwar elections and the conduct and outcomes of electoral processes—this chapter discerns the effects of initial electoral process on statebuilding after civil war.

The chapter's findings are based on a structured, focused comparison of four cases arranged chronologically: Cambodia, South Africa, Afghanistan, and Liberia. The cases chosen for analysis have all had United Nations involvement either in the design of the sequencing of events in critical moments of negotiation, or UN monitoring and observation of the elections, and in each of them the initial transitional electoral process has more or less run its course. While the cases chosen do not allow for a truly long-term assessment of the effects of elections on state viability measured in more than decades, they are sufficiently advanced along a continuum of "progress" toward normality in politics that the issues and concerns about the viability of the new states can be discerned.

Cambodia is an example often cited about how initially problematic elections set up conditions for a weak, captured state; South Africa's 1994 polls are seen as an example of elections that empowered the state (albeit an ANC-dominant one) by rearranging the relationship of the state to its society. In Afghanistan, the inclusion of "warlords" in electoral processes has produced concerns about the ability of the new state to wield monopolistic authority; at the same time, such inclusion did not remove all spoilers from the scene, and escalating violence there suggests that the elected government is insufficiently legitimate to prevent or manage violent challenges. In Liberia, the choice for a presidential election with a runoff raised concerns about whether the loser in the poll would acquiesce to the new government or whether civil war would re-emerge; surprisingly, on the contrary, a newly-empowered state appears to have emerged following voluntary power sharing.

These cases illustrate the central finding of this research: electoral processes are necessary in moving beyond civil war, but path-dependence matters. Sequencing, design, and the extent of international oversight are the key variables explaining the degree to which electoral processes contribute to capable, responsive states and to other alternatives such as captured, fragmented, or weak states. The success of the statebuilding enterprise itself is thus predicated on an electoral process that generates exceptionally broad legitimacy for the immediate, postwar ruling coalition; absent the contingent consent of all parties with the military capacity and ideological or power-seeking interest to spoil the postwar peace, progress toward effective statebuilding remains elusive.

The implication is that those in the international community involved in the peacebuilding-as-statebuilding projects must directly confront the difficulties, contradictions, and dilemmas that postwar electoral processes pose and see them as the principal instrument for defining anew mutually empowering relations between states and societies after civil conflict. On the other hand, getting the initial electoral process "wrong," or being satisfied with a suboptimal process, sets the stage for significant problems in long-term peacebuilding. The task for effective statebuilding is thus not whether or even when to have elections to build effective states for sustainable peace after civil war, but how and how long to stay engaged once the first election has passed.

Perspectives on electoral processes and statebuilding

Many scholars and analysts investigating recent experiences of civil war termination are deeply skeptical of electoral processes in the immediate postwar environment: elections occur in troubled circumstances with deeply fragmented political structures, war-ravaged societies, and, usually, widespread deprivation. Added to this difficult political climate are problems ranging from population displacement, captured or disabled states that are parties to war, and practical challenges such as the absence of a voter's roll or the presence of landmines. This school of thought argues that statebuilding should come first, putting into place viable structure of authority to provide basic security and enhancing service-delivery capacities and economic revival before electoral competition takes place. Statebuilding-first approaches focus on improving economic conditions in postwar environments as a higher priority than fostering political competition (Collier et al. 2003).

Likewise, many observers suggest that postwar electoral processes introduce new uncertainties and that they make war-torn, fragile societies deeply vulnerable to relapse into civil war (Bormeo 1997; Mansfield and Snyder 2005; Höglund 2006). Clearly, the problems associated with immediate postwar elections are acute, suggested that electoral processes held in the wrong circumstances following civil war severely inhibit the building of a functional, capable state because power is distributed along the political lines over which war was fought instead of lines that would contribute to the national integration necessary for long-term state survival. Indeed, this is now a long-standing criticism of the "early" elections held in November 1996 in war-torn Bosnia (Belloni 2008). Related are concerns that indeed democratization itself is an inherently conflict-exacerbating enterprise, fundamentally at odds with the imperatives of conciliation implicit in peacebuilding (Jarstad and Sisk 2008).

Other observers acknowledge that electoral processes are fraught with problems but argue that they are a necessary ingredient to "validating" peace agreements and for providing sorely needed legitimacy for postwar governance.[2] In some circumstances, electoral processes are the critical turning point that ends an uncertain, and usually turbulent, transition period and may in fact be the key ingredient in moving beyond the vulnerabilities of postwar settings to ongoing political violence. For example, it was the transition-culminating elections in South Africa in April 1994 that set the stage for a national unity government that drafted a new constitution, restructured apartheid-era bureaucracies, and allowed for support from society for state development initiatives. In Nepal, in 2008, elections and democratization were key elements of the agreement to end the Maoist rebellion and transform the country's political institutions; they appear to have been a relative success. Beyond celebrated national-level polls, electoral processes such as local-level polls are seen by some development specialists as critical to establishing conditions for the delivery of services that secure public support the peace through tangible and immediate economic gains: in this view, politics must come prior to statebuilding (Risley and Sisk 2005).

Because election *contests* are just that—a competitive game for political power—they heighten social divisions and enhance differences in the political community in a process through which the people choose among alternative views and leaders. Elections are rule-bound competitions over the governance of the state and nature (often, the boundaries) of the "nation." This fact about elections is essentially a paradox for conflict management in those societies that are already deeply divided along ethnic, racial, or religious lines: a popular mandate through an electoral process is necessary to produce a government able to govern with a high degree of legitimacy, but the very way in which the population is required to choose often gives rise to or heightens already deep differences (Ellis 2006). The potentially contradictory aims of potentially divisive, competitive elections and conciliation-oriented peacebuilding, have been pointed out by insightful observers who have looked at efforts to use democratization processes to settle civil strife in deeply divided societies.[3] Pauline Baker has observed:

> Conflict managers tend to concentrate on short-term solutions that address the precipitous events that sparked the conflict; above all they seek a swift and expedient end to the violence. Democratizers tend to concentrate on long-term solutions that address the root causes of the conflict; they search for enduring democratic stability. The former see peace as a precondition for democracy; the latter see democracy as a precondition for peace.
>
> (Baker 1996: 568)

At the crux of the debate on democracy's relationship to conflict management is the challenge of electoral processes in societies prone to, involved in, or emerging from violent conflict. In myriad instances—such as the 1992 presidential elections in Angola, or in the run-up to post-intervention elections in Iraq in 2005—elections and their outcomes can be a strong stimulant for violence by those who expect to lose. On the other hand, inclusion of potential spoilers in some recent instances (including three of the four cases evaluated here) has led to concerns with "warlord" democracy (Wantchekon 2004). Likewise, for incumbents in office who seek to maintain a grip on power, the use of violence and intimidation to assure a win at the polls is an all-too-often practice; in the run-up to the parliamentary elections of March 2005 in Zimbabwe and again in the elections of 2008, opposition leaders were arrested and tortured, the press was intimidated, and international observers kept away.

It is for this reason that in the community of practitioners promoting international peacemaking and peacebuilding, there is widespread concern about the nature, timing, and administration of electoral processes as an instrument for conflict management; indeed, arguably the new focus on statebuilding is a realization that transitional processes—which culminate in elections—are not the end point of peacebuilding. As the authors of the International Peace Academy's "Making States Work" project report:

> Elections are frequently cited as the appropriate endpoint in international engagement in a crisis ... In general, the emphasis has been on form at the expense of substance. The transition to democracy requires a

transformation in public mentality similar to that which underpins a respect for law. Elections may provide evidence of this transformation, but they are only a small part of what is required to realize it. Building robust market economies and resilient civil societies are just as critical for embedding democracy in larger structures that can survive changes of leaders and parties.[4]

Thus, one of the most vexing challenges facing policymakers in the international community, and protagonists in societies deeply divided by internal conflict alike, is the special set of circumstances that occur in immediate postwar elections. From Namibia in 1989 to Nepal in 2008, there have been many instances in which after a civil war a new government is inaugurated in first-ever, postwar elections.[5]

Key considerations in postwar electoral processes

Although each situation is unique, there are common characteristics of elections held in the wake of civil war that can point the way to understanding the conditions under which they are relatively successful in establishing legitimacy for the postwar state, and when they might serve instead to stimulate new fears, provoke new violence, and set back statebuilding rather than advancing it. As Ben Reilly (2003: 174) appropriately observes, "In any transition from conflict to peace, the creation or restoration of some form of legitimate authority is paramount ... the support of the citizenry must be tested and obtained ... The overarching challenge of peacebuilding is to construct a sustainable democratic state that can function without international involvement." This fundamental appreciation that peacebuilding is about democratic statebuilding is coupled with a stark recognition that international efforts to build peace have been lacking in devoting sufficient attention to the local level. Neçla Tscirgi (2003: 1) argues, for example, that "Despite lip service being paid to the centrality of local ownership of peacebuilding, it is not clear that international actors have developed effective strategies for assessing local needs, setting priorities, allocating resources, or establishing accountability."

Among the common challenges are these:

- low trust among protagonists for power, because often there is no external force (such as UN peace operation) capable of enforcing the outcome of elections: parties lack a sense of credible commitment by their opponents to the peace deal and fear cheating or rejection of legitimate election results;
- postwar elections feature high stakes for winning, particularly in those situations of "lootable" commodities: loss of power may endanger economic fortunes;
- postwar environments may be vulnerable to the emergence of wily elites who will mobilize on divisive nationalist, ethnic, or racial themes in their quest for power;

- after civil wars, political parties are often weak and the party system is either underdeveloped or untested: there is high uncertainty regarding relative strengths of the factions, which heightens tensions and fears about winning and losing;[6]
- civil society is weak and populations are traumatized by the effects of war: weak civil society and affected populations are less able to stand up to political forces led by extremists or ideologues; and
- basic state capacities are weak, with governments often unable to ensure proper preparation for elections or to meet other higher-level human needs, rendering elections somewhat surreal as voters vote in conditions that are otherwise fraught with insecurity and destitution.[7]

What are the minimal conditions necessary for a "good" election in high-conflict settings, one that produces a legitimate, stable, and effective government that can make progress toward social goals of human development, human security, and social reconciliation?[8] Can a government created in a process that is essentially conflictual lead a society in a manner that prevents, manages, or transforms social conflict? The answers to these questions are crucial for understanding the conditions under which electoral processes contribute to conflict management and thus statebuilding. Electoral processes require a prior degree of progress on the security front (or demilitarization): disarmament of independent armed forces by factions and political parties, basic safety and security for electoral administration personnel, the elimination of "no-go" zones for campaigning by all parties, and measures to ensure that there is no illegitimate, violent opposition to the outcome (Lyons 2005). How much security is enough? Elections are not an end of the postwar transition, a definitive green-light an international exit strategy or the sole solution to peacebuilding; yet they are a critical turning point of the transition with considerable (if not determinative) implications for statebuidling.

For the case studies in this chapter, it is useful to identify the key variables on which each initial postwar electoral process should be evaluated. These are:

1 How the sequence path is defined, usually in the terms of the war-ending negotiated settlement. The sequence pathway for an electoral process finds its antecedents, path-dependently, in the prior stage of conflict de-escalation, where the formula for settlement of the war—and the way out—is codified. Often, international mediators have significant influence on the nature of settlements, specific sequences of events, and in some instances specific detail such as the electoral system or the creation of a pre-election power-sharing pact.[9]

The question of sequencing equally involves issues of "what" and "when." What needs to occur prior to a relatively free and fair election, such as the review or drafting of an electoral law, voter registration, and the disarmament, demobilization, and reintegration of armed forces, among other desiderata? When, following the end of fighting, should elections be held (with the understanding that they may be two early or too late)? Most observers agree that the November 1996 elections in Bosnia, just a year after the guns fell silent was too soon. But, waiting too long can also be problematic as interim or transitional administrations inherently lack legitimacy. Also, it might make sense to consider local elections first then move to national elections (as in Kosovo), rather the now somewhat standard practice of sequencing national elections first and having local elections thereafter (as in Sierra Leone). In other situations, however, local elections might have deleterious results for peacemaking; each situation needs to be carefully considered for how the sequencing of elections in the postwar environment may affect the prospects for peace and for subsequent democratization (Risley and Sisk 2005).

2   The electoral system. Electoral system choices have strong influences on a variety of outcome variables critical to evaluating critical aspects of statebuilding[10] among them:

- The structure of the party system, such as how many parties form, whether and when they may coalesce, their prospects for gaining power, and potentially their very makeup in terms of the various social divisions that might exist within any given political community (e.g., municipality, region, or country).

- The ways in which candidates craft their appeals. In some situations, it may be possible to induce candidates for certain kinds of candidates for office to adopt certain types of appeals (Lijphart 2004; Reilly 2001). A common example is requirements for a presidential winner to carry a certain minimum percentage of the votes in a very large, and often disperse set of regions. With this rule, it is almost essential that any winner will have had to appeal to at least some voters throughout the country. As a result, it is hoped that presidential candidates will be unifiers, not dividers, of society.

- The overall character of the contest in terms of what the competition is for. The electoral system, which in more technical terms translates votes into particular "seats" or positions, is about determining how ruling coalitions are put together. Winner-take-all systems, including plurality/majority systems, give the winners of a certain threshold of votes—say, 50 percent in strict majority-rule systems—all the power to make decisions for the entire community. Other systems, too, such as the Alternative Vote or Two-Round systems, can have similar winner-take-all effects. Proportional systems give various political parties an equal share in political power for an equal share of overall votes cast. In the former, candidates and parties are competing for unbridled rule, trying to form coalitions of people and groups to garner the magical threshold with a given system that produces a majority.

3 Security and political violence. Electoral processes in conditions of violent conflict require a prior degree of progress on the security front: disarmament of independent armed forces by factions and political parties, basic safety, and security for electoral administration personnel, and the elimination of "no-go" zones for campaigning by all parties. Electoral processes have key, pivotal, decision-making moments in which the process can be tipped in the direction of conflict management on especially divisive issues. It is clear that elections run under conditions where some parties have the capacity to return to widespread violence present special dangers of war recurrence, and that elections conducted in conditions of grave insecurity with regard to street-level political violence are unlikely to produce legitimate or widely accepted results. In the first instance, the 1992 presidential elections in Angola are an oft-cited case of the problems of hasty electoral processes conducted without sufficient disarmament or containment of forces: when the UNITA faction under Jonas Savimbi appeared likely to lose in the second round of voting for the presidency, it returned "to the bush" and the war dragged on for another seven years at a cost of some 150,000 lives.

As in Angola in 1992, much depends on actual or expected exclusion of key protagonists in terms of electoral outcomes. That electoral processes produce winners and losers is an indicator of their capacity to catalyze or to open "windows of vulnerability" to violence: when a strongly insecure party or faction expects to be systematically excluded from political power, they may well turn to violence to either prevent their exclusion or to prevent the election's success (Höglund 2004). Thus, it is likely that at least some of the insurgent violence in Iraq following the US-led coalition's occupation there after 2003 can be explained by the expectations of the Sunni minority of ethnic-census voting elections and thus the likelihood of a Shi'a dominated government that, in coalition with Kurdish parties, would overwhelmingly dominate as far as the eye can see.[11]

4 Electoral management, monitoring, and dispute resolution. The key components of a legitimate electoral process is one that is free and fair in both political and administrative terms, that is inclusive of all elements of society through a well-considered law of citizenship and of voter registration, and that offers meaningful choices to the population (Pastor 1999). Capacities to monitor compliance with international professional best practices, legal requirements, and to deter fraud and intimidation are essential. Likewise, the capacity for electoral dispute resolution is also seen as a key component.[12]

Electoral management in postwar environments occurs in essentially three different ways. First is the full conduct of the election by outsiders, in most instances the United Nations (as in Cambodia) or other international organizations such as the Organization for Security and Cooperation in Europe (as in Bosnia). A second model is joint administration by UN and local electoral management bodies (as in Afghanistan), involving international oversight but with official authority residing in the national electoral commission. Finally, there are some postwar instances in which the entire electoral process is run by insiders (as in South Africa), albeit with the participation of international experts. These choices affect state-building in that they seek to balance the need for professionalized capacity to run an electoral process in a volatile postwar environment with the imperatives of state capacity-building over the long term.

Election observation refers to evaluations of internal and external neutral organizations on all aspects of the electoral process; verification is more extensive, and occurs when such organizations actually oversee and verify that the electoral management body has run the election fairly. The role of international observers has emerged in the 1990s and 2000s as an essential element in postwar elections precisely because domestic observer capacities are weak. Extensive electoral observation in postwar elections is a necessary component if the results are to be accepted both internally and externally as the result of a process that is free and fair in both procedural and substantive terms.

Conversely, perceptions of fraudulent or stolen elections are a strong predictor of violence; thus, a key element of electoral processes for long-term statebuilding is the creation of neutral, autonomous electoral management bodies.[13] At the same time, the presence of extensive international election monitoring missions has likewise been key to address concerns of stolen, managed, or manipulated elections.[14] When domestic capacities for electoral management and monitoring are insufficient, the UN has at times stepped in to oversee polls through UN transitional administrations; while such "trusteeship" appears necessary in failed states, it introduces the paradox of the world body introducing democracy through neo-imperial suzerainty.[15]

Cambodia: a captured state

Cambodia was one of the first post-Cold War multidimensional peace operations through which the international community sought to implement a comprehensive peace agreement, the Paris Peace Accords of 1991 and for this reason it has earned considerable analysis in terms of its implications for understanding and lessons learned on operational matters of peacekeeping and on broader concerns of peacemaking and peacebuilding. The case continues to be useful for analysis because the longer-term legacies of the earlier intervention and the lasting effects of critical decisions taken then can be more fully evaluated for statebuilding given the passing of time (see also the chapter by David Roberts in this volume).

The intent of the United Nations mission, UNTAC (United Nations Transitional Authority in Cambodia) was to rebuild a state that had earlier been complicit in one of the most egregious attacks on its own society: the horrendous genocide unleashed by the Khmer Rouge led by Pol Pot which killed some 1.7 million people. Even prior to the Khmer Rouge killing fields, however, Cambodia had been what in contemporary terms would be deemed a "failed" state, which during the 1960s and early 1970s faced incursions by the North Vietnamese regime, bombing by the US during the Vietnam War, an internal military coup that saw prime minister General Lon Nol assume total power, and an internal guerilla struggle led by the Communist Khmer. During 1977–78, war broke out with Vietnam and eventually, following the fall of Phonm Phen, Hun Sen assumed power in 1985 even as the country remained engulfed in guerilla warfare waged by the deposed Khmer Rouge led by Pol Pot.

The most important issues surrounding the effects of the first elections on statebuilding occurred just prior to, and at the end of, the UNTACT mission. The 1991 Paris Peace Accords reflect a thawing of the Cold War and a high moment in global diplomacy designed to end Cambodia's tragedy, and it included the essential elements of the sequencing that set the stage for the political aspects of statebuidling. Among the critical issues decided in the settlement were: 1) the recognition of the four principal protagonists, the Royalist FUNCIPEC under Prince Norodom Ranariddh as prime minister (with restoration of his father, Sihanouk, as King), the State of Cambodia under Hun Sen, the Republican KPLNF), and the Khmer Rouge to include the latter's formal inclusion in the process of transition (to include, possibly, elections); 2) formation of a transitional authority under the overall supervision of the UN; 3) the election of a constituent assembly under a proportional representation system (closed list, party PR); and 4) the role of the UN as both administrator and mediator of the envisaged electoral process together with the provisional government (the Supreme National Council) under the rubric of "dual control." Thus, the sequence path was set: preparations for relatively quick elections (two years after the accord) for a constitution-making body. In this context, considerable power over the timing and decisions regarding the electoral process were provided to the Special Representative of the Secretary-General (SRSG) Yasushi Akashi.

The story of the Cambodian elections of 1993 has been well told. The most important elements for this analysis are the ways in which the process that subsequently led to the capture of the state by Hun Sen in a series of steps that led him and his CPP to consolidate power exclusively: the post-election mediation by Akashi that created a post-facto, tenuous power sharing relationship between Hun Sen and the Prince Ranariddh, the 1997 coup d'état that ousted Ranariddh, and the revival of a coalition government between 2000 and 2003, and the pivotal 2004 elections that essentially consolidates the power of the CPP under Hun Sen producing what is essentially a captured state. Indeed, the ability of the government to convict Cambodian opposition leader Sam Rainsy of defaming Hun Sen while he is in exile in France is indicative of the extent to which the Cambodian state is a narrow, autocratic, corrupt and kleptocratic one. Key institutions of autonomous state power—the National Election Commission and the Constitutional Council—

have been eviscerated as checks on executive authority. In sum, the Hun Sen regime has been able to consolidate power and thus manipulate and control later electoral processes—the 1998 local elections and the 2004 national elections—after having fully re-captured the state despite a peace settlement and UN transitional administration designed to democratize it.

How much of the captured nature of the present can be attributed to the scene-setting elections of 1993? Several issues deserve to be highlighted. First, the elections were administered by the UN electoral team to the best of their ability given the conditions on the ground, which included a Khmer Rouge boycott and military strikes by their forces on UN personnel, electoral officials, candidates, and voters (especially in the areas they militarily control). Likewise, the electoral system in principle was appropriate for a postwar environment in that there is broad consensus that list-PR can help foster inclusivity, and the elections to constitutional assemblies may leave the door open for "post-settlement" settlements. However, two problems with this electoral system choice can be identified: first is that the closed-list nature of the system gives political parties strong internal power over their own rank-and-file (through the control of candidacy selection) such that the top-level elites normally wield considerable power; closed-list PR systems are power-centralizing. Second, PR on its own (without other aspects of power sharing, such as vetoes, decentralization, or an enforceable code of rights) is insufficient to bring about stable ruling coalitions, especially if a party to the conflict it has other means of power (control of the state's military and police, for example). Indeed, the ironic outcome of the 1993 elections is that FUNCIPEC "won" the elections with a plurality of the vote share (45.3 percent) compared to the next-largest vote share for Hun Sen's CPP (38.7 percent).

The key controversies are related to sequencing and to electoral dispute resolution. The decision to hold the elections despite demobilization and ongoing violence to strategically create what Stedman has referred to as a "departing train" approach to managing spoiler violence was, in hindsight, ill-considered. In such a volatile environment, the security imperatives trumped democratization imperatives and essentially led to a too-hasty departure for the UN, which viewed the elections as an exit strategy. The second was the absence of a prior power-sharing agreement and the efforts by Akashi after the election to, in essence, void the actual outcome of the elections by forging a fractious and indeed ill-fated coalition government. The strategic decision to pursue power sharing despite clear indications that Hun Sen was bent on total power (despite the election outcome) and with evidence that a number of CPP officials had committed grave violations of human rights in efforts to intimidate voters and influence the election's outcome.

Akashi's response to claims of fraudulence in the elections—forging a power-sharing deal between the FUNCINPEC and the CPP—now seems to be the principal ill-considered decision that has allowed Cambodia to become a captured state. The failure to achieve a broader and deeper power-sharing pact prior to the election, the decision to bend to the CPP intimidation tactics just after the election, and the failure to engage over the long term (well into the mid-1990s and especially during the collapse of the coalition during the violence of July 1997) illustrate that electoral process of 1993 and its immediate aftermath set the stage for the type of kleptocratic, authoritarian state seen in Cambodia today.

South Africa: from apartheid to a dominant-party state

Since the celebrated "liberation" elections of April 26–27, 1994, South Africa features a fully-functioning democratic state with a fairly representative parliament, a coherent executive branch led by an indirectly elected President, and an independent and sometimes assertive judiciary. Its civil society is vibrant, and its press is independent. At the same time, the government rules over a de facto one-party (or dominant) state with weak parliamentary opposition; the ANC has increased its majority in the subsequent elections—1999 and 2004—winning with 69.68 percent of the popular vote in the ten years after the April 2004 poll. Nonetheless, the democratic credentials of South Africa's state are not extensively questioned given its adherence to a broadly-accepted constitutional settlement that was reached in 1996. The constitution ("One Law for One Nation") is seen as a model charter for democracy in a diverse society, with well-considered provisions on human rights enforced by a strongly powered Constitutional Court, rights to religious, cultural, and ethnic identity, a popularly-based National Assembly and quasi-federal rights for the country's nine provinces in an upper house (The National Council of Provinces). The implications of the initial election in South Africa provide a distinct counterpoint to the troubled Cambodian process, and thus deserve reflective analysis for how the process differed on several key variables.

From 1948–94, particularly, South Africa was ruled by white nationalists that implemented policies of systematic racial segregation known as apartheid (separateness), depriving the black majority of dignity, citizenship, living wages, and access to land. Apartheid sparked an internal revolt from the disenfranchised black majority, embodied in the anti-apartheid struggle of the African National Congress (ANC) which rebelliously opposed the exclusive white-minority state with non-racial nationalism, socialism, and demands for full-enfranchisement and democratic control of the state. The regime responded with a period of repression and a regional policy of destabilizing its neighbors.

By 1989 the country was at the boiling point, with predictions of an unbridled civil war along racial lines. Remarkably, reason prevailed and white-minority leaders began to negotiate with representatives of the black majority the dismantling of apartheid and the introduction of a new, non-racial democracy. During 1990–94 the country witnessed a remarkable social catharsis in which the principles of tolerance, negotiation, diversity, and democracy prevailed throughout four years of tumultuous talks. It was its culture of negotiation and bargaining over a common future that led to the

Nobel Peace Prizes for the last white-minority president, F.W. de Klerk, and the ANC's Mandela, who was once the state's prisoner #1 yet became the country's first president in the celebrated "liberation" elections in April 1994 (Reynolds 1994; Stedman 1994). It is important to point out in this analysis that the South African state was not fully disabled by the 1970s and 1980s (social conflicts which approached fatality levels equivalent to civil war), but it was highly weakened such that critical areas of the country (especially major urban and peri-urban areas) became ungovernable and the state lacked efficacy and autonomy due to the international anti-apartheid sanctions regime (Price 1991).

The sequencing of the transition was critical to explaining the relative "success" of the transition and the 1994 elections. Initially, the talks that began in 1990 were bilateral—between the NP and ANC led by F.W. de Klerk and Nelson Mandela, respectively—but they eventually became more broadly based to include other parties such as the IFP, homeland leaders, and other opposition parties. Perhaps the most important interim negotiated agreement was the first, known as the Groote Schuur "Minute" of May 1990. This first accord linked commitment to renunciation of the ANC's armed struggle with normalization of political freedoms, the return of exiles, the release of political prisoners and the eventual move to full enfranchisement and elections. The pact defined "nonracial democracy" in a united South Africa as the ultimate outcome of the talks. Subsequent pacts were reached in 1990, 1991, 1992, and 1993.

The talks broadened in 1992 and 1993 to include white parties to the right of the NP (notably, the white right-wing Freedom Front). African opposition to the left of the ANC such as the Pan-Africanist Congress at first opposed talks but also eventually was included in multiparty negotiation. All along, the process of negotiation was smoothed by small, moderate, bridge-building parties such as the Democratic Party (DP). Former homeland governments also participated in the multiparty talks, making the peace process eventually (and especially at the time of the April 1994 elections that ended apartheid), widely inclusive of all the major political forces in the country. This broad inclusion is pointed to as a key element in the success of the transitional negotiations; the inclusive nature of the process is the single most important variable in the analysis of the process of redesign of the apartheid state.

The transition was turbulent and bloody. Political violence was an endemic feature of the transitional period, to the extent where there was in South Africa during the transition an undeclared internal war. Some 16,000 persons lost their lives in political violence between 1990 and 1994. There were several crisis-inducing events that threatened the talks beginning in June 1990, just after the Groote Schuur pact. IFP–ANC faction fighting—mostly the youth wings—was extensive, especially in greater Johannesburg and the KwaZulu Natal region. Much credit for the successful conclusion of the bloody transition goes to the ANC. The ANC leadership, particularly, changed its view and recognized that much of the violence was aimed at derailing its pursuit of power. The ANC's changed position was summed up by key negotiator Kader Asmal, who said in November 1993 that delay of the election would "hold the country hostage to violence and to violent men."[16] Thus, a settlement was clinched in June 1993 despite the ongoing strife on the street.

The negotiators reached a broad-based agreement on formal power sharing in the 1993 Interim Constitution. This agreement was a quintessential political pact, or mutual security agreement, in which democratization occurs with the explicit protection of the interests of the incumbent regime and its military and security forces. Such pact-making and consensus seeking continued after the elections of 1994 and through the period of constitution making by the elected Constitutional Assembly (which also acted as an interim parliament) until the adoption of a permanent constitution and its eventual certification by the Constitutional Court in October 1996. The linchpin feature of the 1993 interim constitution was the agreement by the ANC on a period of transitional power sharing with the former rulers and a pledge to ensure the jobs and livelihood of the civil service, South African Defense Force (SADF, now SANDF) and the police. The power-sharing pragmatism was backed up by political finesse, manifested by the ANC concessions of early 1994 to the right-wing Freedom Front and the IFP. These concessions to potential spoilers of the pact brought these parties into the Government of National Unity at the eleventh hour and averted a bloody showdown during the celebrated liberation elections of April 1994.

In analysis of the election's implications for statebuilding, four key findings emerge. First, the choice for PR was an internal one—made within the ANC—based on the strategic calculus that such a system would not frustrate attempts to form a government that would give it power, but would also allow the inclusion of stronger parties (particularly the white right wing) that, if left out, would violently oppose the new state and prevent its effective functioning. The second implication is that a power-sharing pact was internally derived (based on what Arend Lijphart has insightfully described as a self-negating prediction, or the realization that the failure to share power would induce a worse outcome of violent encounters); it was neither imposed by outsiders such as the United Nations, nor was it seen as a permanent feature of a democracy. Elections followed a power-sharing deal in what virtually all observers at the time, and in hindsight, view as a genuine attempt to prioritize peace. Indeed, the South African process of elections-then-constitution making provides a sequence that allowed for ongoing bargaining on the most divisive issues.

The third variable is of electoral administration and monitoring: the "ownership" of the election-management process was by South Africans themselves and not by the international community. However, international involvement was extensive in the form of the United Nations Observer Mission in South Africa (UNOMSA), which provided sufficient presence to perform at least a modicum of confidence-building among the parties (and within the population) that the electoral process was essentially free and fair. The final explanation of the relative success of the 1994 election in terms of its subsequent effects on statebuilding was that they provided the "New South Africa" state with legitimacy. State strength relies on society's coherence, and abundant research demonstrates that social cohesion has increased considerably in subsequent years following the political pact. As Pierre du Toit observes (2001: 178), "The reconstituted post-apartheid state started with ample amounts of the crucial ingredient of legitimacy, an ideal platform for acquiring the other components of state strength."

However, South Africa's post-apartheid government—led first by Mandela until 1998 and until September 2008 by his protégé Thabo Mbeki—faces deep and intense social and economic challenges. All the danger signs of a weak state—high unemployment, rampant poverty, massive inequalities, lingering racial and ethnic divisions, crime, corruption, disease (especially HIV/AIDS), and tensions over land are present in South Africa today. Although it maybe the strongest and most economically developed state in Africa today, South Africa faces fundamental social challenges that if not addressed, ameliorated, and managed may well create new violent tensions, undermine the transition to democracy, and spell stormy weather for this pivotal state in the region and on the world stage. Statebuilding remains a very much unfinished project in South Africa, despite the overall salutary effects that the initial elections provided.

The principal task ahead is to manage the decline of the ANC as a liberation-legitimized hegemonic state (however benign it has been) into a state whose legitimacy derives from better service-delivery performance and from more normalized democracy. Statebuilding in this context will clearly require a second stage of democratic transition featuring alternation in ruling coalitions stemming from greater electoral accountability. In this regard, the choice for closed PR-list electoral system may yield opportunities and dangers: opportunities in that there is a likelihood of party fragmentation that would include the broad-tent ANC (signs of which are already appearing); dangers in the form of extreme fragmentation that would lead to "polarized pluralism" and thus a weak state unable to coherently address the myriad of social challenges the country faces in the years ahead.

Afghanistan: a state with a chance?

The signing of the Bonn Agreement in December 2001 set the stage for a dramatic redesign of the Afghan state following the thirty years of political instability, foreign occupation, Cold-War proxy conflict, rule by a neo-fascist Islamist Taliban, and fractious civil war. The Afghan story is a long and complicated one, and the Bonn Agreement is but one small part of a broader narrative that took a major turn with the post-September 11, 2001 US-led international intervention (approved with a Security Council mandate) that allowed the rebel Northern Alliance to oust the Taliban from power. For the purposes of this analysis, however, the Bonn Agreement has special significance because of the way the UN-mediated accord established a sequence path through which the Afghan state would be reconstituted following a period of interim transitional rule, a constitution-making process (the Loya Jirga), and eventually presidential and parliamentary elections. The presidential elections that occurred in October/November 2004—which affirmed the presidency of Hamid Karzai, who had been chosen as head of the interim government in Bonn and again at the Loya Jirga of June 2002—and the landmark parliamentary elections of September 2005.

The Afghan state remains a weak one struggling to build capable institutions, hobbled by the incomplete nature of statebuilding that occurred in the past as a result of a highly fragmented society, and with ongoing military challenges from a not-yet-fully-defeated Taliban (Rubin 1995: 2002). With the initial elections having occurred, however, it is possible to evaluate their conduct and to make inferences about the effect they have on the statebuilding enterprise in Afghanistan. The sequence of transition that put national dialogue processes first, the choice for presidentialism, the holding of parliamentary elections that give prominent roles to regional strongmen, the affirmation of women's rights to include the franchise, and the continued presence of the international community in providing security for the electoral event are all critical issues to consider for their implications both for Afghanistan and elsewhere.

The transition sequence in Afghanistan was developed in the context of the history of internecine war that plagued the country for 30 years; its fragmented, devastated, and de-modernized society, the ideological and ethnic orientations of the actors, and the political economy of war and predation (especially with regards to poppy cultivation and heroin production) have deeply shaped the patterns of politics that fed into the calculus of international mediators at Bonn. In the talks, the Afghan protagonists and international actors (through the six-plus-two formula) agreed to the creation of a transitional government to ease the vacuum of power following the Taliban collapse, a national dialogue/constitution-making process of the Loya Jirga (Council of Elders) with preparations by a constitutional commission, and to elections in 2004.

However, Bonn was not a comprehensive peace agreement and indeed it did not address core issues recognized in the peacebuilding literature as essential preconditions to peace, such as the disarmament of key factions; instead, the agreement promised the militias would come under the command of the interim government and that a new Afghan army would subsequently be formed. Given the realities on the ground, Bonn set the stage for a strategy of cooptation rather than confrontation with power-wielding local militias run personalistically by "warlords." Like criticism of Bosnia's Dayton Agreement for embracing ethnic nationalists, critics of Bonn point to the overall strategy of peacemaking as creating the critical problem for post-agreement peacebuilding. A Human Rights Watch report written a year after the agreement identified the challenge of statebuilding as a consequence of Bonn, a challenge that will also be a factor in the analysis of the 2004 and 2005 elections.

> But, because of the conscious choices made by key actors, notably Afghan military leaders and the United States, the processes set in motion by the Bonn Agreement are now faltering in key areas such as human rights, public security, the rule of law, and economic reconstruction. In the area of human rights (as in many other areas), the primary problem is the continuing power of Afghanistan's warlords. When the U.S. confirmed its commitment to the future of Afghanistan, it spoke about the primacy of democratization and human rights. Yet its actions have shown this commitment to be shallow. After the overthrow of the Taliban, it employed a "warlord strategy" in order to relieve it of its security and human rights responsibilities.
>
> (Human Rights Watch 2002)

With the provision of UN-mandated security under the auspices of the International Security Force (ISAF) and the deployment of a multidimensional peacekeeping operation (United Nations Assistance Mission in Afghanistan, UNAMA), the sequence path outlined in the Bonn agreement has remarkably held. The selection process for the Loya Jirga had a certain "democratic" component to it, as regional representatives were selected albeit not without intimidation and control by the regional power-holders. As envisaged, an "Emergency" Loya Jirga was convened by June 2002 that managed to reach agreement on Karzai's continued presidency and to the surprise of many it did not end in deadlock and disintegration but rather managed to affirm the integrity of the state, its multiethnic character, and the thorny relationships between the state, human rights, and Islam.

The convening of the constitution-making Loya Jirga was equally important in setting the stage for the 2004 elections, as it further ossified the power structures of regional warlords and cemented their control over key regions, arguably to the disadvantage of independent voices, advocates of women's rights, and civil society. Key decisions were made on the creation of a strong presidency, some advances on women's and other civil and political rights, the creation of ostensibly strong and independent judicial institutions including a Human Rights Commission, and it vaguely (and some would say inadequately) addresses the relationship between Islam, human rights, and the state.[17]

Despite two delays of the presidential elections over security concerns— involving, among other problems, attacks in UN electoral officials—the Afghan public first voted in presidential elections held on October 9, 2004. The elections were overseen by a Joint Electoral Management Body chaired jointly by a UN electoral official and including a number of prominent Afghans. Despite allegations of irregularity in the polls by several of the losing candidates (who ran independently, but with some affiliation to political parties), the outcome of the election (run on a simple-majority decision rule, but with a built-in second round if no candidate emerged victorious in the first round) was unambiguous: Hamid Karzai garnered 55.4 percent of the vote, more than three times his closest rival (Yunus Qanuni of the Afghan Nationalist Party, a Tajik). Among the most serious problems of the election was that it would run without a valid or fully developed voter registration roll. The principal effect of the election was to affirm what was already assumed: Karzai was a legitimate national leader, able to minimally unify Afghans sufficiently behind the new state despite all the problems associated with its troubled transition. Remarkably, but probably because of the extensive ISAF preparation and deployment, the presidential elections were held with very little political violence.

The September 2005 elections for the Wolesi Jirga (House of the People) were much more contested, with even greater ramifications for the state-building enterprise in Afghanistan. (They were delayed for a full year by Karzai due to the security situation.) Two-hundred and forty-nine seats were contested for the lower house through a system of Single Non-Transferable Vote (SNTV) in multi-member districts which varied in size (Kabul, for example, returned 33 seats), together with the election of 34 provincial councils. Thus, candidates ran as individuals in a fairly complicated electoral system designed to produce overall proportionality (through the mechanisms of SNTV and the choice for multi-member districts; proportionality increases with the district magnitude, or number of candidates returned from an electoral district). This choice led to no small amount of confusion on the part of voters (and perhaps accounted for a lower turnout rate of around 50 percent overall, and lower in Kabul with only 36 percent); more important, however, it led to the election of several candidates in some districts with as little as an 8 percent of the first-preference votes.

Evaluation of the election's outcome indicates a wide variety of celebrations and concerns: violence on election day was again fairly minimal, women in some cases beat strong opponents because they were seen as less likely to engage in corruption (women won six more seats than the 68 that had been reserved through a quota system), and overall the Afghan state now has a broader degree of popular legitimacy ... more than it has ever had (DeGrasse and Hsu 2005). On the other hand, warlords were elected into parliament in many parts of the country, with some 25 seats were won by regional warlords (politicians with their own militias). The election's outcome is ambiguous given the candidacy system, although one observer has described the outcome in terms of 81 members of "pro-government," 84 members as pro-opposition, and 84 members with no factional alignment; likewise, the results have been carefully analyzed according to ethnic identity (roughly proportional to the population) and those with jihadist orientations (Wilder 2005). Additional criticisms of the election is that the choice for SNTV weakened a functioning party system and inhibited the functioning of the parliament because of the unstable nature of coalition politics in the new body.[18]

The election's outcome in Afghanistan does have a significant impact on the prospects for statebuilding in that they have crowned a process that does not bode well for creating the type of mutually empowering state–society relations necessary for effective governance. As Barnett Rubin (2006: 24–25) has observed:

> The convening of the National Assembly on December 19, 2005, following the September 18, 2005 elections to the lower house and provincial councils, effectively completed the Bonn process, which aimed at reestablishing the permanent institutions of government. The election of representatives, however, is a means to the accountable provision of public services by the state. If the state is incapable of providing those public services, elections can lead to kleptocracy rather than democracy, and many Afghans fear that process is already under way.

Liberia: failed states, electoral processes and state resuscitation

President Ellen Johnson-Sirleaf, elected in landmark UN-guided, two-round elections in October and December 2005, has described a key challenge of peacebuilding in her country as the rebuilding of "disabled institutions." That is, Liberia was not necessarily a fully failed state, in terms of the total collapse of the state, but rather that state institutions were deliberately disabled by former regimes and most extensively under the kleptocratic rule of former President Charles Taylor. Surely, Johnson-Sirleaf's election as president in a closely contested poll that took place late 2005, along with parliamentary elections, in a long-term process of the resurrection of society and the rebuilding of state institutions in what all observers agree will be a long-term challenge in war-torn Liberia.

In 14 years of war, Liberia lost over 250,000 people to war in a country of only 3 million. The Liberian war has many facets, but at least one of which was the systematic abuse of the state to loot the country of resources and to facilitate the elite predation that was rampant under the rule of former president Charles Taylor, a former rebel leader who after a series of failed peace agreements and transitional governments managed to win the presidency in elections in 1997. Taylor systematically used the state for his personal enrichment, to include the alleged brokering of diamonds from neighboring Sierra Leone and the later plundering of Liberia's national forests in illicit timber sales.[19] The effect of the war on the Liberian state was pervasive: the security forces under Taylor became a "state within a state," government ministries either collapsed or became mechanisms for rent-seeking and banal graft, service delivery collapsed (especially in ungovernable rebel-held areas), and the country's financial institutions failed to function. Consequently, there was also a deep human-security crisis with widespread recruitment of child soldiers, deployment of landmines and proliferation of small arms, a devastated economic and social infrastructure, and among the lowest human development indicators on the planet (Levitt 2005).

The logjam in the Liberian imbroglio occurred in June 2003, when during peace talks being held in Ghana Taylor was indicted by the UN war-crimes tribunal for Sierra Leone, effectively undermining his ability to survive again by pledging peace while waging war. Further, as the war escalated in mid-1993 and a battle for Monrovia created a humanitarian emergency, the West African regional grouping ECOWAS (Economic Community of West African States) intervened anew to bring the fighting in Liberia to a halt. Following the arrival of Nigerian peacekeepers in August 2003, Taylor was whisked away to exile in Nigeria (from where he was later extradited to Freetown to face justice). At this stage, it was clear that Liberia had a chance for democracy (Sawyer 2005).

It is very likely that no real transformation of the Liberian state would have been possible without the removal of Taylor's grasp on power. Following his demise, the Comprehensive Peace Agreement was signed in Accra, Ghana, by Taylor's remaining loyalists and the two principal rebel forces, the Liberians United for Reconciliation and Democracy (LURD) and the Movement for Democracy in Liberia (MODEL). The agreement paved the wave for the long-planned deployment of a significant Chapter VII UN peace operation with a force of 15,000 troops under the oversight of tough-minded UN SRSG Jacques Paul Klein and pledged the parties to a full peace agreement that featured full disarmament and demobilization of the principal rebel forces, the creation of a transitional government, and the move toward elections under the extant constitution of Liberia. The UN Mission in Liberia (UNMIL) was a classic post-Cold War "multidimensional" peace operation that featured an emphasis on military and police security, the creation and strengthening of justice mechanisms, an emergency relief and crash development program, forward-thinking elements such as an HIV/AIDS policy coordinator and a child-soldier reintegration program ... and an electoral process.

The sequence path defined in the Comprehensive Peace Agreement was less complex than other similar cases, in part because there was not a specific, immediate desire by any party to fully review either the electoral law or the institutional design of the state. As a result, national elections were planned to occur more-or-less all at once to reconstitute the state but not to redesign the institutions themselves. In Liberia, mirroring the US constitution from which it draws its basic design, the President is head of state and the parliament consists of House of Representatives (64 seats) and a Senate (30 seats, two from each province or "county"). The most important aspects of the institutional design for this analysis are that the electoral systems used for executive and legislative outcomes are—in contrast to current theories and recommendations for postwar societies—essentially majoritarian. The president is elected in a two-round, majority-rule system and House and Senate members are both elected under a First-Past-the-Post system.

The presidential election October 11 (first round) and November 8 (second round) reveals a dramatic process that is significant, not for grand reasons of institutional design such as the possible benefits of majoritarian presidentialism, but because it reveals that the essentially peaceful outcome of the elections are *sui generis*: Liberia's first postwar elections ended peacefully because of sheer luck and able leadership. In the first round of elections, former Champions League football star and youthful populist George Weah won a plurality of votes (28.3 percent) and the next most winning candidate was Johnson-Sirleaf with a first-round tally of (19.8 percent). In the second round, however, voters clustered around Johnson-Sirleaf such that she was able to win 59.4 percent of the total votes cast compared with Weah's 40.6 percent. Remarkably, both rounds of elections went off peacefully, in no small measure attributable to the widespread deployment of international election observers and the ability of the UNMIL force to provide security (together with a fairly robust demobilization program having run its course).

In a moment of high drama, it was not clear, however, that Weah's supporters would accept his loss in the second round, and indeed in protests in Monrovia following the poll chanted "No Weah, No Peace;" indeed, into December of 2005 Weah claimed that due to fraud in the second round he had won the presidency. By mid-December, however, Weah conceded the presidency and the inauguration of Johnson-Sirleaf—Africa's first female president—went off without considerable violence. Despite speculation that Johnson-Sirleaf would appoint Weah to her cabinet in an act of voluntary power sharing, she declined to do so.

However, in the parliamentary elections Weah's party (the Congress for Democratic Change, CDC) holds a plurality in the House of Representatives. Moreover, in the House and in other posts are a range of former rebel and government of Liberia commanders and, indeed, Charles Taylor's wife (from whom he is legally separated) and a host of other erstwhile Taylor loyalists. Thus, the Liberian outcome is similar to Afghanistan's: the inclusion through the legislative arena of a number of factions involved in the war who have either emerged as "warlord" figures or whose hands are not clean in terms of the widespread atrocities that occurred. Indeed, several members of the new parliament are on lists of possible indictees in the Sierra Leone war-crimes court. Perhaps the one positive side of the legislative outcomes in Liberia is the relative balance of ethnic interests reflected in the results. Thus, serious problems may lie ahead in the functioning of the parliament as state-(re)building occurs in earnest, foremost among them factionalism, incoherence, and a number of legislators with a long-history of rent-seeking and corruption.

Despite the well-founded concerns about the nature of the Liberian parliament and the possibility of a Taylorist revival, the fact that Liberia was able to move toward a more legitimate state through the election of the widely popular Johnson-Sirleaf is a positive first step toward the enabling of state institutions. Liberia remains a tenuously balanced society with deep insecurities resulting from the devastation of the wars and neglect its people have suffered. With regional instability emanating from Cọte d'Ivoire, a proliferation of small arms, a culture of conflict, and a myopic scale-down of the UN peacekeeping force, Liberia remains at risk for recurrence of conflict. Nonetheless, comparatively, its electoral process has indeed imbued the state with a new legitimacy that for the first time in many years may give Liberia an opportunity to rearrange an erstwhile predatory state's relationship with its people.

Findings and recommendations

The focus on elections as part of postwar statebuilding has suffered from the association of such processes (and especially the national election event itself) as the end-point of a transition from war to peace and as a moment after which the international community can begin to disengage. The electoral processes analyzed here—especially the Cambodia, Afghanistan, and Liberia examples—suggest that this focus on elections as transition-ending has indeed been myopic. Scholars of peacebuilding (and indeed of democratization; see Carothers 2002) have long argued against short-term mentalities and the weaknesses of the standard, transition-driven approaches to building viable states that can provide for human security and development in the long term (Hampson 1996, Paris 2004).

This analysis reaffirms that finding in its evaluation of initial postwar elections in the four cases: electoral processes are critical turning points in transitions; however their outcomes only partially create the conditions for statebuilding and in some instances, such as in Cambodia in 1993, can seriously undermine the legitimacy of the state. Most important, these initial elections set the stage for the nature of state–society relations, for years to come as evidenced by the Cambodia and South Africa cases; in both of these instances, subsequent elections more or less confirmed extant power relations and control of the state by an autocratic regime (in Cambodia) and a dominant-party state (in South Africa). Table 9.1 illustrates the comparison of these cases and helps in the deriving of contingent generalizations from the analysis.

Several conclusions emerge from this analysis. First, electoral processes—despite a myriad of well-founded concerns leveled against them—are essential to statebuilding because they give a modicum of legitimacy and credibility to postwar regimes: South Africa, Afghanistan, and Liberia are all examples. In any situation, electoral processes there are pivotal moments of transition processes linked to a broad sequence of events. Despite a plethora of sensible and well-founded concerns with conducting elections after civil war there remains no alternative, feasible mechanism to test for the legitimacy of a state. Elections—for better or for worse—are an essential step in the process of reconstituting political order after civil war, despite the clear and evident risks they impose for re-igniting violent conflict in the heat and passion of the contest for power. While it might be ideal to delay postwar elections for up to ten years after a civil war—to allow for statebuilding, for reviving the

Table 9.1 Postwar electoral processes: cases considered

	Sequence Path in Peace Accord	Electoral System	Security and Violence	Management and Monitoring	Implications for Statebuilding
Cambodia *Constituent Assembly elections 2003*	1991 Paris Peace Accord Elections to a Constituent Assembly to Draft a New Constitution	Constituent Assembly: Closed Party List PR	UNTAC; Khmer Rouge resistance	UN Transitional Election Management Body	Following the UN-brokered post-election pact, Prime Minister Hun Sen vitiated the power-sharing agreement; a corrupt and exclusive state
South Africa *Elections to Parliament and Constituent Assembly (Indirect Presidential)*	1990 Groote Schuur Minute; 1993 Interim Constitution	Parliamentary: Closed Party-List PR, low (< 1% effective threshold)	South African security with UNOMSA/Interim Government Oversight; extensive pre-election factional violence	Newly Formed Independent Electoral Commission; International (informal) technical assistance	Transitional power-sharing pact gives way to dominant-party state; high legitimacy, mixed capacity

Table 9.1 (continued)

	Sequence Path in Peace Accord	Electoral System	Security and Violence	Management and Monitoring	Implications for Statebuilding
Afghanistan *Presidential Elections, 2004; Parliamentary Elections 2005*	Bonn Agreement of December 2001 defines the sequence path. Interim power-sharing government; 2002 *Loya Jirga*; 2004 *Loya Jirga*, 2004 Presidential Election; 2005 Parliamentary and Provincial Polls	Presidential: Two-Round Majority Parliamentary: SNTV in Multimember constituencies (no political parties) for 249 seats	UNAMA/NATO (2003–); anti-government violence by loyalists of the ousted Taleban, including assassination and bombings	UN–Afghan Joint Electoral Management Body	State enjoys high external legitimacy but faces ongoing violent opposition and debilitating internal divisions and factions
Liberia *Presidential and Parliamentary Elections 2005*	Accra Accord 2003; Established demobilization, disarmament, and reintegration; election timetable	Presidential: Two Round Majority Parliamentary: FPTP	UNMIL; sporadic public-order problems but no organized violence	Liberia National Elections Commission; UN Monitoring, Technical Assistance	Marginal victory by Johnson-Sirleaf mitigated by fractured parliament; highly legitimate state, feeble capacity

economy and improving human development, for changing incentive structures of elite predation, and for fostering trust and reconciliation—practical political imperatives demand faster action.

However, when such processes go awry and power is captured by a narrow faction that was party to the war in the first place, as in Cambodia, electoral processes inhibit the mutually enforcing state–society relations needed for effective states. Much depends on how elections are sequenced in terms of the providing of security, how they are related to power-sharing pacts that limit state capture, and how they are designed in terms of institutional choice. From this analysis, the most important variables in the viability of elections are the provision of security (usually, but not always, by external forces) and the extent of inclusivity in electoral outcomes. These cases give strong credence to the overall finding that security must precede electoral events, not follow them. At the same time, inclusion even of warlords or those who have perpetrated serious human-rights abuses may be necessary to achieve security in the short term, as the parliamentary polls in Afghanistan and Liberia indicate; such a strategy was not successful in Cambodia, however, as inclusion and even amnesty failed to turn the Khmer Rouge away from violently opposing the transition.

Second, the creation of legitimacy and the promotion of mutually reinforcing state–society relations in postwar depends on is the new election of new ruling elites in processes widely perceived as being free and fair. In situations where electoral processes return elites to power who have engaged in war (as in Cambodia, but also in Bosnia or Timor-Leste) they garner less legitimacy. Elite alternation is important, but so too is the integrity of the electoral process itself. Throughout the entire electoral process—from creation of the electoral management body, to evaluation of statutes on political party registration, to voter registration, candidate certification, laws on press freedoms, to design and distribution of ballots, to management of security, to election day itself, and certification of results, the entire process must be considered reasonably legitimate for elections to be legitimate and fair. Unless claims of fraud and abuse can be demonstrably and satisfactorily arbitrated (as in Liberia) or negotiated (as in South Africa), the stage is set for renewed conflict. The declaration of an election's relative freeness or fairness is closely linked with the observation, both by domestic observers (such as official monitors, civil society, or the press) and increasingly by international observers. While "free and fair elections"—whether the electoral process is "credible"—are not in themselves sufficient for conflict management, they are necessary as a critical contribution of democracy to resolving social differences through democratic means.

Third, the choice of electoral system is a pivotal consideration, not just for the first election but in subsequent polls as well. These cases feature a variety of choices, mostly due to historical artifact (in the case of Liberia) and considerations such as a weak party system in the case of Afghanistan. There is a de facto "default preference" by policymakers for closed-list PR as an electoral system choice in postwar environments (used in Cambodia and South Africa, and in many other settings as well): such systems tend to produce inclusivity in parliamentary outcomes—they do not prejudice the emergence of a relatively strong presidency, they are more amenable to facilitating the participation of displaced persons, they may strengthen party systems, and they do not require the delimitation of boundaries and even in some cases a fully finalized voters roll. But list-PR may not be conducive to further democratization that strengthens the state in the long run. As in South Africa, the experience in Kosovo offers further evidence on this score; according to Kosovar analysts,

> The electoral system that Kosovo has had so far, (closed lists-proportional representation) has served its purpose in the first term. It allowed parties to consolidate in the immediate phase after the war, but it was the wrong choice for the second term ... Unfortunately, independent politicians are still considered a nuisance not only to party leaders, but also to those international administrators who think that [final territorial] status and security can be solved without democracy. As a result, this system has discouraged the development of a proper democracy at the expense of some narrow and immediate interests.
>
> (Dugolli and Malazogu 2006: 1)

The concern about list PR suggests there is a longer-term need for combining proportionality with accountability, either through opening up lists or through moving toward candicacy-based systems such as SNTV or increasing district magnitude in a system of MMD; seemingly, open-lists are preferable as the choice for SNTV in Afghanistan demonstrates the problems of this system in terms of complexity. In post-settlement environments, however, the need for certainty at the moment of war termination runs counter to the need to revisit institutional choices down the road. For this reason, Pierre du Toit (2003) has rightly called for the need of the international community to open dialogue on war-terminating choices over time in what he has termed "post-settlement settlements."

Finally, there is strong reason for the international community to stay a strongly engaged actor well beyond the initial elections envisaged in peace accords. In Cambodia, it was some four years after the initial electoral event that Hun Sen seized power ... without a robust response from the international community to prevent or reverse the unilateral capture of the state. As Peter Wallensteen (2008) has argued, it is critical that the international community continue to react to crises of democratization long after peace agreements are reached and implementation processes have run their proverbial course, and that such reaction be closely tied to a keener sense of early warning when democratic accountability is being compromised (as in the removal of judges). Too often, the international community waits—as it did in Cambodia—until it is too late to react to crises of democratization in postwar environments. The attention span of international engagement must last well into the future if electoral processes are to create the mutually empowering state–society relations needed for statebuilding to be effective.

Notes

1 An electoral process is the entire sequence, from the design of the election itself (e.g., presidential or partliamentary, or proportional or majoritarian) and launch in the campaigns through the long lead-up to election day (the electoral "event"), any run-offs that may occur, and including the eventual resolution of post-election disputes.

2 On the function of immediate postwar elections as "validating" peace agreements, see Reilly 2003.

3 For a further articulation of this argument, see and Mansfield and Snyder 1995 and Snyder 2000.

4 See Chesterman et al. 2004.

5 For a comprehensive evaluation of the UN role in promoting democracy, see Brown 2003 and Newman and Rich 2004.

6 Paradoxically, election-related violence is found in situations when the outcome of the election is wholly uncertain—when power is up for grabs—and when there is a high degree of certainty about the outcome, when a particular party or faction is quite expected to win. Much depends on the motivation of prospective losers to do everything they can, including wage a violent struggle, to prevent themselves from losing political power through an electoral process.

7 For an overview, see Kumar 1999.

8 Elklit and Reynolds 2005 argue that electoral processes are too-often dichotomized as either "free or fair" or not, when a better understanding of the evaluation of such processes would suggest the need to understand the extent to which any given election may approach such an ideal; no electoral process is perfect.

9 Conflict-exacerbating election outcomes can be mitigated by a pre-election pact that determines the fate the of the election well before the ballots are cast; nego-tiation of pre-election pacts is strongly encouraged when there are significant spoiler challenges to elections or when an especially powerful party or faction seeks to boycott an election. Pre-election pacts are a form of power sharing. For recent analysis, see Roeder and Rothchild 2005.

10 For details, see Reynolds et al. 2005.

11 For an analysis of the Iraq imbroglio, see Diamond 2005. For a broader analysis of the issues of ethnic census voting, expectations in electoral contests, and the effects of electoral system choice in such considerations, see Horowitz 1985.

12 Procedures for handling electoral disputes through impartial, efficient, and legally valid, and widely accepted mechanisms are crucial even in the most advanced democracies. Accidents happen, mistakes are made, and trust is low: the institu-tions and procedures for dispute resolution need to be established and tested early in the electoral process, such that by the time voting day arrives there is trust in the fairness of the mediation and arbitration process. Without such institutions and mechanisms for dispute resolution, parties may well turn to violent means to press their interests in an election dispute.

13 For comprehensive information on electoral administration, see ACE: The Electoral Knowledge Network at www.aceproject.org.

14 As Eric Bjornlund (2004: 304–5) writes,

> The involvement of multilateral organizations in election monitoring has helped them to strengthen their commitment to promoting genuine democracy

among member states. Meanwhile, non-partisan domestic election-monitoring groups in developing countries have not only deterred fraud and improved public confidence in important elections but have also encouraged citizen involvement in political life more generally.

15 See Chesterman 2004.
16 Quoted in Sisk 1995: 243.
17 For analysis of the latter, see the Human Rights Watch report by Zia-Zarifi, 2004.
18 For analysis, see the International Crisis Group 2006a.
19 For details on Taylor's plundering, see Global Witness 2005.

Part V
Autonomy and dependence

10 The dangers of a tight embrace

Externally assisted statebuilding in Afghanistan

Astri Suhrke

This chapter examines the international assistance to post-Taliban state-building in Afghanistan with a focus on international economic and military assistance. The central argument is that this assistance has had negative as well as positive effects; together they create severe internal tensions in the statebuilding project itself. For all the achievements cited in removing the Taliban and launching an ambitious policy of reconstruction and modernization, the intervention in 2001 and subsequent aid strategies have also created a rentier state that is totally dependent upon foreign funds and military forces for its survival. Furthermore, this state has weak legitimacy and limited capacity to utilize aid effectively, and it faces a mounting insurgency. In this situation, the premises and structure of the statebuilding project invites critical examination.

Analytical perspectives

Much of the present policy-oriented literature on Afghanistan is either project-oriented,[1] or addresses policy within the established framework for international engagement in the post-Taliban years. This literature does raise questions about certain modalities of aid and often ends by recommending change, such as channeling more funds directly through the Afghan government, consulting more with the Afghan government on foreign military operations in the country, and increasing pressure on neighboring Pakistan to suppress the insurgents. Yet there is little critical thinking about the basic framework for international involvement and the underlying assumption that, on balance, it clearly has a positive effect. While the mounting problems in Afghanistan are being recognized, the dominant response from experts has been to call for increased international involvement. The premise evidently continues to be that a "critical mass" of external support—not yet reached—is required to turn things around.[2]

At least until mid-2006, when some hesitancy became evident, the policy of the US, its allies and the major aid agencies operated on a similar premise. The response to the growing problems—violence and corruption, slow institution building and economic recovery, rapid expansion of the opium economy, growing popular unrest, and failure by the central government to expand its hold beyond the capital—was to call for more economic assistance, stronger political commitment, and more foreign troops.[3]

The response reflects what is widely considered to be the main historical lesson from Afghanistan's recent past. The withdrawal of Soviet forces caused the Soviet-backed regime to crumble, the West no longer professed much of an interest in the country, and the mujahedin groups—aided and abetted by Afghanistan's neighbors—turned on each other in a nasty civil war. Neither the US nor the UN intervened to stop the fighting, and the Pakistan-supported Taliban exploited the anarchic violence to seize power, eventually controlling some 90 percent of the territory and giving sanctuary to international terrorists until they were overthrown by the US intervention in 2001. This narrative of international abandonment understandably is a warning against reduction or withdrawal of international assistance at the present time. Instead, a steadfast commitment and more involvement are recommended. "International" in this discourse is typically taken to mean activities undertaken under the auspices of the UN, the Western-led donor community, NATO or the US-led coalition forces. Western analysts often contrast this involvement with "opportunistic" intervention by neighboring states—notably Iran and Pakistan—that are seen as "ready to intervene" if "[the] international community ... reneges on its commitments to help secure and rebuild the country" (Weinbaum 2006).

This narrative has inhibited critical thinking about the fundamentals of the contemporary statebuilding project in Afghanistan. There is, for instance, little if any systematic comparison with the ill-fated Soviet intervention in 1979–89, although the escalating insurgency has made for instructive comparisons (and is a subject of black humor among Afghans).[4]

By contrast, concepts of legitimacy and accountability are central to the analysis of statebuilding in Afghanistan that is set out below. So is the notion that conflict is inherent in the statebuilding enterprise qua social change, and as such will necessarily enter into the relationship between the outside agents and the national or local actors. In this respect, the premise of the present chapter is closer to that of the contribution by Barnett and Zürcher in this volume. A perspective that recognizes the tensions and dilemmas of externally assisted statebuilding—above all when such assistance is largely foreign-directed—is also shared by a small but persistent set of critical voices in the Afghan-specific literature (Johnson and Leslie 2004; Koehler 2005; Ottaway and Lieven 2002; Suhrke and Woodward 2002).[5]

What, then, are these tensions and dilemmas, and are they so stark in the Afghanistan case because of the nature of that particular enterprise?

The Afghanistan case is distinctive for several reasons. Historically, as is often pointed out, the central state has been weak. The point has sometimes been exaggerated—the period since the reforms of Amanullah Shah in the early 1920s was after all marked by the growth of a uniform and nation-wide civil administration and other national institutions such as the police and the courts.[6] Yet more than two decades of war, foreign invasion and various attempts to introduce radical social change had severely damaged the structure and authority of the emerging Afghan central state. By the time the US-led military intervention toppled the Taliban regime and installed a successor, authority and power were fragmented. Instead of a clear center, there were numerous local leaders including commanders, tribal notables and mullahs who had risen to power during and as a result of the war, as well as political leaders, mostly with a religious background, whose stature likewise was shaped by their role in the war against the Soviet-supported regime and the subsequent civil war. This fragmented political landscape interacted negatively with another distinctive dimension of the Afghanistan case—the "bad neighborhood" effect. Located on the cross-roads of Asia, Afghanistan has long been subject to competing and intervening influences from its neighbors as well as large powers further afield. The same was true this time. As outside powers cultivated competing Afghan factions, a centrifugal process was set in motion that exacerbated internal cleavages and fragmented efforts of the UN mission (UNAMA) to forge a common strategy of statebuilding at the central level.

Most important, however, the foundation for the statebuilding enterprise was a foreign military intervention. The origins of the new regime raised serious questions about its legitimacy and its leader—Hamid Karzai—who was chosen by the United States and affirmed as the head of the transitional government. Although later elected president through a popular vote (with much public backing and liberal funding from the US), Karzai's image remained tarnished. When disillusionment and difficulties later appeared, as inevitably would happen in a difficult peacebuilding process, Afghan critics readily compared Karzai to two earlier leaders who likewise had been installed by foreign troops—the exiled Shah Shuja, whom the British had put on the throne in the mid-nineteenth century, and Babrak Karmal, whom the Soviet government had brought back to Afghanistan in late 1979 to assume power. Neither of them had lasted very long.

The other important aspect of the origins of the statebuilding venture was its links to the US-led international "war on terror." The United States had intervened in Afghanistan in order to destroy the Taliban and their international Al-Qaeda supporters. As the "war on terror" escalated—both in Iraq and elsewhere—the difficult state-and-peacebuilding mission in Afghanistan was drawn into its vortex. The intensifying conflict between militant Islam and the West spilled over in Afghanistan. Taliban and their supporters recruited increasingly from the Middle East as a fall-out from the war in Iraq. US and NATO forces started to launch large, offensive operations in the southeast. The political discourse and protests within the country reflected signal issues in the "war on terror" such as the cartoons of the Prophet Muhammad, and US imprisonment of Muslims (including Afghans) at Guantanamo and elsewhere.

On the ground inside Afghanistan, the "war on terror" continued. A principal mission of the US after the initial defeat of Taliban had been to destroy the remaining Islamist militants in the border areas. The strategy of waging war while trying to build peace created serious internal tensions in the statebuilding project. Most obviously, US and later NATO military commanders worked with local "warlords" in the fight against Taliban and foreign militants, thereby empowering local leaders. The result was to undermine the central state, which the US and much of the international community in principle also sought to strengthen. As the insurgency gathered strength, it seemed to further sap the energy of the reconstruction and statebuilding efforts and gave the political discourse a militant Islamic edge. Increasingly pressed to defend its nationalist and Islamic creditentials, the government's balancing act between modernist supporters and traditional critics, and between international patrons and domestic clients, became very difficult.

These conditions sharpened tensions that under more favorable circumstance might have surfaced as lesser problems. But whether appearing in stark or soft form, the most central dilemmas the statebuilding venture seemed to spring from the dangers of a tight embrace. Giving the leader, regime or state to be built too little support could undermine growth, physical protection, effectiveness, and other tangible outputs that external money, technology and troops could help provide, but giving too much support could stifle the sense of ownership, the growth of local capacity and local accountability structures, and more generally, the legitimacy of the enterprise. External aid flows would enhance the power of the local agents through whom the money flows, but it would also underline the fact the handlers were mere agents and, to that extent, weak and dependent. External presence in a post-conflict situation represented a tangible commitment to peace and stability, but it also would create irritants, distortions and generate expectations of change that may be unrealistic. Building a strong national army to replace warring militias would help establish security, which in turn is necessary for reconstruction and statebuilding, but too strong an army might decide to take over the enterprise. Cutting across these are two common sets of tensions: (1) between the production of a certain good, and its legitimacy, and (2) short-term gratification and long-term sustainability.

In theory, contradictory forces of this kind should in each case have an optimal or equilibrium points, for instance where the advantages of importing administrative capacity outweigh its disadvantages. To identify such points, however, is extremely difficult. As a step in this direction, the rest of this chapter will examine such tensions in two areas of a tightly embraced statebuilding in Afghanistan—creating financial and military capacity at the central level.

Structures of dependence

International efforts were essential in getting the post-Taliban statebuilding enterprise off the ground. Initially organized through the UN in an extraordinary show of unity, the states and aid agencies engaged in Afghanistan were generally referred to as "the international community." Each had, of course, distinct interests. Over time, these emerged more clearly as divergent or rival concerns. The major players included the UN mission (UNAMA) and the UN agencies. NATO as an organization underwrote the international peacekeeping and stabilization presence through ISAF (International Security Assistance Force). The international financial institutions (especially the World Bank), the European Union and Japan from the beginning provided much assistance for economic reconstruction and governance. Russia and India reformulated their aid and policy agendas in relation to the post-Taliban order, as did Iran and Pakistan, although Pakistan was handicapped by its past support for the Taliban. Gradually, the new government in Kabul also expanded relations with the smaller republics to the north that had emerged from the disintegration of the Soviet Union. But the United States clearly remained the single most important foreign actor. Initially content to let the UN take the diplomatic lead, in mid-2003, Washington adopted an active policy of "nation-building" that entailed a more politically intrusive role. The US continued to set the ground rules for the international military involvement by virtue of its own combat forces on the ground (in Operation Enduring Freedom, OEF) and as the preeminent member of NATO. The US was a major actor in the economic assistance field as well. In mid-2006 the US transferred more of the military functions to NATO.[7]

For Afghanistan, the dependence on these components of the international community was a fundamental and visible fact of life. Several years after the new government was installed in Kabul, military security and the national budget—the two pillars of the statebuilding agenda—continued to be almost totally dependent on foreign forces and foreign funding. The degree of military dependence is illustrated by President Karzai's amazing public admission of weakness in May 2005. If foreign forces were to leave, he warned, Afghanistan would "go back immediately to chaos … Afghanistan will not make it as a sovereign, independent nation able to stand on its own feet."[8] As for the budget, over 90 percent of the total for 2004–5 came from external funds, with no significant change in this ratio in sight (World Bank 2005a: vii–viii).

Economic dependence

Foreign donors initially prioritized humanitarian aid assistance and the government collected very little tax revenue in 2002, equivalent to less than 10 percent of the national budget. Three years later, domestic tax collection had approximately doubled to around $280 million, but was still quite modest. The revenue-to-GDP ratio was only 5 percent, which was "well below the level even in other very poor countries," the World Bank critically noted (ibid.: viii). The overall expenditure level had also increased, with the result that domestic revenues were expected to cover only 8 percent of the total national budget for 2004–5. The rest was to come from donor funding.[9]

In other words, the ratio of domestic to foreign sources of funding was almost exactly the same as in 2002. The pattern was expected to continue for at least the next five-year period, according to the IMF and President Karzai.[10]

The extreme dependence was underscored by a change in budgetary structures starting in 2004. Instead of an operating and a development budget, as had been the practice before, there was now a core budget, which was handled by the Afghan Ministry of Finance, and an external budget, which was developed in consultation with the Afghan authorities but controlled by the donors. The external budget (2.5 billion dollars in 2004/05) was much larger than the Afghan-controlled budget (865 million dollars for both operating and development expenditures). The external budget included both development and some operating expenses for the army, the police, the health services, education, special national programs like the National Solidarity Program, and the cost of elections. From the Afghan government's perspective, these sectors were beyond its financial control, as the IMF pointed out,[11] and were listed as "off budget" items in major planning documents, including the Afghan National Development Strategy for 2006–10.

How does this revenue ratio compare with the record of previous modernizing regimes in the country? Afghan rulers have long been dependent upon foreign funding, but especially so in two recent periods—during the presidency of Mohammad Daoud (1973–77), and the communist regime (1978–92). These periods therefore are useful points of comparison. As shown in Table 10.1, the comparison is unfavorable for the Karzai government. At both the beginning and end of Daoud's presidency, domestic revenue collection accounted for slightly over 60 percent of total expenditure, even though Daoud had launched grand development schemes that were heavily financed by the US and the USSR. The figures for the early years of the communist regime are in the same range (52–71 percent), even though the government's dependence on the Soviet Union had increased enormously as a result of the invasion and escalating war with the Western-supported mujahedin.[12] By

Table 10.1 Domestic revenue and budget expenditure (Afghanistan)

	Budget expenditure (in mill. afs)		Domestic revenue as percentage of budget expenditure			
	Regular budget	External budget	Operating budget	Development budget	External budget	Total budget
1973	11,318	0	58	42	0	63
1977	24,326	0	49	51	0	61
1979	30,173	0	56	44	0	52
1982	42,112	0	69	31	0	71
2004/2005	41,952	120,144	64	36	8	8

Sources: Rubin (1995), p. 113, 297; World Bank (2005a), pp. 7–8.
Note: The additional "external budget" was first established in 2004.

comparison, after four years the post-Taliban government only collected enough domestic revenue to pay for 8 percent of the total budget, and some 30 percent of the much smaller core budget. The latter mostly covered salaries for government officials on the central level, increasingly also provincial-level officials, but no development project of significance.[13]

Against this background, the intense discussion within the international aid community about the choice of channel for aid transfers becomes less interesting. Channeling more aid through the core budget—as the World Bank and the Afghan government are recommending—would only reduce the government's secondary dependence on the donors.[14] As such, it would go only a small way to close "the sovereignty gap," as former Afghan Finance Minister Ashraf Ghani advocates (Ghani et al. 2005). As long as aid money continued to be the main source of revenue, primary dependence on the donors would remain, and conditions of quasi-sovereignty—to paraphrase Robert Jackson and Carl Rosberg—would prevail (Jackson and Rosberg 1982).

The implications of such extreme dependence on external resources for state survival have been much discussed in the literature on state formation in Africa; for example, in the concept of "extraversion" developed by Jean-François Bayart. Extreme dependence is also part of a broader category of political phenomena called the rentier state. As commonly understood, the rentier state is the exact opposite of what might be said to be the goal of a statebuilding process and, in the case of Afghanistan, as expressed in the formal policy objectives formulated in the Bonn Agreement and related instruments.

The rentier state

As indicated above, the rentier state is a familiar concept in Afghan history. Daoud's presidency is usually singled out as the prototypical rentier state, but other modernizers received substantial foreign funding as well, or subventions, in the language of British imperial officers, who supplied Afghan rulers with funds in the late nineteenth century. The rentier state as it has manifested itself in Afghanistan and elsewhere has been closely studied and has produced a clear conclusion: it is not conducive to either economic development or the evolution of a democratically accountable government.[15]

The main argument regarding democratic development is that accountability follows the direction of resource flows. With the national budget mostly financed by foreign governments and institutions, the Afghan government's major responsibility in accounting for the use of these funds is towards the donors, rather than its own people. The same observation has been made of earlier Afghan regimes that were heavily dependent on external funding. In his seminal study of Afghan political development, Barnett Rubin concludes that Daoud's rentier income from foreign aid and revenue from sales of natural gas had dysfunctional political effects. "Renewed external revenues relieved Daoud of whatever incentives he might have had to make his government accountable [to the population]. He did little to transform the mode of governing to match the means by which he had taken power" (Rubin 1995: 75).

When rebuilding a new order in Afghanistan after the Taliban, most donors insisted on including democratic reforms. Democratic accountability was expected in the long run to contribute to stability, legitimacy and order, and was the reason why the Bonn Agreement and the new Constitution (2003) both provided for a parliament. The parliament elected in 2005 started immediately to flex its muscles. Yet it was unclear what would be its sources of strength if it lacked the power of the purse that historically has forced kings to subject themselves to the scrutiny of the propertied and productive classes. In this context, large aid flows—particularly if they are in the range of 90 percent of the total budget—would tend to marginalize the parliament by giving the donors a more important voice, at least de facto, in setting policy and in holding the government accountable for its use of the funds. The power of the donors in this respect was underlined by the contract-like provisions with the Afghan government in the Afghanistan Compact agreed to at the London conference in 2006. Efficient use of large aid inflows may of course produce some economic development gains, and to that extent also stability. But it is clearly at odds with the long-run goal of promoting democratic government in Afghanistan—which is also central to the state-building agenda—and does little to strengthen the authority and legitimacy of the present government.

To understand the impact of large aid flows on the legitimacy of the government, two factors are critically important: the poppy economy, and the extreme fragmentation of political power. When the new Karzai Administration was installed, the central state appeared as only one of several armed factions. The government controlled the capital but was itself severely factionalized (especially in the first two years), and had only a tenuous hold on the official provincial administration that, almost miraculously, had survived the years of war and turmoil. And while the Karzai government had the enormous advantage of being the internationally recognized party and the formal recipient of aid, some other factions also had external supporters and the additional advantage of exercising control on the ground and having access to significant capital through the opium economy. As the production and trade of poppy rapidly increased and spread to new areas, it underwrote a set of parallel structures of power and authority. This limited the potency of foreign aid in garnering support for the central government.

While the government could use aid resources to provide services and obtain political support, so could rival factions who had other sources of capital. In bargaining for support and political alignment, the fact that the government was dependent on foreign monies undoubtedly was a weakness in two respects. The foreign element was a liability in a political climate increasingly characterized by anti-government and anti-foreign protests, as we shall see below. It was also problematic if viewed from a rational-actor perspective. Dependence on foreign aid exposed the weakness of the government as an autonomous actor. This increased the uncertainty and risks for other actors of aligning with the government, thus introducing a marked hedging effect in the bargaining between the center and local power holders.

It is not difficult to find evidence of hedging. Afghans are acutely aware that in their recent history external patrons have often proved fickle or acted contrary to local interests. Politics traditionally has been based on flexible alignments and shifting alliances. The early Karzai administration was no exception. Both on the central and local level, frequently asked questions were how long the US would support Karzai, and with how much. If Karzai makes a deal and the foreigners break it, the other local party to the agreement has little recourse. The anti-government factions exploit the same logic by capitalizing on the lack of development and sustained presence by government forces in areas that they themselves have made insecure. Hedging adds to the manifest unwillingness to pay taxes and the widespread disregard for the official ban on cultivation and trading of poppy.[16] When the government does obtain compliance, it is typically transitory and in the nature of a spot contract.

The case of the halt in poppy production in Nangarhar province in early 2005 is illustrative. Strong pressure from the central government and promises of generous aid made the governor of Nangarhar (appointed by Kabul) and the local military strongman (self-appointed) impose a temporary ban on poppy production.[17] Production fell by an estimated astounding 96 percent, and made a significant dent in national statistics as well since Nangarhar was a major growing area. After one growing season, however, farmers resumed cultivation. The precise reasons are unclear, but a major argument was that the promised aid had not been forthcoming. Donor spokesmen, in turn, claimed that the provincial population had entertained unrealistic expectations. Aid at any rate needed to go through proper preparation and project cycles. Karzai was publicly silent. He had entered into a contract and could not deliver, and the role of the foreigners overshadowed the deal. Farmers further reported that "the other side" advised them not to cooperate with the foreigners by observing the cultivation ban.

In the short run, while aid provides resources that permit some of the government functions to be undertaken, extreme financial dependence on foreign aid creates a measure of political weakness that cuts against the statebuilding project. As the government in effect plays the role of an agent, rather than one of an owner-patron, to use the language of institutional economics, its credibility to honor long-term political contracts with potential rivals, contesters and supporters is questioned. Instead, spot contracts—ad hoc alignments subject to sudden shift—dominate. Such alignments may well be characteristic of traditional Afghan politics, as is often argued. Yet it certainly differs from the development of stable rules and predictable relationships that are the essence of institution building and associated with the development of an effective state marked by "competence and integrity," as envisaged in the Bonn Agreement.

Sustainability

Even rentier states financed by resources controlled by the state have an element of unsustainability, but domestic natural resources such as oil and diamonds are likely to last longer and have more predictable return than foreign assistance, which is shaped by strategic and therefore inherently shifting interests. Recognizing this as a recurrent feature of their history, the Afghans sought to maximize aid in the short run. This strategy was especially pronounced in the immediate aftermath of the Bonn Agreement, when the government hoped to capitalize on the newsworthiness of the peace. The then-Finance Minister, Ashraf Ghani, argued forcefully that massive aid was necessary for reconstruction and, above all, to drown out the illegal economy. Absent sufficient aid, he warned, Afghanistan would become a "narco-mafia state." His argument underpinned the planning document prepared for the second donor conference in Berlin in March 2004, which called for 28 billion dollars in aid over a seven-year period, and framed the London 2006 conference as well. Billed as a meeting to lay down a political, economic, and social strategy for the next five-year period, the conference produced pledges of over 10 billion dollars for the planning period.

War-devastated and fragmented Afghanistan clearly lacked capacity to absorb aid of this magnitude. Instead of taking a long-haul approach based on a modest inflow of aid that could be equilibrated with the build-up of local capacity, the Ministry of Finance decided to increase absorption levels by importing capacity in the form of international consultants, including expatriate Afghans on international contracts. The consultants took over much of the regular work in the ministries selected for reform (first and foremost, the Ministry of Finance). In August 2004, a total of 224 advisors of this kind were working within the Ministry of Finance, contracted through the international consulting firm Bearing Point under a 95.8 million dollar USAID contract.[18] A European delegation visiting in April 2006 noted that the ministries continued to be "full of external advisors"; many were Afghans from abroad on short-term contracts and with insufficient knowledge of conditions in the country.[19] The scheme was effective in absorbing aid money, but lacked programs for transferring skills (consultants initially worked in office quarters separate from those of the regular Afghan employees, for instance), and raised serious questions about sustainability.

Efforts to link imported capacity to training programs were instituted, but progressed slowly. By mid-2005 development spending was "substantially below budget expectations, essentially due to lack of security and the low capacity of line ministries and implementing agencies to develop and implement projects," the IMF reported (IMF Country Report, July 5, 2005: 6). Some European donors that wanted to shift more funds from international NGOs or UN agencies to the government observed that lack of government capacity was a significant constraint (Strand and Olesen 2005). Some donors increasingly favored channeling aid directly to local authorities or NGOs in areas where their national Provincial Reconstruction Teams (PRTs) were deployed. But capacity constraint was evident on all levels. Even USAID, which mostly worked directly with US contractors and their subcontractors in the field, managed to spend only half of the money appropriated for 2004–5. The US Government Accountability Office reported that many USAID projects were hastily initiated in preparation for the 2004 presidential election in Afghanistan and much of the funding was wasted.[20]

This aid dynamic has had dysfunctional effects in the short run, and seems unsustainable in the longer run. Calls for massive inflows and generous promises generated huge expectations which, unsurprisingly, were not met. The aid discourse contrasted with the reality of slow implementation, visible and widespread corruption, ostentatious displays of new riches, and grinding poverty in large parts of the country, especially in the outlying and insecure areas. Criticism and populist rhetoric mounted. The ubiquitous presence of foreign aid experts on high salaries further fueled political dissatisfaction and unrest, while aid experts pointed to the cost-ineffectiveness of employing foreign consultants or international NGOs rather than using local capacity.[21] By 2006 there were some signs of self-correction in the donor community, as evident in the tougher language on implementation and domestic revenue collection at the London meeting.[22]

Military dependence

The government's five-year plan for 2006–10, the Afghanistan National Development Strategy (ANDS), is prefaced with a poem by the ninth-century Islamic scholar Ibn Qutayba. It begins as follows: "There can be no government without an army ... " The military indeed played a critical role in statebuilding in the early post-Taliban period, although the troops were international rather than national. The new Afghan National Army (ANA) was built up slowly, reaching only 22,000 men by mid-2005, as against the international force level which at that time had stabilized around 30,000.[23] In the meantime, both the US-led combat forces (OEF), and the UN-authorized and NATO-commanded stabilization force (ISAF) sought to achieve three central objectives of statebuilding: disarming opponents, deterring rivals, and defeating the militant opposition to the central state.

ISAF's main task was to deter rivals and encourage opponents to disarm. By securing the capital soon after the fall of the Taliban, ISAF effectively preempted renewed military rivalry among the Afghans factions for the capital (over which they had fought with such devastating consequences in the civil war of 1992–96). Smaller ISAF teams were deployed outside the capital to remind local power holders that Kabul had important external patrons, and additionally undertook civil affairs projects in a "hearts-and-minds" strategy. Formally this was called "extending the authority of the central government in the provinces." ISAF's deterrence effect was reinforced by the much more powerful US military presence. Using "B-52 diplomacy,"

US military personnel appeared at strategic points of conflict to communicate that potentially much larger force could be brought to bear. The threat of international force was the backdrop for Kabul's progress in standing down regional strongmen, especially Dostum in the North and Ismael Khan in the West, and for the gradual marginalization of the powerful Defense Minister, Marshal Fahim in 2003–4.[24] Although not specifically mandated to assist the UN-supervised program to demobilize the various military factions, the presence of ISAF and OEF likewise helped bring the first phase of the program to a completion in September 2005. International military force also helped enforce the new rules of political competition. In the run-up to the elections in 2004 and 2005, ISAF troops were deployed to protect ballot places, and US forces on so-called "full-spectrum missions" encouraged villagers to vote.

The contribution made by international forces to protecting the capital and enforcing the new rules for control over the central state helped preserve a large measure of peace—in the sense of no war—in the capital and initially two-thirds of the country. As a result, people expressed considerable tolerance for their presence despite the legendary Afghan resistance to foreign troops in the past, whether they issued from the Soviet Union or the British imperial army. One widely cited poll in 2005 found that two-thirds of the respondents wanted US forces to remain in the country "until security is restored." If foreign troops stood between them and renewed civil war or a Taliban-style rule, they were welcome.[25]

The insurgency

Yet the welcome seemed to be wearing down over time, as expressed in mounting protests over the conduct of foreign, especially US military forces, and the growing strength of the insurgency. The primary mission of the US forces—to destroy Al-Qaeda bases in Afghanistan and defeat the remnants of the Taliban—produced inconclusive or negative results. The militants responded to the US-led offensives by attacking foreign troops regardless of mission and command, as well as "soft targets," such as foreign-aid personnel and Afghans working with them. Suicide attacks became more common. The tactic had previously not been used in Afghanistan and was attributed to the presence of foreign Islamic fighters. Violent events in the country as a whole increased markedly from 2003 onwards. In the southern and the eastern provinces, the number killed in 2005 was higher than at any time since 2001.[26] Violence intensified further during the first half of 2006 as ISAF forces were preparing to take over from US forces in the southern provinces. Some 300 persons (civilians and military) were reported killed in May and early June alone, and rising to around 600 in July as US-led forces mounted a massive offensive in the southeast designed to root out the insurgents once and for all.[27] Nevertheless, reports indicated that the Taliban-controlled large swaths of territory in the southeast, particularly at night.[28]

Fresh recruits were mobilized locally and from sanctuaries on the Pakistan side of the border, reinforced by foreign jihadi fighters. The decision in late 2005 to increase NATO force levels, as well as the unprecedented scale of the US-led offensive in May–June the following year, amounted to an admission that the insurgents were gaining in strength.

At the village level, it appeared that "the Americans bomb the wrong kind of people and imprison innocent people," as an elder Pashtun in the central Logar province told a foreign visitor (Donini et al. 2004: 32). Foreign troops on search and destroy operations were especially likely to cause local concern, but the distinction between OEF units with a search-and-destroy combat mission and ISAF units with primarily a stabilization mission was not always clear to outsiders.[29] Concerns among Afghans ranged from issues of improper social behavior of foreign soldiers to the widespread disruption, death and other "collateral damage" caused by the counter-insurgency campaign. Major offensives involving dense air strikes and the use of 500-pound bombs in rural areas believed to house insurgents were certain to produce negative reactions regardless of the villagers' initial attitude towards the Taliban. In a case where US air strikes killed 35 villagers in Kandahar province, the elders asked Karzai to tell foreign troops to leave.[30] The southeast, moreover, was the stronghold of tradition-bound Pashtun tribes and the home region of the Taliban. Almost regardless of their actions, foreign forces were handicapped by the very fact of being foreigners and outsiders in a tribal social order. In the poll commissioned by a US television company in 2005, cited above, one-third of the respondents said that attacks on US forces were justified. In subgroups of "socially conservative" respondents, and those who were "dissatisfied with the benefits of peace," the figure rose to 60 percent.

Dependence on foreign military force thus had contradictory effects on the statebuilding process. Fighting the insurgency with foreign troops provided coercive force that the central state lacked, but by virtue of their actions and identity foreign troops also undermined popular support for the government. US forces also collaborated with local powerholders by paying for manpower and intelligence for use in military operations. Widely reported soon after the Karzai government was formed, the practice evidently continued.[31] The result was to empower local groups that were actual or potential opponents of a stronger central state. Finally, the highly unequal nature of the relationship undermined the authority of the Karzai government by demonstrating its subordination to US military priorities. In legal terms, the point was expressed by the absence of the kind of status of forces agreement (SOFA) that normally regulates troop deployments among sovereign states. When incidents involving US forces caused public embarrassment and popular anger, Karzai deplored the events and requested his main ally to change behavior, but with little effect.

A series of incidents in the spring of 2005 proved particularly embarrassing as they came at the time when Washington and Kabul were launching closer military, economic and political cooperation in the form of a "strategic partnership." A UN report had documented illegal arrests, torture, and death of Afghans held by US forces in Afghanistan.[32] US military operations had (again) claimed children among its civilian victims. Coincidentally, reports that US forces had desecrated the Koran while interrogating prisoners at Guantanamo (where a number of Afghans were held), caused violent demonstrations in Afghanistan as elsewhere. Karzai demanded that US forces exercise "extreme caution," asking that the Afghan government be consulted on OEF operations and that Afghan detainees held by US forces in the country be handed over to Afghan authorities.[33] The concessions from the US were mostly symbolic. Some detainees were released, but the government's position of powerlessness was confirmed in both legal and political terms. The terms of the new "strategic partnership" gave the US as well as NATO forces "freedom of action" to conduct military operations, although based on unspecified "consultations and pre-approved procedures." Yet the strategic partnership was just a mutual declaration, not a treaty, and the formulations were vague. Pressed on the meaning of "consultations," President Bush pointedly avoided a commitment by saying "we'll consult with them in terms of how to achieve mutual goals. ... [The United States] will consult with Afghanistan if it perceives its territorial integrity, independence or security is at risk."[34]

The precise damage done to the Karzai government's authority by such heavy-handed military tactics and diplomacy is difficult to assess, but was probably considerable. It seemed to indicate that power relations had not fundamentally changed since US forces invaded the country and installed the new government, despite the fact that Karzai had subsequently been legitimized by traditional means (the Emergency Loya Jirga in 2002), and through presidential elections (in 2004). Dependence again appeared as weakness. If the Karzai government by its own admission was so dependent on foreign forces, and, by the demonstrated heavy-handedness of the US, so unable to influence its larger ally, aligning with the government carried a high risk. The point was underscored by the Taliban, who increasingly targeted both officials and ordinary persons working for the government and its foreign supporters.

Building the Afghan National Army (ANA)

The most obvious way out of the predicament posed by reliance on foreign troops was to build up a national Afghan army. This would also address the problematic fact that the head of the government and the key personal ally of the United States—Hamid Karzai—unlike the other contenders for power did not have his own group of armed followers. Karzai's initial reliance on private US security contractors for bodyguards was a stark reminder of this weakness.

US Special Forces started training and equipping the ANA in early 2002, almost immediately after the invasion (Jalali 2002). The program was accelerated after the Bush administration in mid-2003 changed its Afghanistan policy to stress state- and nation-building. Although British, French, and later Canadian forces assisted, building the ANA was above all a US project. American military trainers were embedded with their Afghan counterparts, equipment was airlifted from the US, and salaries and construction costs were paid by the US. At the US Bagram Air Field base, new sections were established in the Office of Security Cooperation-Afghanistan to oversee the program.

The development of the ANA was almost entirely financed by the United States through the external budget of the Afghan government, that is, the part beyond Kabul's control. For fiscal year 2003/2004, the US funded 618.3 million dollars of a planned budget of 904 million, and the following year contributed over 550 million towards a planned budget of 904 million.[35] Funds came primarily from the Foreign Military Financing (FMF) budget, a long-standing Department of Defense program that in the past has provided military support to US allies in the Middle East, above all Israel, Egypt, and Jordan. Unlike other Afghan development sectors financed by donors through the external budget, funding for the ANA was steady and secure, virtually up-front at the beginning of the budget year. For 2004/2005, 80 percent of the planned expenditure for ANA had been funded as per the mid-year review. By comparison, only 15 percent of the budget for the Livelihood and Social Protection sector had been funded, and 14 percent for the Education and Vocational Training, even though the dollar amount for both education and livelihood combined was far less than the allocation for the ANA.[36] The Pentagon funds covered all aspects of ANA development, including salaries, logistics, training, construction of recruiting stations, rehabilitation of hospitals, construction of garrisons in the southeast and the south, establishment and operation of the four regional commands (Kandahar, Herat, Gardez, and Mazar-e-Sharif). The largest single item was the formation of the central Army Corps of three infantry brigades in Kabul. US funds also supported the development of the ANA Air Corps.

The Afghan government and its Ministry of Defense controlled only a small part of the overall defense budget. A mere 114 million dollars in 2004/2005 was channeled through the core budget, mainly for salaries, including ministry staff. The marginalization of the ministry implied by this budgetary structure was related to other postwar developments. It was originally part of a broader policy to demobilize the remnants of the mujahedin factions—the so-called factional armies that had fought first the communists and subsequently each other in the civil war in the 1990s—and specifically to weaken the power of Marshal Fahim, the Minister of Defense. Fahim commanded a large factional army and was stalling the demobilization program. By early 2004, however, his position had eroded. His lack of cooperation on demobilization and reform of the Ministry of Defense, as well as his identity as an ethnic minority (Tajik from Pansjir) but leader of a militarily powerful faction (Northern Alliance), had attracted a growing number of critics from among modernists, human-rights activists and Pashtun leaders, as well as the US and other donors.

The US-led policy of forming a new, national army, funded and directed by donors, was intended to weaken Fahim and speed up the demobilization program. The strategy also served US interests more directly. An army built, trained, equipped, and financed by Washington would be subject to American influence in numerous direct and indirect ways, from ideological formation to budgetary controls and supply of spare parts. If successful, it would give the US a proxy army to defeat "terrorists" in Afghanistan and support US interests elsewhere in Central Asia. US interests in the region did not necessarily coincide with those of the Afghan government, however. From the perspective of Afghan interests, the arrangement would constrain the pursuit of an independent foreign policy and could make the country vulnerable to enmity in US relations with states in the region. The issue surfaced when Washington in May 2005 announced it would institutionalize its military presence in Afghanistan through a new "strategic partnership." The reaction of Russia, China, and the four Central Asian states bordering on Afghanistan—members of the Shanghai Cooperation Organization formed in 2001—signaled distrust and counter-pressure. While also triggered by Washington's policy towards political unrest in Uzbekistan, a formal communiqué issued in July called for the United States to set a timeline for withdrawing from military bases in Central Asia and suggested there was a declining need for combat operations against the Taliban. Deteriorating relations between the US and Iran caused fears in the western province of Herat that a military confrontation between the two powers might involve the border region as well.[37] Iran's possible membership in the Shanghai group, as discussed in early 2006, further underlined the potential difficulties that continued military dependence on the US might cause in Afghanistan's relations with its neighbors.

After three years of intense efforts, the formation an effective Afghan military force was, by mid-2006, still very much a work in progress. Initial problems of recruitment, retention, training and reliability were reduced, but questions remained about the reliability and effectiveness of the ANA as a fighting force against the Taliban and other enemies of the central government.[38] The ANA remained still highly dependent upon its American mentors, symbolically expressed by the use of English rather than Afghan names for its missions and bases when operating in the field.

In another perspective, the ANA was seen as a relatively privileged institution that raised issues of imbalanced development. The World Bank drew attention to the disproportionately large expenditures for defense, concluding that the policy was clearly unsustainable (World Bank 2005). The UN mission noted in early 2005 that while most state institutions remained "extremely weak"; "[s]o far, only the Afghan National Army program has been able to encompass the various dimensions of institution-building, from in-depth reform of the Ministry itself, to the vetting and training of officers and soldiers, to post-deployment assistance and mentoring."[39] The failure to invest equally in developing civilian institutions of the state and governance, including the sidelining of political parties in the 2004 parliamentary elections, accentuated the comparatively favored position of the armed forces and, in the longer run, the possibility that the statebuilding project might culminate in a military coup, or at least heavy military domination of the government. The historical precedent was certainly there: the Afghan army has twice in recent history (1973 and 1978) been instrumental in bringing about regime change.

Legitimacy

By originating in a foreign military intervention, the statebuilding project in post-Taliban Afghanistan became closely tied to the power of foreign troops and capital in ways that affected the legitimacy of the state. One element of legitimacy is the utilitarian or instrumental dimension, which stems from ability to provide material goods. The impact of the dependence on foreign power in this respect is contradictory. On the one hand, the state has become an important point for transmission of valued funds and services. On the other hand, its extreme dependence on outside sources underscores the government's position as a mere link in the larger transmission belt, and therefore as an unreliable agent.

As for the normative element of legitimacy, the consequences of the foreign-initiated and foreign-dependent statebuilding process are also mixed. The new order had been welcomed by many as a relief from war and the oppressive rule of the Taliban, and as a promise of peace and prosperity to come. Yet the dependence on foreigners carries negative connotations in three major ideological perspectives. First, the development ideology of the importance of "local ownership" is widely cited on all levels in the political discourse, often expressed in the slogan that in rebuilding their state, society and economy, "the Afghans must be in the driver's seat." But, Afghan critics asked, how can we be in the driver's seat when, in fact, the map is produced in New York, Bonn, and London, the fuel bill is paid for at pledging conferences in Tokyo and Berlin, and the foreigners now are doing back-seat driving? Second, Afghan nationalism, however diffuse, has a distinct core defined by pride in a country that was never colonized and a people that repeatedly has driven out foreign invaders. Third and more narrowly defined, the ideology of the militant Islamists specifically attacks the Western foreign presence and development model as illegitimate. In an international context where the US-led "war on terror," invasion of Iraq and support for Israel's warfare against Lebanon have created perceptions of a Western crusade against Islam, the Afghan government's deep support base in the western Christian powers is a liability.

Critical views of the Western alliance of this kind, ultimately rooted in nationalism and Islam, resonate far beyond the number who actively supports the militants. They are powerful tools for focusing and justifying criticism of the government and its foreign supporters. While specific incidents may catalyze protests, the underlying grievances are the driving force, whether related to the failed promises of peace, the direction and pace of the statebuilding project—which has created losers as well as winners—or multiple concerns with the visible and powerful foreign presence in itself. By being so obviously and deeply dependent on the West, the government lays itself open to attack. The expressions are varied and numerous. For instance:

- Populist rhetoric targets "greedy" NGOs and UN personnel who siphon off the aid money and block traffic with their four-wheel drive vehicles. A candidate for parliament wins a seat on this platform (September 2005). The headquarters of a European NGO in Jalalabad with a long history of working in Afghanistan is burnt down in protests triggered by news that American interrogators at Guantanamo have abused the Koran (April 2005).
- In the parliament, political opponents of Karzai complain that the foreigners are obstructing traffic in Kabul by building security barriers in front of their embassies. The barriers must be immediately removed, they say, even those in front of the United States embassy, which has practically blocked off a main street (January 2006).
- Political opponents and independent critics question the Karzai government's eagerness to conclude a "strategic partnership" with the United States (May 2005).
- Violent demonstrations against foreign pillars of the government: The UN offices in Herat are attacked by a mob when the central government tries to remove Ismael Khan (September 2004). Coordinated attacks on ISAF headquarters in three locations are triggered by the Danish cartoons of the Prophet, but seem connected with the agenda of military leaders who all are at odds with the modernists in the central government (February 2006).[40]
- Violent riots, including arson and looting, in Kabul sparked by an accident caused by American military vehicles. Around 20 persons were killed and 160 injured, mostly by gunshot wounds as Afghan and US forces opened fire (May 2006).
- Militants attack foreign troops as well as soft targets (development and humanitarian workers), and Afghan "collaborators," including teachers (continuously).

To avoid being tarred by the anti-foreign brush, the government sought to establish its own sources of normative legitimacy. In part, this was done through Western-modern rituals, notably the 2004 presidential elections, and partly by projecting the traditional image of the central state as a broker of services that enhances the status and power of local authorities, as Roy notes (Roy 2004). Karzai has been increasingly engaged in bargaining with local strongmen and pursuing promotional policies to establish his legitimacy and usefulness as a traditional facilitator of this kind. The practice runs counter to the notion of a strong central state that was at the core of the Bonn Agreement agenda, as well as the interests of many donors who suspect Karzai's bargaining partners are linked with the drug trade, are incompetent in relation to the needs of a modern state, or have bad human rights records.[41] The conflicting nature of traditional and modern sources of legitimacy thus limits the possibility of Karzai—or any head of government in his position—to strengthen his own authority and by implication that of the state. The parliamentary elections in 2005 probably had a more straightforward positive legitimizing effect on the state. By widening the political arena at the central level, it also enhanced the power, saliency and to that extent the legitimacy of politics at the central, as distinct from the local, level.

Conclusions

The present statebuilding project in Afghanistan is carried out under conditions that exacerbate the historical legacy of a weak central state located in a strategically contested part of the world. The project originated in a military intervention that installed a new regime. Its ambitious agenda of reconstruction and reform unfolded against the background of mounting conflict between political Islam and the West. As the first battlefront in the US-led "war on terror" after 9/11, and as a deeply Muslim society, Afghanistan became inextricably linked to the escalating violence of this widening war in Iraq and elsewhere. Within the country, the statebuilding process was from the outset externally driven. Two key elements—capital and military force—were largely provided by foreign powers. This created a series of problems, especially in the third major area required for statebuilding, namely legitimacy.

The statebuilding process consequently has been difficult, plagued by a rapidly expanding insurgency and beset with dilemmas. One of the basic dilemmas stems from the tight embrace of external powers. While also evident during the period of Soviet invasion and tutelage in the 1980s, the dilemma does not simply reflect the centrality of self-determination in the postcolonial world. The British experienced similar problems during their Afghan ventures in the mid-nineteenth century. Having installed Shah Shuja as ruler in Kabul in 1838, the British subsequently wanted to withdraw their troops so as not to incur the cost of a permanent occupation. There was a sticking point, however. The British feared that Shah Shuja would not last long if deprived of the support of British bayonets; at the same time, they recognized that as long as the troops remained, the Shah would be considered a puppet of "infidel foreigners." It was, as a commentator later noted, a dilemma, and it set the scene for the ignoble British defeat in the first Anglo-Afghan war (Macrory 1969: xvi).

The contradictions of the present statebuilding project create policy dilemmas for both donor and recipients. Foreign troops provided critical coercive power in the initial post-Taliban phase and guaranteed the capital area as a neutral site for peaceful political change. Economic and technical assistance made it possible to distribute large-scale relief and launch an ambitious reconstruction and modernization program. The negative consequences of heavy foreign dependence were also evident. Unlike some patterns of dependence that historically have been associated with strong states (for example, in "national security regimes" in South America in the second half of the twentieth century), dependent state formation in post-Taliban Afghanistan has produced weaknesses at the central level of government that may ultimately prove fatal to the whole project.

The signs of weakness were numerous. Accountability structures were established to accommodate external donors rather than domestic constituencies. Dependence was self-perpetuating by favoring imported capacity rather than the slower process of building local capacity. The government's reliance on foreign troops and funding signaled its own weaknesses, thereby encouraging potential supporters to hedge their commitments or enter into "spot contracts" that inhibit institutional development. In a nationalist perspective, the power of foreign troops and money undermined the legitimacy of the government and made it an easy target for genuine and manipulated protest. Representatives of foreign power—whether troops, diplomats or aid workers—were targeted by the militants, as were government "collaborators." By the time of this writing, the attacks had grown into a formidable insurgency spearheaded by a revived Taliban that again received external support.

Some policy decisions lead only to bad choices, and there seem to have been several such junctures in Afghanistan. At present there are no easy choices or clear win-win policy alternatives. Any way one looks at it, there are high risks and costs. Nevertheless, the analysis in this chapter suggests that the dominant response to date—a policy of "more of the same" in terms of international assistance—is not the answer. This prescription is more likely to increase than attenuate the contradictions. This suggests that answers must be sought in departures from the present model.

One alternative is to move towards a more trusteeship model. Possibly, very high levels of foreign funds, troops, administrative expertise, reconstruction, and an unflagging political commitment to staying the course might overwhelm the opposition and outweigh the negative consequences of intrusive assistance. Even if the local resistance were subdued or won over, this course of action would entail a degree of international commitment, presence and control—in effect a new colonialism—for both normative and realpolitik reasons. In the wake of the US intervention in Iraq, this option seems particularly unfeasible.

That leaves open the alternative of scaling down foreign involvement by modifying both the form and the magnitude of international economic assistance. Extending the logic of the analysis of the problems provides some general suggestions. If the bloated rentier state is a problem, its dysfunctional aspects of the rentier state can be reduced by equilibrating levels and types of assistance with a long-term policy of building institutional capacity, as well as "Afghanizing" the reconstruction effort. Given the shortage of Afgan professionals and skilled labor, this would mean a slower rate of reconstruction.

Yet it is likely to spread the gains more evenly, provide less opportunity for large scale corruption, and create a sense of local ownership and accountability. Exploring ways of working with local authorities (even if these are not the choice or to the liking of foreign donors) is another way of addressing issues of absorptive capacity. A decentralized approach would of course raise other problems (notably by creating regional inequalities and encouraging local elites to capture the aid). On the other hand, recent developments around community councils organized in connection with the aid process under the National Solidarity Program, and plans to upgrade these councils to the district and province levels, indicate that structures of accountability and participation are emerging from the bottom up. In the long run, this may be a more viable approach to development and governance than the top-down strategy outlined in the Bonn Agreement.

One reason for the problems at the central level, as discussed above, is the mounting insurgency. In retrospect it seems ironic that the statebuilding project, which increasingly appeared as a casualty of the insurgency, was initially justified by the US and its allies as an instrument for destroying the Islamist militants in the area. The assumption was that a new, democratic, and Western-friendly Afghan government would not only deny sanctuary to terrorists, but actively help to fight them. At the present juncture, it seems, the statebuilding venture can only be rescued if it is separated from the pursuit of the "war on terror," and if the insurgency is successfully dealt with. Since military pressure so far seems to have been counterproductive, the alternative would be to explore negotiations. In practical terms, this would mean efforts to separate the local Taliban from the international militants and to invite the former to participate in reconciliation and power sharing on both the local and the national level. A logical part of this policy would be to pull back US and NATO forces to defensive and stabilizing operations in provincial cities and a continued mission of securing the capital. That way, the past narrative of international abandonment need not be repeated.

Alternative policies of this kind are unlikely to produce the kind of state envisaged in the Bonn Agreement. They may not even lead to the minimal requirements of a state in terms of providing effective and legitimate governmental structures that cover the entire Afghan nation. Violence may continue, yet on a lower level. Local strongmen may continue to rule de facto, though with growing constraint from locally-elected assemblies, and with the central state casting a weaker shadow. In the much longer run, this may add up to a process of state formation, as distinct from the concept of statebuilding with is connotations of social engineering in a shorter-term perspective.

Notes

1 For a review of EU-supported project evaluations, see Strand and Olesen 2005. Donini et al. (eds.) 2004, with contributions mostly from aid workers and UN officials in Afghanistan, addresses both project and policy issues.

2 Barnett R. Rubin, arguably the most knowledgeable and influential of the US experts on Afghanistan, is and an articulate and prolific representative of the "critical mass" school of thought. See, for example, Rubin 2006, 2005. In early 2006, 22 Afghan specialists and former US diplomats signed a letter calling on the U.S. government to provide additional aid in support of the modernization/ statebuilding agenda presented to the January 2006 conference in London (published in the Congressional Publication *The Hill*, February 8, 2006). The view is also endorsed by other Afghanistan experts. See, for example, Maley 2006. For a very strong statement of the argument for more aid, see Rashid 2006.

3 Pledges of 4.5 billion dollars were made at the Tokyo conference in 2002, 8.2 billion in Berlin in 2004, and 10.4 billion in London in 2006, which was not even cast as a pledging conference. The programs of the Asian Development Bank and the World Bank, announced on the eve of the London conference, both emphasized more institution building. NATO had in late 2005 decided to increase its troops with around 6,000, double the announced reduction of US forces around 3,000. Deployment started in early 2006 and brought the total number of foreign troops in Afghanistan to over 30,000, a record high in the post-Taliban period. As the Taliban and their supporters fiercely attacked the new ISAF units, the British sent in an additional 900 men in July the same year.

4 One goes like this: "Question: What is the difference between the Russians and the Americans? Answer: The Americans are better paid."

5 Johnson and Leslie 2004; Koehler 2005; Ottaway and Lieven 2002; Suhrke and Woodward 2002; and Suhrke et al. 2004a, 2004b.

6 See Gregorian 1969; Rubin 2002; and Saikal 2005.

7 A change in ambassador signaled a less intrusive political role, and plans for a reduction of some 3,000 of the 16,000 strong US force in Afghanistan were announced. At the same time, work was going ahead to significantly expand and upgrade the major air bases used by the US in Kandahar and at Bagram, which suggested a long-term presence.

8 Karzai on Voice of America (in Pashto). May 15, 2005, http://www.globalsecurity. org/military/library/news/2005/05/mil-050515-2c7d9c7d.htm.

9 Figures for 2002–3 from Ministry of Finance as cited in the HDR, Afghanistan (note 24).

10 Cooney 2006, citing Karzai and the IMF's representative in Kabul.

11 *Islamic State of Afghanistan: Selected Issues and Appendix.* IMF Country Report, February 2005, pp.17–21.

12 The sale of natural gas was a major source of revenue for both Daoud and the PDPA.

13 In this context, it is misleading to cite only the ratio of domestic revenue to expenditures in the core budget as an indication of growing self-sufficiency, as a recent conference report does: *Post-Conflict Transitions: National Experience and International Reform,* New York: IPA/CIC, March 2005, p. 3

14 The World Bank and the then-Minister of Finance, Ashraf Ghani, early on took the lead in calling for transferring funds through fiduciary or Afghan government channels. By late 2005, more donors were doing so, particularly the European states. The Bank-administered trust fund (ARTF) financed most of the civilian recurrent budget for 2004/5, including around 90 percent of the payroll for the civil servants. World Bank (2005a), pp. 6, 56.

15 The finding holds across disciplines and research areas. Among the vast literature and the variety of types of rentier states, the following should be noted: the early formulation by Beblaw 1990, and more recent work on the rentier effects of the "resource curse" in the Middle East and Africa as inhibiting both modernization and democratization, especially Ross 2001. The reverse dynamic—the bootstrap logic—is identified in a recent study that seeks to document the origins of the

developmental state in Asia. See Doner et al. 2005. Economists of both a rationalist and institutionalist orientation come to similar conclusions; for example, North 1990 supports the conclusion that the fiscal crisis of the English state (the King) "led to the development of some form of representation on the part of constituents" as there was no rentier income (p. 113); Bates confirms this dynamic by observing its opposite among "the third world" governments during the Cold War: "supported by transfers of aid from abroad, [they] did ... [not] need to bargain with their citizens to secure public revenues. They therefore did not need to be responsive to their people or democratic in their politics. ... " (2001: 82).

16 Similarly during the PDPA rule, payment or withholding of taxes was considered a sign of support for, or opposition to, the government. See Giustozzi 2000, p. 167 and passim. This is not to say that Afghans have a record of willingly paying taxes even to strong central leaders. Abdul Rahman Khan, the "Iron Amir" of the late nineteenth century, used to complain that he collected with ease only one-fourth of the taxes due to him, most he had to struggle to get, and for the rest he had to send in the cavalry. Cited in Gregorian (1969).

17 See Koehler (2005), and Afghan press reports distributed by AFGHANDEV@ lists.mcgill.ca.

18 United States Government Accountability Office. Afghanistan Reconstruction. GAO-05-742, July 2005, p. 26, http://www.gao.gov/new.items/d05742.pdf. See also Suhrke et al. 2004a.

19 Confidential report, on file with author.

20 United States Government Accountability Office, Afghanistan Reconstruction. GAO-05-742, July 2005, p. 26, http://www.gao.gov/new.items/d05742.pdf.

21 These critics now included the former Finance Minister, Ashraf Ghani, who had turned a formidable critic of his own previous strategy. See "The Battle to Rebuild Afghanistan," http://212.58.226.50/2/hi/business/4714116.stm.

22 Some signs of corrective tendencies are difficult to assess. The 10 billion dollar pledge in London represents a somewhat lower annual rate than the Berlin conference pledges, but the two pledging periods overlap and makes comparison difficult. The Afghan government, for its part, drastically reduced the estimated need of foreign financing in its development plan for 2006/7–2010/11. The Afghan National Development Strategy (ANDS) projected a financing gap of around 900 million dollars annually (www.reliefweb.nt/library/documents/2006/unama-afg-30jan2.pdf). Given that the external budget for 2004/5 alone was 2.5 billion dollars, however, the budgetary estimates seem seriously disconnected.

23 By early 2006, the Coalition Forces (OEF) had around 19,000 troops (with a scheduled reductions of 3,000), and ISAF had 9,000, with a planned increased of another 6,000.

24 ISAF "rolled out tanks to protect the presidential palace" when pressures to disarm the factions and remove Northern Alliance leader Marshal Fahim in 2003 led to rumors of a coup in September, at the time of Karzai's visit to the United States (Baldauf 2003). Military coups, it will be recalled, brought about two regime changes in the 1970s, the coup by Daoud against the King, and by the PDPA against Daoud. In the confrontation between Kabul and Ismael Khan, US forces played a more direct role. The US had in 2003 established a PRT in Herat. Although newly minted ANA forces were fronting the operation to dislodge Ismael Khan in August the following year, they were flown into Herat in US planes, US forces brought in supplies, and a US Army major accompanied the international press to cover the operation. See "Deploying to Shindand with the Afghan National Army," *Defend America News,* http://www.defendamerica.mil/cgi-bin/prfriendly.cgi?

25 The poll was conducted on behalf of the ABC (US) and released on December 7, 2005, http://abcnews.go.com/International/PollVault/story?id=1363276. A survey

undertaken by a Washington-based program at the same time produced similar results, http://www.ipsnews.net/news.asp?idnews=31737. However, the ABC poll also reported that 42 percent of the respondents had electricity in their homes, of which 19 percent said they were connected to power lines, which suggests that either the sample had a strong urban bias or the answers were untruthful. The World Bank estimated at the same time that only 10 percent of the population as a whole had access to grid power supply. World Bank (2005), p. 80.

26 The government's Afghan National Development Strategy noted that 2005 was "the deadliest twelve-month period for coalition and ISAF forces since 1380 (2001)." See ANDS 2006, pp. 34–35. The BBC on December 8, 2005 reported 1,400 victims killed in the south and the east in 2005. See http://newsvote.bbc.co.uk.

27 *Washington Post*, June 18, 2006.

28 *Le Monde*, June 9, 2006; and *Helmand at War*, The Senlis Council, London, June 2006.

29 ISAF had originally a more restricted mandate, but additional units deployed to the south in early 2006 were expected to operate under more "robust" rules of engagement. The deployment provoked a sharp increase in attack on ISAF units, suggesting an escalation was underway. The command chain and tasks of ISAF and OEF seemed increasingly unclear to outside Western observers as well. In addition, private security contractors dressed in camouflage uniforms participated in highly visible and controversial poppy eradication campaigns in the south. Thus, the Afghan who attacked a Canadian solider with an ax when he was on a civic affairs mission in Kandahar in March 2006 might have acted out of misunderstanding or generalized anger against foreign troops.

30 *New York Times*, May 26, 2006.

31 On Nangarhar in this respect, see '*Killing You is a Very Easy Thing for Us.' Human Rights Abuse in Afghanistan,* Human Rights Watch, vol. 15, no. 5, July 2003, p. 19, http://www.hrw.org/reports/2003/afghanistan0703; and on Helmand, see Walsh 2006.

32 *Report of the Independent Expert on the Situation of Human Rights in Afghanistan, M. Cherif Bassiouni*, UN E/CN.4/2005/122, March 11, 2005. When the report was published the Bush Administration successfully pressured the UN to sack its author, a prominent professor of law teaching in the United States, http://www.law.depaul.edu/institutes_centers/ihrli/pdf/Bassiouni_Afghanistan_Final_05.pdf.

33 Agence France Press, May 1, 2005.

34 Transcript of press conference, May 23, 2005.

35 Afghan sources give 554.04 million, Ministry of Finance, www.af./mof/budget. US sources give 558 million. See "US Military Assistance," http://www.fas.org/asmp/profiles/aid/fy2005/CBJ05_milassist.pdf and http://www.fas.org/asmp/profiles/aid/fy2006/CBJMilAss.pdf.

36 External Development Budget, Funded Programs, National Budget 1384, MYR, www.af.mof/budget.

37 Personal communication with Kristian Berg Harpviken, PRIO, who did fieldwork in Herat in May 2006.

38 The Soviet Union had also sought to build up the Afghan Army as a reliable ally during the 1970s and subsequently as an effective fighting force to defeat the militant Islamist insurgents during the 1980s. Although starting from an army that at the outset was reasonably strong, the policy failed in the 1980s as units increasingly disintegrated or defected to the insurgents.

39 *The Situation in Afghanistan and Its Implications for International Peace and Security*, S/2005/183, March 18, 2005, p. 14.

40 In Maimana, Dostum's stronghold, it was noted that a team from the TV company controlled by Dostum was at hand to film the start of the violent demonstrations against the ISAF base. Demonstrations also occurred in Herat, where Ismael Khan's

infrastructure of power remained at least partially intact. In Kabul, which used to be the stronghold of Bismillah Khan, the main commander of Fahim and present chief of army, ISAF's headquarters were targeted. The demonstrations were closely coordinated in time. See http://www.afnorth.nato.int/ISAF/Update/Press_Releases/speech_8feb06.htm.

41 By June 2006, Western officials were making their complaints public. See Constable 2006.

11 Dilemmas of promoting "local ownership"

The case of postwar Kosovo

Jens Narten

External statebuilding interventions in postwar societies have a common denominator: they all aim at building functioning and self-sustaining state structures, which would, at a later stage, allow external statebuilders to complete their mission and to withdraw from that country, making their capacities available for other regions in the world. From a global or international perspective, this is the main reason why local ownership in statebuilding processes matters. Without a successful handover of control and competencies from external statebuilders to local actors following a period of international involvement, statebuilding missions would either become open-ended and extraordinarily costly, or the missions would come to a sudden end without generating sustainable and self-sustaining local structures.[1]

From a local perspective, (emerging) postwar nations hold the legitimate rights to self-determination and peaceful development under international law and usually have a vested interest in exercising this right. This, in turn, means that if sustainable local ownership is not established in the process of international statebuilding, these rights cannot be effectively enjoyed by a postwar society. International assistance, in this case, would either be a never-ending and, thus, a quasi-colonial external rule, with the inherent risk of increasing resistance from the local population, or the country would be at risk of falling back into violence and chaos.

In the academic and practitioners' communities, surprisingly few systematic efforts have been made to understand these dilemmas and the inherent obstacles to local ownership in postwar statebuilding environments. This essay attempts to help fill this gap and demonstrates a range of structural dilemmas for the promotion of local ownership in statebuilding processes, which regularly jeopardize external interventions. Out of these, three key dilemmas with the potential to endanger the entire statebuilding process are identified. Finally, the essay concludes with practical recommendations that can help external statebuilders remedy or at least mitigate the impact of such dilemmas.

Local ownership as a *conditio sine qua non*?

Demanding local ownership has become common in the international development aid and peacebuilding communities. At the same time, the concept of local ownership has been criticized by some observers, including Scheye and Peake, who warn that "local ownership as currently conceptualized is much more a rhetorical device than an actual guide for implementers [...] and may have more psychological effect than political" (Scheye and Peake 2005: 240). Boughton and Mourmonas also contend that the concept is incoherent and "cannot be conceptually resurrected" due to a lack of observability, loose evidence for its existence, its dynamic and changing target, the high numbers of potential owners, and the heterogeneity of governmental levels (Boughton and Mourmonas 2002). In a similar vein, Reich argues that it "tends to hinder the attainment of the goal of sovereignty of local actors in externally funded projects" and serves more as "an important discursive function, highlighting the necessity for change in present structures and patterns of international cooperation. Local ownership is [rather] a vision to strive towards, but not a practical objective within international funding and working structures" (Reich 2006: 7).

Despite these critical views, a closer look at the development of local ownership as a guiding notion of international assistance underlines its conceptual importance and paradigmatic position in this context. Its roots go back to the mid-1980s, when the idea of participatory development, based on a "people-centred" understanding of development, emerged as a guiding principle of international aid.[2] Ten years later, the OECD's Development Assistance Committee declared that "[f]or development to succeed, the people of the countries concerned must be the 'owners' of their development policies and programmes" in order to "back the efforts of countries and people to help themselves" (OECD Development Assistance Committee 1995: 2). Within the humanitarian aid community, Anderson expresses similar views, focusing on the delivery of postwar humanitarian aid and development assistance in (post)war environments. The principles she developed in a series of workshops with humanitarian aid workers strongly reflect the notion of support for locally owned peace processes (Anderson 1996 and 1999; Anderson and Olson 2003).

In a similar notion and drawing on findings of the foreign and development cooperation ministries of Germany, the Netherlands, Norway, and the United Kingdom since 1999, the influential Joint Utstein Study of Peacebuilding depicted the concept of local ownership as an axiomatic goal in development cooperation, while pointing to the need for "careful research about the identity and background of cooperating partners [...] to increase the degree of local ownership. Otherwise, local ownership risks being a code for working with the most powerful and most opportunistic sectors of society" (Smith 2004: 26f.). Overall, this study reflected the transfer of the concept of local ownership from the field of development aid to related fields, such as postwar peacebuilding or statebuilding. With local ownership considered a "fundamental guiding principle" in this context,[3] Chesterman finds that "[e]very UN mission and development programme now stress the importance of local 'ownership'" (Chesterman 2002: 6).

In the contemporary understanding, local ownership applies to most areas of statebuilding, such as security-sector reform, the promotion of democracy and the rule of law, electoral assistance, transitional justice, civil reconciliation, and the like.[4] In all these sectors, the criteria of local ownership are widely viewed as indispensable to guaranteeing long-term and sustainable implementation of postwar statebuilding and can, thus, be considered a conditio sine qua non of international statebuilding efforts. But what exactly does local ownership mean in practice? Chesterman identifies different objectives that help in understanding the concept. These include responsiveness of international actors, stages of consultation, participation, accountability and effective control, and, finally, full local sovereignty (Chesterman, quoted in Hurwitz 2005: 349).

With a similar logic in respect to operational management aspects of statebuilding processes and their local ownership, reference can be made to a commonality of most statebuilding sectors: Nearly all projects contributing to statebuilding processes share an ideal-type procedural understanding that comprises distinct phases of what is known as project cycle management (PCM). The PCM provides a scheme for the various stages of project management that represents a widely accepted set of standards applied by many international organizations and NGOs, donor communities and their implementing partners.[5] Its constituent components are made up of at least four different steps: 1) The identification and analysis of a problem and the related assessment of needs; 2) the designing of a program to address that problem or need along with adequate tools, including strategies, working methods, staffing and financial resources; 3) the implementation of the program design and its operational elements for the project's beneficiaries; and 4) the intermediate or final evaluation of the program in order to adapt and improve it.[6]

Within this framework, a "high level" of local ownership is the point at which external statebuilders have effectively included local stakeholders at all four levels of the PCM—meaning that local actors have been consulted and included in the process of the problem and needs assessment, project design, and implementation as well as the evaluation and control of the overall process and its outcome. Building on this approach, I would define local ownership in the context of statebuilding as follows:

> Local ownership is the process and final outcome of the gradual transfer to legitimate representatives of the local society, of assessment, planning and decision-making functions, the practical management and implementation of these functions, and the evaluation and control of all phases of statebuilding programs, with the aim of making external peace- and statebuilding assistance redundant.[7]

This definition raises several difficult questions: To which local actors should the statebuilding process be transferred? When is the best moment to pursue that transfer? Which local actors can be considered legitimate for that role? Do the respective local actors also have the necessary skills and capacities for taking over these responsibilities? If not, can external statebuilders provide for the build-up of these capacities? What level of external intrusiveness into local state affairs might be necessary in the overall statebuilding context and where should it end? This list of questions is by no means exhaustive. However, these are among the most important questions, and they confront statebuilding actors with a set of difficult dilemmas, which are identified and explored below.

Key dilemmas in promoting local ownership

Most international peacebuilding or statebuilding missions are confronted with dilemmas relating to the promotion of local ownership.[8] Of course, the precise nature and constellation of such dilemmas varies from one operation to the next, but there are recurring issues and themes: in particular, the problem of external intrusiveness, local dependency, and the "spoiler problem."[9]

Dilemma 1: the need for external intrusiveness vs. creating responsible self-government

The first dilemma relates to a principal paradox of local ownership in most peacebuilding and statebuilding processes.[10] Local ownership can be regarded as the overall goal or outcome as well as the necessary means or process leading to it.[11] In this context, activities of external statebuilders must be regarded as intrusive if they do not allow for input, consultation, and (at a later stage) control by local stakeholders in all phases of project cycle management. That means that external statebuilding can be regarded as less intrusive if statebuilding measures are not imposed but reached in consensus with legitimate local actors. The principal dilemma at this point is that in most postwar environments a certain degree of external intrusiveness is needed to fill a potential vacuum of domestic authority, especially at the beginning of the statebuilding process when political consensus, capacities and resources are absent in the postwar society. At the same time external statebuilders need to help create conditions for sustainable self-government in the society. This creates tension and is something of a conundrum.

If external statebuilders have to exercise some authoritative functions and need, at the same time, to help local actors build their self-governance capacities, the question is what degree of intrusiveness is appropriate, and which sequence and forms of transfer of authority to local actors should be pursued. A reflection on the typology of peacebuilding and statebuilding operations, along with the criteria of external interference into internal state affairs, can help answer this question (Schneckener 2005: 28f). Schneckener distinguishes between four different types of intervention: 1) external consultancy with hardly any direct interference into state authority; 2) operations specialized within a specific field of assistance such as election monitoring, security-sector reform, and the like, with clear-cut monitoring or implementation functions in agreement with the local authorities; 3) multidimensional civil–military operations usually under UN mandate with significant interference into internal affairs, forms of shared sovereignty and a hybrid governance structure; and 4) international transitional or interim administration as a temporary replacement of local state authorities.[12]

In case of highly intrusive international administration over a given post-war territory, different levels or phases of external intrusiveness can also be distinguished. Following Caplan's argumentation, the phase of direct administration by external actors must be distinguished from phases of joint co-administration and local self-administration (with external actors maintaining oversight functions and veto powers) (Caplan 2004: 235ff.). Depending on the types and/or phases of intervention, the levels of intrusiveness will vary. Under a full-fledged international administration, external statebuilders may hold extensive legislative, executive, and judicial authority. In statebuilding missions that have a "light footprint," by contrast, international authority may be of a more consultative nature.[13] It is also possible for certain specific functions to be transferred to local control at different moments, depending on the importance and sensitivity of the function and the corresponding local capacity to manage this function. In short, different degrees of external intrusiveness can prevail in specific statebuilding sectors at the same time. These possibilities demonstrate that developing a detailed and comprehensive categorization of "intrusiveness" would be a very difficult—perhaps impossible—task.

In practical terms, however, statebuilders face real challenges in determining the appropriate degree, time, and sequencing of transfer of authorities and competencies to local actors. If such a transfer occurs too early and in an ad hoc manner, local actors may be unable to take on such responsibilities. But if such transfers happen too late or in a hesitant way, the development of local responsibilities could easily be hampered, either due to the waning willingness of local parties to cooperate with external statebuilders, or the increasing risk of domestic resistance to a statebuilding process, or both. Indeed, if external statebuilders do not succeed in incorporating local needs into their statebuilding agendas in a timely and efficient manner, the danger of alienating local stakeholders from that agenda increases—even to the point that the initial support among the local population for an external presence may be lost as the host society seeks to regain full sovereignty over its territory.[14]

Nevertheless, in the case of a total state collapse or malfunction, external actors often need to pursue the initial statebuilding process unilaterally, with a high level of external intrusiveness into local affairs.[15] This means that the overall basis of the emerging new state is largely predetermined from the outside even before the first set of elections can be held and legitimate local representatives can participate in that process. In such a scenario, (Western) normative values of a "liberal peace" are often introduced from the outside, along with the risk of too rapid political and economic liberalization with all its destabilizing effects.[16] The initial period of international decision-making also runs the risk of artificially creating a need for continuing intrusiveness, should external statebuilders not succeed in gradually transferring their authorities to legitimate local actors after elections. This can be caused by a variety of possible factors. External statebuilders carrying out administrative functions may be reluctant, for internal reasons such as an overly dominant mission bureaucracy or autocratic leadership, to modify their policy of mere local consultation into a policy that allows local co-administration or self-government.[17] But external factors can also be a reason for a delayed transfer—for example, when violent spoilers have won the first postwar elections or when political fragmentation and destabilization processes lead to an emergency situation and recurrence of violence.

Furthermore, there may be only limited windows of opportunity for the effective transfer of executive statebuilding authorities from external actors to their local counterparts. If statebuilders miss these opportunities, the level of external intrusiveness might become excessive and endemic. If this happens, international statebuilders run the risk of imposing their agendas and implementing their statebuilding programs on the society without the necessary incorporation of local stakeholders (Chandler 2004; Scheye and Peake 2005: 245ff.). Such a scenario is reflected in what a number of authors have described using a wide range of terms: international patronage (Caplan 2004), arrogant paternalism (Crawford 2002: 429), neo-trusteeship (Fearon and Laitin 2004: 9ff.; Caplan 2002), benevolent despotism (Beauvais 2001), and "empire lite" (Ignatieff 2003). The political as well as the emotional alienation of large parts of the local society is a constant danger in such kinds of statebuilding environments. This problem is further aggravated when external assistance is made strictly conditional on specific political objectives imposed from the outside (since they do not necessarily meet local needs or build on existing local structures). Local stakeholders may subscribe to such objectives on paper, but this does not mean that they believe in them and are willing to "own" them. In this context, Chanaa refers to an "imposition-ownership divide," aggravating the potential alienation of the local society from external objectives (Chanaa 2002: 64f., 67).[18] An example of such a divide can be seen in situations which the local society perceives as discriminatory, such as widespread judicial immunity against local jurisdiction granted to international staff, by which the local society is largely deprived of its rights to hold external actors liable for violations.[19]

Dilemma 2: prolonging local dependency with short-term vs. long-term requirements

The second dilemma overlaps with the first. The dependency of most postwar societies on external statebuilding assistance, due to partial or total collapse of functioning state structures, requires certain measures of external intrusiveness to address. In this context, the dilemma for statebuilders flows from two contradictory imperatives: On the one hand, there is latent or even manifest pressure on statebuilders from the international donor community to conclude their mandate within short time-frames to allow operational capacities to be redeployed elsewhere, to keep military engagement abroad limited and to save national taxpayers' money. Such pressures may result in the short-term deployment orientation of most governments or organizations sponsoring statebuilding missions. On the other hand, there is an elementary need for thorough capacity-building in almost every postwar society if self-sustaining state structures built on indigenous technical skills, political competences, and a civil culture of tolerant peace and democratic values are to be developed. This makes long-term orientation of external statebuilding assistance necessary.[20]

External statebuilders in the field are regularly subject to these conflicting interests between short-term and long-term oriented statebuilding. However, if assistance is given only on a short-term basis, external measures are likely to prolong or even increase the level of local dependency on such assistance, because there will not be sufficient time to promote the development of sustainable local capacities. Under these circumstances, statebuilders might, at most, succeed in establishing technically functioning state structures in the postwar society, but they will not likely be able to develop a civic culture that can support democracy and rule of law, tolerant pluralism, and civil reconciliation. If such a culture does not receive the necessary time and assistance to develop, the initial postwar dependency of the host society on external assistance is likely to be perpetuated and might even increase. On the other hand, if assistance programs are planned with a long-term orientation but are applied in an overly intrusive way, a statebuilding operation could also cause considerable harm.[21] In such a case, the state of initial postwar local dependency on direct external assistance could be prolonged and aggravated, due to the suppression of self-sustaining local capacities.

When, as a result of any form of ill-delivered external assistance, the level of dependency increases rather than being reduced, this dependency can develop a "structural" quality in the sense that it can become self-perpetuating and resistant to easy solutions. International assistance has the tendency to alter the social fabric of the recipient society in an unintended way. The massive influx of donor money, supplies, and economic assistance can oftentimes endanger remnant local market structures and lead to a massive increase in prices and living costs for the local population. For many post-war economies, international aid is usually a central source of national income, parallel to illegal sources such as smuggling, trafficking, corruption, and organized crime. But the massive influx of international money often seems to increase the incentive for illegal activities and thereby additionally increases local dependency on external assistance (Papic 2003:77). Moreover, recipient societies are often approached with ready-made assistance packages or standardized tool kits for reconstruction and institution-building, which may not reflect the societies' specific needs and cultural circumstances (Pouligny 2005: 505).

Another phenomenon of such protracted forms of local dependency is related to the difficulty of generating sufficient income to cope with exploding living costs. Job opportunities at international field missions on the artificially inflated NGO market (through participation in international reconstruction, institution- or capacity-building programs) are often among the few opportunities for the local population to earn legal money, with salaries much higher than the local average. With their usual recruitment approaches, international missions tend to select young, well-educated, English-speaking local staff and deprive the local economy of most of its innovative and productive human resources. Under these circumstances, young educated people in postwar statebuilding environments often prefer to work as drivers or interpreters for international organizations rather than as local teachers, doctors or engineers.[22] However, when these resources are bound into the artificial job market of international missions, local initiatives to stabilize the nascent local economy are severely hampered. With their recruitment policies, international missions initiate a kind of "brain drain" on the spot, which further aggravates the overall local dependency on external assistance.

The most severe side effects, however, occur when the massive influx of financial resources comes to an abrupt end due to a refocusing of the international donor community on other crisis areas worldwide (Pugh and Cooper 2004: 161f.; Papic 2003: 76ff.). Apart from overall economic and financial dependency, postwar societies often depend on external expertise for institution- and capacity-building programs due to a lack of existing local capacities.[23] Here, the immediate postwar dependency on external capacity-building expertise becomes problematic when statebuilders do not conceptualize and implement their measures using the principle of "help for self-help," or the notion that external aid should aim to help recipient societies overcome their dependency on the transfer of technical know-how and expertise. Such short-sighted forms of capacity-building can have a number of causes, such as insufficient coordination among statebuilding agencies, limited duration of projects, short-term deployment, a high level of staff rotation and "mission jumping" of external staff to other missions, and overall planning insecurity due to unforeseeable budget cuts or ad-hoc exit requirements, all of which undermine long-term statebuilding needs.

To remedy these deficits, external statebuilders need to implement programs with a focus on building capacities of local trainers from the first days of a mission in order to generate indigenous sources for follow-up capacity-building, and to initiate a cycle of self-sustainability. In this context, Hansen concludes that "an appropriate axiom for international assistance [in postwar societies] is therefore always the 'train-the trainers' and 'train-the-managers' principle" in the context of "investing in institutional learning" (Hansen 2005: 326).[24] Using such an approach, local dependency on external expertise can gradually be reduced. In addition, local trainers usually have at their disposal much better insight into and knowledge about the specific cultural and socio-economic circumstances in the recipient society and are therefore better able to adapt methods and contents of training to the local environment (Reychler and Paffenholz 2001: 298). With this approach, all phases of the management cycle for capacity- and institution-building projects could effectively be transferred to local trainers and managers after a certain time, which would decrease the level of local dependency. A train-the-trainers approach seems thus to be equally important both for building postwar state institutions and for outreach activities to promote a corresponding civic culture within the host society.[25] In the medium and long run, participatory forms of intervention, such as the training-of-trainers strategy, are best designed to overcome local dependencies on external statebuilding assistance, promote local ownership of that process and permit a non-harmful exit strategy for external actors.[26]

Dilemma 3: identifying local partners vs. empowering potential spoilers

A third dilemma is related to the difficulties that statebuilders face in identifying appropriate local partners. According to Hansen and Wiharta, statebuilders can, in principle, identify their partners at three distinct levels of the host society: 1) existing authorities and elites; 2) the population in its organizational forms, such as the individual citizen, civil-society groups, and business communities; and 3) individual staff members of state institutions and the respective statebuilding sectors.[27] However, the issue of previous war involvement is also relevant: If statebuilders identify their partners among the former warring parties, they can easily run the risk of benefiting those actors who bear the prime responsibility for the violent action and atrocities during the war (which would conflict with international legal principles and standards). Empowering former "entrepreneurs of violence"[28] would send strong signals to the local population that the use of violence and criminal activities during the war will pay off after the war.

However, because these actors often continue to enjoy strong postwar bases of support in parts of the local population, statebuilding processes may also be at risk if internationals seek to sideline these actors. Statebuilders may therefore face the difficult choice between operational effectiveness by using the popular support and power basis of the already strong or moral legitimacy by claiming international legal principles and agreed norms to support a moral basis for intervention. Further, if the public perception of externally assisted statebuilding deteriorates to a significant extent, public pressure on newly recruited local partners may also increase to the point where they leave the external–local partnership and turn into spoilers in the overall statebuilding process.[29]

Thus, external statebuilders face the necessity of identifying cooperating partners within the local population, without whom local ownership of statebuilding processes could not be realized. In so doing, statebuilders often choose to apply an approach to identification and cooperation that results in a "picking-the-winners" process.[30] As the international community is in control of most of the needed statebuilding resources, external actors are largely free to select their local cooperating partners, who in turn will greatly benefit from the resources available at the expense of those local actors who did not get selected.[31] In picking the winners, statebuilders often prefer those local elites who have a specific set of Western credentials, such as a pluralist orientation and education, English-language proficiency, use of donor vernaculars such as "markets," "reform" and "civil society," and who identify themselves as reformers (Wedel 1996: 575, quoted in Sharman and Kanet 2000: 240).[32] However, non-selected "losers" may maintain their political influence and economic resources at informal levels. In a postwar environment with limited income and career opportunities, one standard strategy of sidelined elites is to generate their income and general power bases from illegal sources (namely, by engaging in the black market or organized crime structures and by seeking political influence through corruption or means of intimidation).[33] In addition, the more the local population feels under threat of becoming losers of postwar reform and economic liberalization, the more easily side-lined elites can recruit political followers. Mobilizing predominantly the frustrated youth of a postwar society through political agitation and the incitement of ethnic hatred can become a basic modus operandi of spoiler groups.

Another set of risks arises when statebuilders choose to build new state structures along ethnic lines, thereby engaging in an ethnicization of the emerging political system. According to Hehir, political entrepreneurs "who have achieved political power by exploiting ethnicity and fomenting fear of the 'other' [ethnic or societal group] have a vested interest in maintaining ethnic polarization, especially if the political administration operates on this basis" (Hehir 2006: 209). If, at the same time, external statebuilders fail to apply a balanced "geographic transfer approach" (Hansen 2005: 311) and do not extend statebuilding measures to all communities and municipalities in their mission area, they can easily trigger the establishment of parallel state institutions and a territorial enclavization along ethnic lines.

When, in addition to that, the levels of external intrusiveness and local dependency increase, statebuilders often prevent local representatives from taking responsibility for the overall statebuilding process. Local actors blaming international ones for the shortcomings in that process might be the consequence (Papic 2003: 76). Even local elites who are promoted as postwar winners can in these circumstances feel pushed to play a more radical or ethno-political role and turn themselves into potential spoilers inside the statebuilding process. If, on top of that, external statebuilders also miss the chance to "immunize" the civil society against ethnic or political radicalization by promoting respect for democratic values and tolerance among the local population, the room for spoilers to maneuver is almost limitless. When the post-war society lacks adequate means of societal correctives, the spoiler problem begins to reinforce itself and the dilemma for statebuilders is perpetuated.

However, there is no simple way to overcome the dilemma of identifying local partners for cooperation and applying a policy that might result in a process of picking winners and empowering certain local actors (with the risk of producing spoilers). This seems to be an almost inevitable problem of postwar statebuilding assisted from outside. There is never a guarantee for external statebuilders that even the most thoroughly scrutinized local part-ners might not turn into spoilers of the statebuilding process at a later stage. However, by explicitly supporting the development of a civic culture of democracy, rule of law, and tolerant pluralism, statebuilders can at least attenuate the negative side effects of this process.

The interaction of local-ownership dilemmas

While each of the three dilemmas identified has its own characteristics, they also have the potential to interact with and reinforce each other. Under-standing the way each dilemma functions is the key to being able to over-come their impacts in the context of statebuilding processes and local ownership. Figure 11.1 illustrates central parts of that mutual interaction and reinforcement.

The figure is meant to demonstrate the close interrelatedness between external intrusiveness, local dependency, and local spoilers. It does not have a distinct starting point or a final end. However, what the figure shows is that the three dilemmas are linked with each other in a system of mutually reinforcing interaction:

- External statebuilding measures with an initially-necessary degree of intrusiveness can easily prolong the host society's dependency if they are

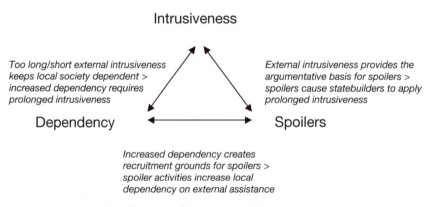

Figure 11.1 Interacting dilemmas of local ownership

applied for either too long or too short a period and if the proper time slot for transfer of ownership of such measures is not being recognized and used.

- At the same time, prolonged local dependency makes the continuation of external assistance necessary, with the result that there is continued application of intrusive measures from the outside (upper-left arrows).
- Moreover, prolonged dependency of the host society creates an ideal recruitment ground for activities of local spoilers, due to high levels of socio-economic frustration, political alienation, and the generation of postwar winners, losers and sidelined elites.
- Parallel to that, successful spoiler activities increase local dependency on external assistance, due to the weakening of the overall political fabric, the security situation, and so on (arrows below).
- Furthermore, destabilizing activities of local spoilers are likely to cause external statebuilders to intensify their intrusive measures and miss the ideal moment for transfer of competencies, due to the sensitive security situation. Or they result in a quick and hasty exit strategy, with measures being too weak to counter spoiler activities.
- Finally, protracted forms of external intrusiveness in the statebuilding process provide an ideal argumentative basis for local spoiler groups to mobilize popular resistance and to recruit violence-prone followers by claiming the host society's right to national self-determination (upper-right arrows). At this point, the cycle of interaction between the three dilemmas can easily develop self-reinforcing spiral dynamics, when starting the cycle anew.

Statebuilding in Kosovo and the dilemmas of promoting local ownership

The UN Mission in Kosovo (UNMIK) provides a good illustration of the impact of the three dilemmas and their interaction. Based on UN resolution 1244, the mandate of UNMIK in Kosovo was to promote substantial autonomy and self-government via the development of local democratic institutions, to which administrative responsibilities could be progressively transferred. Thus, the task of promoting local ownership represented a decisive element of effective statebuilding in Kosovo,[34] both as a means to an end (peace) and an end in itself. However, in implementing their mandate, international statebuilders were confronted with a number of interrelated dilemmas.

External intrusiveness for autonomous self-government?

UNMIK, which includes the OSCE mission and the EU presence in Kosovo in a joint pillar structure, was tasked "to provide a [civil] interim administration for Kosovo under which the people of Kosovo can enjoy substantial autonomy [...] while establishing and overseeing the development of provisional democratic self-governing [local] institutions."[35] This mandate, however, did not include an international agreement on the future status of Kosovo either as an independent state or as a continued province of Serbia, after the end of the UNMIK administration. Overall, UNMIK statebuilders faced the dilemma of exercising a necessarily high level of external intrusiveness in local affairs as a transitional administration and, at the same time, allowing and promoting increased levels of local ownership in order to realize the goal of autonomous self-government for the Kosovar people, in the absence of a clear political status for Kosovo. Put differently, there was no clear overall goal of the postwar statebuilding process. Parallel to this, UNMIK in cooperation with KFOR also had to fill the administrative and security vacuum after the withdrawal of Serb forces in the immediate postwar period. Holding and exercising unrestricted administrative powers in a population whose vast majority of over 90 percent was unwilling to accept anything less than state independence from Serbia, UNMIK was thus trapped by its own mandate. Moreover, the perception by many Kosovars of UN statebuilders changed over time from that of liberators to one of potential occupiers.

Under these circumstances, UNMIK was tasked with implementing (highly intrusive) statebuilding measures. First and foremost, the Special Representative of the UN Secretary-General (SRSG), as the head of the mission, combined the roles of the prime legislator, the chief of the executive and the judiciary in Kosovo. Combining these state powers in one person is reminiscent of forms of autocratic, at best benevolent, despotism. Through the SRSG's office, UNMIK imposed regulations on the applicable law in Kosovo, which led to a confusing legal framework.[36] Aside from directly applicable UNMIK regulations, the SRSG also declared as applicable law the old pre-1989 Yugoslav laws (based largely on the 1974 autonomous Kosovo Constitution) and the International Covenant on Civil and Political Rights (ICCPR), among other international legal documents. Furthermore, in the case of legal gaps, it also made the 1989–99 laws applicable if they complied with human-rights standards. Partially due to this confusing legislation, the local judiciary in Kosovo was scarcely able to commence its work and local judges often refused to apply legislation from the Milosevic era within their jurisdiction. Besides regulating the legal system, UNMIK regulations also foresaw the establishment of central local institutions, such as local courts, currency and fiscal authorities, taxation and trading authorities, consolidated budget, housing and property authorities, the Kosovo Police Service (KPS), and the Kosovo Protection Corps (KPC),[37] as well as registries for business enterprises, media outlets, and NGOs, a civil and voter registry, a political-party registry, electoral codes, and provisions for self-governing municipal structures.[38]

Many of these initial statebuilding measures took place with very limited consultation of local stakeholders. After the end of the war in Kosovo in

early June 1999, it took UNMIK almost ten months to establish local consultative bodies and co-administrative structures under the Joint Interim
Administrative Structure (JIAS). It was not until February 2000 that the
structure went into effect to inform central decision-making of the SRSG
and UNMIK's growing mission bureaucracy (Narten 2006a: 145f.). The role
of the local counterparts within JIAS, however, was limited to giving non-
binding and purely consultative advice to the SRSG and UNMIK departments. This situation of high political intrusiveness into Kosovar political
affairs continued at the municipal level until October 2000 and at the central
level until November 2001. It was at these points that the first municipal
assembly elections and the Kosovo Assembly elections were held,[39] after a
hectic phase of build-up of local political parties and the hammering out
by UNMIK of Kosovo's postwar political system in the Constitutional
Framework.[40]

The fact that this preliminary "constitution" of Kosovo was issued by the
SRSG's office as a mere regulation without the formation of a local constituent assembly is a prime example of the existing imposition-ownership
divide between UNMIK and local stakeholders. Even after the formation of
a local parliamentary structure in form of the Kosovo Assembly and the
Kosovar government, UNMIK departments transferred only some of their
administrative and executive functions and authorities to the new local
ministries of the PISG (Provisional Institutions of Self-Government), withholding a significant number of powers reserved to the SRSG in key political
areas, such as the police and the judiciary. The SRSG also used his veto
powers regularly to block draft legislation of the Kosovo Assembly and the
PISG, and maintained wide-ranging legislative and executive control by
issuing a number of administrative directions and regulations. Such a veto
policy reflected the watchdog function of the SRSG in case norms of the
"liberal" peacebuilding and statebuilding agenda, such as minority protection
or hate incitement, were at stake.[41]

However, UNMIK's former policy of "Standards before Status," formulated by the office of SRSG Steiner in 2002, which imposed eight benchmarks to be fulfilled by the PISG before the future status of Kosovo could
officially be considered, was both intrusive and largely inconsistent in its
application.[42] UNMIK was widely perceived as using these standards to
counter early Kosovar demands for political independence from Serbia
(Buerstedde 2005: 142f.).[43] Furthermore, the benchmarks did not have clear
indicators for their fulfilment. Overall, their development with hardly any
consultation with the PISG can be regarded as an example of imposing a
top-down policy of conditionality on the local government. It was not until
December 2003, that Steiner's successor, Holkeri, changed that UNMIK
policy into a more participatory approach by seeking direct involvement of
the PISG government and close cooperation with local counterparts in the
development of a detailed implementation framework of the individual
standards with the Kosovo Standards Implementation Plan (KSIP).[44]

However, Holkeri's shift of UNMIK's policy from one of high intrusiveness and conditionality to one of rather participatory intervention, allowing more room for local ownership and transparency, suffered a severe setback when large-scale political alienation and economic frustration (particularly among young Kosovars) resulted in a renewed massive eruption of ethnic violence during the Kosovo-wide riots of March 2004, which left nineteen people dead, many Kosovo-Serb settlements destroyed, and their former inhabitants displaced.[45]

In the aftermath of these riots, UN Special Envoy Eide concluded in an evaluation report that UNMIK's standards-before-status approach was "untenable in its current form" and that UNMIK was in a state of "disarray [and] without direction and internal cohesion."[46] Holkeri resigned from office and was succeeded in the summer of 2004 by the new SRSG Jessen-Petersen, who speeded up the handover of authorities from UNMIK to the PISG by establishing PISG ministries in the formerly "reserved power" sectors of policing and jurisdiction, while reducing UNMIK's bureaucracy. Jessen-Petersen also pushed the agenda of determining the future status of Kosovo further, declaring that "UNMIK prepares to close shop in Kosovo" (Jessen-Petersen 2006: 10).[47] Meanwhile, the UN Security Council and the Contact Group on the Balkans initiated a series of status talks between delegations from Belgrade and Prishtina, with the assistance of UN Special Envoy Ahtisaari and, later, under the auspices of the Contact Group itself (see below). Overall, the incoherent and overly intrusive implementation of the standards-before-status policy must be regarded as a symptomatic failure of international statebuilding in Kosovo to promote local ownership. Setting benchmarks of this type assumes that the local actors can achieve these standards and that such a policy is being applied by the external statebuilders in a reliable and stringent manner. However, as this policy was implemented, local actors were not realistically able to fulfill many standards demanded, such as in the areas of policing or the judiciary. These competencies, for example, fell under the reserved powers of the international administration and could not effectively have been influenced by the PISG.

At the same time, the demand to achieve these benchmarks varied significantly from turning down local calls for independence to the point at which the fulfillment of the given benchmarks did not seem to make any difference to the commencement of high-level talks on Kosovo's future status. If setting benchmarks is intended to help determine when a statebuilding mission can be regarded as completed so that external statebuilders can hand over to local control, such an approach needs to be implemented in a coherent and transparent way with a clear determination of timelines and sequencing of power transfer to local representatives. Partially due to the silence of UNMIK's mandate on this point, which postponed clarification on Kosovo's future status to an undefined date, this opportunity was missed and kept the mission's overall statebuilding goal rather ambiguous and open-ended. Nevertheless, if UNMIK authorities had been transferred too early to local representatives, Kosovar political parties and the local government might have been unable to contain ethnically motivated violence or to engage in genuine, democratic elections. Overall, it appears that finding an appropriate moment for a well-balanced and consistent transfer of competencies was missed due to a flawed mandate and an incoherent handover policy, which increased the initial intrusiveness dilemma and led, in the end, to a hasty UNMIK exit strategy and handover to the European Union.

Local dependency externally prolonged?

Despite its rather open-ended mandate and a wealth of initial donor contributions (compared to other crisis areas in the world), UN statebuilders in Kosovo together with KFOR were faced with a constant reduction of available resources after 2001, both financially and with respect to civilian and military manpower.[48] With the developments after 9/11, international statebuilding and reconstruction efforts became increasingly focused on other crisis areas, such as Iraq and Afghanistan.[49] Also, UN statebuilders in Kosovo were usually only able to plan their programs and activities for a time span of a year or a little more, taking into account the annual and often delayed budgeting processes of the international organizations under the UNMIK umbrella. In addition, many staff members of UNMIK were hired for other missions and left Kosovo.[50] Under these circumstances of planning insecurity and high fluctuation of personnel, the operational dilemma between short-term and long-term mission requirements prevailed, significantly affecting the practical work of statebuilding in Kosovo. Following the holding of democratic elections, formal state structures were built up. However, when it came to the development of self-sustaining local capacity-building and the long-term promotion of a civic culture of tolerance and democratic values in postwar Kosovo (as underpinning elements to the overall statebuilding process), external statebuilders were often restricted in their project planning due to a lack of necessary long-term orientation, all of which contributed to the prolongation of Kosovo's dependency on external statebuilding assistance.

Kosovo's society was (and to a large degree still is) very dependent on economic and financial assistance from the outside. This was especially so during the humanitarian crisis and reconstruction phase immediately after the war in the summer of 1999. A large number of international governmental and non-governmental organizations provided the necessary financial resources and technical support, while creating an extended international job market in Kosovo. Apart from the UNMIK proper, the UNHCR until 2001, the OSCE and the EU, most of the bigger UN agencies were present in Kosovo with their programs. The UN Development Group for Kosovo itself comprised more than twelve agencies (such as OCHA, FAO, UNDP, UNICEF, UNOPS, OHCHR, IOM, ILO, WHO, UNFPA, UNIFEM, and

HABITAT) that tried to coordinate a wealth of postwar reconstruction and institution-building activities.[51] With respect to local job opportunities, UNMIK with its some 3,800 international officers employed over 2,600 local staff, while the OSCE with about 320 international officers hired over 1,000 local staff. KFOR as the main military component in Kosovo comprised about 17,000 troops from 23 NATO countries and 13 non-NATO countries with many more local employees than the civilian components of UNMIK and OSCE together.[52]

Moreover, it is estimated that about 50,000 Kosovars found employment in more than 380 international NGOs active in Kosovo in 2003 and a possibly much larger number in the more than 2,000 local NGOs (Holzner 2003: 11; Kramer and Dzihic 2005: 36).[53] With the massive influx of international donor money, the number of local NGOs increased from about 110 local NGOs in early 2000 to 2,394 four years later. This explosion in the number of NGOs illustrates what an enormous inflationary impact external assistance in statebuilding environments has had on the local market.[54] However, the low quality of this artificial job market becomes obvious if one considers the effective output of the local NGOs. It is estimated that no more than 10 percent of all registered local NGOs in Kosovo were actually implementing projects, which means that the vast majority of them must be regarded as non-operational "shadow" NGOs boosted up by international money.[55]

The recruitment approach used by most international governmental as well as non-governmental organizations in Kosovo followed the pattern of preferred sets of specific credentials. Western-educated, young local English-speakers had the best chances of becoming employed at IGOs and NGOs at high salaries.[56] Their massive recruitment resulted in forms of local brain drain depriving the local labor market of its most productive and innovative human resources and leaving the less educated behind in the vast semi-legal sectors of the economy.[57] Another striking example of negative consequences of the massive influx of donor money for the statebuilding process of Kosovo after 1999 can be seen with organized crime. The presence of, at times, more than 20,000 international staff, both military and civilian, can be linked not only to a suddenly inflated job market with all its positive and negative consequences but also to a massive increase in organized crime, such as gun smuggling, trafficking in human beings, and prostitution. It has been alleged that international staff members were involved in high-level embezzlement, smuggling of arms and forced prostitution (Kramer and Dzihic 2005: 134; Davis 2002: 57, quoted in Khakee and Florquin 2003:30; and Mendelson 2005: 8ff.). Moreover, UN statebuilders did not succeed in creating a comprehensive economic development strategy and a self-sustaining local economy. This was seen as being hampered by unclear property titles, a low foreign investment rate, and a flawed privatization process of formerly socially-owned enterprises (mainly due to Kosovo's unresolved political status) (ICG 2004a: 3, 38).[58] This turn of events was all the more surprising, considering that an estimated 20 billion euros or 25 billion US dollars was spent on Kosovo by international organizations and donors in total, over the period from 2000 to 2004.[59]

Apart from these forms of prolonged socio-economic dependency in Kosovo, a need for external expertise and technical know-how for building local capacities and postwar institutions also prevailed. The 2004 report of UN Special Envoy Eide that assessed the role of UNMIK with respect to the March riots, recommended that a transfer of powers to Kosovo institutions "should be accompanied by a more ambitious and systematic policy of capacity-building" due to the weakness and inexperience of the PISG, to which "along with greater ownership [...] must be provided relevant knowledge and expertise" (UN Doc. S/2004/932, first Eide Report: 18). Citing the establishment of the Kosovo Police Service as a successful example of a well-trained multi-ethnic local institution, Eide found that "capacity-building efforts have tended to be sporadic, uncoordinated and of limited duration, carried out by a number of actors" and that "under such circumstances the impact will necessarily be limited." Having consulted with local stakeholders, Eide recommended a "more systematic approach and [...] ensuring that the qualifications of those involved match the needs on the ground," while asking the OSCE to identify areas for capacity-building (ibid.).

In spite of such fundamental criticism, at least two capacity-building programs led by the OSCE mission in Kosovo provided interesting examples of how a better balance could be achieved between externally intrusive and locally owned capacity building. Besides running the Kosovo Police Service School, the OSCE took the lead role in building the capacities of the Kosovo Assembly following the 2001 elections, with one of its main activities being the Assembly Support Initiative (ASI). This program, established in early 2002 by the Central Assembly Support Unit of the OSCE mission, aimed at developing the professional skills of the new Kosovo assembly members, based on the principle of institutional learning. However, in contrast to the SRSG's Assembly Task Force (which was responsible for developing assembly rules and regulations) and UNMIK's International Secretariat at the assembly, the OSCE refrained from imposition. Instead it created the ASI program as an open working forum of a group of cooperating partners. These partners included international actors, such as the European Agency for Reconstruction, the Inter-Parliamentary Union, national political foundations from abroad, international and local NGOs and the parliamentary parties, comprising 24 participating partners in total (Narten 2006a: 151).

ASI was based on a system of regular consultation on specific issues of parliamentary support without a centralized system of imposed decision-making and with a growing level of local ownership. While the participatory working style of ASI can be considered as an advantage in promoting the local ownership of capacity-building programs, UNMIK, symptomatically, chose not to participate in that program expressing its concerns about being coordinated by the OSCE (ibid.). Overall, the ASI activities comprised a whole range of capacity-building support from the planning of conferences to providing training and assistance for parliamentary groups, including working visits to parliaments abroad, conducting advisory oversight to the Assembly on procedural rules, public hearings, and providing technical support for reviewing draft laws for compliance with EU standards.[60] Having generated largely self-sustaining management capacities, the ASI support functions were progressively handed over to the local counterparts by the end of 2005.

Another example of the OSCE's local ownership-oriented capacity-building approach could be seen in its comprehensive National Professional Officers (NPO) program for training and enabling segments of its local staff to progressively take over the functions of seconded international personnel. The OSCE provided them with a combination of training courses and fieldwork under direct mentorship by international officers. In its Human Rights Department, for example, the NPOs learned on the job about aspects of legal and judicial human rights, reporting and team-building skills, techniques of mediation and conflict resolution as well as skills for project planning and implementation.[61] The program focused to a large extent on building local trainer and managerial capacities that enabled the NPOs to adapt working concepts and methods for self-identified local audiences. Having received this kind of training and on-the-job learning, the NPOs worked as local trainers and fully-fledged human rights, elections and democratization officers in their respective local communities and transmitted their knowledge and expertise in self-designed outreach activities to other Kosovar multipliers, such a teachers, civil servants, and NGO activists.

The two examples of the ASI and NPO programs show that, despite overall planning insecurity and a general short-term orientation as opposed to actual statebuilding needs in Kosovo, the dilemma of prolonged local dependency on external assistance could be (at least partially) overcome by focusing on those capacity-building programs that would generate local trainer and/or manager capacities in a relatively short time. Based on such local capacities for the statebuilding process in Kosovo, a self-sustaining cycle of long-term capacity-building by local resources was promoted, allowing local ownership in nearly all phases of project management and, in the long run, helping develop an understanding of democratic values and societal tolerance with locally-designed outreach activities. In other sectors, however, such as economic development or the rather sensitive areas of jurisdiction and security, a general dependency on external assistance remained virulent and was further aggravated by short-term mission requirements. In the end, this contributed to UNMIK's sudden "closing-the-shop" policy and a hasty transfer of reserved competencies to the local government and/or other international actors under leadership of the European Union.

Identifying partners, empowering spoilers?

UNMIK faced the immediate postwar problem of identifying appropriate local partners for cooperation and, ever since, has been confronted with a progressive spoiler dilemma at different levels. The Serb-dominated state apparatus had left Kosovo immediately after the war, while the Albanian underground structures were at odds with each other and split between the (exile) government of moderate Ibrahim Rugova and the Kosovo Liberation Army (KLA) led by Hashim Thaci, Ramush Haradinaj and Agim Ceku, all of whom later became high ranking "state" representatives in postwar Kosovo. After the war, there was also a period of reverse violence against the minority population, which led to continued displacement and destruction. In such a context, UNMIK had to build up its initial operational capacities, inevitably needing to identify and select local cooperating partners to promote the local ownership of the statebuilding process. In making this selection, UNMIK faced the difficult choice of working with still powerful, former warring parties that were also engaged in postwar crime activities, with unofficial and non-elected underground structures or with newly recruited (but hardly available) professional staff from among the local population

UNMIK knew that without the support of the local population, which widely sympathized with the KLA and the underground structures, stable local ownership of the statebuilding process would be unlikely to be achieved and tasked with building up a functioning local self-government and new democratic institutions. Therefore, it faced the dilemma of identifying local partners while running the risk of empowering as official partners potential spoilers or sidelined elites, many of whom enjoyed wide popular support and were in powerful positions after the war.

It was in this context immediately after the war that units of the KLA installed self-appointed municipal governments throughout most regions in Kosovo with their commanders in charge of entire municipalities (while taking control of private apartments, commercial properties and formerly socially-owned enterprises) (Wennmann 2005: 485). This early take-over of illegal revenues laid the foundation for certain parts of today's parallel economy and mafia structures and provided a form of KLA warlordism in Kosovo in 1999, accompanied by large-scale acts of ethnic revenge against minority groups and political opponents (Heinemann-Grüder and Paes 2001: 34ff.; Heinemann-Grüder and Grebenschikov 2006: 46). As a consequence, one of KFOR's and UNMIK's early statebuilding efforts concentrated on disarmament, demobilization, and reintegration programs for members of the KLA. Many of the KLA officers applied to and were integrated into the newly established Kosovo Police Service (KPS) and the Kosovo Protection Corps (KPC). Although conceptualized as a civilian Kosovar institution, the KPC was commonly perceived as the nucleus of a future Kosovo-Albanian army-in-waiting for the status of independence (while the KPS was regarded as an overall success story for multiethnic policing) (ibid.; Jessen-Petersen 2006: 8; Simonsen 2004: 299).

External statebuilders also sought to transform the political arm of the KLA into UNMIK-registered political parties. The most prominent of these parties were the PDK with its political leader Hashim Thaci and the AAK under former KLA commander and then Kosovo Prime Minister Ramush Haradinaj, who was later indicted by the International Criminal Tribunal for the Former Yugoslavia (ICTY) in The Hague. UNMIK's strategy of allowing former KLA elites to participate in the nascent political system was also illustrated by the election of another former KLA commander, Agim Ceku, as Prime Minister. Prior to this function, Ceku served as the Kosovar head of the KPC. Instead of identifying and promoting new, non-elite people as local partners for cooperation, UNMIK opted to rely largely on those elites among the Kosovo-Albanian community who were already powerful before and during the war. This happened in spite of the fact that some key figures of the new postwar institutions and local government might have been responsible for illegal activities and war crimes during and after the war. All together, UNMIK's "picking-the-winners" strategy predominantly benefited prewar and wartime elites from the ethnic majority. This selection approach is based on the logic of picking those people who are perceived as strongmen and who have certain sets of Western credentials preferred by internationals and a self-identification as reformers (despite allegations of criminal activities).

While picking such winners inside the statebuilding process resulted in a kind of "virtual" peace in Kosovo (Richmond 2004: 96), the international administration "failed to read the mood in the population and to understand the depth of the dissatisfaction of the majority and the vulnerability of the minorities."[62] Renewed ethnic violence swept through Kosovo in the March 2004 riots and saw an estimated 50,000–060,000 mainly Kosovo-Albanian protesters take to the streets.[63] A high unemployment rate (60–70 percent especially among young Kosovars) and a high level of political alienation from UNMIK (which was perceived as blocking Kosovo's way to independence) were cited by observers as evidence of UNMIK's failure "to understand the potential for extremists to mobilize support for ethnic violence and the vulnerability of minorities."[64] This assessment refers to the strong potential for radicalization of sidelined spoilers outside the official statebuilding process, which exists on both sides of the main ethnic divide in Kosovo where large parts of the population perceived themselves as losers in postwar reform and economic liberalization. The list of actual or potential spoilers outside the statebuilding process is long and comprises factions, such as the Albanian National Army, KLA veterans' associations,[65] radicalized former KLA commanders, the so-called Serb bridge watchers in north Mitrovica, and non-violent factions such as the student movement for self-determination "Vetevendosje," as well as more radical political figures of the Serb National Council from its North Mitrovica branch and the parallel institutions in Kosovo-Serb communities.[66] Overall, as UNMIK was progressively seen by the majority population as changing its role from liberator to occupier, international statebuilders in Kosovo were less and less welcomed by the local population and numerous local stakeholders, regardless of their ethnic or societal affiliation.

The dynamics of the March 2004 riots also illustrate how easily local cooperating partners can turn into spoilers who contribute to the incitement of ethnic hatred and violence. For example, one parliamentarian of the Kosovo Assembly, in an interview broadcast on television, declared the riots to be "a legitimate revolt by the Albanian population" and "a lesson for the international community."[67] Other parliamentarians interviewed on television during those days engaged in ethnic stereotyping which, in sum, must be considered to have helped fuel the March riots. After the riots, the international community demanded that all legal means be applied to prosecute all of the perpetrators. However, the apparent reluctance of the (Kosovo-Albanian dominated) local judiciary to convict fellow-Albanian perpetrators, resulted in "a low number of court cases and convictions in relation to the large number of participants in the riots and the scale of the events that took place throughout Kosovo in March 2004" and gave "the impression of impunity among the population for such kinds of ethnically motivated crimes."[68]

Statebuilders' decisions also arguably contributed to an "institutionalization of ethnicity" in the political and institutional system of postwar Kosovo (Hehir 2006: 202, 205). From the beginning of the operation, local institutions were composed in accordance with an ethnic quota. Examples of this process are the pre-election Interim Administrative Council, as an ethnically composed consultative organ of JIAS, the formation of ethnicity-based political parties for the following elections, the 120-seat parliamentary Kosovo Assembly with its 20 reserved seats for ethnic minorities and the reservation of committee posts in the assembly and of minister posts in the PISG government. Moreover, Eide found that "the development of new institutions is undermined by a strong tendency among politicians to see themselves as accountable to their political parties rather than to the public they serve. Appointments are ... regularly made on the basis of political and clan affiliation." In addition he found that, "the privatization process [of the Kosovar economy] could lead to discrimination along ethnic lines and affect the sustainability of minority communities."[69] Hehir argues similarly that "UNMIK established ethnicity as the defining social characteristic in Kosovo and [that] the administration embedded ethnic identity in the new political system, making it a crucial factor in the apportioning of power." He continues that this "decreased the chances that a multiethnic, democratic society can be created in the province," while the international community appeared to be in considerable denial about its own failures (Hehir 2006: 201f. and 210).[70]

In today's Kosovo, "multi-ethnicity" remains little more than rhetoric. It has not resonated within the local society or led to the establishment of a civil culture of ethnic tolerance and rule of law. In the longer term, the large-scale outbreak of ethnic violence in the March 2004 riots did not lead to a stricter application of normative standards to be fulfilled before considering Kosovo's future status, but rather to the practical abandonment of these standards and an accelerated commencement of a series of status talks, along the lines of UN Special Envoy Eide's recommendations.[71] The first round of these talks was led by the office of the UN's Special Envoy for Kosovo (UNOSEK) Ahtisaari over a period of 13 months, starting in January 2006. For this process, the Contact Group (consisting of France, Germany, Italy, Russia, United Kingdom, and the US) issued ten "Guiding Principles," which ruled out a return of Kosovo to its prewar status, its partition or union with neighboring countries or parts thereof, and made clear that the status "settlement must be acceptable to the people of Kosovo."[72] Until September 2006, a total of 15 rounds of direct talks between the Belgrade and Prishtina negotiating teams were held in Vienna, with an agenda largely imposed by UNOSEK and with hardly any non-Serb minority representatives involved.[73] With both sides diametrically opposed to each other (Belgrade only willing to grant Kosovo wide-ranging autonomy within Serbia, and Prishtina insisting upon state independence), Ahtisaari decided to end these series of talks and submitted his own Comprehensive Proposal for the Kosovo Status Settlement to the UN Security Council in March 2007. His proposal foresaw internationally supervised independence for Kosovo and far-reaching provisions of municipal self-government for Kosovo-Serb communities.[74]

However, Russia indicated that it would veto the Ahtisaari proposal (proposed as a follow-up to resolution 1244), and rejected five draft resolutions sponsored by Western powers in the council. This led to a new round of direct "negotiations" between Belgrade and Prishtina in the second half of 2007 facilitated by a Contact Group troika of an EU, a US, and a Russian representative. Following another period of shuttle diplomacy and additional meetings between the parties in Vienna, New York, and Brussels, the troika was to submit a report to the UN Secretary-General on December 10. As these talks also appeared to have become blocked in the old positions, the Prishtina delegation and many Western member states of the Contact Group regarded this as the final attempt to achieve a negotiated settlement before Prishtina declared Kosovo's independence unilaterally.[75] In preparation for Kosovo's path to independence (to be recognized bilaterally by most Western states),[76] the Kosovo Assembly earlier declared (in April 2007) its acceptance of and commitment to the full implementation of the Ahtisaari proposal as "legally binding upon Kosovo."[77] Meanwhile, the PISG and the Kosovo-Albanian (multi-partisan) Unity Team for the negotiation process has intensified its cooperation with the planning teams of the Ahtisaari-proposed police and justice mission of the EU and the EU-led International Civilian Office (ICO) in order to take over control functions from UNMIK after a settlement, and to prepare draft laws and the future Kosovar constitution.

By the end of 2007, UNMIK's role had almost been reduced to one of a passive observer, preparing for its own exit. Moreover, the entire statebuilding consensus between the PISG/Unity Team and its Western protagonists within the EU and the Contact Group must be regarded as an extremely fragile one, which has come under intense pressure from all sides of civil society. In November 2006 and again in February 2007, the student move-ment "Vetevendosje" (Self-determination) organized mass demonstrations in Prishtina against the decentralization plans of the Ahtisaari proposal and the PISG's intentions to accept those. This, in turn, led to violent clashes with the UN police and to two tragic casualties. In this context, the movement, under its leader, Albin Kurti, ran a campaign, which again described UNMIK as an undemocratic and neo-colonial regime, using the slogan "decentralization = partition = war."[78] In February 2007 the Kosovo-Serb community also organized mass demonstrations with about 7,000 protesters in North-Mitrovica, at which Milan Ivanovic, one of the key figures of the Serb National Council in Kosovo, declared that "if independence [of Kosovo] is imposed on us, [Kosovo-] Serbs have the right to self-determination."[79] This development indicated all the more how easily the official statebuilding partnership between UNMIK and the political elite of the PISG could reinforce the spoiler dilemma and empower civil resistance movements against the statebuilding agenda, while the status negotiations were being held.

All in all, there was no ideal solution for UN statebuilders in Kosovo to overcome the inevitability of identifying local cooperating partners in the statebuilding process in the face of a lack of sufficient local professional staff (not suspected of violent or criminal activities during or after the war), the risk of empowering spoilers and Kosovo's unclear status. While UNMIK unwillingly contributed, with this identification process, to the generation of political and socio-economic winners in the statebuilding process, sidelined but powerful elites were progressively able to exploit widespread political alienation and economic frustrations among the local population. All this provided an explosive environment for the postwar statebuilding process. The UN's only practical option to reduce the spoiler dilemma might have been to concentrate, early on, on educating newly-recruited local staff as cooperating partners and to promote their local power base without falling back on a policy of ethnicization. In addition, they could have focused on outreach activities to the local population to reduce the power base of potential spoilers. However, this chance was largely forfeited as UNMIK was not able to resolve the contradiction between the need for operational effectiveness (by cooperating with old powerful elites) and moral legitimacy (by building non-suspect state structures with new personnel).

Findings from Kosovo: interacting dilemmas of promoting local ownership

The Kosovo case illustrates not only the three major dilemmas of promoting local ownership, but also how closely interlinked these dilemmas are with each other. Given an unspecific and rather open-ended mandate and lacking any clear indication of Kosovo's future status as a guiding overall goal for the statebuilding process, UNMIK had a double function to fulfill: 1) to provide international administration for the territory of Kosovo in the absence of functioning state structures after the war using highly intrusive measures of postwar statebuilding with almost unlimited, quasi-autocratic powers; and 2) to create local structures of responsible self-government, to which these powers could progressively be transferred without knowing exactly what kind of state was to be built and which powers to withhold. UN statebuilders were, therefore, caught in the dilemma of promoting local ownership in a process of building self-governing structures and needing to apply measures of external intrusiveness without clarity about the final outcome. This overall dilemma interacted with (and was aggravated by) the operational contradiction between short-term mission requirements in terms of external financial, logistical and human resources, and the long-term needs of the host society for a sustainable postwar statebuilding process. One consequence of this was the prolonged dependency of the Kosovar society on external assistance in many statebuilding sectors, which resulted in continued intrusive measures by international actors for a period of more than eight years.

Another dilemma stemmed from the fact that UNMIK had to identify cooperating local partners for the statebuilding process, while lacking sufficiently available, educated local staff not suspected of having a violent past or involvement in criminal activities. UNMIK had the choice between relying on already powerful local actors and building-up new local partners and their capacities. The first option promised quick operational effectiveness, the other required long-term involvement but implied higher legitimacy in international terms. UN statebuilders selected the first option and initiated a process of picking winners, leaving sidelined elites and larger groups of the population feeling they were becoming losers in the statebuilding process. This increased the risk of empowering local spoilers who periodically threatened to undermine the entire statebuilding process. This spoiler dilemma interacted with the dilemmas of high external intrusiveness and prolonged local dependency. Kosovo's ongoing dependency in socio-economic and capacity-building terms provided an ideal mobilization and recruitment ground for local spoilers, who claimed the right to self-determination and utilized economic frustration and political alienation from a statebuilding process commonly perceived as overly long and progressively intrusive. The activities of local spoilers in Kosovo, in turn, made a prolonged security and veto presence of international actors necessary, constituting a kind of vicious circle among the three dilemmas.

In sum, UNMIK missed the critical point for a well-balanced identification and strenghthening of local partners through a consistent transfer of powers, and by not setting transparent, fair, and realistically achievable benchmarks with clearly defined indicators of achievement for local counterparts. UNMIK also lacked a stringent policy for local capacity-building and outreach activities to promote self-sustaining local resources and an underpinning for a civic culture of democratic values. Later it pursued a rather uncoordinated closing-the-shop policy of quick transfer of reserved powers to local actors (and to EU-led successor missions) at the end of its presence in Kosovo. Over a period of almost a decade of international administration in Kosovo since 1999, the statebuilding policy of UNMIK left the impression of incoherence and poor coordination with respect to the promotion of local ownership in the statebuilding process. During most of its presence, UNMIK conducted statebuilding measures (like the standards-before-status policy) in a highly intrusive but inconsistent manner. After the March riots of 2004 and following the Eide reports, a sudden policy shift toward a quick and hasty exit strategy took place, which prevented a thoroughly planned and sustainable final handover of authority.

At this later stage, the UN statebuilders were trapped (and to a certain degree had trapped themselves) by a progressively self-enforcing dilemma of ill-applied external intrusiveness, through which the local society was kept dependent on ongoing external guidance. A handover of oversight competencies to the EU police and justice mission and the EU-led ICO in accordance with the Ahtisaari proposal could not effectively overcome the existing dilemmas of promoting local ownership in the statebuilding process. A future state of Kosovo will become little more than a para-state under international supervision (comparable with Bosnia but without international recognition at UN level). The envisaged EU-controlled international oversight and NATO's continued military presence will continue to apply measures of external intrusiveness and create further local dependencies in the areas of military security, policing, justice, and minority rights for an indefinite period of time. Altogether, it is likely to provoke further civil resistance among spoiler groups in the Kosovar society in the future. All of this will, then, create a continuum in which each of the local ownership dilemmas identified will reproduce itself and reinforce other ones.

Conclusion and recommendations

Kosovo represents a special example of external statebuilding assistance in light of UNMIK's all-encompassing authorities as an international interim administration and given Kosovo's unclear political status. However, the analysis of such a statebuilding environment provides a distinct analytical advantage: relevant socio-political interaction processes become more apparent under such conditions, which, in turn, allows for a much clearer understanding of the underlying processes and problems of coping with the dilemmas of promoting local ownership. Overall, the Kosovo example demonstrates that the prevailing dilemmas interacted with and significantly reinforced each other and prevented the consistent promotion of local ownership. External statebuilders can easily get trapped in such an evolving cycle of mutually interacting and reinforcing dilemmas of: 1) external intrusiveness vs. creating self-governing local structures; 2) prolonged dependency by short-term vs. long-term operational requirements; and 3) identifying local partners vs. empowering potential spoilers. By drawing on the findings of the Kosovo case and by trying to identify how the negative impact of the dilemmas identified can effectively be mitigated (if their existence cannot be prevented as such), the following recommendations to statebuilders of future UN missions can be made.

The principal dilemma between external intrusiveness and the (early) creation of local self-government cannot be overcome as such. What can be done, however, is to deploy statebuilding missions only when they have a mandate that clearly defines the final outcome of the process with minimal room for misinterpretation. If at the level of the UN Security Council, for example, such a clear-cut mandate cannot be achieved and UN statebuilders are nevertheless tasked with exercising an international administration over a given territory, there needs to be a transparent and fair process for setting benchmarks vis-à-vis local actors that clearly defines realistically achievable indicators. Uncertainty about the processes and overall goals of a state-building mission risks unleashing a progressively worsening "imposition-ownership-divide." A field-based emphasis on gradual (co-)ownership between external and local actors (based on a clear set of expectations and objectives) needs to be embraced instead. With such a policy, a higher level of under-standing and popular support among the local population might be achieved, which would help reduce the recruitment and mobilization grounds of local spoilers.

At the same time, the impact of short-term orientated mission requirements for planning, financing, and deployment ought to be reduced (specifically by issuing longer-term staffing contracts and project budgeting as well as by a policy of early recruitment of trainer-of-trainers staff and related programs). This would enable longer-term cycles of local capacity-building and the generation of competent local staff to take over central competencies of the international administration. In addition, a well-planned and early con-centration on self-reproducing local resources and skills would help reduce the statebuilders' dilemma of identifying appropriate local partners in the mid-term period and would allow for a constant, progressive integration of local partners at all levels of the management cycle. The capacity-building programs descibed above show how important it is to reduce prolonged local dependency with measures that create self-generating local trainer and manager capacities. Such indigenous resources seem to be better equipped to develop and implement outreach activities that promote an understanding of democratic values and societal tolerance among the local population. In some sectors (such as economic development), a similar process would be much harder to initiate. However, improved planning security and the con-centration on self-reproducing local resources with a multiplying effect is applicable to all sectors of importance for the statebuilding process.

The dilemma of empowering potential local spoilers by initiating the necessary identification and selection process of local partners will continue to prevail in most statebuilding environments. However, the impact of this dilemma could effectively be reduced if were to would invest more in educational projects for the general public, and in employment and activity programs especially for the youth in a postwar society. This could help diminish the power bases of potential spoilers. If statebuilders were to succeed in doing this, the latent or manifest pressure by the population on selected local cooperation partners to leave the statebuilding consensus and to join the activities of violent spoilers would also be alleviated. However, this would be dependent on careful policy-making by external statebuilders aiming at a broad social contract without further promoting ambivalent policies such as ethnicization of the postwar social and political fabric. Such measures would also be the key to securing the ground for a common understanding of the overall statebuilding process and reducing the room for local spoilers to maneuver.

If such farsighted mandating, planning, and application of external statebuilding measures could be achieved, the publicly accepted time span for an adequate and appropriate transfer of powers to legitimate local representatives would expand significantly and allow external statebuilders more time for a sustainable completion of their mandate. In such a case, the host society would be given the necessary time to develop the ground for a sound political and civic culture, underpinning new state institutions and allowing more democratic pluralism and tolerance to develop. With such a process, external statebuilders might feel less pressure to impose overly intrusive measures and could afford to involve democratically elected and thus legitimate representatives in all phases of the management cycle. Only under such circumstances, and with a well-regulated and reflected exit strategy for external statebuilders, would it be possible for the intrusive statebuilding phase to be succeeded by a phase of consecutive monitoring. If this could be achieved, external statebuilders would leave behind more sustainable and responsible structures of local self-government, fulfilling the requirement of local ownership in the overall statebuilding process.

Notes

1 Hansen and Wiharta argue that "the international effort is almost always limited due to a lack of resources; manpower, funds and [...] a limited attention span. Therefore, the sooner responsibility can transition to less transient stakeholders, the better." (Hansen and Wiharta 2006: 14).
2 See Cernea 1985; Chambers 1984 and 1997; and Jennings 2000.
3 See Canadian Peacebuilding Coordinating Committee 2005: 5; and Smith 2004: 26.
4 In that order, see Hansen 2005: 295; Sisk and Risley 2005: 3f.; Hurwitz 2005: 348f.; and Mobekk 2005a: 289.
5 As an example of the PCM as an applied working tool see European Commission 2002: 3ff.; and OSCE Training Section 2005: 4.
6 Hansen identifies similar phases for local participation in a post-conflict reform process, such as fact-finding and diagnostics, planning and design, program development, and sustainability (Hansen 2005: 295 and 308).

7 There is an ongoing debate on whether local ownership of peacebuilding and statebuilding processes must be sought from the very beginning, including the involvement in setting the agenda and leading the process (Tschirgi 2004: 9), or if local ownership is "usually not intended to mean control and often does not even imply a direct input into political questions. [...] Local ownership, then, must be the end of a transitional administration, but it is not the means" (Chesterman 2003: 4). In her findings, Reich goes one step further by questioning local ownership as a concrete project objective in general and by demanding a shift in the focus "to a discussion of the relationships between outsiders and insiders" (Reich 2006: 30). As a practical alternative for project management, she proposes instead applying the concept of mutual "learning sites," by which insiders and outsiders would learn to alter their own views to overcome existing and patronizing asymmetries and disparities (ibid.: 23ff. and 30).

8 For the purpose of this analysis, "dilemma" will be used in the following to describe the condition of difficult and complex choices between competing imperatives or objectives for external statebuilders, with the effect that pursuing one objective has the potential of working against achieving another objective.

9 Hansen identifies four dilemmas in the context of building local capacities for public security: process vs. outcome, finding appropriate partners, opposing time frames, and local dependency (Hansen 2005: 304ff.).

10 See Scheye and Peake 2005: 235f.; and Champagne 2005: 7.

11 See Chesterman 2007.

12 Other authors used the distinction of statebuilding environments with missions of so-called light footprint from those of international transitional administration holding full executive authorities with respect to their level of external intrusiveness (Chesterman 2002: 9); or they distinguished between various degrees of intervention from enforcement, to reform to monitoring (Hansen 2005: 301ff.); while Krasner introduced the concept of "shared sovereignty as a compromise between light footprint interventions and full-scale transitional administration" (Krasner 2004: 108ff.).

13 However, in light-footprint operations as well, external consultancy based on partnership with local actors might be linked to political and/or financial conditionality, thus indirectly raising the level of intrusiveness again (see Keane 2005).

14 In the context of military interventions, Edelstein labels such a situation as one of "obsolescing welcome" (Edelstein in this book).

15 However, statebuilding missions may opt to establish broad consultative forums of local stakeholders from all groups of civil society prior to elections to inform external decision-makers.

16 The liberal peace concept is largely based on principles of democracy, human rights, the rule of law, and a free market economy, which directly influences UN state- and peacebuilding agendas. This approach is critically reflected as *mission civilisatrice* (Paris 2003). Moreover, too early liberalization in the statebuilding process might be counterproductive if applied prior to the establishment of stable local institutions (Paris 1997: 89 and Paris 2004: 187f.).

17 Chesterman argues that "funds for post-conflict reconstruction are notoriously supply-rather than demand-driven. This leads to multiplication of bureaucracy in the recipient country [...] and a focus on projects that may be more popular with donors than they are necessary in the recipient country" (Chesterman 2003: i and 7).

18 See also Eide et al. 2005: 34f.

19 For the security sector, problems of accountability of international authorities in a postwar mission environment are exemplified in Mobekk 2005b: 391f.

20 See Hansen and Wiharta 2006: 37.

21 An extensive debate with a number of lessons learned around this question has been developed for the field of humanitarian assistance and development aid by

the NGO network *Collaborative for Development Action* in its two projects on *Local Capacities for Peace* and *Reflecting on Peace Practice* (Anderson 1996; Anderson 1999; and Anderson and Olson 2003).

22 At the same time, most of these job opportunities exist only in urbanized areas of the local capital or provincial towns, in which international offices are based. This often leads to an aggravation of income discrepancies between urban and rural areas.

23 Hansen states that the "capacities to undertake reform may simply be non-existent" and that the "lack of capacity may indeed be what triggered the intervention in the first place" (Hansen 2005: 305).

24 See International Alert 2002; and Strimling 2002: 271 and 282.

25 Outreach activities are recommended in the context of integrated missions (Eide et al. 2005: 40). Hansen defines rule-of-law culture as a behavioral (apart from a structural) dimension of capacity-building (Hansen 2005: 315 and 323).

26 Chopra and Hohe (2004) introduce the term "participatory intervention" in this context. In a similar understanding, Barnett uses the term "republican peace-building" as an alternative to liberal peacebuilding for an incremental, more integrative and deliberative process of peace- or statebuilding that "allows space for societal actors to determine for themselves what a good life is and how to achieve it" (Barnett 2006: 90).

27 See Hansen and Wiharta 2006: 31 ff.

28 A discussion on entrepreneurs of violence can be found in Zürcher and Koehler 2001: 49ff.

29 A definition of spoilers can be found in Stedman 1997.

30 A notion introduced by Sharman and Kanet 2000: 240, quoted in Sinanovic 2003: 120.

31 This applies especially to the early statebuilding period prior to holding first elections, but can, to some degree, also be effective in later periods.

32 See also Pouligny 2005: 507.

33 Chanaa therefore stresses the importance of managing corruption in the early context of postwar reform (Chanaa 2002:71ff.).

34 The mandate of UNMIK in Security Council Resolution 1244 (UN Doc. S/RES/1244) does not mention Kosovo as a state but reaffirms the territorial integrity of Yugoslavia (now Serbia), of which Kosovo is a province in international legal terms. Consequently, the mandate refers only to the establishment of substantial autonomy and provisional institutions of self-government (PISG) pending a political settlement of Kosovo's future status (Art. 10 and 11). However, UNMIK and its co-missions of the OSCE and the EU have treated Kosovo through all their programs as a quasi-state. In early 2006, a negotiation process on the future status of Kosovo was commenced. For reasons of better analytical compatibility, this study uses the notion of statebuilding for Kosovo although its status of statehood has not yet officially been determined.

35 Ibid.: Art. 10.

36 UNMIK Regulation 1999/24 amended by UNMIK Regulation 2000/59, available at http://www.unmikonline.org/regulations/index.htm (June 2006).

37 KPS and KPC recruited large numbers of fighters from the former Kosovo Liberation Army (KLA).

38 Available at http://www.unmikonline.org/regulations/index.htm (June 2006).

39 It took until early 2002 before the first central local government of the two big Kosovo-Albanian parties of LDK and PDK could be formed, following strong political intervention by SRSG Steiner.

40 UNMIK Regulation 2001/9, available at http://www.unmikonline.org/regulations/index.htm (June 2006).

41 One illuminating example of this was the vetoing by the SRSG of the draft law of the assembly on war veteran values and their status in the Kosovo society.

42 These benchmarks comprised the following elements: functioning democratic institutions, the rule of law, freedom of movement, returns and reintegration, the economy, property rights, dialogue with Belgrade, and the Kosovo Protection Corps (UN Mission in Kosovo 2002).

43 See UN Doc. S/2004/932 (first Eide Report): 15.

44 UNMIK/PISG 2004. In mid-2006, the KSIP was replaced by the European Partnership Action Plan, agreed between the EU and the PISG, which embedded the KSIP values and principles in the EU's integration process for Kosovo; see UN Doc. S/2006/707.

45 Ibid. On the incidents during the March riots see *inter alia* Human Rights Watch 2004; and International Crisis Group 2004a.

46 UN Doc. S/2004/932 (first Eide Report): 3 and 10.

47 In June 2006, Jessen-Pettersen resigned from his office as SRSG and was succeeded in September 2006 by the former head of UNMIK's EU pillar for reconstruction Rücker, who declared in his first press conference in this position that he considered himself the last SRSG of UNMIK.

48 See the figures provided in Kramer and Dzihic 2005: 125.

49 However, in the statebuilding context of Kosovo, the impact of the terrorist attacks of and after September 11, 2001, and the subsequently declared war on terror was of only very minor importance for two reasons. First, the international involvement with Kosovo pre-dated the developments of 9/11 and was based on a UN mandate unchanged since then. Second, fundamentalist Islam does not play a prominent role in the Kosovar society. For example, only a tiny part of the population belongs to Wahhabi Islam (International Crisis Group 2006b: 8). However, American and British involvement in Afghanistan and Iraq since 9/11 led to a reduced international military and financial engagement in Kosovo.

50 Even local Kosovar staff were recruited for these countries (Information provided to the author by former UNMIK personnel in Kosovo).

51 See http://www.undg.ks.undp.org/ProjectList.aspx (June 2006).

52 On the figures on UNMIK, the OSCE, and KFOR, see Kramer 2005: 25ff.

53 Based on reports on Kosovo of the United Nations Secretary-General in the period from 1999–2003.

54 Kosovar Civil Society Foundation 2000; and Nietsch 2005: 5, footnote 16. The peak of international NGO and IGO assistance was reached between 1999 and 2001 after which the donor community re-focused on other crisis areas worldwide (see Kramer and Dzihic 2005: 36).

55 Ibid. An UNMIK list of Serbian NGOs in Kosovo provides data on 269 NGOs declared to be operational in the Kosovo-Serb enclaves (UNMIK 2005: Annex XX).

56 With living costs similar to western European countries for imported goods, the average income in Kosovo per person is calculated at about 90 euros per month (United Nations Development Programme 2004: 125). By contrast, the salary of local staff at international organizations can easily amount to ten times this much.

57 Calic argues that most of the 30,000–50,000 small private enterprises are regarded as being hesitant to pay taxes and show a certain susceptibility to criminal activities (Calic 2004: 21).

58 See UN Doc. S/2004/932 (first Eide Report): 18.

59 This includes the UNMIK budget, EU reconstruction aid, KFOR military expenditures, and contributions of international NGOs and donors (Kramer and Dzihic 2005: 125).

60 A list of ASI activities in 2004 is available at http://www.osce.org/documents/mik/2004/05/2931_en.pdf (June 2006).

61 OSCE Mission in Kosovo 2003a: 23. On the overall work of the OSCE Human Rights Department, see Narten 2006b.

62 UN Doc. S/2004/932 (first Eide Report): 3.
63 OSCE Media Representative 2004: 5.
64 UN Doc. S/2004/932 (first Eide Report): 10.
65 KLA war veterans associations, for example, described UNMIK as "neo-colonial" and as "carrying out the same policies applied by Serbia" (Human Rights Watch 2004: 18, quoted in Hehir 2006: 205).
66 UNMIK first chose to ignore the Kosovo-Serb and Belgrade-sponsored parallel structures active in the areas of internal security and policing, jurisdiction, administration, education, health, etc. (Wennmann 2005: 485; and OSCE Mission in Kosovo 2003b).
67 Ibid.: 12.
68 OSCE Mission in Kosovo 2005: 4 and 34. In this context, Human Rights Watch speaks of a "failure to bring to justice many of those responsible for the violence and destruction of March 2004" and that there is a real danger that if the status quo on impunity continues, Kosovo risks becoming a "failed state" in which lawlessness and arbitrariness, not transparent, democratic rule will reign, regardless of the identity of the future leadership of the province (Human Rights Watch 2006: 65).
69 UN Doc. S/2005/635 (second Eide Report): 2f.
70 See also Human Rights Watch 2004: 3.
71 UN Doc. S/2005/635 (second Eide Report): 4f.
72 Statement by the Contact Group on the future of Kosovo, London, January 31, 2006.
73 Author's interview with the Deputy Special Envoy for Kosovo Rohan, Venice, December 11, 2006; also see Waringo 2006: 1.
74 UN Doc. S/2007/168 and S/2007/168/Add.1.
75 Statements by Kosovo-Albanian politicians at http://www.reliefweb.int/rw/rwb.nsf/db900sid/SSHN-785GLB?OpenDocument&cc=srb as well as http://www.reliefweb.int/rw/rwb.nsf/db900sid/SHES-76KN6V?OpenDocument&rc=4&cc=srb (October 2007).
76 George W. Bush declared on June 10, in Tirana: "[Y]ou've got to say enough is enough, Kosovo is independent." Available at http://www.state.gov/p/eur/rls/rm/86260.htm; for the EU see http://www.reliefweb.int/rw/rwb.nsf/db900sid/EMAE-78BM5W?OpenDocument&cc=srb (October 2007).
77 Kosovo Assembly Declaration, April 5, 2007, available at http://www.kuvendikosoves.org (April 2007).
78 See Vetevendosje website at http://vetevendosje.org/decentralizimi.pdf (February 2007).
79 Statement available at www.reliefweb.int/rw/RWB.NSF/db900SID/YSAR-6Y9LZT?OpenDocument&rc=4&cc=srb (February 2007).

Part VI
Reflections and conclusions

12 Statebuilding after Afghanistan and Iraq

Miles Kahler[1]

Over the past half-decade, three logics, supported by powerful intellectual and political constituencies, have converged to elevate fragile states and state-building on the international agenda. The humanitarian motivation, oldest of these logics, emphasizes the human and international costs of internal conflict and genocide. Humanitarian concentration on short-term, apolitical relief of human suffering was transformed during the 1990s to include attention to longer-term—and intensely political—causes of internal conflict, particularly weak institutions.

A second logic for statebuilding emerged from concern with economic development among the poorest countries. The economic consequences of violent internal conflict became clear: "development in reverse" (Collier 2007: 27). Good governance was closely linked with effective use of foreign aid and successful economic development. This new emphasis on institutional criteria for targeting aid threatened to marginalize fragile and failed states, however. New forms of international engagement with those states were required to avoid punishing poorly-governed societies, whose populations were among the most economically deprived in the world.

Finally, the terrorist attacks of September 11, 2001 reoriented US and NATO security policy toward risks emanating from territories that were not effectively policed. Afghanistan, a neglected and chaotic backwater since the end of the Cold War, had become a key base for al-Qaeda. International public "bads" of all kinds, from infectious disease to refugee flows, were linked to failed states. Widespread skepticism toward interventionist "social work" during the 1990s quickly changed to statebuilding as a strategic necessity.[2]

The proponents of each of these logics often agreed on little more than the importance of a shifting cluster of states labeled fragile or failed. Definitions of fragile and failed states depended on ultimate policy aims—an end to civil war, economic development and poverty alleviation, or a reduction in security threats. Those most concerned with security—either human security of those in the failed and fragile states, or national security interests of more powerful states—defined the boundaries of state fragility by the incidence of violent conflict. Fragile and failed states were, in this view, beset by or emerging from internal conflict.[3] The World Bank and other development agencies accepted this association of internal conflict and state fragility. However, the Bank defined its larger universe of "Low-Income Countries Under Stress" (LICUS, recently renamed fragile states) by poverty and "weak policies, institutions, and governance."[4] Overshadowing all of these larger groups of poor and generally small states are the cases of Afghanistan and Iraq, one an example of state failure long ignored by the international community and now a centerpiece of the United States Global War on Terror; the latter a case of state failure induced by military invasion, an intervention ill-prepared for its subsequent statebulding enterprise.

At least rhetorically, these statebuilding projects converged on a model—the New York Consensus—that found an ideological home at United Nations headquarters. As Roland Paris and Timothy Sisk point out, the complexity and transformational ambitions of the UN's role in fragile and failed states grew over the course of the 1990s. At the same time, an increasingly rigid and detailed template has defined international statebuilding goals—the creation of liberal democratic polities that preside over vibrant civil societies and market economies. This template became as powerful as its much-criticized analogue in economic policy, the Washington Consensus.

The ambitions of the New York Consensus now meet with increasing skepticism. The cases of Afghanistan, analyzed by Astri Suhrke in this volume, and Iraq have clearly contributed to this increasingly pessimistic evaluation. Even without those faltering (or catastrophic) efforts, however, each of the contending constituencies would have been challenged by recent statebuilding results. United Nations programs that once had been portrayed as successful models, such as Kosovo and Timor Leste, now demonstrate the uncertain results of large-scale statebuilding interventions. Albanian Kosovars have grown increasingly resistant to UN tutelage; riots erupted in March 2004, directed at both the United Nations Mission in Kosovo (UNMIK) and the remaining Serb population. As designated trustee for Timor Leste from 1999 until independence in 2002, the United Nations had enjoyed a broad mandate, substantial powers to fulfill that mandate, and resources on a large scale. Nevertheless, by May 2006, violence in the capital of Timor Leste had produced a state teetering on the brink of failure. Renewed international military intervention was required to restore the peace.

Development agencies have produced equally uncertain results with their efforts to improve the governance of fragile states. The first independent review of the World Bank's LICUS (fragile states) initiative questioned the Bank's track record in improving governance (World Bank 2006). Although the latest World Bank governance report describes both improvements and declines in governance indicators for regions such as sub-Saharan Africa, the team concludes "we do not have as yet any convincing evidence of significant improvements in governance worldwide" (Kaufman, Kraay and Mastruzzi 2007: 22).

On the effectiveness of international intervention to end violent conflict, contemporary pessimism may be overdrawn. The Human Security Report argues that the new century's decline in internal conflict is owed to an increase in International involvement to settle ongoing civil wars (Human Security Centre 2005). Scholarly investigation supports this minimalist measure of international success in peacebuilding (Fortna 2004). The counterfactual cannot be readily dismissed: although the results to date have been disappointing, internal conflict and poor governance might have been even worse in the absence of international assistance to fragile and failed states.

Whether the mixed results of statebuilding are best viewed as predictable and even promising, given the complexity of the task, or mediocre, given the resources devoted to statebuilding over the past decade, a diminishing number of practitioners and analysts argue for more of the same. As Paris and Sisk observe, the reinvestment option—staying the course by devoting more resources and more time to the existing model of statebuilding—has relatively few supporters in the wake of Afghanistan, Iraq, and other cases of ineffective international intervention. Instead, two alternatives, both critical of the New York Consensus and existing statebuilding practices, point toward a rethinking and redesign of international intervention. A strategy of disengagement was rarely advocated after 9/11, as humanitarians, military interventionists, and proponents of good governance agreed on the importance of international support for statebuilding. Disengagement now claims substantial support for statebuilding through local initiative, initiative that is often stifled by international actors, however well intentioned. Revisionists, a second group of critics, are more sanguine that reformed international strategies can promote statebuilding in fragile and failed states.[5]

The contributors to this volume are uniformly skeptical of the New York Consensus, whether they endorse a revision of the Washington Consensus or disengagement. In both their analysis of international intervention in fragile and failed states and their policy recommendations based on that analysis, the authors deviate from the "stay the course" remedies of more resources and more time. Revisionist analysis, described in the next section, questions the unit of analysis for policy intervention and the key variables that shape strategic interaction between those intervening and those with local political power. The policy prescriptions described in the final section suggest that rethinking of the New York Consensus is unlikely to produce yet another monolithic international consensus on statebuilding. Instead, if the authors here are representative, the next round of international intervention will witness an ongoing debate between those who espouse revised and more modest forms of engagement—but engagement nonetheless—and those who favor disengagement in favor of local solutions and local empowerment.

Revisionist analysis: thinking outside the state

Although fragile states by definition have weak control over their own borders and limited capacity to prevent meddling by outside parties, those who explain and evaluate statebuilding outcomes have often assumed a fixed and relatively closed territorial space in which intervention takes place. Accuracy demands that the radical openness of these societies, an openness that they often cannot control, be taken into account in any assessment of their prospects for statebuilding.

State fragility is often linked to regional effects. Bad neighborhoods make it more difficult to end civil wars and to establish new institutions of governance. Regional neighborhoods may alter the incentives of local political actors within fragile states; regional actors also directly, if covertly, intervene in the politics of those states. In many respects, the relevant unit of analysis is a failed region rather than failed states: regions in which norms against violent intervention are weak or non-existent, economic exchange is low, and regional institutions play a minor or ineffective role in quelling conflict. West Africa, with its extensive spillovers of rebel armies and contraband trade, was an exemplar of a failed region during the 1990s, a particularly striking case in light of its past of relative prosperity and peace. Northeast Africa is now a site for covert and overt intervention by neighboring states and by great powers, drastically lowering the prospects for alleviating conflict and re-establishing political order in Somalia and Ethiopia. Post-apartheid South Africa, in contrast, has served as an anchor of regional stability, lending economic and political support to successful statebuilding in Mozambique and Namibia.

Changes in regional configurations of power can also diminish conflict, even if statebuilding success is not guaranteed. The eruption and decline of conflict in the Balkans and the former Soviet Union can be explained in part by the internal demise of hegemonic communist parties and the regional retreat of the Soviet empire before new hegemonic powers, the European Union and NATO, could replace them. Cambodia's civil war ended when both the great powers and its regional neighbors—Vietnam and the Association of Southeast Asian Nations (ASEAN)—accepted that further conflict was no longer in their interest. Cambodia's evolution, into a relatively peaceful but corrupt and authoritarian state, was cemented by its membership in ASEAN and by the acquiescence of those same neighbors. Private-security companies (PSCs) have played an ambiguous role in developing the military capacity of post-conflict states. Deborah Avant awards "democratically dense" regional institutions a primary role in determining the effects of PSC intervention in fragile states. In the presence of a democratic regional network, PSCs are more likely to strengthen a centralized state apparatus; PSC involvement in the absence of such a network undermines statebuilding by fragmenting political and military power.[6]

The global political and military environment also shapes statebuilding outcomes. The ambiguous effects of the Cold War's end—eliminating destabilizing interventions in Central America and Cambodia, and, at the same time, removing foreign subsidies that propped up dependent states—took more than a decade to resolve. David Edelstein notes that the international threat environment widens tolerance for military intervention in local populations. If the intervening force is perceived as a shield against neighboring predatory states (Serbia in the case of Kosovo or Indonesia for Timor Leste), external military force and international trusteeship may continue without a concomitant increase in local resistance.[7] A primary determinant of international intervention and its scale is the attitude of the major powers. If no major power perceives a strategic or political interest in a particular fragile state, international involvement will be less likely; if it occurs, fewer resources will be mobilized.

International economic and political networks are another, less noted, feature of the global environment in which fragile states are embedded. As nodes in global networks for contraband goods (diamonds, illicit drugs), states such as Sierra Leone, Haiti, and Afghanistan have been overwhelmed by network resources in the hands of local political competitors. In similar fashion, diaspora networks linked to conflict and post-conflict states can provide both political incentives and resources for either peacebuilding or continued conflict (Lyons 2005).

If revisionist analysis of statebuilding interventions forces attention to regional and global environments, disaggregation of the state as sole unit of analysis is another revisionist move. Entire states are typically arrayed on the spectrum of state fragility and failure. Despite disclaimers, the construction of lists, such as the World Bank's LICUS or fragile states category, tends to make state fragility one half of a dichotomous distinction: states are fragile or failing, or they are not. States, however, may fail in only parts of their domain: sub-national and spatial circumscription of state failure is often ignored. In such territories as the Federally Administered Tribal Areas (FATA) in Pakistan, northwest Kenya, or northern Uganda, the central government's authority is minimal or absent, and violent conflicts of differing intensities may persist for years. (None of these states appears on the World Bank's list of fragile states.) A second filter may screen out states where low and persistent levels of violence have serious consequences for political stability and economic development, even if that conflict does not threaten a civil war. In Nigeria, for example, the National Commission for Refugees has estimated that more than three million Nigerians were driven from their homes between 1999 and 2005; at least 14,000 died in ethnic, religious, or communal fighting during the same period.[8] Despite this level of persistent violence, Nigeria is often omitted from lists of fragile and failed states.

Statebuilding outcomes as strategic interaction

The outcomes of international intervention in fragile and failed states are best modeled as the result of strategic interaction between those intervening and an array of local actors, some welcoming the intervention and others hostile to it. Michael Barnett and Christoph Zürcher model a game among peacebuilders (PBs), state elites (SEs), and subnational elites (SNEs) in order to explain why, given their initial goals of social and economic change, so many peacebuilding ventures produce conservative results: consolidating the power of existing state and rural elites.[9] Whether one accepts their specific model or not, Barnett and Zürcher's approach illuminates a critical feature of statebuilding that is often ignored in evaluating particular cases: progress in statebuilding does not result solely from the aims, intentions, or errors of the peacebuilders. Peacebuilders do not act on a tabula rasa; rather, their programs become part of an intricate set of political calculations on the part of existing elites and their rivals. Whatever the asymmetries in power, local actors possess bargaining power and often use it effectively. Even in the aftermath of violent conflict and apparent state collapse, local political actors and their response to the peacebuilding program will be critical to any explanation of the outcome.

This strategic approach suggests one likely prerequisite for success: sophisticated political analysis by international statebuilders that allows them to play this game with maximum sophistication. Case studies, however, suggest that peacebuilders often rely on rules of thumb or unreliable allies. As Jens Narten documents in the case of Kosovo, peacebuilders are likely to choose local partners on the basis of superficial characteristics (language skills or rhetorical support for the intervention's goals) rather than careful analysis of converging political interests.[10] The importance of local knowledge also undermines efforts to construct universal templates for intervention: each statebuilding game will incorporate different players with different preferences and bargaining advantages.

State control and capacity as a baseline

How do the preferences, resources, and strategies of the key players vary to produce progress or stalemate in statebuilding? A systematic answer to that question can shed light on the ability of international intervention to further statebuilding under specific political conditions. One of those conditions is particularly important in determining the bargaining power of local actors in fragile and failed states: the baseline of state control and capacity that they enjoy when international intervention begins. At least three variants of initial state capacity can be identified. Each, in the hands of local political actors, can transform the statebuilding bargain.

Violent internal conflict need not result in a weakening of the state. The American Civil War, the bloodiest in US history, is only one example of an internal conflict that strengthened and expanded state institutions on the winning side. International intervention in such cases is typically directed toward the reform of an existing state in the interests of peace, rather than building a new state. Outside guarantors often insure a power-sharing arrangement that awards some control over the state apparatus to the contending parties and prevents the use of state coercion by one party against the other. The presence of a state apparatus, even if its writ does not extend throughout the national territory, might seem to simplify the task of international statebuilders, since state reform is less complicated than state construction. Control of the state provides a key bargaining resource to local actors, however, and transforms the bargaining relationship with international peacebuilders. The paradoxical result may be a successful end to conflict, but less external influence on the future state and its reform.

Cambodia and El Salvador provide examples of this trajectory and its hazards. Cambodia's statebuilding, described by David Roberts, began with Hun Sen and his regime in control of a party-state apparatus that reached to the village level.[11] The Paris Peace Agreement of 1991 had set a liberal-democratic state as Cambodia's political goal. Instead, following surprisingly free and fair national elections in November 1992, Cambodia's state remained rooted in traditional networks of patronage and clientelism. Power-sharing meant the construction of a second, parallel patronage network to support the royalist FUNCINPEC.[12] Despite large infusions of foreign aid over more than a decade, Cambodia's state remains corrupt and largely unaccountable, even though peace has been maintained.[13] El Salvador is another instance of successful international peacebuilding without thoroughgoing reform. The military regime accommodated its leftist opponents by opening the political process, although reform of the military and police were difficult and imperfect. State-led social and economic reforms, designed to attack the original causes of violent conflict, were largely set aside (Doyle and Sambanis 2006: 200–208; Paris 2004: 122–28).

In a second cluster of fragile and post-conflict states, the reconfiguration of state power becomes a key issue in postwar political conflict. In these cases, the repressive apparatus of the state (military, secret police, paramilitaries) is well developed, but other political goods are inadequately provided or provided according to political or ethnic criteria to selected portions of the population. North Korea is an extreme example of such a state: fully capable of maintaining political control of its population through a massive security apparatus, but incompetent in providing food security and economic development.[14]

For international actors, states of this second type endanger statebuilding by placing the state itself at the center of political conflict. South Africa and Iraq illustrate two contrasting outcomes for over-developed, repressive states. South Africa was able to maintain its existing state apparatus under new political management through commitments to both policy change and political incorporation of the majority population. That bargain maintained political stability and international confidence during a difficult transition, a remarkable achievement in the absence of more intrusive forms of international intervention. In Iraq, the newly-empowered Shiite majority (or self-appointed spokesmen for that majority) insisted on measures that effectively demolished the Iraqi state, particularly a sweeping de-Baathification and a dismantling of the Iraqi military. These steps are now uniformly viewed as fatal blows to subsequent efforts to construct a new, more legitimate political order in Iraq. In contrast to South Africa, the contending Iraqi parties and the international coalition (the United States and the United Kingdom) were unable to overcome their distrust to forge a credible bargain that would have reformed the state without destroying it.

Finally, in a third cluster of cases, state capacity is inadequate for provision of the key political good of security or any of the ancillary goods that are necessary for successful statebuilding. Under these circumstances, the bargaining game changes once again. Local political actors may possess resources, but their bargaining chips do not include a state apparatus. International statebuilders confront a new paradox: political elites may have few incentives to build state institutions that deliver critical political goods to the entire population. If, as Barnett and Zürcher accurately stipulate, the principal goal of local actors is to maintain themselves in power, then obtaining an adequate supply of external, private goods for their own selectorate—those enfranchised to choose the local leadership—will be their primary goal.[15] Statebuilding that dilutes those resources among the population at large (or even among a minimum winning coalition) may seem unnecessary or even dangerous.

Under these circumstances, international statebuilders confront the "dangers of a tight embrace" described by Astri Suhrke.[16] As local elites underperform at statebuilding (in order to extract more resources for their own political supporters), international peacebuilders are tempted to pour in more resources, often using their own personnel (trusteeship) or expatriates (such as Avant's private-security companies). The capabilities of the local state fail to improve; the moral hazard created by the flood of resources produces even lower effort on the part of local elites, and the cycle continues. Many policy recommendations in this volume and elsewhere center on this dilemma and to the need to create local capacity from the earliest stage of the statebuilding intervention.[17]

Explaining bargaining power: international statebuilders

Although an asymmetry of power between international statebuilders and local actors often appears overwhelming, international statebuilders vary substantially in their preferences, resources, and instruments. As described earlier, at least three political constituencies, varying in influence across the industrialized countries, compete to define the bargaining preferences of international statebuilders: human security (an end to internal conflict), economic development (good governance), and national security (defined post-9/11 as an end to terrorist sanctuaries and regional instability). Multilateral institutions are often important contributors to statebuilding, with authority delegated by their members for designing and implementing programs. Ultimately, however, one or more of these three logics of intervention, refracted through the aims of their most powerful member governments, also sets their institutional preferences.

Barnett and Zürcher argue that security, defined as political stability, will dominate the aims of international statebuilders, although the presence of that bias requires empirical verification. Subordination of liberalization—the creation of a liberal-democratic and market-oriented regime—to stability is key to their finding that co-opted peacebuilding is the likeliest outcome. Such a clear ordering of preferences within the international coalition is unlikely, however. More likely is competition among constituencies with different statebuilding goals, producing volatility in the preference ordering of the coalition and a weakening of their collective bargaining posture.

Available resources also influence bargaining outcomes between external statebuilders and local political actors in fragile and failed states. Political pressure in donor countries for less costly intervention reinforces preferences for stability over political change. Resource availability is set primarily by the major powers, which adds weight to their preferences within the international statebuilding coalition. As a recent RAND report concluded, "full-scale peace enforcement actions are feasible only when the intervening authorities care a great deal about the outcome, and even then, only in relatively small societies" (Dobbins et al. 2007: xxxvii). Michael Doyle and Nicholas Sambanis, echoing the UN's Brahimi Report, argue that successful peacebuilding requires a match between resources and mandate, and that both must fit the "ecology of authority" on the ground (Doyle and Sambanis 2006).

Revisionist analysis suggests, however, that the absolute level of resources alone is unlikely to predict statebuilding progress. The effective deployment of aid and other resources in a bargaining setting is often difficult. In bargaining with local actors, credible promises to provide resources must be coupled with credible threats to withdraw those resources. Conditionality of this kind has been ineffective in changing the behavior of established governments, even when it could be implemented.[18] Little evidence exists that conditionality will be more successful in the political conditions of fragile states. Major powers have often undermined the conditionality of multilateral organizations in favor of their strategically important clients. International financial institutions and bilateral aid agencies also have powerful incentives to continue financial assistance, even when conditions have not been met. The threat to withdraw resources has, as a result, seldom been credible. Because threats to reduce or suspend resources are not credible, revisionists note that large-scale resource flows may have perverse effects, creating moral hazard and reducing local incentives for statebuilding and reform. In the case of Afghanistan, Astri Suhrke describes the purchase of stability through construction of a dependent, rentier state that fails to develop either autonomy or capacity.[19]

Resources are related to bargaining outcomes through the mediation of policy instruments available to the statebuilding coalition. The menu of those instruments is often more restricted than official accounts allow. Categories of foreign assistance are often labeled statebuilding or nationbuilding in post-conflict settings, even though they have only modest effects on building local capacity and institutions. Available instruments are also scattered across a fragmented international coalition. No multilateral organization has a primary mandate to build local institutional capacity; expertise is found in myriad bilateral agencies and multilateral institutions, often with over-lapping mandates. The International Monetary Fund offers technical assistance for building central banks and other fiscal and monetary institutions. Assistance to key elements of the security sector, such as police, is divided among national and multilateral agencies: United Nations Civilian Police (CIVPOL), regional organizations, and a growing number of bilateral assistance programs (Call and Barnett 2000: 47–50). New actors, particularly non-governmental organizations (NGOs), have expanded their operations to include support for civil society and democratization. Neither NGOs nor the PSCs described by Avant can be defined as "instruments," however, since they are only partially funded by the intervening governments. They add both new capabilities and additional fragmentation to the statebuilding mix.

In reviewing statebuilding outcomes, one puzzle recurs: the absence of a clear relationship between an apparent asymmetry in bargaining power between the international coalition and local political agents on the one hand, and statebuilding outcomes on the other. Revisionist analysis of bargaining between international and local actors explains this apparent disjuncture between power and outcome. Local actors may control some portion of a nascent or derelict state apparatus, awarding local actors a substantial advantage through access to those institutions. Even when statebuilding begins at ground zero, local actors may choose to divert external assets toward maintaining themselves in power rather than building effective institutions.

The international coalition, on the other hand, finds it difficult to translate resources into success: squabbling over immediate goals (as between the United States and its NATO allies in Afghanistan), failing to manage myriad agencies that claim a statebuilding role, and swamping local institutions because of political pressure to show short-term results. The policy instruments at hand, whether bilateral or multilateral, are often ill suited for statebuilding. All of these weaknesses redress the apparent imbalance between international and local actors. The outcome, though often more complex in its origins than indicated in the model of Barnett and Zürcher, is the same: co-opted or captured peacebuilding, in which resources serve primarily to maintain post-conflict political elites in power. That outcome, often far from the liberal state of the New York Consensus, has produced revisionist rethinking of the goals of statebuilding and a parallel re-examination of statebuilding strategies.

Recalibrating goals and strategies

As the option of reinvestment or staying the course has declined in appeal, those counseling disengagement and those recommending a revised engagement with fragile and failed states increasingly dominate debate over statebuliding goals and strategies. Advocates of disengagement do not argue primarily on the basis of cost or lack of progress. Rather, they claim that the international coalition fails because it swamps local solutions and local empowerment. Loosening the "tight embrace" becomes a means to more successful statebuilding in the longer run.

Supporters of disengagement share a vision of bottom-up, organic evolution in indigenous political institutions that may, under certain conditions, produce an effective state. In certain respects, their perspective replicates arguments for indirect rule during the colonial era: reliance on local elites (and their local knowledge) to guarantee minimum conditions of order. Jeremy Weinstein, for example, claims that war making leads to statebuilding, which he labels autonomous recovery, under certain "rare and difficult to create" conditions (Weinstein 2005). The key incentives for statebuilding must be generated internally and autonomously: external intervention in most cases will only interfere with those indigenous processes, by either creating a dependent, rentier state (Suhrke) or undermining the statebuilding effects of warfare (Weinstein). In both cases, less international intervention may produce state formation in the "much longer run" rather than statebuilding "with its connotations of social engineering in a shorter-term perspective."[20] Somalia, particularly breakaway Somaliland, which has developed indigenous political institutions and a functioning economy in the absence of recognition or official development assistance, figures prominently in discussions of positive disengagement (Menkhaus 2006/2007).

The inevitability of aid dependence, the moral hazard that it creates, and its erosion of local capacity is one issue that divides those promoting disengagement from revisionists who advocate a reformed version of the New York Consensus. Another disagreement centers on the time horizon permitted any foreign intervening power. Advocates of disengagement view any foreign intervention as necessarily short-lived, too short-lived for institution-building that will last; revisionists are more willing to contemplate strategies that will reduce, though not eliminate, what Edelstein terms the duration dilemma.

The revisionist response

Although revisionists and those who favor disengagement share a critical view toward the New York Consensus, revisionists advance a set of policy recommendations that will sustain international engagement with fragile and failed states in the interests of statebuilding. They envisage reforms that will make international intervention more effective and less self-defeating over time. Five revisionist policy responses can be identified among the authors in this volume and in the wider policy debate: a lowering of expectations in favor of "good enough governance"; earlier and more intensive concentration on local ownership; effective multilateral coordination; new means for maintaining a less intrusive presence in fragile states over the longer term; and finally, an experimental outlook that both supports promising local initiatives and subjects international policies to rigorous evaluation.

No single aspect of statebuilding better illuminates the sharpening debate among proponents of the original New York Consensus, revised engagement, and disengagement than democratization and elections. Revisionists increasingly accept political outcomes that postpone or set aside transformation of political institutions and processes. Subversion of the liberal statebuilding project by local elites, the most likely outcome in many cases, now "might be the best of all possible worlds."[21]

The issue of democratization and elections illuminates variations on a revisionist theme. The New York Consensus had incorporated democratization and respect for human rights as a necessary element in statebuilding for several reasons. A liberal-democratic internal peace was viewed as a safeguard against a new eruption of civil conflict. Democracy insured effective governance through transparency and accountability. Elections were a key means for legitimating new state institutions. Contemporary controversy over the necessity or even the desirability of electoral democracy for statebuilding is particularly striking, since democratization has long been part of the foreign-policy agenda for most industrialized democracies.

The critics of early electoral democracy level several distinct charges. First, elections and democratic political competition may undermine other goals of statebuilding, particularly political stability and a fragile internal peace. Roland Paris has argued in favor of "institutionalization before liberalization" (IBL), timing elections only when conditions will permit them without endangering political stability and effective administration. Political competition in the IBL model is also circumscribed through a ban on organizations that advocate inter-group violence and a prohibition of hate speech on the public media (Paris 2004). Paris does not dismiss the ultimate value of democratization; democratization and particularly elections should simply follow other, more critical items on the statebuilding agenda.

Others are more critical of elections as a necessary element in state legitimation. David Lake, for example, argues that the legitimacy of political authority is based primarily on its provision of political goods, including security, for the population that it governs. A successful international trustee must first provide those goods in order to sustain the legitimacy of its intervention. The trustee must then transfer that legitimacy to indigenous political authorities if statebuilding is to succeed in the longer run (Lake 2007). Michael Barnett has pointed to risks associated with liberal democratic statebuilding (and the low probability of its success), urging instead a more modest republican model that encourages deliberation, constitutionalism, and representation. This alternative model for political legitimacy renders formal liberal institutions, such as elections, less essential (Barnett 2006).

Finally, liberal statebuilding may be an unwarranted imposition on local political practices, interfering with the development of indigenous institutions. David Roberts portrays much of the liberal program as a failure to accept the "otherness" and durability of local political institutions. Democratic imposition becomes an analogue to economic shock treatment: a painful and destructive effort to jump-start political change that is likely to fail. Roberts' account of Cambodian politics converges with the endorsement of co-opted statebuilding by Barnett and Zürcher: elites will aim to maintain themselves in power; international actors should accommodate themselves to that intractable reality.[22]

These criticisms of democratic institution building are met with skepticism by other revisionists who admit the importance of sequencing and appropriate constitutional design. Timothy Sisk, for example, views continuing international engagement after elections as essential to maintaining the course toward liberal statebuilding.[23] Elections have too often served as a false panacea for post-conflict societies, providing useful political cover for a precipitous end to international intervention. Declaring democracy and then departing is no substitute for a more durable commitment that would ensure the security of political institutions. Ill-timed or ill-designed elections may produce captured statebuilding, in which entrenched elites prevent further political and economic reform. At the same time, Sisk claims that democratic elections make a central contribution to the legitimacy of any modern political order, in the eyes of both the international community and the local population.

The elitist perspective accepted by some revisionists and proponents of disengagement leaves the less powerful with little recourse if their prospects for economic development and political empowerment are crushed by the greed and ruthlessness of those elites; little recourse, that is, apart from a return to violence. Even if those elites are successful at providing political goods for their populations in the absence of democratic institutions, long-term state legitimacy is not guaranteed. After all, many colonial rulers and authoritarian regimes, such as the Shah's Iran, were relatively successful at such goods provision. Nevertheless, their political opponents were able to successfully undermine the regime's legitimacy and ultimately, the social order through attacks on their international backing and lack of democratic standing.

The debate over democratization reflects revisionist acceptance of an end to the perfectionism of the New York Consensus, accepting "good enough governance" rather than a model of states based on the Western (and Asian) industrialized world.[24] Barnett's republicanism represents a retreat from liberal democratic standards for institutions, one that is more accommodating of local political conditions. Political institutions that are both inclusive— avoiding political divisions that could lead to violent conflict—and open to the future political change could provide another, more modest alternative to liberal statebuilding. Minimal political standards might also be framed with regard to outputs: decent (if not good) governance, a permissive economic environment (no political predation), and broad provision of human security. Violation of other international standards, such as the outbreak of genocidal violence, would continue to require more forceful international intervention.

Both revisionists and proponents of disengagement advocate a second change: local ownership of statebuilding and rapid development of local capabilities for governance. Revisionists, however, believe that current statebuilding practices can be changed to encourage, rather than undermine, local initiative. Narten, for example, urges "building capacity of local trainers from the first days of their presence in a postwar environment." In similar fashion, Edelstein presses for building of local security forces from the start of an intervention.[25] Although lip service to local empowerment and capacity is a familiar mantra in the statebuilding liturgy, early dedication of resources to building local capacity would break with past practices and override political incentives for short-term results. Statebuilders have often relied on expatriate contract personnel for many of their immediate statebuilding needs, since few local personnel appear to be qualified. Building local qualifications has uniformly ceded priority to efficient and rapid supply of key political goods. Breaking those powerful precedents would require both new international instruments and a willingness to pay political costs for failures and poor performance on the part of local personnel.

Faulty management of large and unwieldy international coalitions has led to persistent calls for better coordination, or, under its most recent label, harmonization. Paris suggests that coordination often provides cover for deeper disagreement in the donor community on the aims and methods of statebuilding, rather than a solution to those disagreements.[26] Revisionists accept that calls for coordination are often rhetorical shams. Nevertheless, developing a more coherent ordering of statebuilding priorities among donors, particularly the major powers, remains a worthwhile goal.

Achieving coherence among aid donors and multilateral institutions could satisfy two different purposes, however. One of these would clearly benefit the governments of fragile states: reducing the burden of negotiation and implementation that is imposed on overstretched officials by multiple international partners. More controversial, however, is the aim of increasing donor bargaining power through a coordinated strategy. Coordination could also produce a clear division of labor among international actors, one that would increase overall levels of expertise and capacity through specialization. However defined, recent multilateral steps to improve coordination, such as the new UN Peacebuilding Commission described by Paris, are unlikely to overcome competition and disagreement in the donor coalition. The most successful route to such harmonization in particular countries may be the designation of lead roles for the most engaged national governments (or the European Union), embedding those leading actors in a multilateral process of consultation. This route may have advantages over more unwieldy formal mechanisms or the unilateral route taken by the United States in Iraq. Multilateral forums will remain valuable for the exchange of new knowledge and for establishing best practices. The latter role, which has been undertaken by the OECD, may be deepened by the UN Peacebuilding Commission.

Maintaining engagement over the Long Run

Revisionists part company with advocates of disengagement in their fourth proposal for reform: a search for ways to maintain engagement beyond an initial and costly period of direct intervention. The strategies that they contemplate resemble the "off-shore" redeployments of military force that have been recommended in Iraq. After establishing minimal standards of governance, longer-run means of monitoring performance and calibrating resources to that performance must be designed: "trusteeship lite," or, to borrow a term from the International Monetary Fund, enhanced surveillance. The regional environment and regional institutions can provide one, less intrusive means for such monitoring. Unfortunately, regional institutions in many parts of the developing world are underdeveloped or unwilling to intrude in matters of domestic governance. Paul Collier recommends governance conditionality, rather than policy conditionality: requirements that governments be accountable to their own citizens, ownership writ large. Collier also suggests military guarantees of constitutional governments as another form of more distanced yet effective shaping of broader political development (Collier 2007). In designing these mechanisms for less intrusive surveillance, revisionists seek to avoid intensive oversight that erodes local confidence and impedes the development of indigenous solutions to local problems. At the same time, such initiatives would accept that building legitimate and effective political institutions, often in the face of local opposition, will require long-term engagement.

Finally, revisionists stand ready to support promising local initiatives in statebuilding and governance, whenever they appear. The attitude of international actors should become more experimental; their stance should more closely resemble a venture capitalist investing in promising, locally-generated innovations in governance. At the same time, measurement of progress should be grounded in more systematic evaluation of what works in different contexts. The often narrowly-conceived statebuilding prescriptions of the New York Consensus would be tested thoroughly in the demanding environments of fragile states. One dismal failure of statebuilding over the past fifteen years has been its inability to move beyond "lessons learned" to develop more rigorous evaluation protocols.

Each revisionist prescription carries risks. "Good enough" governance and temporary retreats from democratization may produce second-class governance and toleration of elite abuses in the name of public order. An immediate emphasis on local ownership and capacity building, endorsed by both revisionists and advocates of disengagement, will almost certainly impose lower levels of service provision and higher degrees of corruption on the populations of fragile states. Coordination based on the multilateral leadership of major powers will fail if no power accepts responsibility. Low-profile strategies of engagement for the longer run may cause important constituencies in the donor countries to lose interest in the statebuilding project, while failing to satisfy those opposed to international tutelage in fragile states. Finally, international actors could capture any turn toward an experimental stance, promoting their own programs and priorities as locally grown.

After allowing for these risks, the revisionist agenda faces tests of political feasibility in both the major donors, particularly the EU and the United

States, and in the societies of fragile states. The incremental and tentative character of the revisionist program is unlikely to win it much political applause. Advocates of disengagement will continue to note cases of aid dependence and institutional backsliding. Revisionist recommendations are unlikely to satisfy simultaneously the security, development, and humanitarian constituencies that have supported statebuilding in recent years: too activist for those searching for political stability, not activist enough for many NGO advocates of human rights and human security. Nevertheless, alternative approaches—the New York Consensus and the disengagement option—are arguably more difficult to sustain politically. Perhaps, however, the best outcome will not be another monolithic consensus, whatever its label. With states from Angola to Pakistan confronting crises of governance that have momentous regional and global implications, the debate over statebuilding has only begun. For now, continuing that debate is likely to produce a sturdier and more reliable revision of the statebuilding formulas that have produced such mixed results.

Notes

1 I would like to thank Roland Paris, Timothy Sisk, Jens Narten, Astri Suhrke, and David Edelstein for comments on an earlier draft of this chapter. Jeremy Horowitz and Benjamin Graham provided invaluable research assistance.
2 Michael Mandelbaum (1996) leveled this criticism against Clinton Administration interventions in Somalia, Bosnia, and Haiti.
3 Exemplars of this view are the State Failure Task Force (Goldstone et al. 2000; now the Political Instability Task Force: http://globalpolicy.gmu.edu/pitf/) and the Foreign Policy/Fund for Peace Failed States Index ("The Failed States Index," www.fundforpeace.org). The former equates state failure to "serious political instability," defined by four categories. Three of those four include internal conflict or state-led violence. The latter index purports to measure "vulnerability to violent internal conflict."
4 Three out of four fragile states, as measured by the World Bank, are "affected by on-going armed conflict." The World Bank measures quality of governance through the Bank-generated Country Policy and Institutional Performance Assessment (CPIA). This internally generated metric includes sixteen criteria grouped into four clusters: economic management, structural policies, policies for social inclusion/equity, and public sector management and institutions.
5 Roland Paris and Timothy Sisk identify those who reject "reinvestment" as either those who counsel retreat ("scaling back international statebuilding efforts") or those who urge continuing engagement after a rethinking of existing strategies. Their categories are similar to those used here.
6 Deborah Avant, Chapter 5 in this volume.
7 David Edelstein, Chapter 4 in this volume.
8 "Violence Left 3 Million Bereft in Past 7 Years, Nigeria Reports," *New York Times*, March 14, 2006. Also "Internal Displacement in Nigeria: A Hidden Crisis," Norwegian Refugee Council, Global IDP Project, February 1, 2005 (www.idpproject.org).
9 Michael Barnett and Christoph Zürcher, Chapter 2 in this volume.
10 Jens Narten, Chapter 11 in this volume.
11 David Roberts, Chapter 7 in this volume.

12 FUNCINPEC: The National United Front for an Independent, Neutral, Peaceful and Co-operative Cambodia.

13 Between 1999 and 2003, World Bank CPIA scores for three of the five governance indicators remained largely the same or declined, with slight increases in two dimensions. Cambodia in 2003 scored worse than the average for IDA recipients in all five governance criteria, an outcome that reduced the World Bank's IDA allocation for the country (World Bank 2004: 122).

14 On famine and food security in North Korea, see Haggard and Noland 2007.

15 On the selectorate and the provision of private goods, see Bueno de Mesquita et al., 2003, pp. 42–43.

16 Astri Suhrke, Chapter 10 in this volume.

17 For example, Narten, who argues for immediate "training of trainers" so that capacity building can be assumed early on by local personnel (Chapter 11 in this volume).

18 For a critique, Collier 1997.

19 Suhrke, Chapter 10 in this volume.

20 Ibid.

21 Barnett and Zürcher, Chapter 2 in this volume.

22 Roberts, Chapter 7 in this volume.

23 Sisk, Chapter 9 in this volume.

24 I have borrowed the phrase "good enough governance" from Grindle 2004, although giving it a somewhat different meaning.

25 Narten, Chapter 11 in this volume; Edelstein, Chapter 4 in this volume.

26 Paris, Chapter 3 in this volume.

13 Conclusion

Confronting the contradictions

Roland Paris and Timothy D. Sisk

"Frankly, we aren't doing enough," United Kingdom Foreign Security David Miliband remarked to the United Nations Security Council, in a special all-day debate on the state of UN efforts to build peace in war-torn societies in May 2008.[1] While there had been some admirable efforts by the UN to conduct peacebuilding operations, he contended, these cases were the "exception and not the rule." In the context of deep concern about the efficacy and performance of UN-led operations in war-shattered countries, the UK convened the special Security Council debate on peacebuilding during its tenure as president of that body in order to put the spotlight on three critical gaps in the international community's ability to foster sustainable peace after civil war, namely developing local capacities for leadership and governance, rapidly fielding capable civilians to conduct the ambitious statebuilding tasks, and devising more rapid and flexible mechanisms for funding. Violent challenges to peacebuilding in Afghanistan and Sudan—which teeter between progress toward peace and recurrence of war—loomed large in the collective soul-searching on the challenges of peacebuilding.

Foreign Minister Miliband was correct to assert the UN has not always done enough to secure peace after civil war. Nonetheless, we argue in this book that the larger challenge is not simply to "do more." The more crucial, but perplexing, challenge is to manage the difficult and deep contradictions of post-conflict peacebuilding, particularly those involved in efforts to strengthen or construct effective and legitimate state institutions as a foundation for security, human development, and other public goods within societies emerging from war.

This concluding chapter is divided into three parts. First, we identify the principal contradictions and policy dilemmas of postwar statebuilding that emerged from the analyses of the preceding chapters. Second, we propose a new analytical tool called "dilemma analysis" as a method of anticipating and managing the contradictions inherent in postwar statebuilding. Third, we present a series of reflections on the findings of the volume relating to the record of peacebuilding and its possible future as this grand experiment arrives at a crossroads.

The contradictions and dilemmas of statebuilding

In Chapter 1, we argued that there are deep contradictions and tensions in the idea of statebuilding, which in turn give rise to difficult policy dilemmas for international and local participants in these missions. The recurring problems and shortcomings of statebuilding, in other words, are not simply the result of inadequate coordination or a lack of adequate resources. Understanding these problems requires a deeper investigation of the "conflicted" nature of statebuilding itself.

At the most basic level, these contradictions are unchanging and unchangeable; they are embedded in the very idea of externally assisted statebuilding. The contributions to this volume suggest that five such embedded or core contradictions stand out as particularly fundamental:

1   *Outside intervention is used to foster self-government.* Even though statebuilding missions are designed to create the conditions for sustainable self-government in host states, by providing assistance to national authorities rather than imposing foreign rule, in practice the power exercised by international statebuilding actors is intrusive, no matter how well meaning it may be. This tension is at the heart of practical challenges such as defining the conditions of legitimacy (and perceived legitimacy) for statebuilding operations, designing transitional governance structures, providing security and delivering public services, determining how long a mission should take place and in what form, and addressing questions of transitional justice.

2   *International control is required to establish local ownership.* If full local ownership of the domestic affairs in the host state could be achieved without outside direction, there would be no need for robust, multifunctional statebuilding missions in the first instance. But identifying who the local "owners" should be, or devising a process for allocating ownership rights, necessarily involves decisions and actions that will favor some parties over others, thereby defying the principle of local ownership itself. This contradiction not only makes for difficult policy choices, but potentially calls into question the legitimacy and sustainability of any ensuing ownership arrangements.

3   *Universal values are promoted as a remedy for local problems.* Civil wars have both international and domestic drivers, and they often spill over national borders, but at bottom they are predominantly local phenomena, fought and experienced by individuals and groups who live in a particular socio-cultural context. Many of the policy dilemmas faced by statebuilding actors derive from incongruities between the universal values (predominantly those in the liberal tradition of individual human rights, democratic governance, and market-oriented economics) espoused by international organizations and donor governments on one hand, and the values, social practices, political traditions, and cultural expectations of

the host society on the other. This tension, like the previous two, also contributes to the problem of defining statebuilding policies that are appropriate, effective, and legitimate not only in the eyes of the interveners but also in eyes of local elites and masses.

4 *Statebuilding requires both a clean break with the past and a reaffirmation of history.* Moving from war to peace entails continuity as well as change. Statebuilding operations cannot "remake" war-torn societies. Indeed, international actors often underestimate the persistence and resilience of the deeply engrained patterns of political and economic life. That said, statebuilding must in some measure involve the introduction of new approaches to conflict resolution and management, which can and do challenge traditional practices. Although the old and the new may blend into new hybrid forms of political and social organization, they often generate conflicts and transformational tensions that are not uncommon in developing societies undergoing rapid change. These can serve as a dangerous source of destabilization in the particularly fragile conditions of countries just emerging from civil wars.

5 *Short-term imperatives often conflict with longer-term objectives.* In the early stages of a statebuilding operation, outside actors typically face strong pressures to behave in ways that make sense in the short term but run counter to the longer-term requirements for establishing effective, legitimate state institutions. Preserving a ceasefire and managing potential "spoilers," for example, often involve making explicit or tacit bargains with ruling elites whose continued power (whether this power is formally recognized or informally exercised) can ultimately present a significant obstacle to building "depersonalized" state institutions and broadening political representation beyond the parties that fought the preceding war. Similar tensions between short-term and long-term imperatives also pose a problem for the planning of economic reconstruction and aid delivery, security sector reform, and transitional justice goals.

These embedded contradictions exist at a relatively high level of abstraction from the day-to-day realities of statebuilding operations. Yet they are ultimately the source of concrete policy dilemmas that the practitioners of statebuilding routinely have to struggle with. These dilemmas, in other words, are the visible, policy-level manifestations of statebuilding's under-lying contradictions. We use the term "dilemmas" advisedly: they are, by definition, problems that defy easy solutions because they present choices between multiple, conflicting imperatives.

Among the various policy dilemmas explored in this book, the following five are noteworthy because they each appear in several of the chapters:

1 *Footprint dilemmas.* The "footprint" of an operation refers to its degree of intrusiveness in the domestic affairs of the host state, which in turn is a reflection of (i) the size of the international presence, (ii) the breadth of

tasks that external actors take on, and (iii) the assertiveness of the external actors in pursuing these tasks. The dilemma is that, on one hand, a dominant international presence (a "heavy footprint") may be required to maintain security and to oversee (or even enforce) the implementation of a peace agreement, including the process of initiating political and economic reforms; on the other hand, a less intrusive international presence (a "light footprint") may be required to allow local political, social, and economic life to achieve a post-conflict equilibrium on its own terms, without the distorting effects of powerful external actors. David Edelstein examines this dilemma as it relates to the military aspects of externally-assisted statebuilding, but the "footprint dilemma" appears in nearly all the chapters in relation to both military and non-military issues. Astri Suhrke's study, for example, finds that the *economic* footprint of state-building efforts in Afghanistan since the defeat of the Taliban regime has served to weaken, not strengthen, the legitimacy and capacity of that country's government.

2 *Duration dilemmas.* Difficult choices relating to the duration of an inter-national statebuilding operation are explored in several of the chapters. On one hand, statebuilding is necessarily a long-term enterprise. Elections can be held quickly, but the political institutions to which public officials are elected take much longer to consolidate. Economic reforms can be started right away, but in the absence of administrative capacity in the host government and at least a minimal system to uphold the rule of law, these reforms have the potential to go awry. But while statebuilding is a lengthy process, there are countervailing pressures and imperatives that militate against a prolonged or open-ended international deployments. First, over time, important segments of the local population tend to grow increasingly irritated—or even hostile—towards the continued presence of powerful outside actors, which can, in turn, undermine externally-assisted statebuilding efforts. Second, very lengthy or open-ended missions can produce quite a different problem: passivity within the local population, including a lack of interest in taking on the responsibilities of self-government (see "Dependency dilemmas" below). In addition, the inter-national resources for statebuilding operations are often limited, both in scale and duration. Few donor countries or international organizations are willing to "sign up" for more than a few years of statebuilding in any given country. Nevertheless, there is no denying that the objectives that these donors and organizations continue to articulate require lengthy commit-ments—a tension which raises questions about the credibility of the objectives that statebuilders articulate and their willingness to cut corners, as Michael Barnett and Christoph Zürcher suggest in their chapter.

3 *Participation dilemmas.* Factional leaders do not necessarily represent the population of their countries, yet they are typically the individuals who are involved in peace negotiations and therefore remain central political actors in the period immediately following the conflict. As Kirsti Samuels

argues in her chapter, a key challenge for statebuilders is to strike a balance between maintaining the cooperation of former fighters and potential spoilers, while simultaneously drawing in other groups and ultimately the population as a whole into the postwar political process. If factional leaders are too powerful, new institutional structures may be viewed as illegitimate by other groups and individuals who believe that these leaders are unrepresentative, corrupt—or, worse, criminals.

Compounding this dilemma is the danger that the international presence may itself constrain political participation: first, by diverting civil-society activity towards externally-defined objectives rather than allowing local groups to pursue their goals in a more undirected manner; and second, by exercising de facto decision-making power that is not itself subject to popular control and accountability. Further, as noted earlier, while promoting local ownership is an important and essential goal for statebuilding, there is no simple way (particularly for powerful outsiders) to determine who the "owners" should be. The very act of stimulating participation and local ownership can lead to perverse results, no matter how well-intentioned the international actors, simply because an international mission by its very presence has distorting effects on local politics: like a powerful magnet in an electric field.

4   *Dependency dilemmas.* Related to both the footprint and duration dilemmas is the danger of fostering dependency among local elites and the general population of a host state on the international presence. The goal of postwar statebuilding is to foster the conditions for self-sustaining peace through effective, legitimate self-governance. Yet large flows of outside assistance and the "hands on" role of international actors in facilitating the implementation of peace settlements can create new political and economic patterns in the host society that rely on a continuation of large-scale external aid and guidance. If these expectations and dependencies harden, statebuilding missions risk working against their own ultimate goal of fostering self-government in the society. Worse, they risk morphing into indefinite trusteeship arrangements that raise additional problems, which may include—paradoxically—a growing resistance to the international presence in some parts of the population. This combination of dependency and resistance has the potential to produce pathological patterns reminiscent of colonial societies, which proved to be unsustainable in the past. But if statebuilding simultaneously requires a measure of international control (particularly at the outset of a mission) and a long-term process of institution-construction, then some measure of dependency may be unavoidable. Squaring this circle is the core challenge of dependency dilemmas; and like the other dilemmas described here, it is a problem that emerges from underlying tensions and contradictions in the idea of externally-assisted statebuilding.

5   *Coherence dilemmas.* Statebuilders face two kinds of coherence dilemmas: (i) organizational coherence and (ii) normative coherence. Organizational

coherence involves the need for coordination among the myriad international actors involved in such operations, including national donors, regional organizations, international financial institutions, specialized international agencies, global bodies such as the UN, and non-governmental organizations. However, coordination is difficult due to confusing or competing lines of authority and budgetary autonomy among entities within the UN system, in particular. In addition, as Roland Paris argues in his chapter, efforts to improve coordination can serve as a substitute for addressing substantive disagreements on how to analyze and respond to the dilemmas of statebuilding.

Beyond the issue of coordination among international actors, there is also a need for organizational coherence among the legitimate representatives of the host society itself, so that international actors can engage effectively with national leaders. The danger, however, is that efforts to identify national-level interlocutors can result in an over-emphasis on elites based in the capital, to the expense of regional and local institution-building.

The second kind of coherence dilemma—at the "normative" level— arises from disjunctures and inconsistencies in the values that statebuilders articulate (often drawn from universal norms) versus the values that are reflected in the actual policies that statebuilders pursue in the field and the results of these policies. Principles such as democratic accountability, national self-determination, the rule of law, and good governance all tend to be compromised—to varying degrees—by the very fact of international intervention, and by pragmatic imperatives to (i) cooperate with powerful local actors and (ii) tailor institutional designs to reflect the distinctive patterns of political and economic life within the society.

Anticipating and managing the dilemmas

The authors in this book do not offer falsely simple prescriptions for what it takes to consolidate peace in countries that are emerging from civil war. On the contrary, the research pointedly highlights both the deep-rooted complexities of statebuilding and the need for a better understanding of these complexities— from the unanticipated consequences of promoting political and economic liberalization in deeply-divided societies, to the awkward disjuncture of international guidance versus local control. At best, the many dilemmas of postwar statebuilding can only be managed, not resolved. Occasionally, innovative policies or clever decisions can ameliorate them, but effective management must itself be based on a careful analysis of the underlying contradictions and tensions that give rise to these dilemmas. It must also be based on extensive knowledge of the host country, and careful consideration of the long-term consequences of initial short-term stabilization and recovery efforts.

There are, of course, limits to how "rational" policy making can be in any organization, be it a national government, an international agency (especially the unique, global bureaucracy that is the UN), a non-governmental entity, or—for that matter—the congeries of actors involved in postwar statebuilding operations. As Charles Lindblom pointed out some fifty years ago in his classic examination of public administration in the United States, "muddling through" is more typical in policy making than the rationalist archetype of means–ends planning (Lindblom 1959). This muddling metaphor clearly characterizes the early years of earlier efforts described in Chapter 1.

We argue that relying on muddling through is not the best option for the international community in responses to the horrors of contemporary civil wars. Given the nature of statebuilding—its many actors, the scope of its task, and the relatively high level of uncertainty regarding its impacts and outcomes—there will always be significant elements of improvisation and "irrationality" in statebuilding policy. This reality, however, should not be taken as a license for complacency or to yield the debate to critics of international efforts to build sustainable peace after war from either critical or realist perspectives. The design and conduct of statebuilding operations *can* be more rational and better informed than they have been in the past. The stakes are too high, and the consequences of failure too great, to resign oneself to the limitations of muddling through. As Miles Kahler writes in his chapter, "With states from Angola to Pakistan confronting crises of governance that have momentous regional and global implications, the debate over statebuilding has only begun. For now, continuing that debate is likely to produce a sturdier and more reliable revision of the statebuilding formulas that have produced such mixed results."

For this reason, we recommend that statebuilding actors at least take the step of conducting "dilemma analyses" prior to and during their operations. The more typical approach to mission planning involves identifying a sequence of steps to be completed at particular moments by particular actors, with the moments defined either according to a timeline or on the basis of having achieved specific prerequisite conditions; current policy instruments designed to aid decision-making tend to be based on this essential premise.[2] By contrast, dilemma analysis begins from the assumption that many of the elements of statebuilding will not fit together easily. Rather, they will often work at cross-purposes. In fact, some of these elements are likely to interact in ways that have the potential to undercut, not advance, the goal of establishing legitimate, effective state institutions in war-torn countries.

Such an analysis is crucial, in our view, to dealing more effectively with the dilemmas of statebuilding. It does not replace a more conventional planning process, but supplements it. The key questions, for those who wish to do dilemma analysis on ongoing or contemplated statebuilding mission, are:

- To what extent, and exactly how, might these statebuilding dilemmas manifest themselves in a given operation?
- What are the particular features of the local environment that make it more (or less) likely that certain dilemmas will become particularly problematic?
- What are the underlying tensions or "drivers" of the anticipated dilemmas?

- How might each dilemma interact with, or give rise to, other dilemmas?
- Which of the anticipated dilemmas has the potential to be most problematic, and why?

One benefit of conducting such analysis is that it requires deep local knowledge and can therefore expose knowledge gaps that might otherwise go unnoticed in a conventional planning process. It also focuses attention on the deeply engrained continuities in the political, social, and economic life of a society emerging from war, which have tended to be under-appreciated. Further, it is a necessarily multidisciplinary exercise (due to the thematic span of the dilemmas themselves) and consequently creates incentives to bring together teams of analysts with different expertise—and from different statebuilding organizations—thereby helping to break down disciplinary and organizational "silos."

Ultimately, however, the primary purpose of dilemma analysis is to inform the process of devising more nuanced and effective statebuilding strategies. To this end, navigating dilemmas should be at the center of statebuilding policy, recognizing that in most cases the challenge is to find a "sweet spot" that comes closest to balancing competing imperatives. It is also crucial to scrutinize both the intended and possible unintended consequences of policy action within the context of these dilemmas. Finally, short-term decisions must be evaluated in the light of their longer-term implications for institution-building.

More awareness, scrutiny, and understanding of these contradictions and dilemmas should also yield more realistic expectations of what can be achieved during an initial period of post-conflict statebuilding and in the ensuing period. One of the weaknesses of recent missions has been the gap between the stated objectives and the actual performance and outcomes of statebuilding efforts, which can foster disappointment and perceptions of disingenuousness—or worse, hypocrisy—that risk undermining the legitimacy of, and support for, these efforts. Greater sensitivity to the inherent tensions and contradictions of statebuilding should (among other things) highlight the limited ability of outsiders to effect profound and truly far-reaching transformations in the workings of any society. Bringing expectations into closer alignment with possibilities would itself strengthen the prospects for effective statebuilding.

Learning from the past, looking to the future

Any evaluation of the future of peacebuilding benefits from a review of learning from the mostly UN-led peace operations during the post-Cold War period. Because there is a fairly high rate of war recurrence following negotiated agreements (some 25 percent of wars recur, according to Suhrke and Samset 2007), peacebuilding is critical for international peace and security: warring factions must be disarmed, power must be shared, new constitutions negotiated, elections held to legitimate newly formed governments (or in some instances determine the sovereign status of disputed territory), and relief and reconstruction must take place in situations where rival factions retain power and sometimes military control of territory. Yet, because most wars in the post-Cold War period terminate at the negotiating table and not on the battlefield, local protagonists are not powerless subjects that the international actors can manipulate at will. As Michael Barnett and Christoph Zürcher argue in their evaluation of the "peacebuilder's contract," international actors are dependent on, and often manipulated by, local power elites in a complex web of interdependencies and bargaining power. The outcome of this relationship is often "captured" peacebuilding, in which the ambitious goals of international interventions are arrested by relation-ships on the ground. Thus, much of the frustration of peacebuilding efforts stems from these mutually-dependent relationships among peacebuilders and local elites.

The authors in this book derive some additional key observations regarding the roles and structures of key players in the international system; practices and policies have indeed evolved considerably in the 1990s and 2000s, including new approaches (such as "integrated missions") and new institutions and resources devoted to the task of rebuilding war-torn states. Yet, much of this change has focused on the organizational aspects of peacebuilding. Roland Paris's chapter shows that this concern with coordi-nation continues today, both at the global level of the UN and perhaps even more importantly in regional contexts such as the further development of peace operations where collective security organizations such as NATO are working with regional organizations and the UN (for example, in Kosovo and Darfur). However, fixing failed states by improving coordination is only one part—a small part—of the challenge.

Because the danger of war recurrence is real (Darby 2006), security imperatives remain central, but it is in this realm that some of the stark contradictions of statebuilding can be found. As David Edelstein shows, there is a short window of opportunity when international military power alone can provide security before the welcome wanes for foreign troops and local perceptions of legitimacy "obsolesce." But international efforts to build national capacity for security are also fraught with peril, as Deborah Avant's research underscores. Relying on private-sector actors to train integrated national security forces can undermine statebuilding goals if these efforts are not informed by professional norms.

Security, in turn, may be unsustainable if the incentives of the economic system do not reinforce efforts to create capable and legitimate states. The authors in this volume emphasize the critical relationships among state capacity, socio-economic development, and the mitigation of "root causes" of conflict such as scarcity and inequality. Often, as we saw in the chapters by David Roberts on Cambodia, Astri Suhrke on Afghanistan, and Chris-topher Cramer on economic "trajectories of accumulation," it is the persis-tent and deeply-entrenched patterns of economic accumulation and distribution that hinder the progress toward sustainable peace. Aid flows and even global trade relationships can also reinforce weak statehood.

The contributions to this volume also underscore the observation that peacebuilding and statebuilding are indeed about politics—most notably when they involve efforts to reform political systems through constitution-making and to empower new political elites through electoral processes. Yet these processes are fraught with difficulties, too. Kirsti Samuels's chapter on constitution-making processes, for example, finds that there is no "one-stop shopping" for institutional designs that can reinforce peace. Processes of constitution-making that emphasize inclusion, participation, and mutually reinforcing bargaining relationships will vary by context and during different phases of a peacebuilding effort. Nor do early imperatives always line up with longer-term needs. The chapter by Timothy Sisk on postwar electoral processes, for example, makes the point that ill-chosen institutions—especially the blind pursuit of power sharing—can lead to long-term state capture by authoritarian elites (as in Cambodia after 1993). Institutions that are more tailored to context can in fact yield mutually-beneficial state–society relations (as in South Africa), which, in turn, can reinforce state strength.

The fact that peacebuilding is fundamentally political also gives credence to the call—often heard from members of the Global South—for more local ownership. Over time, the international community should support efforts to create representative institutions and public policy processes that are self-sustaining, suitable to local conditions, and accountable to the societies they are intended to serve. Even the best-intentioned efforts (such as the massive aid flows that have been pledged in post-Taliban Afghanistan) may have deleterious unintended consequences. Nevertheless, calls for local ownership not easily implemented, as Jens Narten shows in his chapter on Kosovo, and translating these calls into practical action is a particularly difficult thing to do, especially when there is an imminent risk of resurgent violence. In some cases, the imperative of keeping peace may be a higher-order priority for international peacebuilders than handing over authority to local actors in the name of "ownership." Over the longer term, however, statebuilding processes that are not locally owned are likely to produce resentment and rejection.

The next challenge for statebuilding: sustainability

Designing and conducting statebuilding missions based on greater under-standing of these contractions and dilemmas is a crucial and immediate need, but over the longer-term international actors should focus more attention on tackling the problem of "sustainability" in peacebuilding and statebuilding. The idea of sustainability is two-fold. First and most obviously, it means sustaining international attention and resources on states that are currently hosting (or have recently hosted) peacebuilding missions. (This is one of the laudable goals of the UN Peacebuilding Commission.) However, sustain-ability also implies developing mission strategies with longer-term results in mind. Today's peacebuilding approaches still tend to be rooted in short-term thinking and needs, focusing on the initial period following the termination of a conflict. For these strategies and missions to produce more sustainable results, they need to be viewed not simply as "post-conflict" operations, but rather as the first of many phases of international engagement in recovering countries, most of which will remain fragile long after the formal termination of the initial mission. For example, threats to a postwar democratization process can manifest themselves over many years, not only in the first or second electoral contests.

Subsequent phases of statebuilding may be conceived as "successive missions" aimed at the gradual stabilization of political and economic conditions within the country. This does not necessarily mean open-ended military or security deployments. Rather, once initial transitional tasks are completed—such as disarmament, demobilization, return of refugees, interim government, and elections—the international role should gradually shift towards a more "ordinary" international development and monitoring presence. Further analysis is required to evaluate what different types of successive missions (involving fewer military deployments but still providing for security and credible commitment to peace agreements and protection to vulnerable UN and other international staff) are best deployed to fill the gap between the full-scale peace operation and a "normal" development presence.

The idea of successive missions also calls into question the usefulness and appropriateness of thinking about "exit strategies" for statebuilding operations. As Dominik Zaum (2007) writes, "Exit should best be seen as a process, not an event, and therefore does not mean disengagement." Rather than "exiting," external actors should explicitly remain involved in promoting (and to some extent overseeing) the statebuilding process in progressively less intrusive ways. These might involve long-term international police missions, deployment of significant numbers of UN civilian personnel, further security-sector reform activities, rule of law and judicial reform, working with parliament and political parties, training for future elections observers, building civil-society or community-level conflict resiliency, and developing the capacity and dispute resolution skills of electoral management bodies. A key challenge for international statebuilders is to incorporate planning for these subsequent phases directly into the initial design of the mission, thereby reducing some of the contradictions between short-term and long-term statebuilding needs.

Statebuilding at a crossroads

The future of postwar statebuilding (and the larger peacebuilding project, of which it is a part) remains uncertain. Nevertheless, demands on the UN to field new missions continue to grow. A widespread loss of confidence in international statebuilding would make it more difficult to provide assistance to countries in dire need, including Afghanistan, Darfur, Haiti, southern

Sudan, and Somalia. In the most extreme case, a rejection of statebuilding could effectively abandon tens of millions of people to lawlessness, predation, disease, and fear. Making statebuilding more effective, and more sustainable, is therefore a pressing objective at this moment in history.

The contributors to this volume have attempted to present a constructive approach to improving the effectiveness of post-conflict peacebuilding and statebuilding efforts. In his chapter, Miles Kahler describes this as a revisionist approach to peacebuilding—and we agree. Rather than advocating a retreat from these efforts (which would create more problems than it would solve) or making deceptively simplistic calls for greater investment or improved coordination, this book has investigated the deeper contradictions and dilemmas that render postwar statebuilding so intrinsically difficult in practice. Our hope is that this analysis will spur other scholars to investigate such tensions and dilemmas in further detail, and to develop robust instruments of assessment that incorporate the contradictions into policy-planning, and that these findings will also encourage policy practitioners to design and implement more nuanced and longer-term approaches based on a greater awareness of the underlying tensions and limitations of such interventions.

The dilemmas of statebuilding will never go away, but they can be managed more successfully than they have been in the past. The first step, however, is to deepen existing understandings of these dilemmas, their underlying causes, and their interactions and implications.

Notes

1 Quoted in "Security Council Hears 60 Speakers, Asks Secretary-General to Advise Organization," United Nations Department of Information, May 20, 2008, at www.un.org/news/press/docs/2008/sc9333.doc.htm.
2 For example, see the "Essential Tasks Matrix" prepared for the US Department of State (available at http://www.state.gov/s/crs/rls/52959.htm). We find such analytical tools valuable and well-intentioned; however, they do not explicitly provide policymakers with sufficient methodologies for understanding the contradictory nature of the statebuilding tasks and may in fact lead to the type of sequential or sector-specific thinking that has proven problematic in the past.

References

"A Nation Resolved to Overcome Its Tough Heritage." 2002. *International Special Reports* – Croatia, March 10: http://www.internationalspecialreports.com/europe/01/croatia/anationresolved.html.

Abdullah, Ibrahim. 1998. "Bush Path to Destruction: the Origin and Character of the Revolutionary United Front/Sierra Leone." *Journal of Modern African Studies* 36 (2): 203–35.

Ackerman, Bruce A.1992. *The Future of Liberal Revolution.* New Haven: Yale University Press.

Ackerman, Bruce A. 1989. "Constitutional Politics, Constitutional Law." *Yale Law Journal* 99: 453–547.

Adekanye, Bayo. 1998. "Power-Sharing in Multi-Ethnic Political Systems." *Security Dialogue* 29 (1): 25–36.

Addison, Tony. 2005. "Does the Global Economy Work for Peace?" Discussion Paper No. 2005/05, UNU/WIDER: Helsinki.

Addison, Tony and Mark McGillivray. 2006. "Aid to Conflict-Affected Countries: Lessons for Donors." In *Security and Development: Investing in Peace and Prosperity,* eds. R. Picciotto and R.Weaving. Oxford: Routledge.

Addison, Tony, Philippe Le Billon and Mansoob Murshed. 2001. "Finance in Conflict and Reconstruction." Discussion Paper 2001/44, Helsinki: WIDER.

Ahmed, Salman, Paul Keating and Ugo Solinas. 2007. "Shaping the Future of UN Peace Operations: Is There a Doctrine in the House?" *Cambridge Review of International Affairs* 20 (1): 11–28.

Akiner, Shirin. 2001. *Tajikistan. Disintegration or Reconciliation?* (Central Asian and Caucasian Prospects). London: RIIA.

Akiner, Shirin and Catherine Barnes. 2001. "The Tajik Civil War: Causes and Dynamics." In *Politics of Compromise: The Tajikistan Peace Process,* eds. Ksmoludin Abdullaev and Catherine Barnes. London: Conciliation Resources.

Alborghetti, Igor. 1995. "MPRI, Croatia – An Example for B&H?" *Globas* 254 (October) http://www.bosnet.org/archive/bosnet.w3archive/9511/msg00448.html.

Alexander, Ernest R. 1995. *How Organizations Act Together: Interorganizational Coordination in Theory and Practice.* Luxembourg: Gordon and Breach.

Allen, Christopher. 1995. "Understanding African Politics." *Review of African Political Economy* 65: 301–20.

Allen, Christopher. 1978. "Sierra Leone." In *West African States: Failure and Promise,* ed. John Dunn. Cambridge: Cambridge University Press.

Amnesty International. 1998. "Croatia: Impunity for the Storm." Amnesty International Report, AI Index EUR 64/004/1998. London: Amnesty International. http://asiapacific.amnesty.org/library/Index/ENGEUR640041998?open&of=ENG-HRV

Amnesty International. 1998. "Croatia: Statistics and Laws Alone Will Not End Torture and Ill-Treatment" AI Index: EUR 64/09/08. Amnesty International News Service220/98. London: Amnesty International. http://www.amnesty.org/en/library/asset/EUR64/009/1998/en/dom-EUR640091998en.html.

Amsden, Alice. 2007. *Escape from Empire: the Developing World's Journey through Heaven and Hell*. Cambridge, Mass.: MIT Press.

Amsden, Alice. 2001. *The Rise of the Rest: Challenges to the West from Late-Industrializing Economies*. Oxford: Oxford University Press.

Amsden, Alice. 1997. "Editorial: Bringing Production Back In – Understanding Government's Economic Role in Late Industrialization." *World Development* 25 (4): 469–80.

Anderson, Mary B. 1999. *Do No Harm: How Aid can Support Peace – or War*. Boulder: Lynne Rienner.

Anderson, Mary B. 1996. *Do No Harm. Supporting Local Capacities for Peace through Aid*. Cambridge: Collaborative for Development Action

Anderson, Mary B. and Lara Olson. 2003. *Confronting War: Critical Lessons for Peace Practitioners*. Cambridge: Collaborative for Development Action.

Andreasson, Stefan. 2006. "Stand and Deliver: Private Property and the Politics of Global Dispossession." *Political Studies* 54 (1): 3–22.

Associated Press. 2000. "Generals Criticize war crimes crackdown." *St. John's Telegraph* 30 (September): 16.

Atkin, Muriel. 1999. "Tajikistan: A Case Study for Conflict Potential." *The Soviet and Post-Soviet Review* 24 (3): 175–203.

Atzili, Boaz. 2007. "When Good Fences Make Bad Neighbors: Fixed Borders, State Weakness, and International Conflict." *International Security* 31 (3): 139–73.

Avant, Deborah. 2005. *The Market for Force: the Consequences of Privatizing Security*. Cambridge: Cambridge University Press.

Ayoob, Mohammed. 1995. *The Third World Security Predicament: Statemaking, Regional Conflict, and the International System*. Boulder: Lynne Rienner Press.

Bain, William. 2006. "In Praise of Folly: International Administration and the Corruption of Humanity." *International Affairs* 82 (3): 525–38.

Baker, Pauline. 1996. "Conflict Resolution versus Democratic Governance." In *Managing Global Chaos: Sources of and Responses to International Conflict*, ed. C. A. Crocker, F. O. Hampson, and P. Aall. Washington, D.C.: U.S. Institute of Peace.

Baldauf, Scott. 2003. "Afghan Military Tied to Drug Trade." In *Christian Science Monitor*, 4 September.

Barfield, Thomas J. 2004. "Problems in Establishing Legitimacy in Afghanistan." *Iranian Studies* 37 (2): 263–93.

Barnett, Michael. 2006. "Building a Republican Peace: Stabilizing States after War." *International Security* 30 (4): 87–112.

Barnett, Michael. 2001. "Authority, Intervention and IR Theory." In *Intervention and Transnationalism in Africa*, eds. Thomas Callaghy, Ronald Kassimir, and Robert Latham. Cambridge: Cambridge University Press.

Barnett, Michael, David Kim, Madalene O'Donnell, and Laura Sitea. 2007. "Peacebuilding: What's in a Name?" *Global Governance* (13) 3: 35–58.

Barnett, Michael and Martha Finnemore. 1999. "The Politics, Power and Pathologies of International Organizations." *International Organization* 53 (4) (Autumn): 699–732.

Barnett, Michael, Songying Fang, and Christoph Zürcher. "The Game of Peacebuilding." In progress.

Bastian, Sunil and Robin Luckham, eds. 2003. *Can Democracy be Designed? The Politics of Institutional Choice in Conflict-Torn Societies.* London: Zed.

Bates, Robert H. *Prosperity and Violence.* New York: Norton

Baunsgaard, Thomas and Michael Keen. 2005. "Tax Revenue and (or?) Trade Liberalization." IMF Working Paper 05/112, Washington: IMF, June.

Bayart, Jean François. 1993. *The State in Africa: The Politics of the Belly.* Longman Group United Kingdom.

Beauvais, Joel C. 2001. "Benevolent Despotism: A Critique of UN Statebuilding." *Journal of International Law and Politics* 33 (4): 1101–78.

Beblaw, Hazem. 1990. "The Rentier State in the Arab World." In *The Arab State*, ed. Giacomo Luciani. London: Routledge: 80–85.

Becker, Marcus C. 2004. "Organizational Routines: A Review of the Literature." *Industrial and Corporate Change* 13 (4): 643–77.

Beetham, David. 1996. *Bureaucracy*, 2nd ed. Minneapolis: University of Minnesota Press.

Bellamy, Alex J. and Paul D. Williams. 2005. "Who's Keeping the Peace? Regionalization and Contemporary Peace Operations." *International Security* 29 (4): 157–95.

Belloni, Roberto. 2008. *Statebuilding and International Intervention in Bosnia.* London: Routledge.

Bendaña, Alejandro. 2005. "From Peacebuilding to Statebuilding: One Step Forward and Two Steps Back?" *Development* 48 (3): 5–15.

Bergner, Daniel. 2003. *In the Land of Magic Soldiers.* New York: Farrar, Straus and Giroux.

Betts, Richard. 1994. "The Delusion of Impartial Intervention." *Foreign Affairs* 73 (6): 20–33.

Bhatia, Michael, Kevin Lanigan, and Philip Wilkinson. 2004. *Minimal Investments, Minimal Results: The Failure of Security Policy in Afghanistan.* AREU Briefing Paper.

Biedermann, Ferry. 2007. "Lebanon's Divide Hampers War Reparation." *Financial Times*, July 11.

Bjornlund, Eric. 2004. *Beyond Free and Fair: Monitoring Elections and Building Democracy.* Baltimore and London: Johns Hopkins University Press.

Blair, Harry and Katarina Ammitzboell. 2007. "First Steps in Post-Conflict Statebuilding: A UNDP-USAID Study." Washington, D.C.: USAID.

Bormeo, Nancy. 1997. "Myths of Moderation: Confrontation and Conflict During Democratic Transition." *Comparative Politics* 29 (3): 305–22.

Boughton, James and Alex Mourmonas. 2002. "Is Policy Ownership an Operational Concept?" International Monetary Fund Working Paper 02/72;, New York, April.

Bourgois, Philippe. 2004. "The Continuum of Violence in War and Peace: Post-Cold War Lessons from El Salvador." In *Violence in War and Peace: An Anthology*, eds. Nancy Scheper-Hughes and Philippe Bourgeois. Oxford: Blackwell.

Boutros-Ghali, Boutros. 1995. "Supplement to An Agenda for Peace," UN document A/50/60-S/1995/1, January 3.

Boutros-Ghali, Boutros. 1992. *An Agenda for Peace: Preventive Diplomacy, Peacemaking and Peace-keeping.* New York: United Nations.

Boyce, James K., ed. 1996. *Economic Policy for Building Peace: Lessons Learned from El Salvador.* Boulder: Lynne Rienner.

Boyce, James K.. 2002. *Investing in Peace.* New York: Oxford University Press.

Boyce, James K. and Madalene O'Donnell, eds. 2007. *Peace and the Public Purse: Economic Policies for Postwar Statebuilding.* Boulder: Lynne Rienner.

Brahimi, Lakhdar. 2007. "State Building in Crisis and Post-Conflict Countries," paper prepared for the 7th Global Forum on Reinventing Government, Vienna, Austria (June 26–29), http://unpan1.un.org/intradoc/groups/public/documents/UN/UNPAN026305.pdf.

Bratton, Michael and Nicolas van de Walle. 1997. *Democratic Experiments in Africa: Regime Transitions in Comparative Perspective.* Cambridge: Cambridge University Press.

Bremer, L. Paul. 2006. *My Year in Iraq: The Struggle to Build a Future of Hope.* New York: Simon and Schuster.

Brömmelhörster, Jörn, ed. 2000. *Demystifying the Peace Dividend.* Baden-Baden: Nomos.

Brown, Frederick Z. and David G. Timberman. 1998. *Cambodia and the International Community: The Quest for Development, Peace and Democracy.* Singapore: Institute of Southeast Asian Studies.

Brown, Mark Malloch. 2003. "Democratic Governance: Toward a Framework for Sustainable Peace." *Global Governance* 9: 141–46.

Brown, MacAlister and Zasloff, Joseph, 1998. *Cambodia Confounds the Peacemakers 1979–98.* Cornell: Cornell University Press.

Bueno de Mesquita, Bruce, Alastair Smith, Randolph M. Siverson, and James D. Morrow. 2003. *The Logic of Political Survival.* Cambridge, Mass.: MIT Press.

Bukovansky, Mlada. 2002. *Legitimacy and Power Politics: The American and French Revolutions in International Political Culture.* Princeton: Princeton University Press.

Bunce, Valerie. 2000. "Comparative Democratization: Big and Bounded Generalizations." *Comparative Political Studies* 33 (6/7;): 703–34.

Buerstedde, David. 2005. "Violence in Kosovo Calls for a Fresh Look at the Mission's Priorities." OSCE Yearbook 2004, Institute for Peace Research and Security Policy at the University of Hamburg/IFSH. Baden-Baden: Nomos (135–45).

Burbach, Roger, Orlando Nunez, Orlando Núñez Soto, and Boris Kagarlitsky. 1997. *Globalization and Its Discontents: The Rise of Postmodern Socialisms.* London: Pluto Press.

Bures, Oldrich. 2006. "Regional Peacekeeping Operations: Complementing or Undermining the United Nations Security Council?" *Global Change, Peace and Security* 18 (2) (June): 83–99.

Burin, Frederic S. and Kurt L. Shell, eds. *Politics, Law, and Social Change: Selected Essays of Otto Kirchheimer.* New York: Columbia University Press.

Calic, Marie-Janine. 2004. *Kosovo 2004. Optionen deutscher und europäischer Politik* [Options for German and European Policy-Making], Study of the Stiftung Wissenschaft und Politik/SWP, No. S 01, Berlin, January.

Call, Charles T. 2005. "Institutionalizing Peace: A Review of Post-Conflict Peacebuilding Concepts and Ideas for DPA." Paper prepared for the Policy Planning Unit of the UN Department of Political Affairs, January 31.

Call, Charles T. and Elizabeth M. Cousens. 2008. "Ending Wars and Building Peace: International Responses to War–Torn Societies," *International Studies Review* 9: 1–21.

Call, Charles T. and Michael Barnett. 2000. "Looking for a Few Good Cops: Peacekeeping, Peacebuilding and CIVPOL." In *Peacebuilding and Police Reform*, ed. Tor Tanke Holm and Espen Barth Eide. London: Frank Cass (43–68).

Campbell, Donald T. 1969. "Reforms as Experiments." *American Psychologist* 24: 409–29.

Canadian Peacebuilding Coordinating Committee. 2005. Canada and the Pursuit of Peace. Summary. A submission to the House of Commons Standing Committee on Foreign Affairs and International Trade, Ottawa, November.

Candio, Patrick and Roland Bleiker. 2001. "Peacbuilding in East Timor." *The Pacific Review.* 14 (1): 63–84.

Caplan, Richard. 2005a. *International Governance of War-Torn Territories: Rules and Reconstruction*. New York: Oxford University Press.

Caplan, Richard. 2005b. "Who Guards the Guardians? International Accountability in Bosnia." *International Peacekeeping* 12 (3): 463–76.

Caplan, Richard. 2004. "Partner or Patron? International Civil Administration and Local Capacity-building." *International Peacekeeping* 11 (2): 229–47.

Caplan, Richard. 2002. "A New Trusteeship? The International Administration of War-torn Territories." International Institute for Strategic Studies Adelphi Paper No. 341. Oxford: University Press, February.

Caplan, Richard and Béatrice Pouligny. 2005. "Histoire et contradictions du state-building." *Critique Internationale* 28 (July–September).

Carbonnier, Gilles. 2002. "The Competing Agendas of Economic Reform and Peace Process: A Politico-Economic Model Applied to Guatemala." *World Development* 30 (8): 1323–39.

Carnegie Commission on Preventing Deadly Conflict. 1997. *Preventing Deadly Conflict: Final Report*. Washington, D.C.: Carnegie Commission on Preventing Deadly Conflict.

Carothers, Thomas. 2002. The End of the Transition Paradigm. *Journal of Democracy* 13 (1): 5–21.

Cernea, Michael. 1985. *Putting People First. Sociological Variables in Rural Development*. Oxford: Oxford University Press.

Chambers, Robert. 1997. *Rural Development: Putting the First Last*. London: Intermediate Technology Publications.

Champagne, Hélène. 2005. "Peacebuilding: Toward a Global Ethic of Responsibility?" *Peace, Conflict and Development* 6 (6): 1–30.

Chanaa, Jane. 2002. *Security Sector Reform: Issues, Challenges and Prospects*, Adelphi Paper No. 344, International Institute for Strategic Studies. Oxford: Oxford University Press.

Chandler, David. 2006. *Empire in Denial: The Politics of Statebuilding*. London: Pluto Press.

Chandler, David. 2005. "From Dayton to Europe: International Accountability in Bosnia." *International Peacekeeping* 12 (3): 336–49.

Chandler, David. 2004. "The Responsibility to Protect? Imposing the 'Liberal Peace'." *International Peacekeeping* 11 (1): 59–81.

Chandler, David. 2000. *Bosnia: Faking Democracy After Dayton*. London: Pluto Press.

Chandler, David P. 1993a. *A History of Cambodia*. Bangkok: Silkworm Books.

Chandler, David P. 1993b. *The Tragedy of Cambodian History: Politics, War, and Revolution Since 1945*. Bangkok: Silkworm Books.

Chang, Ha-Joon. 2002. *Kicking Away the Ladder: Developmental Strategy in Historical Perspective*. London: Anthem Press.

Chang, Ha-Joon. (Forthcoming). "The Trope of Ownership. Transfer of Authority in Post-Conflict Operations." In *Rule of Law in Conflict Management: Security, Development and Human Rights in the 21st Century*, ed. Agnes Hurwitz. Boulder: Lynne Rienner/International Peace Academy.

Chang, Ha-Joon. 2002. "Tiptoeing Through Afghanistan: The Future of UN State-building", International Peace Academy Report. New York, September.

Chang, Ha-Joon and Ilene Grabel. 2004. *Reclaiming Development: An Alternative Economic Policy Manual*. London and New York: Zed Books.

Checkel, Jeffrey T. ed. 2007. *International Institutions and Socialization in Europe*. New York: Cambridge University Press.

Checkel, Jeffrey T., ed. 2005. "International Institutions and Socialization in Europe." *International Organization*, 59 (4) (Fall): 801–26.

Chesterman, Simon. 2007. "The Trope of Ownership. Transfer of Authority in Post-Conflict Operations." In *Civil War and the Rule of Law Security, Development, Human Rights*, eds. Agnes Hurwitz and Reyko Huang. Boulder: Lynne Rienner/International Peace Academy.

Chesterman, Simon. 2005. "From State Failure to State-Building: Problems and Prospects for a United Nations Peacebuilding Commission," *Journal of International Law and International Relations* 2 (1): 155–175.

Chesterman, Simon. 2004. *You, the People: The United Nations, Transitional Administration, and Statebuilding*. New York: Oxford University Press.

Chesterman, Simon. 2003. "Ownership in Theory and in Practice: Transfer of Authority in UN Statebuilding Operations." *Journal of Intervention and Statebuilding* 1 (1): 3–26.

Chesterman, Simon. 2002. "Tiptoeing Through Afghanistan: The Future of UN State-Building," International Peace Academy Report. New York. September.

Chesterman, Simon, Michael Ignatieff, and Ramesh Thakur. 2004. *Making States Work: From State-Failure to Statebuilding*. International Peace Academy and the United Nations University, www.ipacademy.org/PDF_Reports/MAKING_STATES_WORK.pdf.

Chingono, Mark. 1996. *The State, Violence and Development: the Political Economy of War in Mozambique, 1975–92*, Aldershot: Avebury.

Chisholm, Donald. 1989. *Coordination without Hierarchy: Informal Structures in Multiorganizational Systems*. Berkeley: University of California Press.

Chopra, Jarat. 2002. "Building State Failure in East Timor." *Development and Change* 33 (5): 979–1000.

Chopra, Jarat. 2000. "The UN's Kingdom of East Timor." *Survival* 42 (3): 27–39.

Chopra, Jarat and Tanja Hohe. 2004. "Participatory Intervention." *Global Governance* 10 (3): 289–305.

Clapham, Christopher. 1996. *Africa and the International System: The Politics of State Survival*. New York: Cambridge University Press.

Clingendael Institute. 2005. *The Stability Assessment Framework: Designing Integrated Responses for Security, Governance and Development*. Netherlands Ministry of Foreign Affairs and the Clingendael Institute.

Cohen, Roger. 1995. "US Cooling Ties with Croatia After Winking at its Buildup." *New York Times*, October 28, A1.

Collier, Paul. 2007. *The Bottom Billion: Why the Poorest Countries Are Failing and What Can Be Done About It*. New York: Oxford University Press.

Collier, Paul. 1997. "The Failure of Conditionality." In *Perspectives on Aid and Development*, eds. Catherine Gwin and Joan M. Nelson. Washington, D.C.: Overseas Development Council, (51–77).

Collier, Paul and Anke Hoeffler. 2001. *Greed and Grievance in Civil War*. Policy Research Working Paper 2355. World Bank, Washington, D.C.

Collier, Paul et al. 2003. *Breaking the Conflict Trap: Civil War and Development Policy*. Washington, D.C.: The World Bank and Oxford, UK: Oxford University Press.

Constable, Pamela. 2006. "Afghan Leader Losing Support," *Washington Post*, June 26.

Constitutional Court of Bosnia and Herzogovina. 2000. Request for Evaluation and Constitutionality of Certain Provisions of the Constitution of Republica Srpska and the Constitution of the Federation of BiH. Partial Decision U 5/98 III. July 1. http://www.ccbh.ba/eng/odluke/povuci_html.php?pid=22214.

Cooley, Alexander. 2005. *Logics of Hierarchy: The Organization of Empires, States, and Military Occupations*. Ithaca: Cornell University Press.

Cooley, Alexander. 2003. "Western Conditions and Domestic Choices: The Influence of External Actors on the Post-Communist Transition." In *Nations in Transit 2003: Democratization in East Central Europe and Eurasia*. Lanham MD: Rowman & Littlefield.

Cooley, Alexander and James Ron. 2002. "The NGO Scramble: Organizational Insecurity and the Political Economy of Transnational Action." *International Security* 27 (1): 5–39.

Cooney, Daniel. "Afghanistan Hails Debt Cancellation," *Washington Post*, February 8, 2006

Cooper, Ian. 2006. "The Watchdogs of Subsidiarity: National Parliaments and the Logic of Arguing in the EU," *Journal of Common Market Studies* 44 (2): 281–304.

Cooper, Neil. 2005. "Picking Out the Pieces of the Liberal Peaces: Representation of Conflict Economies and the Implications for Policy," *Security Dialogue* 36 (4): 463–78.

Cotton, James. 1999. " 'Peacekeeping' in East Timor: An Australian Policy Departure." *Australian Journal of International Affairs* 53 (3): 237–46.

Cousens, Elizabeth M. 2001. "Building Peace in Bosnia." In *Peacebuilding as Politics: Cultivating Peace in Fragile Societies*, eds. Elizabeth M. Cousens and Chetan Kumar with Karin Wermester. Boulder: Lynne Rienner, pp. 113–52.

Cousens, Elizabeth, Chetan Kumar, with Karen Wermester, eds. 2000. *Peacebuilding as Politics: Cultivating Peace in Fragile Societies*. Boulder: Lynne Rienner.

Cramer, Christopher. 2006a. *Civil War is Not a Stupid Thing: Accounting for Violence in Developing Countries*. London: Hurst.

Cramer, Christopher. 2006b. "Review of EPA Impact Assessment: 'Impact and Sustainability of Economic Partnership Agreements for Angola.'" Brussels: EU (available from author).

Cramer, Christopher. 2001. "Privatization and Adjustment in Mozambique: A Hospital Pass?" *Journal of Southern African Studies* 27 (1): 79–103.

Cramer, Christopher. 1999. "Can Africa Industrialize by Processing Primary Commodities? The Case of Mozambican Cashew Nuts." *World Development* 27 (7): 1247–66.

Crawford, Neta C. 2002. *Argument and Change in World Politics. Ethics, Decolonization, and Humanitarian Intervention*. Cambridge: Cambridge University Press.

"Croatian government welcomes IMF Credit." 1997. Agence France Presse, March 14.

Crocker, Chester A., Fen Osler Hampson, and Pamela Aall, eds. 1999. *Herding Cats: Multiparty Mediation in a Complex World.* Washington, D.C.: United States Institute of Peace Press.

Curtin, Philip D. 2000. *The World and the West: The European Challenge and the Overseas Responses in the Age of Empire.* New York: Cambridge University Press.

Cutillo, Alberto. 2006. "International Assistance to Countries Emerging from Conflict: A Review of Fifteen Years of Interventions and the Future of Peacebuilding." International Peace Academy report, New York.

Daalder, Ivo and James Goldgeier. 2006. "Global NATO." *Foreign Affairs* (September/October): 105.

Dahrendorf, Nicola, ed. 2003. *A Review of Peace Operations: A Case for Change.* London: King's College London, Conflict, Security and Development Group. http://ipi.sspp.kcl.ac.uk/index.html.

Danner, Mark. 1998. "Operation Storm." *New York Review of Books*, October 22.

Darby, John, ed. 2006. *Violence and Reconstruction.* South Bend, Indiana: University of Notre Dame Press.

Davenport, Christian. 2005. "Freedom under Fire: Repression, Context and Fragility of the Domestic Democratic Peace," Paper presented at the annual meeting of the International Studies Association, Honolulu, Hawaii, March 5.

Davenport, Christian. 1996. "'Constitutional Compromises' and Repressive Reality: A Cross-National Time-Series Investigation of Why Political and Civil Liberties are Suppressed." *Journal of Politics* 58 (3): 627–54.

Davis, Ian. 2002. *Small Arms and Light Weapons in the Federal Republic of Yugoslavia: The Nature of the Problem.* London: Saferworld.

de Coning, Cedric. 2007. "Coherence and Coordination in United Nations Peacebuilding and Integrated Missions – A Norwegian Perspective." Norwegian Institute of International Affairs.

de Coning, Cedric. 2004. "Coherence and Integration in the Planning, Implementation and Evaluation of Complex Peacebuilding Operations." *Conflict Trends* 1 (April). Durban, South Africa: ACCORD.

de la Rey, Cheryl and Susan McKay. 2006. "Peacebuilding as a Gendered Process." *Journal of Social Issues* 62 (1): 141–53.

de Soto, Alvaro and Graciana del Castillo. 1994. "Obstacles to Peacebuilding." *Foreign Policy* 94 (Spring): 69–83.

DeGrasse, Beth and Emily Hsu. 2005. "Afghanistan: Old Problems, New Parliament, New Expectations." Washington, D.C.: United States Institute of Peace briefing.

Department for International Development, Government of the United Kingdom. 2002. "Decentralization and Governance," Key sheets no. 11 (May).

Department of Foreign Affairs and International Trade, and Canadian International Development Agency. 2002. *Canadian Peacebuilding Initiative: Strategic Framework.* Ottawa: Government of Canada.

Di John, Jonathan. 2006. "The Political Economy of Taxation and Tax Reform in Developing Countries." Research Paper No.2006/74. Helsinki: UNU/WIDER.

Diamond, Larry. 2005 *Squandered Victory: The American Occupation and the Bungled Effort to Bring Democracy to Iraq.* New York: Times Books.

Diamond, Larry, Juan Linz and Seymour Martin Lipset. 1999. *Democracy in Developing Countries.* Boulder: Lynne Rienner.

Diehl, Paul F. 1994. *International Peacekeeping.* Baltimore: Johns Hopkins University Press.

Dietl, Gulshan. 2004. "War, Peace and the Warlords: The Case of Ismael Khan of Heart in Afghanistan." *Alternatives* 3 (23): 41–66).

Dobbins, James, Seth G. Jones, Keith Crane, and Beth Cole DeGrasse. 2007. *The Beginner's Guide to Nation-Building*. Santa Monica, CA: RAND Corporation.

Doner, Richard F., Bryan K. Ritchie, and Dan Slater. 2005. "Systemic Vulnerability and the Origins of Developmental States: Northeast and Southeast Asia in Comparative Perspective," *International Organization* 59 (Spring): 327–61.

Donini, Antonio. 2004. "Principles, Politics, and Pragmatism in the International Response to the Afghan Crisis." In *Nation-Building Unraveled? Aid, Peace, and Justice in Afghanistan*. ed. Antonio Donini, Norah Niland, and Karin Wermester. Bloomfield, CT: Kumarian Press, pp. 117–42.

Donini, Antonio et al., eds. 2004. *Nation-building Unraveled? Aid, Peace and Justice in Afghanistan*. Bloomfield, CT: Kumarian Press.

Donini, Antonio. 1996. "The Policies of Mercy: UN Coordination in Afghanistan, Mozambique and Rwanda," Thomas J. Watson Jr. Institute for International Studies Occasional Paper no. 22, Brown University.

Douglass, Ian. 1999. "Fighting for Diamonds in Sierra Leone." In *Peace, Profit, or Plunder: the Privatization of Security in War-Torn African Societies*, eds. Jakkie Cilliers and Peggy Mason. Pretoria: Institute for Security Studies.

Doyle, Michael and Nicholas Sambanis. 2006. *Making War and Building Peace. United Nations Peace Operations*. Princeton: Princeton University Press.

Doyle, Michael and Nicholas Sambanis. 2000. "International Peacebuilding: A Theoretical and Quantitative Analysis."*American Political Science Review* 94 (4): 779–801.

Drogin, Bob. 2000. "A Success Story in the Balkans: Croatians Celebrate Mesic's Inauguration." *The Gazette* (Montreal) February 19.

Duffield, Mark. 2001. *Global Governance and the New Wars: The Merging of Development and Security*. London: Zed Books.

Duggan, Colleen. 2004. "UN Strategic and Operational Coordination: Mechanisms for Preventing and Managing Violent Conflict." In *Conflict Prevention from Rhetoric to Reality: Organizations and Institutions*, vol 1. ed. Albrecht Schnabel and David Carment. New York: Lexington Books, pp. 345–62.

Dugolli, Igor and Leon Malazogu. 2006. "Voting Trends and Electoral Behavior in Kosovo, 2000–2004." Prishtina: Kosovar Institute for Policy Research and Development, Policy Paper No. 6. Available at: www.kipred.net/UserFiles/File/Trends_english.pdf.

Dunn, James. 2003. *East Timor: A Rough Passage to Independence*. New South Wales: Longueville.

Durch, William J. 1996. *UN Peacekeeping, American Politics, and the Uncivil Wars of the 1990s*. New York: St. Martin's Press.

Durch, William J., ed. 1993. *The Evolution of UN Peacekeeping: Case Studies and Comparative Analysis*. Palgrave Macmillan

Du Toit, Pierre. 2003. "Why Post-Settlement Settlements?" *Journal of Democracy* 14 (3): 104–18.

Du Toit, Pierre. 2001. *South Africa's Brittle Peace: The Problem of Post-Settlement Violence*. London: Palgrave.

Dziedzic, Michael J. and Michael K. Seidl. 2005. *Provincial Reconstruction Teams and Military Relations with International and Nongovernmental Organizations in Afghanistan*. Washington, D.C.: United States Institute of Peace.

Easter, Gerald. 2000. *Reconstructing the State: Personal Networks and Elite Identity in Soviet Russia*. New York: Cambridge University Press.

Economist, 2006. "A Geographical Expression in Search of a State," *The Economist*, July 8: 24.

Edelstein, David M. 2008. *Occupational Hazards: Success and Failure in Military Occupation*. Ithaca, N.Y.: Cornell University Press.

Edelstein, David M. 2004. "Occupational Hazards: Why Military Occupations Succeed or Fail." *International Security* 29 (1): 49–91.

Eide, Espen B., Anja T. Kaspersen, Anja T., Randolph Kent, and Karin von Hippel. 2005. *Report on Integrated Missions: Practical Perspectives and Recommendations*. New York: Study for the Expanded UN ECHA Core Groups.

Eisenstadt, Shmuel, and Louis Roniger. 1984. *Patrons, Clients and Friends*. Cambridge: Cambridge University Press.

Eisenstadt, Shmuel, and Louis Roniger. 1980. "Patron-Client Relations as a Model of Structuring Social Exchange." *Comparative Studies in Society and History* 22 (1): 42–77.

Elson, Robert E. 1997. *The End of the Peasantry in Southeast Asia: A Social and Economic History of Peasant Livelihood, 1800–1990s*. London: Macmillan.

Elklit, Jørgen and Andrew Reynolds. 2005. "A Framework for the Systematic Study of Election Quality," *Democratization* 12 (2): 1–16.

Ellis, Andrew. 2006. "Dilemmas in Representation and Political Identity." In *Democracy, Conflict, and Human Security: Further Readings* (Volume II), eds. Judith Large and Timothy D. Sisk. Stockholm: International IDEA.

Encarnación, Omar. 2005. "Do Political Pacts Freeze Democracy? Spanish and South American Lessons." *West European Politics* 28 (1): 182–203.

Englebert, Pierre and Denis M. Tull. 2008. "Postconflict Reconstruction in Africa: Flawed Ideas about Failed States," *International Security* 32 (4) (Spring): 106–39.

European Commission. 2002. *Project Cycle Management Handbook*. Brussels: Evaluation Unit of the EuropeAid Co-operation Office.

Fauvet, Paul and Marcelo Mosse. 2003. *Carlos Cardoso: Telling the Truth in Mozambique*. Cape Town: Double Storey.

Fearon, James D. and David D. Laitin. 2004. "Neotrusteeship and the Problem of Weak States." *International Security* 28 (4): 5–43.

Feldman, Noah. 2004. *What we Owe Iraq: War and the Ethics of Nation Building*. Princeton: Princeton University Press.

Findlay, Trevor. 1995. *Cambodia: The Legacy and Lessons of UNTAC*. SIPRI Research Report 9. Oxford: Oxford University Press.

Fine, Ben, Costas Lapavitsas and Jonathan Pincus, eds. 2001. *Development Policy in the Twenty-First Century: Beyond the Post-Washington Consensus*, London and New York: Routledge.

Fisher, Sharon. 2000. "Croatia's EU Odyssey." *Central Europe Review* 2 (19), May 15.

Føllesdal, Andreas. 1998. "Survey Article: Subsidiarity." *Journal of Political Philosophy* 6 (2): 190–218.

Foner, Eric. 1988. *Reconstruction: America's Unfinished Revolution, 1863–77*. New York: Harper and Row.

Foreign Policy. 2006. "The Failed States Index." *Foreign Policy*, May/June: 50–58.

Fortna, Virginia Page. 2004. "Does Peacekeeping Keep Peace? International Intervention and the Duration of Peace after Civil War." *International Studies Quarterly*, 48 (2): 269–92.

Fortna, Virginia Page. 2003. "Inside and Out: Peacekeeping and the Duration of Peace after Civil and Interstate Wars" *International Studies Review* 5 (4): 97–114.

Fraenkel, Jon. 2001. "The Alternative Vote System in Fiji: Electoral Engineering or Ballot-Rigging?" *Journal of Commonwealth and Comparative Politics* 39 (2): 1–31.

Fritz, Verena and Alina Rocha Menocal. 2007. "Understanding State–Building from a Political Economy Perspective: An Analytical and Conceptual Paper on Processes, Embedded Tensions and Lessons for International Engagement." Report for DFID's Effective and Fragile States Teams, London: Overseas Development Institute.

Fukuyama, Francis. 2004. *State-Building: Governance and World Order in the 21st Century.* Ithaca, N.Y.: Cornell University Press.

Gannon, Kathy. 2004. "Afghanistan Unbound," *Foreign Affairs.* 83 (3): 35–46.

Gardish, Hafizullah. 2004. "Hamed Karzai: Re-Election Seen as Done Deal." Afghan Recovery Report 139.

Gaul, Matt. 1998. "Regulating the New Privateers: Private Military Service Contracting and the Modern Marque and Reprisal Clause." *Loyola Law Review* (June).

Gerth, Hans and C. Wright Mills. 1978. *From Max Weber: Essays in Sociology.* Oxford: Oxford University Press.

Ghani, Ashraf. 2005. "The United Nations High-Level Panel on Threats, Challenges and Change: Assessing the Options and Exploring the Reactions to the Report's Postwar Peacebuilding Recommendations." Speech at the meeting of the Center for Strategic and International Studies, Washington, D.C., March 10.

Ghani, Ashraf, Clare Lockhart, and Michael Carnahan. 2006. "An Agenda for Statebuilding in the Twenty-First Century." *Fletcher Forum on World Affairs* 30 (1) (Winter): 101–24.

Ghani, Ashraf, Clare Lockhart, and Michael Carnahan. 2005. "Closing the Sovereignty Gap: an Approach to Statebuilding." Working Paper 253, London: Overseas Development Institute, http://www.odi.org.uk/publications/working_papers/wp253.pdf

Giddens, Anthony. 1993. Sociology, 2nd ed. New York: Polity Press.

Gill, Graeme. 2000. *The Dynamics of Democratization: Elites, Civil Society and the Transition Process.* London: Macmillan.

Giustozzi, Antonio. 2006. "War and Peace Economies of Afghanistan's Strongmen." *International Peacekeeping* 14 (1): 75–89.

Giustozzi, Antonio. 2005. "The Debate on Warlordism: the Importance of Military Legitimacy." Discussion Paper No. 13, Crisis States Programme, DESTIN, London: LSE, www.crisisstates.com

Giustozzi, Antonio. 2004. "Good" State vs. 'Bad' Warlords? A Critique of State-building Strategies in Afghanistan," Working Paper Series No. 51. Crisis States Programme, DESTIN, London, LSE.

Giustozzi, Antonio. 2003. "Respectable Warlords? The Politics of Statebuilding in Post-Taleban Afghanistan," Working Paper Series No. 33, Crisis States Programme, DESTIN, London, LSE.

Giustozzi, Antonio. 2000. *War, Politics and Society in Afghanistan, 1978–1992,* Washington, D.C.: Georgetown University Press.

Gleditsch, N.P., O. Bjerkholt, A. Cappelen, R. Smith, and P. Dunne, eds. 1996. *The Peace Dividend.* London: Elsevier.

Global Witness. 2005. *Timber, Taylor, Soldier, Spy.* London: Global Witness.

Goldgeier, James. 1999. *Not Whether But When.* Washington, D.C: Brookings Institution Press.

Goldstone, Anthony. 2004. "UNTAET with Hindsight: The Peculiarities of Politics in an Incomplete State." *Global Governance* 10: 83–98.

Goldstone, Jack A. et al. 2000. "State Failure Task Force Report: Phase III Findings." McLean Science Applications International Corporation. September 30. http://globalpolicy.gmu.edu/pitf/SFTF%20Phase%20III%20Report%20Final.pdf.

Goodhand, Jonathan. 2004. "From War Economy to Peace Economy? Reconstruction and Statebuilding in Afghanistan." *International Affairs* 58 (1): 155–74.

Goodhand, Jonathan and Mark Sedra. 2006. "Afghanistan Peace Conditionalities Study." London: Department for International Development.

Goodison, Paul and Colin Stoneman. 2005. "Trade, Development and Cooperation: Is the EU Helping Africa." In *Trade, Development, Cooperation – What Future for Africa?*, ed. Henning Melber. Uppsala: Nordic Africa Institute.

Goodson, Larry. 2005. "Afghanistan in 2004: Electoral Progress and an Opium Bloom." *Asian Survey* 45(1): 88–97.

Goodson, Larry. 2004. "Afghanistan in 2003: The Taliban Resurface and a New Constitution is Born." *Asian Survey* 44 (1): 14–22.

Goodson, Larry. 2003. "Afghanistan's Long Road to Reconstruction." *Journal of Democracy* 14 (1): 82–99.

Gorjao, Paulo. 2002. "The Legacy and Lessons of the United Nations Transitional Administration in East Timor." *Contemporary Southeast Asia* 24 (2): 313–36.

Goulet, Yves. 1998. "MPRI: Washington's Freelance Advisors." *Jane's Intelligence Review* 10 (7) (July).

Grant, J. Andrew. 2005. "Diamonds, Foreign Assistance and the Uncertain Prospects for Post-conflict Reconstruction in Sierra Leone." *The Round Table* 94 (381) (September): 443–57.

Greenhill, Kelly M. and Solomon Major. 2006/07. "The Perils of Profiling: Civil War Spoilers and the Collapse of Intrastate Peace Accords." *International Security* 31 (3) (Winter): 7–40.

Gregorian, Vartan. 1969. *The Emergence of Modern Afghanistan: Politics of Reform and Modernization, 1880–1946.* Stanford: Stanford University Press.

Grigg, William Norman. 1997. "Selective 'Justice' Turns Blind Eye to Croatian Atrocities." *The New American* 3 (21), http://thenewamerican.com/tna/1997/vol3no21/vol3no21_croatian.htm.

Grindle, Merilee S. 2004. "Good Enough Governance: Poverty Reduction and Reform in Developing Countries." *Governance* 17 (4): 525–48.

Gryzmala-Busse, Anna and Pauline Luong. 2002. "Reconceptualising the State: Lessons from Post-Communism." *Politics and Society* 30 (4): 529–54.

Gupta, Sanjeev, Shamsuddin Tareq, Benedict Clements, Alex Segura-Ubiergo and Rina Bhattacharya. 2004. "Rebuilding Fiscal Institutions in Postconflict Countries." Fiscal Affairs Department, Washington D.C.: IMF.

Gurr, Ted R. 2000. *People versus States: Minorities at Risk in the New Century.* Washington D.C.: United States Institute of Peace Press.

Haas, Michael. 1991. *Cambodia, Pol Pot and the United States: The Faustian Pact.* New York: Praeger.

Haggard, Stephan and Marcus Noland. 2007. *Famine in North Korea: Markets, Aid, and Reform.* New York: Columbia University Press.

Hameiri, Shahar. 2007. "Failed States or a Failed Paradigm? State Capacity and the Limits of Institutionalism." *Journal of International Relations and Dvelopment* 10: 122–49.

Hampson, Fen Osler. 1996. *Nurturing Peace: Why Peace Agreements Succeed or Fail*. Washington, D.C.: United States Institute of Peace Press.

Hanlon, Joseph. 2005. "Is the International Community Helping to Create the Preconditions for War in Sierra Leone?" *The Round Table* 94 (381) (September): 459–72.

Hanlon, Joseph and Teresa Smart. 2006. "The Manica Miracle Is Over," http://www.open.ac.uk/technology/mozambique/p5.shtml.

Hansen, Annika S. 2005. "Building Local Capacity for Maintaining Public Security." In *After Intervention: Public Security Management in Post-Conflict Societies – From Intervention to Sustainable Local Ownership*, eds. Anja H. Ebnöthe and Philipp H. Fluri. Partnership for Peace Consortium Working Group on Security Sector Reform, Vienna/Geneva, pp. 293–331.

Hansen, Annika and Sharon Wiharta. 2006. "The Transition to Order after Conflict," SIPRI Policy Report (Draft), 5.

Harris, Peter and Ben Reilly, eds. 1998.*Democracy and Deep-Rooted Conflict: Options for Negotiators*. Stockholm: International IDEA.

Hart, Vivien. 2001. "Constitution-Making and the Transformation of Conflict. *Peace & Change* 26 (1): 153–76.

Hashim, Ahmed S. 2006. *Insurgency and Counter-Insurgency in Iraq*. Ithaca, N.Y.: Cornell University Press.

Heder, Steve. 1995. "Cambodia's Democratic Transition to Neoauthoritarianism." *Current History: A Journal of Contemporary World Affairs* 94 (596): 425–29.

Heder, Steve and Judy Ledgerwood, eds. 1996. *Propaganda, Politics and Violence in Cambodia: Democratic Transition under United Nations Peacekeeping*. Armonk, NJ: ME Sharpe.

Hedges, Chris. 1997. "Nationalists in Croatia Turn Away from West," *New York Times*, April 27, A9.

Hegre, Håvard, Tanja Ellingsen, Scott Gates, and Nils Peter Gleditsch. 2001. "Toward a Democratic Civil Peace? Democracy, Political Change, and Civil War, 1816–1992." *American Political Science Review* 95 (1): 33–48.

Hehir, Aidan. 2006. "Autonomous Province Building: Identification Theory and the Failure of UNMIK." *International Peacekeeping* 13 (2): 200–13

Heinemann-Grüder, Andreas and Igor Grebenschikov. 2006. "Security Governance by Internationals: The Case of Kosovo." *International Peacekeeping* 13 (1): 43–59.

Heinemann-Grüder, Andreas and Wolf-Christian Paes. 2001. "Wag the Dog: The Mobilization and Demobilization of the Kosovo Liberation Army." Brief No 20. Bonn: Bonn International Center for Conversion.

Heininger, Janet E. 1994. *Peacekeeping in Transition: The United Nations in Cambodia*. New York: Twentieth Century Fund Press.

Herbst, Jeffrey. 2003. "Let Them Fail: State Failure in Theory and Practice: Implications for Policy." In *When States Fail: Causes and Consequences*, ed. Robert I. Rotberg: Princeton: Princeton University Press.

Herodotus, and Edward Blakeney. 1910. *The History of Herodotus*, trans. George Rawlinson. London: J.M. Dent & Sons Ltd.

Herrhausen, Anna. 2007. "Coordination in United Nations Peacebuilding: A Theory-Guided Approach," discussion paper SP IV 2007–2301, Wissenschaftszentrum Berlin für Sozialforschung [Social Science Research Center], Berlin, Germany.

High Level Panel on Threats, Challenges and Change. 2004. *A More Secure World: Our Shared Responsibility*. New York: United Nations.

Hillen, John. 2000. *Blue Helmets: The Strategy of UN Military Operations*. London: Brassey's.

Hirsch, John L. 2001. "War in Sierra Leone." *Survival* 43 (2) (Autumn): 145–62.

Hirschman, Albert Otto. 1977. *The Passions and the Interests: Political Arguments for Capitalism before its Triumph*. Princeton: Princeton University Press.

Höglund, Kristina. 2004. "Violence in the Midst of Peace Negotiations: Cases from Guatemala, Northern Ireland, South Africa, and Sri Lanka." Research Report No. 69. Uppsala, Sweden: Uppsala University Department of Peace and Conflict.

Holbrooke, Richard. 1999. *To End A War*. New York: Random House.

Holzner, Mario. 2003. "Kosovo: A Protectorate's Economy." *Vienna Institute Monthly Report* 1: 9–18.

Horowitz, Donald L. 2002. "Constitutional Design: Proposals versus Processes." In *The Architecture of Democracy: Constitutional Design, Conflict Management, and Democracy*, ed. Andrew Reynolds. Oxford: Oxford University Press.

Horowitz, Donald L. 1985. *Ethnic Groups in Conflict*. Berkeley and Los Angeles: University of California Press.

Howard, Michael. 1978. *War and the Liberal Conscience*. New Brunswick: Rutgers University Press.

Howe, Herbert. 2001. *Ambiguous Order: Military Forces in African States*. Boulder: Lynne Rienner.

Howe, Herbert. 1998. "Private Security Forces and African Stability: the Case of Executive Outcomes." *Journal of Modern African Studies* 36 (2): 307–31.

Human Rights Watch. 2006. "Afghanistan: Bush, Musharaff, Karzai Must Act Now to Stop Militant Abuses." September 27. http://hrw.org/english/docs/2006/09/27/afghan14272.htm.

Human Rights Watch. 2006. "Not on the Agenda. The Continuing Failure to Address Accountability in Kosovo Post-March 2004." HRW Report 18 (4).

Human Rights Watch. 2004. *Failure to Protect: Anti-Minority Violence in Kosovo*, March, HRW Report 16 (6).

Human Rights Watch. 2003. "World Report 2003: Africa/Sierra Leone." New York: Human Rights Watch.

Human Rights Watch. 2002. "Afghanistan's Bonn Agreement One Year Later." New York: Human Rights Watch, www.hrw.org/backgrounder/asia/afghanistan/bonn1yr-bck.htm.

Human Security Centre. 2005. "Human Security Report." University of British Columbia. http://www.humansecurityreport.info/

Human Security Centre. 2008. "Human Security Brief 2007." Simon Fraser University, http://www.humansecuritybrief.info.

Human Security Centre. 2006. Human Security Brief 2006. Vancouver: Human Security Centre, University of British Columbia.

Hurd, Ian. 2003. "Legitimacy and Authority in International Politics." *International Organization* 53 (2) (Spring): 379–408.

Hurrell, Andrew. 2005. "Power, Institutions, and the production of Inequality." In *Power in Global Governance*, eds. Michael Barnett and Raymond Duvall. Cambridge: Cambridge University Press.

Hurwitz, Agnes. 2005. "Rule of Law Programs in Multidimensional Peace Operations: Legitimacy and Ownership." In *After Intervention: Public Security Management in Post-Conflict Societies – From Intervention to Sustainable Local Ownership*, eds. Anja H. Ebnöther and Philipp H. Fluri. Partnership for Peace

Consortium Working Group on Security Sector Reform: Vienna/Geneva, pp. 333–56

Hyung-Gon, Paul Yoo. 2003. "Corruption, Rule of Law and Civil Society: Why Patronage Politics Is Good for Developing Markets and Democracies." *International Affairs* 12 (1): 24–45.

IEG. 2006. "Engaging with Fragile States: An IEG Review of World Bank Support to Low-Income Countries under Stress." Washington, D.C.

Idris, SM Mohammed. 1998. "The Message from Calicut – 500 Years after Vasco da Gama." *Third World Resurgence* 96: 22–23.

Ignatieff, Michael. 2003. *Empire Lite. Nation-building in Bosnia, Kosovo and Afghanistan.* New York: Vintage.

Inoguchi, Takashi, Edward Newman and John Keane. 1998. *The Changing Nature of Democracy.* New York: United Nations University Press.

International Alert. 2002. "Supporting and Enhancing Community-Based Peace-building." Global Issues Policy Notes 1.

International Crisis Group. 2006a. "Afghanistan's New Legislature: Making Democracy Work." Washington: ICG Asia Report 116. Available at www.crisisgroup.org/home/index.cfm?l=1&id=4108.

International Crisis Group. 2006b. "An Army For Kosovo?" ICG Europe Report 174. Brussels: International Crisis Group.

International Crisis Group. 2005. "Kosovo after Haradinaj." ICG Europe Report 163. Pristina, Brussels: International Crisis Group.

International Crisis Group. 2004a. "Collapse in Kosovo." Europe Report 15. Pristina, Belgrade, Brussels: International Crisis Group.

International Crisis Group. 2004b. "Liberia and Sierra Leone: Rebuilding Failed States." Crisis Group Africa Report 87. Dakar and Brussels: International Crisis Group.

International Crisis Group. 2003. "Afghanistan: The Constitutional Loya Jirga." Asia Briefing 29. Kabul and Brussels: International Crisis Group.

International Crisis Group. 2002. "Sierra Leone's Truth and Reconciliation Commission: A Fresh Start?" Africa Briefing 12. Freetown/Brussels: International Crisis Group.

International Crisis Group. 2001. "Sierra Leone: Time for a New Political and Military Strategy." Africa Report 28. Freetown, Brussels and London: International Crisis Group.

International Crisis Group. 2001. "Sierra Leone: Managing Uncertainty." International Crisis Group Africa Report 35. Freetown, Brussels: International Crisis Group.

International Organization of Migration. 2003. "Labor Migration from Tajikistan. Typoscript." Dushanbe: International Organization of Migration.

International Peacekeeping. 2007. Special issue on "Afghanistan in Transition: Security, Governance and Statebuilding," 14 (1) (February).

Irvine, Jill. 1997. "Ultranationalist Ideology and Statebuilding in Croatia, 1990–96." *Problems of Post-Communism* 44 (4) (July/August): 30–44.

Ishizuka, Katsumi. 2003. "Peacekeeping in East Timor: The Experience of UNMISET." *International Peacekeeping* 10 (3): 44–59.

Issacharoff, Samuel. 2004. "Constitutionalizing Democracy in Fractured Societies." *Journal of International Affairs* 58 (1) (Fall): 73–93.

Jackson, Robert H. 1990. *Quasi-States: Sovereignty, International Relations, and the Third World.* Cambridge: Cambridge University Press.

Jackson, Robert and Carl G. Rosberg. 1982. "Why Africa's Weak States Persist: The Empirical and the Juridical in Statehood." *World Politics* 35 (1): 1–24.

Jalali, Ali A. 2002. "Rebuilding Afghanistan's National Army." *Parameters* 32 (3) (Autumn): 72–86. http://www.carlisle.army.mil/usawc/parameters/02autumn/jalali.htm.

Jarstad, Anna K. and Timothy Sisk, eds. 2008. *From War to Democracy: Dilemmas of Peacebuilding*. New York: Cambridge University Press.

Jennings, Ray. 2000. "Participatory Development as New Paradigm: The Transition of Development Professionalism." Paper prepared for the "Community Based Reintegration and Rehabilitation in Post-Conflict Settings" conference, October, Washington, D.C.

Jeong, Ho-Won. 2005. *Peacebuilding in Postconflict Societies: Strategy and Process*. Boulder: Lynne Rienner.

Jeong, Ho-Won. 2002. "Peacebuilding: Operational Imperatives and Organizational Coordination." *Hiroshima Peace Science* 24 (1)–19.

Jervis, Robert and Jack Snyder. 1999. "Civil War and the Security Dilemma." In *Civil Wars, Insecurity and Intervention*, ed. Barbara Walter and Jack Snyder. New York: Columbia University Press.

Jessen-Petersen, Soren. 2006. "Challenges of Peacebuilding: The Example of Kosovo." *S+F Sicherheit und Frieden/Security and Peace* 24 (1): 6–10.

Johnson, Chris and Jolyon Leslie. 2004. *Afghanistan: The Mirage of Peace*. New York: Zed.

Jones, Bruce. 2003. "Evolving Models of Peacekeeping: Policy Implications and Responses." paper prepared for the UN Department of Peace-keeping Operation's Best Practices Unit.

Jones, Bruce. 2001. "The Challenges of Strategic Coordination: Containing Opposition and Sustaining Implementation of Peace Agreements in Civil Wars." International Policy Paper Series on Peace Implementation. New York: International Peace Academy.

Jones, Bruce and Rahul Chandran with Elizabeth Cousens, Jenna Slotin, and Jake Sherman. 2008. "From Fragility to Resilience: Concepts and Dilemmas of Statebuilding in Fragile State." Research paper for the OECD Fragile States Group (March 4).

Jones, Seth. 2006. "Averting Failure in Afghanistan." *Survival* 48 (1): 111–28.

Joseph, Richard. 1999. "Democratization in Africa after 1989: Comparative and Theoretical Perspectives." *Transitions to Democracy*, ed. Lisa Anderson. New York: Columbia University Press, pp. 237–60.

Joseph, Richard. 1997. "Democratization in Africa after 1989: Comparative and Theoretical Perspectives." *Comparative Politics* 29: 363–82.

Junne, Gerd and Willemijn Verkoren, eds. 2005. *Postconflict Development: Meeting New Challenges*. Boulder: Lynne Rienner Publishers.

Kalyvas, Stathis. 2006. *The Logic of Violence in Civil Wars*. Cambridge: Cambridge University Press.

Kasfir, Nelson. 2003. "Domestic Anarchy, Security Dilemmas, and Violent Predation: Causes of Failure." In *When States Fail*, ed. Robert Rotberg. Princeton: Princeton University Press, pp. 53–76.

Kaspersen, Anja T. and Ole Jacob Sending. 2005. "The United Nations and Civilian Crisis Management." Oslo: Norwegian Institute of International Affairs.

Kaufman, Daniel, Aart Kraay, and Massimo Mastruzzi. 2007. "Governance Matters VI: Aggregate and Individual Governance Indicators, 1996–2006." World Bank Research Working Paper 4280. Washington, D.C.: The World Bank.

Kaufman, Daniel, Aart Kraay, and Massimo Mastruzzi. 2005. "Governance Matters IV: Governance Indicators for 1996–2004." World Bank Research Policy Working Paper 3630. Washington, D.C.: The World Bank.

Keane, Rory. 2005. "The Partnership-Conditionality Binary in the Western Balkans: Promoting Local Ownership for Sustainable Democratic Transition" *Cambridge Review of International Affairs* 18 (2): 247–57.

Keefer, Philip and Stephen Knack. 1997. "Why Don't Poor Countries Catch Up? A Cross-National Test of Institutional Explanation." *Economic Inquiry* 35 (3) (July): 590–602.

Keohane, Robert. 2003. *Humanitarian Intervention: Ethical, Legal and Political Dilemmas*. Cambridge: Cambridge University Press.

Khakee, Anna and Nicolas Florquin. 2003. "Kosovo and the Gun: A Baseline Assessment of Small Arm and Light Weapons in Kosovo." Study of the United Nations Developments Programme, Prishtina/Pristina.

Khalilzad, Zalmay. 2005. "How to Nation-Build: Ten Lessons from Afghanistan." *National Interest* (Summer): 19–27.

Khan, Mushtaq. 2004. "State Failure in Developing Countries and Strategies of Institutional Reform." In *Annual World Bank Conference on Development Economics Europe (2003): Toward Pro-Poor Policies: Aid Institutions and Globalization*, eds. Bertil Tungodden, Nicholas Stern, and Ivar Kolstad. Proceedings of Annual World Bank Conference on Development Economics, Oxford: Oxford University Press and World Bank. Available at: http://www-wds.worldbank.org/servlet/WDS_I Bank_Servlet?pcont=details&eid=000160016_20040518162841.

Khan, Mushtaq. 2002. "Corruption and Governance in Early Capitalism: World Bank Strategies and their Limitations." In *Reinventing the World Bank*, Jonathan R. and Jeffrey A. Winters, eds. Ithaca and London: Cornell University Press, pp. 164–84.

Kiernan, Ben, ed. 1993. *Genocide and Democracy in Cambodia: The Khmer Rouge, the United Nations and the International Community*. New Haven: Yale University Press.

Kirchheimer, Otto. 1969. "Changes in the Structure of Political Compromise." In *Politics, Law, and Social Change: Selected Essays of Otto Kirchheimer*, eds. Frederic S. Burin and Kurt L. Shell. New York: Columbia University Press, pp. 131–59.

Kitschelt, Herbert. 2000. "Linkages between Citizens and Politicians in Democratic Polities." *Comparative Political Studies* 33 (6/7): 845–79.

Klein, Maury. 1968. "Southern Railroad Leaders, 1865–93: Identities and Ideologies." *Business History Review* 42 (3): 288–310.

Klijn, Erik-Hans and Joop F. M. Koppenjan. 2000. "Public Management and Policy Networks: Foundations of a Network Approach to Governance." *Public Management* 2 (2): 135–58.

Klug, Heinz. 2000. *Constituting Democracy: Law, Globalism and South Africa's Political Reconstruction*. Cambridge: Cambridge University Press.

Koehler, Jan. 2005. "Conflict Processing and the Opium Economy in Jalalabad." PAL Internal Document 5 (June). Jalalabad/Berlin: Analysis Research Consulting. http://www.arc-berlin.com/pdf-sept/Drugs_and_Conflict_full.pdf.

Kosovar Civil Society Foundation. 2000. *List of Kosovo NGOs*, 1st edition. Prishtina/Pristina.

Krain, Matthew and Marissa Edson Myers. 1997. "Democracy and Civil War: A Note on the Democratic Peace Proposition." *International Interactions* 23 (1): 109–18.

Kramer, Helmut and Vedran Dzihic. 2005. *Die Kosovo-Bilanz. Scheitert die internationale Gemeinschaft [The Kosovo Balance. Does the International Community Fail?]*, LIT Verlag: Vienna.

Krasner, Stephen D. 2004. "Sharing Sovereignty. New Institutions for Collapsed and Failing States." *International Security* 29 (2): 85–120.

Kriger, Norma. 2003. *Guerrilla Veterans in Postwar Zimbabwe*. Cambridge: Cambridge University Press.

Kritz, Neil. 2003. "Constitution-Making: Lessons for Iraq." Testimony before a Joint Hearing of the Senate Committee on the Judiciary, Subcommittee on the Constitution, Civil Rights and Property Rights, and the Senate Committee on Foreign Relations, Subcommittee on Near Eastern and South Asian Affairs, June 25.

Kuhner, Jeffrey Thomas. 1999. "Croatia at Crossroads: Tudjman Has Choice of embracing Pro-democracy Movement or Trying to Crush It," *The Gazette* (Montreal), August 19, p. B3.

Kumar, Krishna, ed. 1999. *Post-conflict Elections, Democratization, and International Assistance*. Boulder: Lynne Rienner.

Lacina, Bethany and Kristian S. Gleditsch. 2005. "Monitoring Trends in Global Combat: A New Dataset of Battle Deaths." *European Journal of Population* 21 (2–3): 145–66.

Lake, David. 2007. "Building Legitimate States after Civil Wars: Order, Authority, and Institutions." Paper presented at the conference on Building Peace in Fragile States, La Jolla, CA, April 27–28.

Lake, David and Robert Powell. 1999. *Strategic Choice and International Relations*. Princeton: Princeton University Press.

Lake, David A. and Donald Rothchild, eds. 1998. *The International Spread of Ethnic Conflict: Fear, Diffusion, and Escalation*. Princeton: Princeton University Press.

Large, Judith and Timothy D. Sisk. 2006. *Democracy, Conflict and Human Security: Pursuing Peace in the 21st Century*. Stockholm: International IDEA (Institute for Democracy and Election Assistance).

Ledgerwood, Judy, ed. 2002. *Cambodia Emerges from the Past: Eight Essays*, Northern Illinois University, DeKalb, IL: Center for Southeast Asian Studies.

Levitt, Jeremy. 2005. *The Evolution of Deadly Conflict in Liberia: From "Paternaltarian-ism" to State Collapse*. Durham: Carolina Academic Press.

Lichtenstein, Alex. 1996. *Twice the Work of Free Labor: the Political Economy of Convict Labor in the New South*. London and New York: Verso.

Licklider, Roy. 1995. "The Consequences of Negotiated Settlements in Civil Wars, 1945–1993." *American Political Science Review* 89 (3): 681–90.

Lijphart, Arend. 2004. "Constitutional Design for Divided Societies." *Journal of Democracy* 15 (2): 96–109.

Lijphart, Arend. 2002. "The Wave of Power-Sharing Democracy." In T*he Architecture of Democracy: Constitutional Design, Conflict Management, and Democracy*, ed. Andrew Reynolds. Oxford: Oxford University Press, pp. 37–54.

Lijphart, Arend. 1999. *Patterns of Democracy: Government Forms and Performance in Thirty-Six Countries*. New Haven: Yale University Press.

Lijphart, Arend. 1985. *Power-Sharing in South Africa*. Berkeley: Institute of International Studies.

Lijphart, Arend. 1984. *Democracies: Patterns of Majoritarian and Consensus Government in Twenty-One Countries*. New Haven: Yale University Press.

Lijphart, Arend. 1977. *Democracy in Plural Societies: A Comparative Exploration.* New Haven: Yale University Press.

Lindblom, Charles. 1959. "The Science Of Muddling Through." *Public Administration Review* 19: 79–88.

Lipson, Michael. 2007a. "Interorganizational Coordination in Complex Peace Operations: Perspectives from Organizational Theory," unpublished paper delivered at the conference on "Public Administration Meets Peacebuilding," University of Kostanz, Germany, June 15–16.

Lipson, Michael. 2007b. "Peacekeeping: Organized Hypocrisy?" *European Journal of International Relations* (March), pp. 5–34.

Lister, Sarah and Tom Brown, with Zainiddin Karaev. 2004. "Understanding Markets in Afghanistan: A Case Study of the Raisin Market," Case Studies Series. Kabul: Afghanistan Research and Evaluation Unit (AREU), www.areu.org.af.

Lister, Sarah and Adam Pain. 2004. "Trading in Power: The Politics of 'Free' Markets in Afghanistan," Briefing Paper. Kabul: AREU, www.areu.org.af.

Lizée, Pierre. 2000. *Peace, Power and Resistance in Cambodia: Global Governance and the Failure of International Conflict Resolution.* London: Macmillan.

Luckham, Robin Anne Marie Goetz, and Mary Kaldor. 2003. "Democratic Institutions and Democratic Politics." In *Can Democracy Be Designed? The Politics of Institutional Choice in Conflict-Torn Socities,* eds. Sunil Bastian and Robin Luckham. London: Zed

Lumumba-Kasongo, Tukumbi, ed. 2005. *Liberal Democracy and its Critics in Africa: Political Dysfunction and the Struggle for Social Progress.* London: Zed.

Lund, Michael. 2003. "What Kind of Peace Is Being Built? Taking Stock of Post–Conflict Peacebuilding and Charting Future Directions." Paper prepared for the International Development Research Centre (January).

Luttwak, Edward. 1999. "Give War a Chance." *Foreign Affairs* 78 (4).

Lyons, Terrence. 2005. "Diasporas and Homeland Conflict." In *Territoriality and Conflict in an Era of Globalization,* eds. Miles Kahler and Barbara F. Walter. Cambridge: Cambridge University Press, pp. 111–129.

Lyons, Terrence. 2002. "Post Conflict Elections, War Termination, Democratization, and Demilitarizing Politics." Working Paper 20. George Mason University Institute for Conflict Analysis and Resolution, www.gmu/depts/icar/Work_Paper20.pdf.

Mackinlay, John, Larry Minear, and Jarat Chopra. 1993. "A Draft Concept of Second Generation Multinational Operations." Thomas J Watson Institute for International Studies, Providence: Brown University.

MaClean, Sandra J. 1999. "Peacebuilding and the New Regionalism in Southern Africa." *Third World Quarterly* 20 (5) (October): 943–56.

Macrory, Patrick, ed. 1969. *A Journal of the First Afghan War by Lady Florentia Sale.* Oxford: Oxford University Press.

Makarenko, T. 2002 "Crime, Terror and the Central Asian Drug Trade," *Harvard Asia Quarterly* (6) 3.

Maley, William. 2006. *Rescuing Afghanistan.* London: Hurst.

Mandelbaum, Michael. 1996. "Foreign Policy as Social Work." *Foreign Affairs* 75 (1): 16–32.

Mann, Michael. 1993. *The Sources of Social Power: Vol. II, The Rise of Classes and Nation States, 1760–1914.* Cambridge: Cambridge University Press.

Mann, Michael. 1984. "The Autonomous Power of the State: Its Origins, Mechanisms and Results." *Archives Europa Sociologica* 25: 185–213.

Mansfield, Edward and Jon Pevehouse. 2006. "Democratization and International Organizations." *International Organization* 60 (1) (Winter): 137–67.

Mansfield, Edward and Jack Snyder. 2005. *Electing to Fight*. Cambridge, Mass.: MIT Press.

Mansfield, Edward and Jack Snyder. 1995. "Democratization and the Danger of War (Correspondence)." *International Security* 20 (4): 197.

March, James G. and Johan P. Olsen. 1989. *Rediscovering Institutions: The Organizational Basis of Politics*. New York: Free Press.

Marglin, Angus and Juliette Schor, eds. 1990. *The Golden Age of Capitalism: Reinterpreting the Postwar Experience*. Oxford: Clarendon Press.

Marques, Rafael. 2006. Operacao Kissonde: Os Diamantes da Humillação e da Miséria, www.cuango.net/kissonde/texto.

Marten, Kimberly Zisk. 2004. *Enforcing the Peace: Learning from the Imperial Past*. New York: Columbia University Press.

Marten, Kimberly. 2007. "Statebuilding and Force: The Proper Role of Foreign Militaries," *Journal of Intervention and Statebuilding* 1 (2) (June): 231–47.

Martin, Ian and Alexander Mayer-Rieckh. 2005. "The United National and East Timor: From Self-Determination to Statebuilding." *International Peacekeeping* 12 (1): 125–45.

Mayall, James., ed. 1996. *The New Interventionism, 1991–1994: United Nations Experience in Cambodia, Former Yugoslavia and Somalia*. Cambridge University Press.

McCargo, Duncan. 1998. "Elite governance: business, bureaucrats and the military." In *Governance in the Asia-Pacific Richard Maidment*, eds. David Goldblatt, and Jeremy Mitchell. London: Open University Press.

McCloud, Donald G. 1995. *Southeast Asia: Tradition and Modernity in the Contemporary World*. Boulder: Westview Press.

McCoy, Alfred W. 1999. "Requiem for a Drug Lord: State and Commodity in the Career of Khun Sa." In *States and Illegal Practices*, ed. Josiah McC Heyman. Oxford and New York: Berg.

McGinnis, Michael. 2006. "Partners, Partisans, Proselytizers: Games Played by International Faith-Based Organizations." Paper prepared for 64th Annual National Conference of the Midwest Political Science Association, Chicago.

McMillan, Margaret, Dani Rodrik and Karen Horn Welch. 2002. "When Economic Reform Goes Wrong: Cashews in Mozambique." CEPR Working Paper 3519. London: Centre for Economic Policy Research.

Mendelson, Sarah E. 2005. "Barracks and Brothels. Peacekeepers and Human Trafficking in the Balkans," Report of the Center for Strategic and International Studies (CSIS), Washington.

Menkhaus, Ken. 2006/2007. "Governance without Government in Somalia: Spoilers, Statebuilding, and the Politics of Coping." *International Security* 31 (3): 74–106.

Menkhaus, Ken. 2004. "Somalia: State Collapse and the Threat of Terrorism," Adelphi Paper No. 364. Oxford: Oxford University Press.

Menon-Johansson, Anatole S. 2005. "Good governance and good health: The role of societal structures in the human immunodeficiency virus pandemic." *BMC International Health and Human Rights* 5 (4) (April). http://www.biomedcentral.com/content/pdf/1472-698X-5-4.pdf.

Meyer, John and Brian Rowan. 1977. "Institutional Organizations: Formal Structure as Myth and Ceremony." *American Journal of Sociology* 83: 340–63.

Miall, Hugh. 2007. "The EU and the Peacebuilding Commission." *Cambridge Review of International Affairs* 20 (1) (March): 29–45.

Migdal, Joel Samuel. 1988. *Strong Societies and Weak States*. Princeton: Princeton University Press.

Migdal, Joel Samuel. 1974. "Towards a New Theory of Change amongst Individuals in the Process of Modernisation." *World Politics* 14 (2): 189–206.

Migdal, Joel Samuel, Atul Kohli, and Vivienne Shue. 1994. *State Power and Social Forces: Domination and Transformation in the Third World*. Cambridge: Cambridge University Press.

Migdal, Joel Samuel, Atul Kohli, A and Vivienne Shue. 1994. "The State in Society: An Approach to Struggles for Domination," and "State Power and Social Forces: On Political Contention and Accommodation in the Third World." In *State Power and Social Forces*, ed. Joel Migdal. Cambridge: Cambridge University Press, pp. 1–36, 293–326.

Milliken, Jennifer and Keith Krause. 2002. "State Failure, State Collapse, and State Reconstruction: Concepts, Lessons and Strategies." *Development and Change* 33 (5): 753–74.

Milward, Alan S. 1992. *The Reconstruction of Western Europe, 1945–51*. London: Routledge.

Mobekk, Eirin. 2005a. "Transitional Justice in Post-Conflict Societies – Approaches to Reconciliation." In *After Intervention: Public Security Management in Post-Conflict Societies – From Intervention to Sustainable Local Ownership*, ed. Anja H. Ebnöther and Phillipp H. Fluri. Vienna/Geneva: Partnership for Peace Consortium Working Group on Security Sector Reform, pp. 261–92.

Mobekk, Eirin. 2005b. "Conference Report." In *After Intervention: Public Security Management in Post-Conflict Societies – From Intervention to Sustainable Local Ownership*, ed. Anja H. Ebnöther and Phillipp H. Fluri. Vienna/Geneva: Partnership for Peace Consortium Working Group on Security Sector Reform, pp. 378–421.

Moehler, Devra C. 2006. "Public Participation and Support for the Constitution in Uganda." *Journal of Modern African Studies* 44 (2).

Mollett, Howard, Jennifer Smith and Annie Street. 2007. "Consolidating the Peace? Views from Sierra Leone and Burundi on the United Nations Peacebuilding Commission." Report produced by Actionaid, CAFOD and Care International.

Moore, Mick and James Putzel. 2000. "Politics and Poverty: A Background Paper for the World Development Report, www1.worldbank.org/prem/poverty/wdrpoverty/dfid/synthes.pdf.

Musah, Abdul-Fatau 2000. "A Country Under Siege: State Decay and Corporate Recolonisation in Sierra Leone." In *Mercenaries: An African Security Dilemma*, eds. Abdul-Fatau Musah and J. Kayode Fayemi. London: Pluto Press.

Mysliwiecz, Eva. 1988. *Punishing the Poor: The International Isolation of Kampuchea*. Oxford: Oxfam.

Nakaya, Sumie. 2004. "Women and Gender Equality in Peacebuilding." In *Building Sustainable Peace*, eds. Tom Keating and W. Andy Knight. Tokyo: United Nations University Press, pp. 143–66.

Narten, Jens. 2006a. "Building Local Institutions and Parliamentarianism in Postwar Kosovo: A Review of Joint Efforts by the UN and OSCE from 1999–2006." *Helsinki Monitor* 17 (2): 143–58.

Narten, Jens. 2006b. "The Human Dimension: The OSCE's Approach to Human Rights." In *Human Rights in Europe. A Fragmented Regime?*, ed. Malte Brosig. Peter Lang Verlag: Frankfurt, pp. 101–17.

NATO Ministerial Communique. 1994. "Partnership for Peace: Framework Document." Statement issued by the North Atlantic Cooperation Council, NATO Headquarters, Brussels, January 10–11, http://www.nato.int/docu/comm/49–95/c940110b.htm.

NATO Ministerial Communique. 1991. "Partnership with the Countries of Central and Eastern Europe." Statement issued by the North Atlantic Council Meeting in Ministerial Session, Copenhagen, June 6–7, http://www.nato.int/docu/comm/49–95/c910607d.htm.

Newman, Edward and Roland Rich. 2004. *The UN Role in Promoting Democracy.* Tokyo: United Nations University Press.

Newman, Edward and Oliver Richmond, eds. 2006. *Challenges to Peacebuilding: Managing Spoilers During Conflict Resolution.* Tokyo: United Nations University Press.

Nietsch, Julia. 2005. Kosovo/Kosova Länderbericht [Country Report]. Duesseldorf: Institute for Foreign and Security Policy.

Norberg, Annika Hilding. 2003. "Challenges of Peace Operations." *International Peacekeeping* 10 (4) (Winter): 94–103.

North, Douglass C. 1990. *Institutions, Institutional Change and Economic Performance.* Cambridge: Cambridge University Press.

Obradovic, Stojan Obradovic. 2001. "Indictment Not Only Against Generals." *NIJ Weekly Service* 231, July 20.

O'Brien, Patrick. 1988. *The Economic Effects of the American Civil War.* Basingstoke: Macmillan.

Ochiltree, Ian. 2004. "Mastering the Sharecroppers: Land, Labour and the Search for Independence in the US South and South Africa." *Journal of Southern African Studies* 30 (1): 41–61.

O'Donnell, Guillermo A., Philippe Schmitter, and Laurence Whitehead, eds. 1986. *Transition from Authoritarian Rule.* Baltimore: Johns Hopkins University Press.

O'Donnell, Madalene. 2005. "Literature Review: Post-conflict Public Finance." Program on Post-Conflict Statebuilding, Center on International Cooperation, New York: CIC.

OECD (Organization for Economic Cooperation and Development) Development Assistance Committee. 1995. Development Partnerships in the New Global Context. Meeting of the members of the OECD's Development Assistance Committee at the level of Development Co-operation Ministers and Heads of Aid Agencies, Paris, May 3–4.

OECD (Organization for Economic Cooperation and Development). 2007. "Principles for Good International Engagement in Fragile States and Situations" (April), http://www.oecd.org/dataoecd/61/45/38368714.pdf.

O'Laughlin, Bridget. 1996. "Through a Divided Glass: Dualism, Class and the Agrarian Question in Mozambique." *Journal of Peasant Studies* 23 (4): 1–39.

Olson, Lara and Hrach Gregorian. 2007. "Side By Side or Together: Working for Security, Development and Peace in Afghanistan and Liberia." Peacebuilding, Development and Security Program, Centre for Military and Strategic Studies, University of Calgary (October).

O'Neill, William G. 2002. *Kosovo: An Unfinished Peace.* Boulder: Lynne Rienner.

Orr, Robert. 2004. "The United States as Nation Builder". In *Winning the Peace: an American Strategy for Post-Conflict Reconstruction*, ed Robert Orr. Washington, D.C.: CSIC Press.

Osborne, Milton. 1997. *Southeast Asia: An Introductory History*, New South Wales: Allen and Unwin.

OSCE Media Representative. 2004. "The Role of the Media in the March 2004 Events in Kosovo." Report of the OSCE Representative on Freedom of the Media, Vienna.

OSCE Mission in Kosovo. 2005. "The Response of the Justice System to the March 2004 Riots." Report of the Legal System Monitoring Section of the Department of Human Rights and Rule of Law, Pristina, December.

OSCE Mission in Kosovo. 2003a. "Departmental Guide of Human Rights and Rule of Law Department." Pristina, May.

OSCE Mission in Kosovo. 2003b. "Parallel Structures in Kosovo," Report of the Department of Human Rights and Rule of Law, Pristina, October.

OSCE Training Section. 2005. "Project Management Case Study." Vienna: Organization for Security and Co-operation in Europe, February.

Ottaway, Marina. 2003. "Rebuilding State Institutions in Collapsed States." In *State Failure, Collapse and Reconstruction* ed. Jennifer Milliken. Oxford: Blackwell, pp. 245–66.

Ottaway, Marina. 2002. "Rebuilding State Institutions in Collapsed States." *Development and Change* 33 (5): 1001–23.

Ottaway, Marina. 1994. *Democratization and Ethnic Nationalism: African and Eastern European Experiences*. Washington, DC: Overseas Development Council.

Ottaway, Marina and Anatol Lieven, 2002. "Rebuilding Afghanistan: Fantasy versus Reality." Policy Brief 12 (January). Washington, D.C.: Carnegie Endowment for International Peace. http://www.carnegieendowment.org/publications/index.cfm?fa=view&id=883.

Ovesen, Jan, I.-B. Trankell and J. Ojendal. 1996. "When Every Household is an Island.." Uppsala Reports in Cultural Anthropology, No. 15.

Packer, George. 2005. *The Assassins' Gate: America in Iraq*. New York: Ferrer, Straus and Giroux.

Pak, K, V. Horng, S. Ann, and T.N. Ngo. 2005. "Strengthening Provincial Governance in Cambodia's Decentralization and Deconcentration Reforms: Accountability in the New Management System." Phnom Penh: Cambodia Development Resource Institute.

Papagianni, Ekaterini. 2003. "European Integration and Eastern European Nationalism: A Comparative Study of Minority Policies in Estonia, Latvia, Romania and Slovakia." Ph.D. Thesis, Columbia University.

Papic, Zarko. 2003. "Ownership versus Democracy. Lessons (Not) Learnt in Bosnia and Herzegovina." In *Ownership Process in Bosnia and Herzegovina. Contributions on the International Dimensions of Democratization in the Balkans*, ed. Christophe Solioz, and Svebor Dizdarevic. Baden-Baden: Nomos, pp. 76–85.

Paris, Roland. 2004. *At War's End: Building Peace after Civil Conflict*. Cambridge: Cambridge University Press.

Paris, Roland. 2003. "Peacekeeping and the Constraints of Global Culture." *European Journal of International Relations* 9 (3): 441–73.

Paris, Roland. 2002. "International Peacebuilding and the 'Mission Civilisatrice.'" *Review of International Studies* 28 (4): 637–56.

Paris, Roland. 1997. "Peacebuilding and the Limits of Liberal Internationalism." *International Security* 22 (2): 54–89.

Pastor, Robert A. 1999. "A Brief History of Electoral Commissions." In *The Self-Restraining State: Power and Accountability in New Democracies*, ed. Andreas Schedler, Larry Diamond, and Marc F. Plattner. Boulder: Lynne Rienner Publishers.

Patey, Luke A. and W. Donald Macnamara. 2003. "Non-Governmental Organizations and International Conflict: An Annotated Bibliography." Unpublished manuscript.

Patrick, Stewart and Kaysie Brown. 2007. *Greater than the Sum of Its Parts: Assessing "Whole of Government" Approaches to Fragile States*. New York: International Peace Academy.

Pearce, Jenny. 1999. "Peace-building in the Periphery: Lessons from Central America." *Third World Quarterly* 20 (1): 51–68.

Pevehouse, Jon. 2002. "With a Little Help From My Friends? Regional Organizations and the Consolidation of Democracy." *American Journal of Political Science* 46 (3) (July): 611–22.

Picard, Elizabeth. 2000. "The Political Economy of Civil War in Lebanon." In *War, Institutions, and Social Change in the Middle East*, ed. Steven Heydemann. Berkeley and LA: University of California Press, pp. 292–324.

Pitcher, M. Anne. 2002. *Transforming Mozambique: the Politics of Privatization, 1975–2000*. Cambridge: Cambridge University Press.

Pouligny, Beatrice. 2005. "Civil Society and Post-Conflict Peacebuilding: Ambiguities of International Programmes Aimed at Building 'New' Societies." *Security Dialogue* 36 (4): 495–510.

Powell, Walter W. 1990. "Neither Market Nor Hierarchy: Network Forms of Organization." *Research in Organizational Behavior* 12: 295–336.

Price, Robert. 1991. *The Apartheid State in Crisis: Political Transformation of South Africa, 1975–90*. New York: Oxford University Press.

Prunier, Gerard and Rachel Gisselquist. 2003. "The Sudan: A Successfully Failed State." In *State Failure and State Weakness in a Time of Terror*, ed. Robert Rotberg. Washington, D.C.: World Peace Foundation/Brookings Institution Press, pp. 101–28.

Prusher, Ilene R. 2002. "Battling Warlords Try Civility." *Christian Science Monitor*, May 9.

Pugh, Michael. 2005. "Transformation in the Political Economy of Bosnia Since Dayton." *International Peacekeeping* 12 (3): 448–62.

Pugh, Michael. 2004. "Peacekeeping and Critical Theory." *International Peacekeeping* 11 (1): 39–58.

Pugh, Michael and Neil Cooper. 2004. *War Economies in a Regional Context. Challenges of Transformation*. Boulder: Lynne Rienner

Pugh, Michael and Waheguru Pal Singh Sidu, eds. 2003. *The United Nations and Regional Security: Europe and Beyond*. Boulder: Lynne Rienner.

Quinlivan, James T. 1995. "Force Requirements in Stability Operations." *Parameters* 25: 59–69.

Randall, Vicky and Robin Theobald. 1985. *Political Change and Underdevelopment: A Critical Introduction to Third World Politics*. London: Macmillan.

Rashid, Ahmed. 2006. "Afghanistan: On the Brink." *New York Review of Books* 53 (11): June 22.

Ratner, Steven R. 1995. *The New UN Peacekeeping: Building Peace in Lands of Conflict After the Cold War*. London: St. Martin's Press.

Reich, Hannah. 2006. Local Ownership." In *Conflict Transformation Projects. Partnership, Participation or Patronage?* Berghof Occasional Paper No. 27. Berlin: Berghof Research Center for Constructive Conflict Management, http://www.berghof-center.org/uploads/download/boc27e.pdf.

Reilly, Benjamin. 2003. "Democratic Validation." In *Contemporary Peacemaking: Conflict, Violence and Peace Processes*, ed. John Darby and Roger MacGinty. London: Palgrave, pp. 174–83.

Reilly, Benjamin. 2001. *Democracy in Divided Societies: Electoral Engineering for Conflict Management*. Cambridge: Cambridge University Press.

Reinicke, Wolfgang, Francis Deng and Jan Marten Witte. 2000. *Critical Choices: The United Nations, Networks, and the Future of Global Governance*. Ottawa: International Development Research Centre.

Reno, William. 1999. *Warlord Politics in African States*. Boulder: Lynne Rienner Press.

Reno, William. 1997. "Privatizing War in Sierra Leone." *Current History* (May): 227.

Reychler, Luc and Thania Paffenholz. 2001. *Peacebuilding. A Field Guide*. Boulder: Lynne Rienner.

Reynolds, Andres, ed. 1994. *Election '94 South Africa: An Analysis of the Campaign, Results and Future Prospects*. New York: St. Martin's Press.

Reynolds, Andrew, Ben Reilly, and Andrew Ellis et al. 2005. *Electoral System Design: The New International IDEA Handbook*. Stockholm: International IDEA.

Richards, Paul, ed. 2005. *No Peace No War: An Anthology of Contemporary Armed Conflicts*. Athens and Oxford: Ohio University Press and James Currey.

Richmond, Oliver P. 2006. "The Problem of Peace: Uunderstanding the 'Liberal Peace.'" *Conflict, Security & Development* 6 (3): 291–314.

Richmond, Oliver P. 2004. "UN Peace Operations and the Dilemmas of the Peace-building Consensus." *International Peacekeeping* 11 (1): 83–101.

Ricigliano, Robert. 2003. "Networks of Effective Action: Implementing an Integrated Approach to Peacebuilding." *Security Dialogue* 34 (4): 445–62.

Riley, Major General Jonathan P. 2006. "The UK in Sierra Leone: A Post-Conflict Operation Success?" Heritage Lecture #958 (10 August). Washington, D.C.: The Heritage Foundation.

Ripley, Tim. 1997. *Mercenaries: Soldiers of Fortune*. London: Paragon.

Risley, Paul and Timothy D. Sisk. 2005. *Democracy and Peacebuilding at the Local Level: Lessons Learned*. International IDEA.

Roberts, Nancy C. and Raymond Trevor Bradley. 2005. "Organizing for Peace Operations." *Public Management Review* 7 (1): 111–33.

Roberts, David. 2006. "Human Security or Human Insecurity: Moving the Debate Forward." *Security Dialogue* 37 (2): 249–61.

Roberts, David. 2005. "Empowering the Human Security Debate: Making it Coherent and Meaningful." *International Journal on World Peace* 22 (4): 3–16.

Roberts, David. 2002. "Political Transition and Elite Discourse in Cambodia, 1991–99." *Journal of Communist Studies and Transition Politics* 18 (4): 101–18.

Roberts, David. 2001. *Political Transition in Cambodia, 1991–99: Power, Elitism and Democracy*. London: Curzon.

Roberts, David. 1996. "The United Nations and Peacekeeping in Cambodia, 1979–93." Ph.D. Thesis, Staffordshire University.

Robinson, Ronald. 1986. "The Excentric Idea of Imperialism, With or Without Empire." In *Imperialism and After*, ed. Wolfgang Mommsen and Juergen Osterhammel. Boston: Allen and Unwin.

Rodrik, Dani, ed. 2003. *In Search of Prosperity: Analytic Narratives on Economic Growth*. Princeton: Princeton University Press.

Rodney, Walter. 1973. *How Europe Underdeveloped Africa*. Dar-Es-Salaam: London and Tanzanian Publishing House, Bogle L'Ouverture.

Roeder, Philip and Donald Rothchild, eds. 2005. *Sustainable Peace: Power and Democracy after Civil War*. Ithaca: Cornell University Press.

Ross, Michael. 2004. "What Do We Know About Natural Resources and Civil War?" *Journal of Peace Research* 41 (3): 337–56.

Michael Ross. 2001. "Does Oil Hinder Democracy?" *World Politics*, 53 (3) (April): 325–61.

Rothchild, Donald. 2002. "Settlement Terms and Postagreement Stability." In *Ending Civil Wars: The Implementation of Peace Agreements*, ed. Stephen John Stedman, Donald Rothchild, and Elizabeth M. Cousens. Boulder: Lynne Rienner Publishers, pp.117–40.

Roy, Oliver. 2004. "Development and Political Legitimacy: the Cases of Iraq and Afghanistan." *Conflict, Security & Development*, 4 (2) (August): 167–79.

Rubin, Barnett R. 2006. *Afghanistan's Uncertain Transition from Turmoil to Normalcy*. New York: Center on Preventive Action, Council on Foreign Relations.

Rubin, Barnett R. 2005. "Constructing Sovereignty for Security." *Survival* 47 (4) (Winter): 93–106.

Rubin, Barnett R. 2004. "Crafting a Constitution for Afghanistan." *Journal of Democracy* 15 (3): 5–19.

Rubin, Barnett R. 2002. *The Fragmentation of Afghanistan: State Formation and Collapse in the International System*, 2nd edition. New Haven: Yale University Press.

Rubin, Barnett R. 1998. "Russian Hegemony and State Breakdown in Periphery: Causes and Consequences of Civil War in Tajikistan." In *Post-Soviet Political Order: Conflict and Statebuilding*, ed. Barnett R. Rubin and Jack Snyder. New York: Routledge, pp. 128–62.

Rubin, Barnett R. 1995. *The Search for Peace in Afghanistan: From Buffer State to Failed State*. New Haven: Yale University Press.

Saba, Daoud and Omar Zakhilwal. 2004. *Security with a Human Face: Challenges and Responsibilities*. Islamabad: UNDP Afghanistan National Human Development Report.

Saikal, Amin. 2005. *Modern Afghanistan, A History of Struggle and Survival*. London: I.B. Tarius.

Sambanis, Nicholas. 2000. "Partition as a Solution to Ethnic War: An Empirical Critique of the Theoretical Literature." *World Politics* 52 (4): 437–83.

Samuels, Kirsti. 2005. *Constitution Building Processes and Democratization: A Comparison of Twelve Case Studies*. Stockholm: International IDEA.

Sawyer, Amos. 2005. *Beyond Plunder: Toward Democratic Governance in Liberia*. Boulder: Lynne Rienner Press.

Scheye, Eric and Gordon Peake. 2005. "Unknotting Local Ownership." In *After Intervention: Public Security Management in Post-Conflict Societies – From Intervention to Sustainable Local Ownership*, eds. Anja H. Ebnöther and Philipp Flüri. Partnership for Peace Consortium Working Group on Security Sector Reform. Vienna/Geneva, pp. 235–60.

Schneckener, Ulrich. 2005. "Frieden Machen: Peacebuilding und Peacebuilder [Making Peace: Peacebuilding and Peacebuilders]." *Die Friedenswarte – Journal of International Peace and Organization* 80(1–2): 17–40.

Scott, James Campbell. 1985. *Weapons of the Weak: Everyday Forms of Peasant Resistance*. New Haven: Yale University Press.

Schwartz, Herman. 1994. *States versus Markets: History, Geography, and the Development of the International Political Economy*. New York: St. Martin's.

Scruton, Roger. 1982. *A Dictionary of Political Thought*. London: Macmillan.

Sedra, Mark, ed. 2003. "Confronting Afghanistan's Security Dilemma: Reforming the Security Sector." Brief 28. Bonn: Bonn International Centre for Conversion.

Sen, Amartya. 1999. *Development as Freedom*. New York: Anchor Books.

Sens, Allen. 2004. "The United Nations and Peace-building: Building the (Liberal) Peace?" In Richard Price and Mark Zacher, eds. *The United Nations and Global Security*. London: Palgrave.

Sharman, Jason C. and Roger E. Kanet. 2000. "International Influences on Democratization in Post-communist Europe." In *Pathways to Democracy: The Political Economy of Democratic Transitions*, ed. James F. Hollifield and Calvin Jillson. New York: Routledge, pp. 226–41.

Shearer, David. 1998. *Private Armies and Military Intervention*. New York: Oxford University Press.

Simmons, P.J. and Chantal de Jonge Oudraat, eds. 2001. *Managing Global Issues: Lessons Learned*. Washington, D.C.: Carnegie Endowment for International Peace.

Simonsen, Sven Gunnar. 2004. "Nationbuilding as Peacebuilding: Racing to Define the Kosovar." *International Peacekeeping* 11 (2): 289–311.

Sinanovic, Ermin. 2003. "Building Democracy Top-down: The Role of International Factors in Promoting Civil Society and Democracy in Bosnia and Herzegovina." In *Ownership Process in Bosnia and Herzegovina. Contributions on the International Dimensions of Democratization in the Balkans*, ed. Christophe Solioz and Svebor Dizdarevic. Baden-Baden: Nomos, pp. 120–28.

Singer, Peter Warren. 2003. *Corporate Warriors*. Ithaca: Cornell University Press.

Sisk, Timothy. 2003. "Power-Sharing after Civil Wars: Matching Problems to Solutions." In *Contemporary Peacemaking: Conflict, Violence and Peace Processes*, ed. John Darby and Roger MacGinty. Basingstoke: Palgrave Macmillan

Sisk, Timothy. 2001. "Violence: Intrastate Conflict." In *Managing Global Issues: Lessons Learned*, ed. P.J. Simmons and Chantal de Jonge Oudraat. Washington, D.C.: Carnegie Endowment for International Peace.

Sisk, Timothy. 1995. *Democratization in South Africa: The Elusive Social Contract*. Princeton, N.J.: Princeton University Press.

Smart, Alan. 1999. "Predatory Rule and Illegal Economic Practices." In *States and Illegal Practices*, ed. Josiah McC Heyman. Oxford and New York: Berg.

Smith, Anthony L. 2004. "Timor Leste: Strong Government, Weak State." *Southeast Asian Affairs*: 279–94.

Smith, Anthony L. 2002. "Timor Leste, Timor Timur, East Timor, Timor Lorosa'e: What's in a Name?" *Southeast Asian Affairs*: 54–77.

Smith, Dan. 2004. "Toward a Strategic Framework for Peacebuilding: Getting Their Act Together. Overview Report of the Joint Utstein Study of Peacebuilding. Evaluation Report 1/2004." Oslo: Royal Norwegian Ministry of Foreign Affairs.

Snyder, Jack. 2000. *From Voting to Violence: Democratization and Nationalist Conflict*. New York: W.W. Norton.

Sommers, Marc. 2000. "The Dynamics of Coordination," Occasional Paper No. 40, Watson Institute for International Studies, Brown University, Providence, Rhode Island.

Sørensen, Georg. 2006. "Liberalism of Restraint and Liberalism of Imposition: Liberal Values and World Order in the New Millennium." *International Relations* 20 (3): 251–72.

Spearin, Christopher. 2001. "Private Security Companies and Humanitarians." *International Peacekeeping* 8 (1) (Spring): 20–43.

Spears, Ian. 2002. "Africa: The Limits of Power-Sharing." *Journal of Democracy* 13 (3): 123–36.

Stedman, Stephen John. 1997. "Spoiler Problems in Peace Processes." *International Security* 22 (2): 5–53.

Stedman, Stephen John. 1994. *South Africa: The Political Economy of Transformation.* Boulder: Lynne Rienner.

Steiner, Michael. 2003. "Seven Principles for Building Peace." *World Policy Journal* (Summer): 87–93.

Stewart, Frances. 2000. "Crisis Prevention: Tackling Horizontal Inequalities." QEH Working Paper 33. Oxford: Queen Elizabeth House.

Stewart, Frances and Meghan O'Sullivan. 1998. "Democracy, Conflict and Development – Three Cases." QEH Working Paper 15. Oxford: Queen Elizabeth House.

Stiglitz, Joseph. 1998. "More Instruments and Broader Goals: Moving Toward the Post-Washington Consensus." WIDER Annual Lecture, January 7, Helsinki: WIDER.

Strand, Arne and Gunnar Olesen. 2005. *Humanitarian and Reconstruction Assistance to Afghanistan, 2001–2005.* Copenhagen: Ministry of Foreign Affairs, Danida Evaluation Series, www.cmi.no/pubs.

Strimling, Andrea L. 2002. "Building Capacity for Just Peace: Design, Implementation and Evaluation of Training Programs." in *Second Track/Citizens' Diplomacy. Concepts and Techniques for Conflict Transformation*, ed. John Davies and Edward Kaufman. Oxford: Rowman & Littlefield, pp. 265–83.

Suhrke, Astri. 2006. "The Limits of Statebuilding: The Role of International Assistance in Afghanistan." Paper presented at the International Studies Associated annual meeting. San Diego, CA. March 21–24.

Suhrke, Astri. 2001. "Peacekeepers as Nation-Builders: Dilemmas of the UN in East Timor." *International Peacekeeping* 8 (4): 1–20.

Suhrke, Astri and Ingrid Samset. 2007. "What's in a Figure? Estimating Recurrence of Civil War." *International Peacekeeping* 14 (2): 195–203.

Suhrke, Astri and Susan L. Woodward. 2002. "Make Haste Slowly in Assistance for Afghanistan." *International Herald Tribune*, January 21.

Suhrke, Astri, Kristian Berg Harpviken, and Arne Strand. 2004a. *Conflictual Peacebuilding: Afghanistan Two Years after Bonn.* Bergen: Chr. Michelsen Institute for Development Studies and Human Rights, www.cmi.no/pubs.

Suhrke, Astri, Arne Strand and Kristian Berg Harpviken. 2004b. "After Bonn: Conflictual Peacebuilding." In *Reconstructing War-Torn Societies: Afghanistan*, ed. Sultan Barakat. New York: Palgrave Macmillan, pp. 75–92.

Suhrke, Astri, Arne Strand and Kristian Berg Harpviken. 2002. "After Bonn: Conflictual Peacebuilding." *Third World Quarterly* 23 (5): 875–91.

Suhrke, Astri, Torunn Wimpelmann and Marcia Dawes. 2007. "Peace Processes and Statebuilding: Economic and Institutional Provisions of Peace Agreements." Report prepared for the World Bank and UNDP by the Chr. Michelsen Institute, Bergen, Norway (March).

Tambiah, Stanley J. 1977. "The Galactic Polity: the Structure of Traditional Kingdoms in Southeast Asia." *Annals of the New York Academy of Sciences* 293 (Anthropology and the Climate of Opinion): 69–97.

Tatalovic, Sinisa. 1996. "Military and Political Aspects of the Croato-Serbian Conflict." *Politicka Misao* 33 (5).

Tegegn, Melakou. 1997. *Development and Patronage: A Development in Practice Reader,* ed. Deborah Eade. Oxford: Oxfam.

Tenbensel, Tim. 2005. "Multiple Modes of Governance: Disentangling the Alternatives to Hierarchies and Markets." *Public Management Review* 7 (2): 267–88.

Terry, Fiona. 2002. *Condemned to Repeat? The Paradox of Humanitarian Action.* Ithaca: Cornell University Press.

Thier, J. Alexander. 2004. "The Politics of Peacebuilding Year One: From Bonn to Kabul." In *National Building Unraveled? Aid, Peace, and Justice in Afghanistan,* ed. Antonio Donini, Karin Wermester, and Norah Niland. Bloomfield: Kumarian, pp. 39–60.

Thier, J. Alexander and Jarat Chopra. 2002. "The Road Ahead: Political and Institutional Reconstruction in Afghanistan." *Third World Quarterly* 23 (5): 893–907.

Thies, Cameron G. 2006. "Public Violence and State Building in Central America." *Comparative Political Studies* 39 (10): 1263–82.

Thirlwall, Anthony P. 2002. *The Nature of Economic Growth: An Alternative Framework for Understanding the Performance of Nations.* London: Edward Elgar.

Thoms, Oskar N.T., James Ron, and Roland Paris. 2008. "The Effects of Transitional Justice Mechanisms: A Summary of Empirical Research Findings and Implications for Analysts and Practitioners." Working Paper, Centre for International Policy Studies, University of Ottawa (April).

Thomson, Alex. 2000. *An Introduction to African Politics.* London: Routledge.

Tietel, Ruti. 1997. "Transitional Jurisprudence: The Role of Law in Political Transformations." *Yale Law Journal* 106: 2009–80

Tilly, Charles. 1999. *Durable Inequality.* Berkeley: University of California Press.

Tilly, Charles. 1992. *Coercion, Capital and European States, AD 990–1992.* Cambridge: Blackwell.

Toft, Monica. 2003. "Peace through Victory?" Paper presented at the Annual Meeting of the American Political Science Association, Philadelphia, Pennsylvania, August 27–31.

Tschirgi, Necla. 2004. "Post-Conflict Peacebuilding Revisited: Achievement, Limitations, Challenges." Report of the International Peace Academy's Peacebuilding Forum Conference, New York, October 7.

Tschirgi, Necla. 2003. *Peacebuilding as the Link between Security and Development: Is the Window of Opportunity Closing?* New York: International Peace Academy.

Tschirgi, Necla. 2002. "Making the Case for a Regional Approach to Peacebuilding." *Journal of Peacebuilding and Develeopment* 1 (1): 25–38.

Tsebelis, George. 1991. *Nested Games: Rational Choice in Comparative Politics.* Berkeley: University of California Press.

UNCTAD. 2006. Trade and Development Report. UNCTAD/TDR/2006. New York and Geneva: United Nations Conference on Trade and Development.

United Nations. 1996. *The Adibjan Peace Accord.* November 30.

United Nations Development Programme. 2004. "Human Development Report Kosovo 2004." The Rise of the Citizen: Challenges and Choices. Pristina: United Nations Development Programme.

United Nations Mission in Kosovo. 2005. "Report Submitted by UNMIK Pursuant to Article 2.2 of the Agreement between UNMIK and the Council of Europe Related to the Framework Convention for the Protection of National Minorities."

2 June. Council of Europe Document ACFC(2005)003. Pristina: United Nations Mission in Kosovo

United Nations Mission in Kosovo. 2004. "Provisional Institutions of Self-Government/ PISG. Kosovo Standards Implementation Plan." March 31. Pristina: United Nations Mission in Kosovo.

United Nations Mission in Kosovo. 2002. "Standards before Status." April. Pristina: United Nations Mission in Kosovo.

UN Office for Coordination of Humanitarian Affairs. 2004. "Sierra Leone: Disarmament and Rehabilitation Completed after Five Years." IRIN News Brief, February 4, http://www.irinnews.org/Report.aspx?ReportId=48444.

UNRISD. 1993. *Rebuilding Wartorn Societies*. Geneva: United Nations Research Institute for Social Development.

US Department of Defense and US Department of State. 2000. *Foreign Military Training and DOD Engagement Activities of Interest, in Fiscal Years 1999 and 2000*, Vol. I. Joint Report to Congress, March 1, http://www.fas.org/asmp/campaigns/training/fmtrep.htm.

Uvin, Peter. 2002. "The Development/Peacebuilding Nexus: A Typology and History of Changing Paradigms." *Journal of Peacebuilding and Development* 1 (1): 5–24.

Vankovska, Biljana. 2002. "Privatization of Security and Security Sector Reform in Croatia." Typescript.

Venter, A.J. 1995. "Sierra Leone's Mercenary War for the Diamond Fields." *International Defense Review* 28 (11) (November): 65.

Vickery, Michael. 1993. "Talk at the Cambodia Coordinating Center." St. 360, Phnom Penh, June 3.

Vickery, Michael. 1984. *Cambodia 1975–82*. Boston: Southend.

Vigoda, Eran. 2002. "From Responsiveness to Collaboration: Governance, Citizens, and the Next Generation of Public Administration." *Public Administration Review* 62 (5): 527–40.

Vines, Alex. 1999a. "Gurkhas and the Private Security Business in Africa." In *Peace, Profit or Plunder the Privatization of Security in War-Torn African Societies*, ed. Jakkie Cilliers and Peggy Mason. Pretoria: Institute for Security Studies.

Vines, Alex. 1999b. "Mercenaries and the Privatization of Security in Africa in the 1990s." In *The Privatization of Security in Africa*, ed. Greg Mills and John Stremlau. Johannesburg: SAIIA 1999.

Virtanen, Pekka and Dag Ehrenpreis. 2007. "Growth, Poverty and Inequality in Mozambique." Country Study No.10, Brasilia: International Poverty Centre. http://www.undp-povertycentre.org/pub/IPCCountryStudy10.pdf.

Vukadinovic, Rudocar and Lidiji Cehulic. 2001. "Development of Civil-Military Relations in Croatia." In *Civil–Military Relations in South Eastern Europe: A Survey of the National Perspectives and of the Adaptation Process to the Partnership for Peace Standards*. Ed. Plamen Planter, Partnership for Peace Consortium, Working Group on Crisis Management in South Eastern Europe.

Waldner, David. 1999. *Statebuilding and Late Development*. Ithaca: Cornell University Press.

Wallensteen, Peter. 2008. "International Responses to Crises of Democratization in Postwar Societies." In *War-to-Democracy Transitions: Dilemmas of Democratization in War-Torn Societies*, eds. Anna Jarstad and Timothy Sisk. Cambridge: Cambridge University Press, pp. 213–38.

Walsh, Declan. 2006. "Welcome to Helmand." *Guardian Weekly Review*, February 10–16.

Walter, Barbara F. 2002. *Committing to Peace: The Successful Settlement of Civil Wars.* Princeton, N.J.: Princeton University Press.

Wantchekon, Leonard. 2004. "The Paradox of 'Warlord' Democracy: A Theoretical Investigation." *American Political Science Review* 98 (1): 17–33.

Waringo, Karin. 2006. "Kosovo: The Missing." Report of *Transition Online*, May 17.

Weber, Max. 1978. *Economy and Society: An Outline of Interpretive Sociology.* Berkeley: University of California Press.

Wedel, Janine. 1996. "Clique-run Organizations and U.S. Economic Aid: An Institutional Analysis." *Demokratizatiya: Journal of Post-Soviet Expansion* 4 (4): 571–602.

Weinstein, Jeremy. 2005. "Autonomous Recovery and International Intervention in Comparative Perspective." Working Paper Number 57. Washington, D.C.: Center for Global Development.

Weinbaum, Marvin G. 2006. Afghanistan and Its Neighbors. Special Report No. 162. Washington, D.C.: United States Institute of Peace.

Weinberger, Naomi. 2002. "Civil–Military Coordination in Peacebuilding: The Challenge in Afghanistan," *Journal of International Affairs* 55 (2) (Spring): 245–74.

Weller, Marc and Stefan Wolff. 2006. "Bosnia and Herzegovina Ten Years After Dayton: Lessons for Internationalized Statebuilding." *Ethnopolitics* 5 (1): 1–13.

Wennmann, Achim. 2005. "Resourcing the Recurrence of Intrastate Conflict: Parallel Economies and Their Implications for Peacebuilding." *Security Dialogue* 36 (4): 479–94.

Wilder, Andres. 2005. "A House Divided? Analyzing the 2005 Afghan Elections." Kabul: Afghan Research and Development Unit, www.areu.org.af/publications/A %20House%20Divided.pdf.

Willett, Susan. 1995. "Ostriches, Wise Old Elephants and Economic Reconstruction in Mozambique." *International Peacekeeping* 2 (1) (Spring): 34–55.

Woodhouse, Tom and Oliver Ramsbotham.2005. "Cosmopolitan Peacekeeping and the Globalization of Security." *International Peacekeeping* 12 (2): 139–56.

Woodward, Susan. 2002. "Economic Priorities for Successful Peace Implementation." In *Ending Civil Wars: The Implementation of Peace Agreements*, eds. Stephen John Stedman, Donald Rothchild, and Elizabeth M. Cousens. Boulder: Lynne Rienner, pp. 183–214.

Woodward, Susan. 1995. *Balkan Tragedy: Chaos and Dissolution after the Cold War.* Washington, D.C.: Brookings Institution.

Woodward, Susan L and Astri Suhrke. 2002. "Make Haste Slowly in Assistance for Afghanistan." *International Herald Tribune*, January 21.

World Bank. 2006. *Engaging with Fragile States: An IEG Review of World Bank Support to Low-Income Countries Under Stress.* Washington, D.C.: The World Bank.

World Bank. 2005a. *Afghanistan. Managing Public Finance for Development.* Washington, D.C.: The World Bank

World Bank. 2005b. *Economic Growth in the 1990s – Learning from a Decade of Reform.* Washington, D.C.: World Bank.

World Bank. 2004. *Cambodia at the Crossroads: Strengthening Accountability to Reduce Poverty.* Washington, D.C.: The World Bank.

Wuyts, Marc. 2003. "The Agrarian Question in Mozambique's Transition and Reconstruction." In *From Conflict to Recovery in Africa*, ed. Tony Addison. Oxford: Oxford University Press, pp.141–54.

Yannis, Alexandros. 2004. "The UN as Government in Kosovo." *Global Governance* 10: 67–81.

Yannis, Alexandros. 2001. "Kosovo under International Administration." *Survival* 43 (2): 31–48.

Young, Tom. 1994. "'A Project to be Realised': Global Liberalism and Contemporary Africa." *Millennium: Journal of International Studies* 24 (3): 527–46.

Zahar, Marie–Joelle. 2004. "Reframing the Spoiler Debate in Peace Processes." In *Progressing Towards Settlement*, eds. John Darby and Roger McGinty. London: Palgrave.

Zakaria, Fareed. 2003. *The Future of Freedom: Illiberal Democracy at Home and Abroad*, 1st ed. New York: W.W. Norton & Co.

Zakaria, Fareed. 1997. "The Rise of Illiberal Democracy." *Foreign Affairs* (November–December): 22–44.

Zaum, Domink. 2007. "The Politics of Exit: Transition and Exit from Post-Conflict Statebuilding Operations." Paper presented at the annual conference of the American Political Science Association, Chicago, Illinois, August 30.

Zanotti, Laura. 2006. "Taming Chaos: A Foucauldian View of UN Peacekeeping, Democracy and Normalization," *International Peacekeeping* 13 (2) (June): 150–67.

Zia-Zarifi, Sam. 2004. "Losing the Peace in Afghanistan." New York: Human Rights Watch, www.hrw.org/wr2k4/5.htm.

Zürcher, Christoph. 2006. "Is More Better? Evaluating External-Led Statebuilding after 1989." CDDRL Working Papers 54. Stanford: Center on Democracy, Development, and the Rule of Law, Stanford Institute on International Studies, April.

Zürcher, Christoph and Jan Koehler. 2001. "Institutions & Organized Violence in Post-Socialist Societies." *Berliner Osteuropa Info* 17: 48–53.

Zunec, Ozren. 1996. "Civil–Military Relations in Croatia." In *Civil–Military Relations in the Soviet and Yugoslav Successor States*, eds. Constantine P. Danopoulos and Danile Zirker. Boulder: Westview.

Index

absolutism in Cambodia 150–51, 152, 154, 157–58, 159, 161

acceptance: of peacebuilding 30; of statebuilding within international community 10–11

accountability: in Afghanistan 228, 230, 233–34, 237, 246; coordination and 63; electoral processes, postwar context 196; of Peacebuilding Commission (UN) 72

accumulation: Afghanistan, example of 132, 133, 134, 135, 136, 137–38, 139, 145; changes in patterns of 147n6; contradictory outcomes, generation of 138–39; economic interests, statebuilding and 134–35, 136; export of processed commodities 137–40; fiscal policy 142–43, 145; force, balance and distribution of 133–34; illicit commodity production 136; inequalities, patterns of 140; international politics 136–37; labor mobilization 135–36; liberalization 140–41; market transformation and trajectories of 16–17; Mozambique, example of 130–31, 131–33, 134, 137–38; neoliberal economic policy, transition costs and 140–41, 145–46; "peace-war-peace-continuum" 129–30, 134–35; peacetime, rearrangements of 133–34; power, sources of 134; privatization 141–42; regional interests 136–37; revenue streams, access to 130–37; risk and return 133–34; service-delivery and 129; South Africa, example of 131–32; stabilization 140–41; trade policy 143–44, 145–46; trajectories of 17, 129–46, 147n4, 312–13; vicious

market fundamentalism 133; war entrepreneurs 131; war rents 133; war-to-peace transitions, assumptions on 129; war-warped patterns of 1

Ackerman, Bruce A. 174

ACP (African, Caribbean and Pacific) countries 143

Addison, Tony 142, 144, 148n22

Adekanye, Bayo 179, 190

Ademi, General Rahim 119

Afghanistan 2, 17, 25–26, 58, 67, 91–92, 93–94, 95, 99, 105, 130, 131, 137–38, 174, 177, 203, 217, 227–51, 267, 287, 288, 290, 296, 307, 313, 315; accountability 228, 230, 233–34, 237, 246; accumulation in 132, 133, 134, 135, 136, 137–38, 139, 145; ANA (Afghan National Army) 45, 237, 240–43; ANA (Afghan National Army), building up 240–43; analytical perspectives 227–30, 245–47; ANDS (Afghanistan National Development Strategy) 232, 237, 249n22, 250n26; Bonn agreement on (2001) 42, 43, 51n27, 91–92, 102–3n26, 210–12, 214, 233, 234, 235, 236, 244–45, 247; captured peacebuilding in 46; Compact on, London conference (2006) 47, 234; compromised peacebuilding in 45; conditionalities, reluctance to impose 43; dependence, structures of 230–43, 246–47; economic dependence 231–33, 246–47; electoral processes, postwar context 196–97, 210–14, 219; Finance Ministry in 232, 236, 248n9, 250n35; flagship project 42; hedging, evidence of 235; historical perspective 228–29; infrastructure, destruction of